H. Willis

Vauxhall Viva HB Owners Workshop Manual

by J H Haynes
Associate Member of the Guild of Motoring Writers

and D H Stead

Models covered:

1159 cc Saloon, Saloon De-luxe,
SL De-luxe 90, SL90
Estate cars (De-luxe, SL and 90)

September 1966 to October 1970.
September 1966 to October 1970.
June 1967 to October 1970

ISBN 900550 26 0

© Haynes Publishing Group 1971   2333/026

Printed in England

HAYNES PUBLISHING GROUP
SPARKFORD YEOVIL SOMERSET ENGLAND
distributed in the USA by
HAYNES PUBLICATIONS INC
861 LAWRENCE DRIVE
NEWBURY PARK
CALIFORNIA 91320
USA

Acknowledgements

Thanks are due to Vauxhall Motors Limited, for the assistance given in the supply of technical material and illustrations, and to the Champion Sparking Plug Company for the illustrations showing the spark plug conditions. The bodywork repair photographs used in this manual were provided by Lloyds Industries Limited who supply 'Turtle Wax', 'Dupli-color Holts', and other Holts range products. The help of Mr. R.T. Grainger and Mr. L. Tooze must be specially acknowledged in the preparation of the technical photographs; and that also of Col. F. T. Nicholson in helping to guide the text along.

Although every care has been taken to ensure the correctness of data used, it must be borne in mind that alterations and design changes can occur within the production run of a model without specific reclassification. No liability can be accepted for damage, loss or injury caused by errors or omissions in the information given.

Photographic Captions & Cross References

The book is divided into twelve chapters. Each chapter is divided into numbered sections which are headed in **bold type** between horizontal lines. Each section consists of serially numbered paragraphs.

There are two types of illustration. (1) Figures which are numbered according to Chapter and sequence of occurrence in that Chapter and having an individual caption to each figure. (2) Photographs which have a reference number in the bottom left-hand corner. All photographs apply to the chapter in which they occur so that the reference figures pinpoint the pertinent section and paragraph numbers.

Procedures, once described in the text, are not normally repeated. If it is necessary to refer to another chapter the reference will be given in chapter number and section number thus:- Chapter 1/6.

If it is considered necessary to refer to a particular paragraph in another chapter the reference is 'Chapter 1/6:5'. Cross references given without use of the word 'Chapter' apply to sections and/or paragraphs in the same chapter, e.g., 'see Section 8' means also 'in this chapter'.

When the left or right-hand side of a car is mentioned it is as if one was looking in the forward direction of travel.

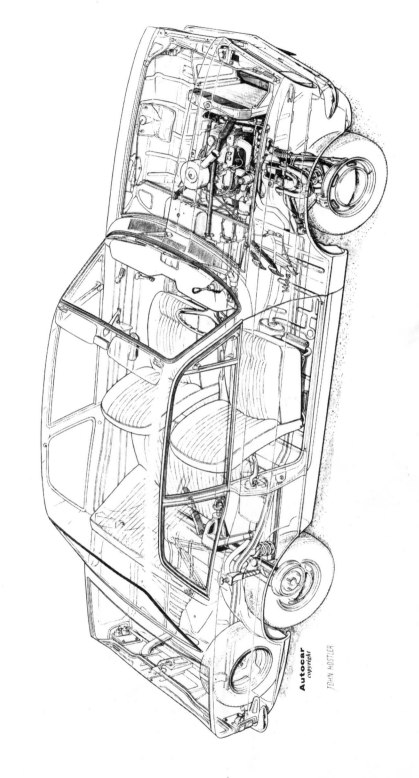

Autocar
copyright

JOHN HOSTLER

A SECTIONED VIEW OF THE VIVA HB SHOWING THE POSITION OF ALL MAJOR COMPONENTS

Introduction

This owners workshop manual is intended for the owner of an HB series Vauxhall Viva, who, having acquired his car either new some years ago, or second-hand recently, does not wish to spend a fortune in keeping it in a safe, economical and good value condition.

No one, however, particularly with all round commitments and interests wishes to spend all his leisure time in looking after his transport. This manual is designed therefore to enable the practically minded owner to maintain his car and at the same time show him the way to carry out most of the repairs that a car normally requires during its life as economically and quickly as possible.

The modern trends in motor car design and production are towards the fitting of components which are renewed completely if they fail — the economics being that the cost of the time required to repair them is little less than the combined cost of labour and material needed to produce them in the first place. However, this trend has not yet moved things completely out of the owner's control and many items such as starter motors, dynamos, fuel pumps, distributors, brake cylinders, and so on can be repaired for an expenditure of pence (new!) on parts where replacement would cost pounds Where a component is only obtainable as a complete unit, an owner should be quite able to install it correctly with the aid of this manual.

Now that vehicles over three years old require annual safety checks the need to know where to look for deterioration in the safety areas is impressed on the owner even more forcibly. Failure will result in loss of use and all the consequent inconvenience and expense.

This manual enables the owner to examine the vehicle himself and so ensure its continued safety well before the date of inspection is due.

For the more ambitious owner, this manual gives step by step details of all the other repairs and overhauls which we consider are within the capabilities of a practically minded person who is in possession of a reasonably comprehensive set of tools. With regard to the latter, this is one area where only good quality equipment will do. The authors also discourage the borrowing of tools except for certain special items which may only be used once in a blue moon. Certainly we would say that you should not be annoyed if someone should refuse to lend them. Appreciate how much they cost if lost or damaged — apart from the fact that keen owners regard their tools as particularly personal belongings.

Much of the work involved in looking after a car and carrying out repairs depends on accurate diagnosis in the first place. Where possible, therefore, a methodical and progressive way of diagnosis is presented. The time that can be wasted in hopping from one possible source of trouble to another, suggested at random quite often by self styled 'experts' must have been experienced by many people. It is best to say at the start therefore, 'This could be one of several things—lets get the book out'.

Contents

Routine Maintenance

Maintenance should be looked upon as essential for ensuring safety, and desirable for the purpose of obtaining economy and performance from the car.

By far the largest element of the maintenance routine is visual examination.

Each chapter of the manual gives details of the routine maintenance requirements. In the summary given here the safety items are shown in **bold type.**

These must be attended to regularly in the interests of preventing accidents and possible loss of life.

Neglect of other items results in unreliability, overall increased running costs and more rapid depreciation of the value of the car.

500 miles

EVERY 500 mile intervals/weekly.

ENGINE

Check oil level in sump and top up as required.
Check radiator coolant level and top up as required.
Check battery electrolyte level and top up as required.

STEERING
Check tyre pressures.

Examine tyres for wear and damage.
Is the steering still smooth and accurate?
Check hydraulic fluid reservoir level. If a significant drop is apparent examine system for leaks immediately.
Is there any reduction in braking efficiency? Try an emergency stop. Is adjustment necessary?

LIGHTS
Do all bulbs work at front and rear?
Are headlamp beams correctly aligned?

3,000 miles

EVERY 3,000 mile intervals/4 monthly, or if indications are that safety items in particular are not performing correctly.

ENGINE
Drain sump of oil when hot and refill with fresh oil.
Check fan belt tension and adjust as necessary.
Check spark plug electrode gap.

CLUTCH
Check clutch cable for adjustment and for fraying and operation.

STEERING
Is there any free play between the steering wheel and road wheels?
Examine all steering linkage rods, joints and bushes for signs of wear or damage.

BRAKES
Examine pads and shoes to determine the amount of friction material remaining. Renew as necessary.

6,000 miles

EVERY 6,000 mile intervals/8 monthly, or if indications are that safety items in particular are not performing correctly.

ENGINE
Renew oil filter element.
Check valve clearances and adjust as necessary.
Clean the fuel pump filter.
Lubricate the distributor.
Lubricate the generator rear end bush.

STEERING
Check front wheel hub bearings and adjust if necessary.
Examine steering gear rubber boots for signs of deterioration and/or oil leakage.

BRAKES
Examine all hydraulic pipes, cylinders and unions for signs of corrosion, dents, chafing or any other form of deterioration or leaks.

SUSPENSION
Examine all suspension mounting bushes and joints for signs of looseness or wear.

12,000 miles

EVERY 12,000 miles/annually, or if indications are that safety items in particular are not performing correctly.

ENGINE
Fit new distributor contact points.
Fit new spark plugs.
Fit new carburetter air cleaner element (or clean washable variety).
Flush out the cooling system.

GEARBOX
Check oil level and top up as required.

BACK AXLE
Check oil level and top up as required.

STEERING
Remove front wheel bearings, flush, inspect and re-pack with grease.

BODY FRAME
Examine for rust where suspension is attached.

SUSPENSION
Grease front suspension arm ball joints.

BRAKES
Renew servo unit air filter (disc brake models.)

24,000 miles

GEARBOX
Drain and replenish oil.

REAR AXLE
Drain and replenish oil.

Non-Specified Intervals

CLEANING
Examination of components requires that they be cleaned. The same applies to the body of the car, inside and out, in order that deterioration due to rust or unknown damage may be detected. Certain parts of the vehicle body frame if rusted badly, can result in its being declared unsafe, and it will not pass the annual test for roadworthiness.

EXHAUST SYSTEM
An exhaust system must be leakproof and the noise level below a certain minimum. Excessive leaks may cause carbon monoxide fumes to enter the passenger compartment. Excessive noise constitutes a public nuisance. Both these defects may cause the vehicle to be kept off the road. Repair or replace defective sections when symptoms are apparent.

RECOMMENDED LUBRICANTS

COMPONENT	TYPE OF LUBRICANT OR FLUID	CORRECT CASTROL PRODUCTS
ENGINE	Multi-grade engine oil...	Castrol 'G.T.X'.
GEARBOX & REAR AXLE	Gear oil of S.A.E.90 E.P. standard	Castrol 'Hypoy' gear oil
STEERING GEAR...	Gear oil of S.A.E.90 E.P. standard...	Castrol 'Hypoy' gear oil
SUSPENSION, STEERING & BALL JOINTS	Heavy duty graphite or molybdenum base grease	Castrol M.S.3 grease
FRONT WHEEL BEARINGS	Medium grade multi-purpose grease	Castrol L.M. grease
DISTRIBUTOR, STARTER & GENERATOR BUSHES	Engine or light oil	Castrol 'G.T.X.' and 'Castrolite'
CONTACT BREAKER CAM & BATTERY TERMINALS... ...	Petroleum jelly...	
CARBURETTER DASHPOT...	... ...	'Castrolite'
UPPER CYLINDER LUBRICANT...	... ...	'Castrollo'
HYDRAULIC PISTONS & WATER PUMP SEAL	Rubber grease	Castrol rubber grease
BRAKE MASTER CYLINDER RESERVOIR	Hydraulic fluid...	Castrol/Girling 'Crimson'

Additionally Castrol 'Everyman' oil can be used to lubricate door, boot and bonnet hinges, and locks, pivots etc.

LUBRICATION CHART

EXPLANATION OF SYMBOLS

CASTROL GTX
An ultra high performance motor oil incorporating for the first time every necessary high performance quality in one oil. Recommended for the engine in summer and winter.

CASTROL ST.
A light-bodied gear oil recommended for gearbox lubrication.

CASTROL HYPOY
A powerful extreme pressure gear oil essential for the lubrication of the hypoid rear axle.

CASTROL MS 3 GREASE
A high melting point, lithium grease containing molybdenum disulphide recommended for grease gun lubrication.

CASTROL LM GREASE
A lithium base grease recommended for the front wheel bearings.

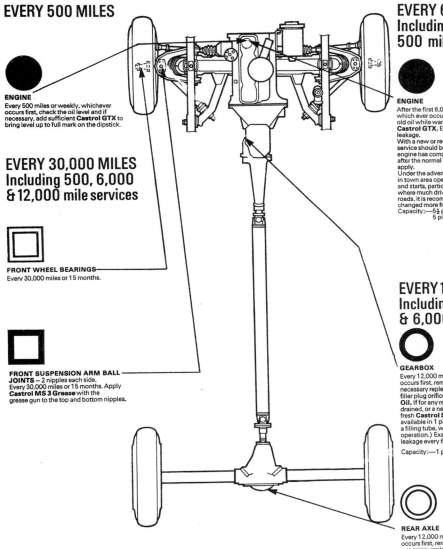

EVERY 500 MILES

ENGINE
Every 500 miles or weekly, whichever occurs first, check the oil level and if necessary, add sufficient **Castrol GTX** to bring level up to full mark on the dipstick.

EVERY 30,000 MILES
Including 500, 6,000 & 12,000 mile services

FRONT WHEEL BEARINGS
Every 30,000 miles or 15 months.

FRONT SUSPENSION ARM BALL JOINTS – 2 nipples each side. Every 30,000 miles or 15 months. Apply **Castrol MS 3 Grease** with the grease gun to the top and bottom nipples.

EVERY 6,000 MILES
Including 500 mile service

ENGINE
After the first 6,000 miles, or 3 months which ever occurs first, drain off the old oil while warm and refill with fresh **Castrol GTX.** Examine engine for signs of leakage.
With a new or reconditioned engine this service should be carried out when the engine has completed 1,000 miles, thereafter the normal 6,000 mile service should apply.
Under the adverse conditions encountered in town area operation with frequent stops and starts, particularly in cold weather or where much driving is done over dusty roads, it is recommended that the oil is changed more frequently.
Capacity:—5½ pints, dry. 4½ pints, refill. 5 pints, filter element change

EVERY 12,000 MILES
Including 500 & 6,000 mile service

GEARBOX
Every 12,000 miles or 6 months, whichever occurs first, remove the filler plug and if necessary replenish to the bottom of the filler plug orifice with **Castrol ST Gear Oil.** If for any reason the gearbox has been drained, or a new gearbox fitted, refill with fresh **Castrol ST Gear Oil** (Castrol ST is available in 1 pint "Handipacks" fitted with a filling tube, which greatly facilitates this operation.) Examine casing for signs of leakage every 6,000 miles.

Capacity:—1 pint HB

REAR AXLE
Every 12,000 miles or 6 months, whichever occurs first, remove filler plug and if necessary replenish to the bottom of the filler plug orifice with **Castrol Hypoy Gear Oil.** (Castrol Hypoy is available in 1 pint "Handipacks" fitted with a filling tube which greatly facilitates this operation.) If for any reason the axle has been drained or dismantled before the first 10,000 miles are completed, consult the handbook for special instructions. Examine casing for signs of leakage every 6,000 miles.

Capacity:—1¼ pints.

Ordering Spare Parts

Buy genuine Vauxhall spares from a Vauxhall dealer direct or through a local garage. If you go to an authorized dealer the correctly fitting genuine parts can usually be supplied from stock which of course is a greatly added convenience.

Always have details of the car's serial number and engine number available when obtaining parts. If you can also take along the part to be renewed it is helpful. Modifications are continuously being made and many are not publicized. A storeman in a parts department is quite justified in saying that he cannot guarantee the correctness of a part unless the relevant numbers are available.

The vehicle identification plate is attached to the forward end of the left-hand wheel arch under the bonnet. It gives details of the model and all items other than the engine. The engine number is marked on the right-hand side of the engine block underneath Nos.1 and 2 spark plugs.

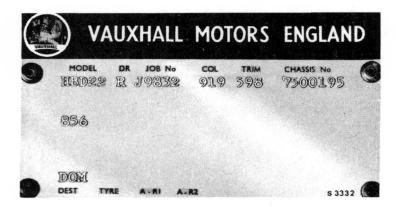

Model Identification Plate

Engine Number

Chapter 1/Engine

Contents

Specifications — Engine Specifications & Data HB22 and HB23

Engine - General

Type	4 cylinder in line O.H.V. pushrod operated
Bore	77.7 mm. (3.062 in.)
Stroke	61.0 mm. (2.400 in.)
Cubic capacity	1159 c.c. (70.7 cu.in.)
Weight	227 lb. (with gearbox 270 lbs) approx.

Compression Ratios

Standard HB22	8.5 : 1
Low compression HB22 (optional)	7.3 : 1
HB23...	9.0 : 1

Firing Order ... ...   1, 3, 4, 2.

Location of No.1 cylinder ... ...   Front of engine next to radiator

Minimum compression pressure (hot).. ... ...   125 lbs/in^2 HB22
                                                     135 lbs/in^2 HB23

Camshaft & Bearings

Camshaft drive..	Single row endless chain
Bearings	3 renewable shell type
Camshaft journal diameter - Front..	1.6127 - 1.6132 in.
- Rear	1.5733 - 1.5738 in.
Camshaft clearance in bearing	.0010 to .0025 in.
Camshaft end float	.006 to .013 in.

Cam dimension - peak to base:-	Intake	Exhaust
HB22	1.3185 in.	1.3125 in.
HB23	1.3222 in.	1.3222 in.
Minimum cam wear HB22	1.2980 in.	1.2920 in.
HB23	1.3017 in.	1.3017 in.
Camshaft thrust plate thickness	.119 into .122 in.	

Connecting Rods & Big End Bearings

Bearing type	Shell
Bearing material	White metal/lead indium Aluminium/tin (HB23)
Connecting rod endfloat on crank pin	.004 in. to .010 in. .
Bearing housing bore...	1.8960 in. to 1.8965 in.
Crank pin diameter - Standard	1.7705 in. to 1.7712 in.
- Grade 'P'	1.7605 in. to 1.7612 in.
Crank pin to bearing clearance...	.0010 in. to .0029 in.
Crank throw	1.197 in. to 1.202 in.

Crankshaft & Main Bearings

Bearing type	Shell
Journal diameter - Standard..	2.1255 in. to 2.1260 in.
- Grade 'J'..	2.1155 in. to 2.1160 in.
Journal to bearing clearance	.0010 in. to .0025 in.
Crankshaft flange diameter	2.998 in. to 3.002 in.
Crankshaft end float	.002 in. to .008 in.
Crankshaft run-out	.0015 in. maximum
Main bearing housing bore	2.2835 in. to 2.2840 in.
Main bearing centre upper half width...	1.287 in. to 1.289 in.
Thrust washers	Incorporated in the upper half of centre main bearing shell

Cylinder Block & Crankcase

Type	Cast iron - cylinders cast integrally with upper half of crankcase
Water jackets	Full length
Oversize bores	.005 in., .020 in., .040 in.
Permissible distortion on top face - Longitudinal	.005 in. maximum
- Transverse	.003 in. maximum
Minimum block depth after re-facing (top face to bearing cap face)	7.508 in.

Cylinder Head & Valves

Permissible distortion on mating face - Longitudinal	.005 in. maximum
- Transverse	.003 in. maximum
- Manifold faces.. ...	.002 in. maximum
Permissible head depth HB22	3.185 in. minimum
HB23	3.157 in. minimum
Porting	Inlet ports on top of head, exhaust ports at side
Valve stem bore	.2765 in. to .2773 in.
Valve seating angle	45º
Valve seating width - Inlet	.05 in. to .06 in.
- Exhaust	.06 in. to .08 in.
Rocker stud diameter - Standard	.3535 in. to .3543 in.
Rocker stud height above cylinder head top face	1.08 in. to 1.12 in.
Rocker ball clearance on stud	.0006 in. to .0028 in.
Valve seat angle	44º
Valve stem diameter - Intake	.2748 in. to .2755 in.
- Exhaust...	.2745 in. to .2752 in.
Valve head thickness - Inlet	.03 in. minimum
- Exhaust..	.04 in. minimum
Valve springs - assembled height	1.34 in. maximum
- nominal free length	1.48 in. maximum
- load at 1.31 in.	46 to 54 lbs.
Tappet diameter	.4712 in. to .4718 in.

Valve timing - Inlet valve open maximum ... ...   107° A.T.D.C.
Valve clearance - Hot
        HB22 - Inlet... ... ...   .006 in.
            - Exhaust... ... ...   .010 in.
        HB23 - Inlet & Exhaust ... ...   .008 in.

Pistons & Piston Rings (including gudgeon pins)

Piston clearance in cylinder bore ... ...   .0009 — .0014 in.
Ring gap in cylinder bore ... ...   .009 — .014 in.
Ring thickness - Top ... ...   .077 — .078 in.
            - Centre ... ..., ...077 — .078 in.
            - Scraper... ... ...   .1865 — .1875 in.
Ring clearance in piston groove - Top... ... ...   .0019 — .0039 in.
                      - Centre ... ...   .0016 — .0026 in.
                      - Scraper ... ...   .0015 — .0035 in.

Piston size		Grade	Dimensions
Standard	... ...	5	3.06085 to 3.06110 in.
		6	3.06110 to 3.06135 in.
		7	3.06135 to 3.06160 in.
		8	3.06160 to 3.06185 in.
.005 in. oversize	... ...	5	3.06585 to 3.06635 in.
		8	3.06635 to 3.06685 in.
.020 in. oversize	... ...	5	3.08085 to 3.08135 in.
		8	3.08135 to 3.08185 in.
.040 in. oversize	... ...	5	3.10085 to 3.10135 in.
		8	3.10135 to 3.10185 in.

Gudgeon pin ... ...   Semi-floating interference fit in connecting rod. Vauxhall only supply complete piston/connecting rod assemblies as spares

Lubrication System

Oil Pump
Driving impeller spindle diameter ... ...   .4327 - .4331 in.
Spindle to bush clearance ... ...   .0006 - .0017 in.
Spindle endfloat ... ...   .007 - .010 in.
Driven impeller spindle diameter ... ...   .4303 - .4307 in.
Spindle fit in body ... ...   .0015 - .0026 in. interference

Impellers
Teeth backlash ... ...   .004 to .008 in.
Driving impeller to spindle fit ... ...   .0009 to .0021 in. interference
Driven impeller to spindle fit ... ...   .0003 to .0015 in. clearance
End float in body... ... ...   .002 to .005 in.
Radial clearance in body.. ... ...   .002 to .005 in.
Drive gear - bore diameter ... ...   .3221 — .4325
          - spindle fit ... ...   .0002 — .0010 interference
Oil pressure relief valve - plunger diameter ... ...   .4353 — .4358
                - plunger fit in cover.. ... ...   .0012 — .0027 clearance
                - spring free length ... ...   1.92 in.
                - spring load at 1.66 in ... ...   6 lbs. 10 oz. to 6 lb. 14 oz.
Oil pressure - hot ... ...   35 — 45 lbs/in^2 @ 3000 r.p.m.
            - pressure switch opens at ... ...   3 — 5 lbs/in^2
Oil capacity - total ... ...   5½ pints Imp.
Oil change capacity ... ...   4½ pints Imp.
Oil change capacity with new filter element .. ..   5 pints Imp.

Torque Wrench Settings

Big end bearing cap bolts ... ...   25 lb/ft. oiled threads
Main bearing cap bolts ... ...   58 lb/ft. oiled threads
Flywheel bolts.. ... ...   25 lb/ft. sealed threads
Cylinder head bolts ... ...   43 lb/ft. dry threads
Valve rocker stud adjusting nuts ... ...   3 lb/ft. min. oiled threads
Oil filter housing bolt.. ... ...   14 lb/ft. dry threads

Brake Horse Power

HB22 8.5 : 1 CR (nett)   56 b.h.p. @ 5,400 r.p.m.
HB22 7.3 : 1 CR (nett)   52 b.h.p. @ 5,400 r.p.m.
HB23 9.0 : 1 CR (nett)   69 b.h.p. @ 5,800 r.p.m.

1. General Description

The 1159 c.c. engine is an oversquare, four cylinder, overhead valve pushrod operated type, with a high standard compression ratio, with an optional low compression version available. (This is achieved by the simple expedient of fitting a thicker cylinder head gasket).

Two valves per cylinder are mounted at an inclination in line, in a cast iron cylinder head. They are operated by tappets, short pushrods and rocker arms from a camshaft located to the right side of the cylinder bores. Adjustment of valve to rocker clearances is effected by a ball joint pivot on which each rocker arm bears and is adjustable on the mounting stud.

The cylinder block/crankcase casting is distinctive for its width relative to depth, even though the centre line of the crankshaft is at the level of the lower edge of the casting. This is due to the oversquare nature of the design and the unusual inlet porting in the head which has the manifold mounted on top, with the exhaust ports coming from the side.

The crankshaft is mounted in three bearings and the top half of the centre bearing shell is flanged to control crankshaft endfloat.

The camshaft is driven by a single timing chain from the forward end of the crankshaft and a mechanical tension adjuster is fitted.

Pistons have a solid cut-away skirt and have three rings, two compression and one oil control. The gudgeon pin floats in the piston and is an interference fit in the connecting rod.

The centrifugal water pump and cooling fan are V-belt driven from a crankshaft pulley wheel. The distributor is mounted at the left side of the engine and is advanced by centrifugal and vacuum means. There is no vernier control for the static ignition setting.

The oil pump is of the gear type and is driven from the camshaft skew gear.

The clutch is a single dry plate diaphragm type operated mechanically by Bowden cable.

The engine and transmission unit is supported at three points: on each side of the engine between crankcase and chassis frame and underneath the gearbox casing to a crossmember bolted to the bodyshell.

2. Routine Maintenance

1. Once a week remove the dipstick and check the engine oil level which should be at the 'FULL' mark. Top up with the recommended grade (see page 8 for details).

Do not let the level of oil drop below the 'Add oil' mark under any circumstances, and if a weekly check reveals this regularly, the oil level should be checked more often and consideration given to the condition of the engine and what remedial action to take.

The quantity of oil needed to bring the level from the 'ADD OIL' to the 'FULL' mark is two pints (Imp.).
2. Every 6,000 miles run the engine until it is hot; place a container with a minimum capacity of six pints under a drain plug in the sump; undo and remove the drain plug and allow the old oil to drain out for at least ten minutes. At the same time renew the oil filter element as described in Section 26.
3. Clean the drain plug, ensure the washer is clean and intact and replace the plug in the sump, tightening it firmly. Refill the engine with five pints of the recommended grade of oil. (Details on page 8).
4. In very hot and/or dusty conditions, or in cold weather with a lot of slow stop/start motoring, using the choke a lot, it is beneficial to change the oil every 3,000 miles.

3. Major Operations with Engine in Place

The following work may be conveniently carried out with the engine in place:
1. Removal and replacement of the cylinder head assembly.
2. Removal and replacement of the clutch assembly.
3. Removal and replacement of the engine front mountings.

The following work can be carried out with the engine in place, but is inadvisable unless there are very special reasons:
4. Removal and replacement of the sump (the front suspension assembly must be removed first).
5. Removal and replacement of big end bearings (after sump removal).
6. Removal and replacement of pistons and connecting rods (after removing cylinder head and sump).
7. Removal and replacement of the flywheel (after removing the clutch).
8. Removal and replacement of the timing chain and sprockets (after removal of the sump), See Section 1.16.
9. Removal and replacement of the oil pump (after removal of the sump).

4. Major Operations For Which The Engine Must Be Removed

1. Removal and replacement of crankshaft and crankshaft main bearings.
2. Removal and replacement of flywheel.
3. Removal and replacement of rear crankshaft oil seal.

5. Methods of Engine Removal

1. The engine complete with gearbox can be lifted as a unit from the engine compartment. Alternatively the engine and gearbox can be split at the front of the bellhousing, the gearbox supported and left in position and the engine removed. Whether or not components like the carburetter, manifolds, dynamo and starter are removed first depends to some extent on what work is to be done.

6. Engine Removal — With Gearbox

1. The average do-it-yourself owner should be able to remove the engine fairly easily in about 3½ hours. It is essential to have a good hoist, and two strong axle stands if an inspection pit is not available. Engine removal will be much easier if you have someone to help you. Before Beginning work it is worthwhile to get all the accumulated debris cleaned off the engine unit at a service station which is equipped with steam or high pressure air and water cleaning equipment. It helps to make the job quicker, easier and of course much cleaner. Decide whether you are going to jack up the car and support it on axle stands or raise the front end on wheel ramps. If the latter, run the car up now (and chock the rear wheels) whilst you still have engine power available. Remember that with the front wheels supported on ramps the working height and engine lifting height is

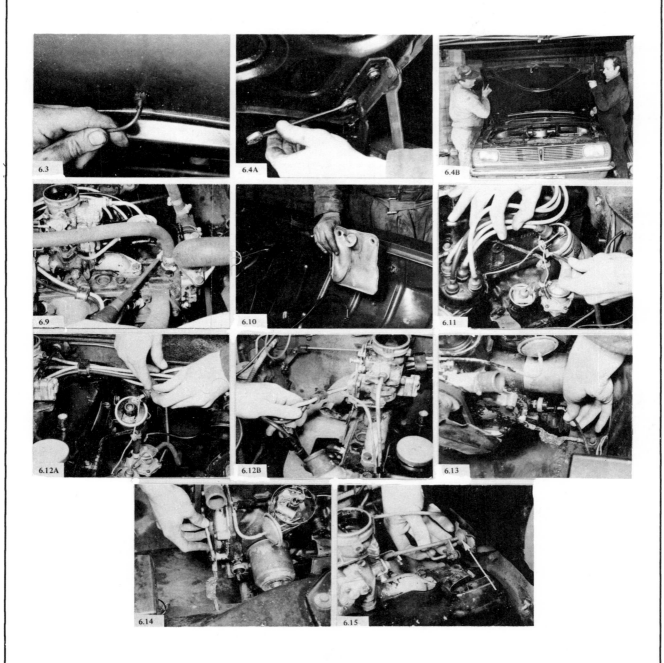

6.3   6.4A   6.4B

6.9   6.10   6.11

6.12A   6.12B   6.13

6.14   6.15

going to be increased.

2. Open the bonnet and prop it up to expose the engine and ancillary components. Disconnect the battery leads and lift the battery out of the car. (Turn to Chapter 10, Section 2 for details and photos). This prevents accidental short circuits while working on the engine.

3. Remove the windscreen washer pipe from the rear underside of the bonnet (photo).

4. Undo the two nuts and bolts from the bonnet side of the hinges (photo A) and lift the bonnet off (photo B). Place it somewhere safe where it will not be knocked over or bumped into.

5. Drain the cooling system as described in Chapter 2, Section 3.

6. Remove the sump drain plug and drain the oil out of the engine into a container of a minimum capacity of six pints.

7. There is no gearbox drain plug. As there will certainly be some small spillage from the gearbox rear cover extension later when the propeller shaft comes out, provide another tray—like receptacle with shallow sides to catch any oil which may drip out before the hole can be plugged. (Makeshift oil receptacles can be made from 1—gallon oil tins from which one of the large sides has been cut out).

8. Remove the air cleaner assembly from the carburetter as described in Chapter 3, Section 5.

9. Remove the radiator and the water hoses which connect it to the engine as described in Chapter 2, Section 6. If a heater is fitted in the car remove also the hose which connects it to the cylinder head (photo).

10 On the right-hand side of the engine compartment the windscreen washer reservoir hangs from two hooks. Remove the cap together with the pipe and then lift out the reservoir (photo).

11 Remove the electrical lead from the terminal marked 'SW' (or +) on the ignition coil (photo). (The other wire in this photograph attached to the same terminal normally runs to a radio suppressor).

12 Remove the cap from the distributor and take the leads from the sparking plugs. Remove also the H.T. lead from the centre terminal of the coil (photo A). Two of the plug leads should be detached from the clip secured to the inlet manifold (photo B).

13 Disconnect the oil pressure switch sender lead from the sender unit on the engine next to the oil filter. Disconnect also the lead to the water temperature gauge fitted at the forward end of the cylinder head (photo).

14 Disconnect the braided earthing wire which connects the engine to the bodyframe by undoing the nut where it is attached to the timing cover (photo).

15 Remove the circlip and spring connecting the intermediate rod to the carburetter throttle lever. Then remove the clip securing the accelerator rod to the intermediate rod which can be moved out of the rubber mounting bush (arrowed in photo).

16 Disconnect the choke cable as described in Chapter 3, Section 5.

17 Remove the starter motor cable from the terminal on the solenoid switch (Chapter 10, photo 18.5) It is easier to remove the lead at this terminal than at the starter terminal.

18 Disconnect the exhaust pipe from the exhaust manifold. This is done by removing the two brass nuts (photo). The nuts may be quite easy to move, in which case an open ended spanner is adequate. If tight however a ring, socket or box spanner should be used to avoid the possibility of burring over the flats in the soft metal. Do not attempt to force the pipe flange off the manifold studs at this stage.

19 Remove the fuel line from the suction side of the fuel pump (Chapter 3, photo 5.4).

20 From inside the car remove the knob from the gear change lever by slackening the locknut underneath it and screwing it off. Lift off the rubber grommet from around the base of the lever.

21 Through a hole in the floor tunnel another rubber cover can be seen round the lever at its base. This covers the screw cap which holds the gear lever in position in the gearbox extension tube. Grip the rubber cover with the cap underneath it and unscrew it.

22 When the cap is unscrewed the gear lever complete with cap, spring and retaining plate may be lifted out.

23 Work may now start on disconnecting the various necessary items under the car. If it has not already been raised on wheel ramps jack the car up at the front so as to give sufficient working clearance underneath and support it on proper stands or blocks. Position the stands under the front crossmember braces where they run back to the bodyframe. Under no circumstances use odd tins, the vehicle jack or other makeshift devices to support the car - it is foolishly dangerous.

24 Undo the knurled screw on the end of the speedometer drive cable where it goes into the gearbox casing at the rear on the right-hand side. Take care not to lose the oil seal disc (which is a free fit) after the cable is removed (Photo A and B).

25 Remove the clutch operating cable from the clutch operating lever and bellhousing as described in Chapter 5 Section 3.

26 Unhook the clutch lever return spring.

27 Remove the nut and large washer from the centre of the crossmember supporting the gearbox by the rear cover (Chapter 6, photo 3.4).

28 The gearbox should next be supported just forward of the crossmember by a jack or blocks.

29 The engine/gearbox unit is now free except for the forward engine mounting brackets which should be detached from the flexible mounting studs by undoing the single nut at each side (photo A and B).

30 Because the engine/gearbox are being taken out of the car together they will have to be tilted to a very steep angle. It is easier therefore if the sling for lifting is only a single loop to facilitate tilting the unit. The sling should pass BEHIND (i.e. the gearbox side) the engine mounting brackets. These, being still attached to the engine, will provide the main lifting lugs.

31 When the mounting bolts have been removed set the sling so that the lifting hook of the hoist is as close to the engine as possible. A lift of at least 3 feet will be necessary to enable the unit to come out clear of the body.

32 When the weight has been taken by the sling, draw the engine forward and up at the front.

33 Prepare for the disengagement of the propeller shaft which will come off the splines at the rear of the gearbox. If you are short handed put something soft on the floor to absorb the shock as it drops; and provide a tray to catch the oil which will drain from the gearbox as soon as the prop shaft comes out.

34 Once the rear of the gearbox is clear it is then simply a question of raising and tilting the unit until it is finally completely clear of the car.

35 At all times ensure that the sling is secure and not straining against any ancillary parts on the engine which could be damaged.

7. Engine Removal - Without Gearbox

1. Begin by following the instructions in Section 6, from paragraphs 1—25 inclusive.

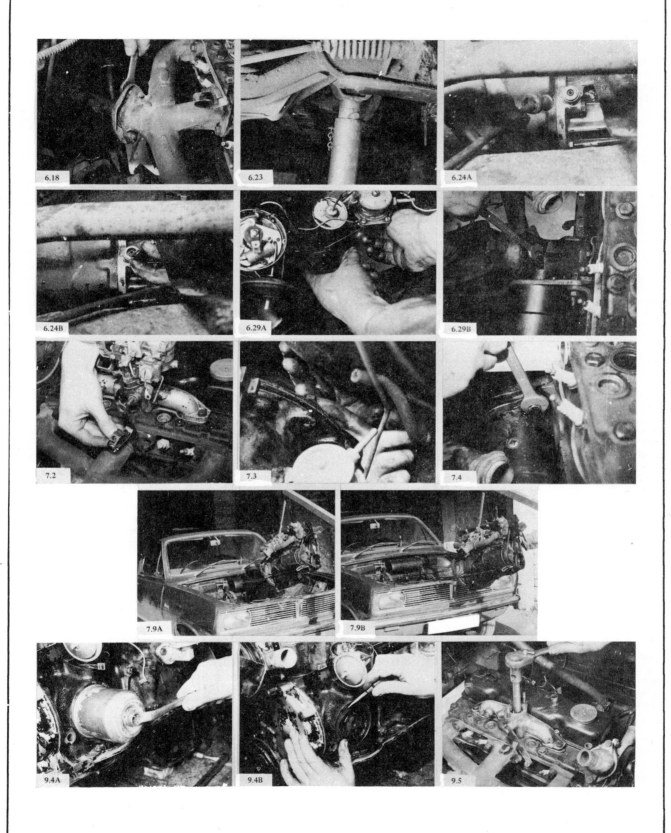

2. Remove the exhaust manifold from the engine by undoing the six mounting bolts. One of these bolts holds a bracing strip attached to the inlet manifold. Remove the other bolt on this brace and take if off (photo).

3. Remove the bolts securing the engine to the gearbox bellhousing. Some of these are accessible from above and others from below (photo).

4. Two of the bolts also locate the starter motor which should be removed when free (photo).

5. Undo the two forward engine mounting bolts (one each side) which hold the brackets to the flexible mountings (Section 6.30).

6. Now support the engine in a sling. As it does not come out at such an acute angle as with the gearbox attached, it requires support. Make sure the hoist hook is as close to the engine as possible when slung, in order to provide maximum lift.

7. Support the gearbox forward of the crossmember by a jack or block. Otherwise, when the engine is drawn away, the full weight of the gearbox will try and pivot forward, imposing a severe strain on the rear mounting.

8. Lift the engine a little and draw it forward so that the clutch is drawn off the gearbox input shaft splines. It is important not to raise or tilt the engine until it is clear, otherwise serious damage could be caused to either the shaft, clutch mechanism or both.

9. Once clear the engine can be lifted up and away (Photo A and B).

8. Engine Dismantling — General

1. Really keen owners who dismantle a lot of engines will probably have a stand on which to mount them but most will make do with a work bench which should be large enough to spread the inevitable bits and pieces and tools around on, and strong enough to support the engine weight. If the floor is the only possible place try and ensure that the engine rests on a hardwood platform or similar rather than concrete (or beaten earth!!).

2. Spend some time on cleaning the unit. If you have been wise this will have been done before the engine was removed, at a service bay. Good solvents such as 'Gunk' will help to 'float' off caked dirt/grease under a water jet. Once the exterior is clean, dismantling may begin. As parts are removed clean them in petrol or paraffin (do not immerse parts with oilways in paraffin—clean them with a petrol soaked cloth and clear oilways with pipe cleaners. If an air line is available so much the better for final cleaning off. Paraffin, which could possibly remain in oilways would dilute the oil for initial lubrication after reassembly)

3. Where components are fitted with seals and gaskets it is always best to fit new ones — but do NOT throw the old ones away until you have the new ones to hand. A pattern is then available if they have to be specially made. Hang them on a convenient hook.

4. In general it is best to work from the top of the engine downwards. In any case support the engine firmly so that it does not topple over when you are undoing stubborn nuts and bolts.

5. Always place nuts and bolts back together in their components or place of attachment if possible—it saves so much confusion later. Otherwise put them in small, separate pots or jars so that their groups are easily identified.

9. Engine Dismantling — Ancillary Components

1. If you are obtaining a factory replacement recondi-tioned engine all ancillaries must come off first—just as they will if you are doing a thorough engine inspection/ overhaul yourself. These are:—

Dynamo	(Chapter 10)
Distributor	(Chapter 4)
Thermostat and cover	(Chapter 2)
Oil filter and cover	(Section 9)
Carburetter	(Chapter 3)
Inlet manifold	(Section 9)
Exhaust manifold	(Section 7)
Water pump	(Chapter 2)
Fuel pump	(Chapter 3)
Engine mounting brackets	(Section 9)
Spark plugs	(Chapter 4)

2. If you are obtaining what is called a 'short engine' (or sometimes 'half-engine') comprising cylinder block, crankcase, crankshaft, pistons, and connecting rods all assembled, then the cylinder head, flywheel, sump and oil pump will need removal also.

3. Remove all the ancillaries according to the removal instructions for them described in the chapters and sections as indicated in paragraph one.

4. Oil Filter and Cover — Removal

a) Undo the centre bolt holding the cover to the side of the crankcase (photo) and pull off the cover. Discard the oil filter element.

b) Remove the sealing ring from the groove in the crank-case (photo).

5. Inlet manifold — Removal.
   Unscrew the two holding bolts one at each end of the manifold and with a socket wrench unscrew the third bolt located inside the intake orifice (photo).

6. Exhaust manifold — Removal.
   See Section 7, paragraph 2.

7. Engine front mounting brackets — Removal.
   Each bracket is held to the block by three bolts. These bolts have been sealed in, so will require considerable torque to turn them. Do NOT use anything other than a ring or socket spanner to remove them. Note which side of the engine each bracket comes from as they are not interchangeable. The brackets may be removed if necessary, with the engine still in place. The engine should be supported underneath and the bolts securing them to the engine and frame removed. In this way the flexible mountings may also be renewed.

10. Cylinder Head Removal — Engine Out of Car

1. Position the engine on a bench (or floor) with the cylinder head uppermost.

2. Remove the four screws holding the rocker cover and lift it off together with the cork sealing gasket which may be re-used if it is not over compressed or damaged.

3. Remove the carburetter (Chapter 3). The inlet and exhaust manifolds may be removed but it is not essential.

4. Slacken off the rocker clearance adjusting nuts (in the centre of each rocker arm) just enough (2—3 turns) to permit each one to be swung aside when the valve is closed so that the pushrods may be lifted out. The crankshaft will need rotating to do this. If it is intended to remove the valves anyway in due course, then it will save time if the rocker arms are removed completely at this stage.

5. Put the pushrods into a piece of pierced cardboard so that each can be identified to its relative valve (photo 23.1.).

6. Slacken off the ten cylinder head holding down bolts in the reverse order of tightening sequence. (See Fig.1.4).

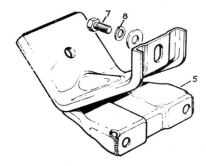

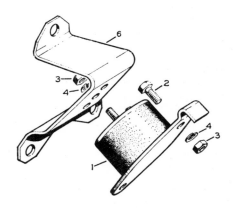

Fig.1.1. EXPLODED DRAWING OF ENGINE MOUNTING BRACKETS AND FLEXIBLE MOUNTINGS

1. Flexible mounting	3. Nut	5. Bracket - right-hand	7. Bolt
2. Bolt	4. Lockwasher	6. Bracket - left-hand	8. Lockwasher

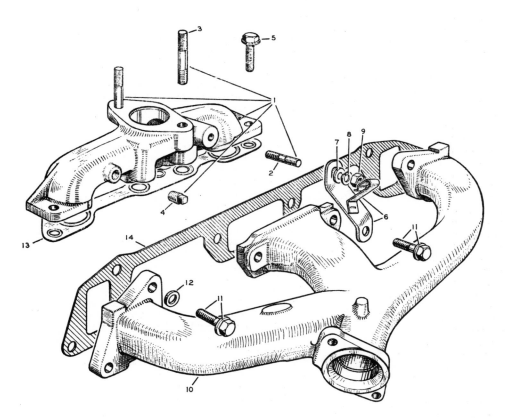

Fig.1.2. INLET & EXHAUST MANIFOLDS — HB22 ENGINE

1. Inlet manifold and studs assembly	stud	7. Plain washer	11 Exhaust manifold mounting bolt
2. Brace mounting stud	4. Blanking plug	8. Lockwasher	12 Washer
3. Carburetter flange mounting	5. Inlet manifold mounting bolt	9. Nut	13 Inlet manifold gasket
	6. Manifold brace	10 Exhaust manifold	14 Exhaust manifold gasket

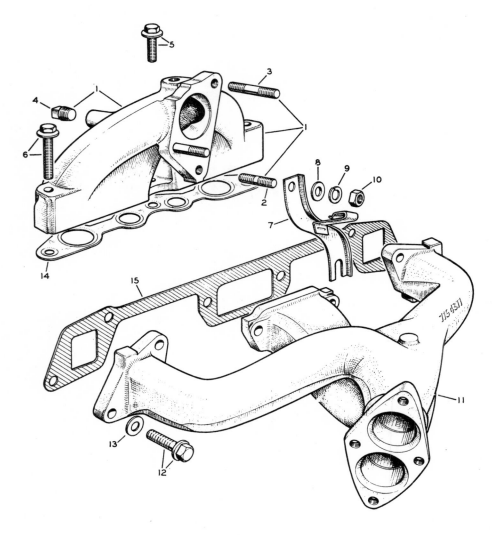

Fig.1.3. INLET & EXHAUST MANIFOLDS — HB23 ENGINE

1. Inlet manifold and studs assembly
2. Brace mounting stud
3. Carburetter mounting stud
4. Blanking plug
5. Inlet manifold mounting bolt
6. Inlet manifold mounting bolt
7. Manifold brace
8. Plain washer
9. Lockwasher
10. Nut
11. Exhaust manifold
12. Exhaust manifold mounting bolt
13. Plain washer
14. Inlet manifold gasket
15. Exhaust manifold gasket

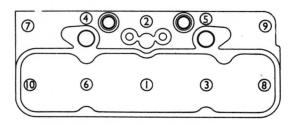

Fig.1.4. Diagram showing sequence of tightening cylinder head studs.

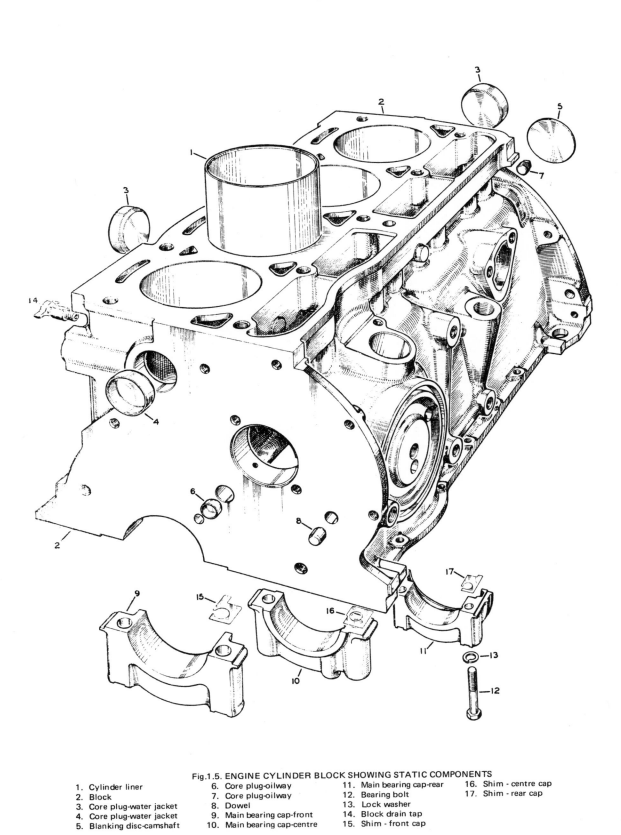

Fig.1.5. ENGINE CYLINDER BLOCK SHOWING STATIC COMPONENTS

1. Cylinder liner
2. Block
3. Core plug-water jacket
4. Core plug-water jacket
5. Blanking disc-camshaft

6. Core plug-oilway
7. Core plug-oilway
8. Dowel
9. Main bearing cap-front
10. Main bearing cap-centre

11. Main bearing cap-rear
12. Bearing bolt
13. Lock washer
14. Block drain tap
15. Shim - front cap

16. Shim - centre cap
17. Shim - rear cap

7. The cylinder head should now lift off easily. If not, try turning the engine over by the flywheel (with the spark plugs in position) so that compression in the cylinders can force it upwards. A few smart taps with a soft headed mallet or wood cushioned hammer may also be needed. Under no circumstances whatsoever try to prise the head off by forcing a lever of any sort into the joint. This can cause damage to the machined surfaces of the block and cylinder head.

11. Cylinder Head Removal — Engine in Car

1. Before proceeding as described for 'Cylinder Head Removal — Engine Out of Car' it is first of all necessary to carry out the following, including the removal of the parts as stated:
2. Disconnect both battery leads.
3. Drain the cooling system.
4. Remove the hoses from the water pump.
5. Remove the carburetter air cleaner unit.
6. Disconnect the vacuum advance suction pipe from both the carburetter and distributor, unclip it from the fuel feed pipe and take it off.
7. Disconnect the fuel feed pipe by unscrewing the union at the carburetter. To move the pipe out of the way slacken one of the two clips on the flexible connection at the fuel pump and turn the pipe away. Try and avoid bending the pipe.
8. Disconnect the accelerator linkage by removing the clip which holds the cranked arm to the carburetter throttle actuating arm.
9. Disconnect the 'Lucar' connector for the lead from the water temperature gauge sender unit in the cylinder head.
10 Remove the distributor cap complete with the plug leads and coil lead which should be disconnected at the plugs and coil respectively.
11 Proceed as for removing the head with the engine out of the car (Section 10). If the engine needs turning to assist in breaking the joint, reconnect the battery leads and give the engine a quick turn with the starter motor.

12. Valve Rocker Arms — Removal

1. The rocker arms can be removed as soon as the rocker cover is off. Each arm is located on a stud and is lightly supported on the stud by an inverted cone shaped coil spring. The vertical location of each rocker arm is controlled by a hemispherical ball on which the rocker pivots, and which is held in position by a self locking nut.
2. When the nut is removed the rocker can be lifted off, followed by the spring and washer at the base of the stud.

13. Valves — Removal

1. Remove the cylinder head (Sections 10 and 11).
2. Remove all the rocker arms.
3. The valves are located by a collar on a compressed spring which grips two colletts (or a split collar) into a groove in the stem of the valve. The spring must be compressed with a special G clamp in order to release the colletts and then the valve. Place the specially shaped end of the clamp over the spring collar with the end of the screw squarely on the face of the valve. Screw

up the clamp to compress the spring and expose the colletts on the valve stem. Sometimes the spring collar sticks and the clamp screw cannot be turned. In such instances, with the clamp pressure still on, give the head of the clamp (over the spring) a tap with a hammer, at the same time gripping the clamp frame firmly to prevent it slipping off the valve.

Take off the two colletts, release the clamp, and the collar and spring can be lifted off. The valve can then be pushed out through its guide and removed. Make sure that each valve is kept in a way that its position is known for replacement. Unless new valves are to be fitted each valve MUST go back where it came from. The springs, collars and colletts should also be kept with their respective valves. A piece of card with eight holes punched in is a good way to keep the valves in order.

14. Valve Guides — Reconditioning

If the valves are a slack fit in the guides, i.e. if there is noticeable movement when side to side pressure is exerted on the stem whilst in the guide, then the procedure is to ream out the valve guide bores and fit new valves with oversize stems.

Reaming is a skilled operation and the non-qualified owner would be well advised to have this done by a fitter.

15. Sump Removal

The engine must be out of the car in order to remove the sump unless you wish to remove the front suspension and axle assembly which we do not recommend. With the engine out, it is better to wait until the cylinder head is removed. Then invert the engine and undo the set screws holding the sump to the crankcase and lift it off. If the cylinder head is not being removed (for example if the oil pump only is being removed) the engine should be placed on its side and the sump removed as described.

16. Crankshaft Pulley, Timing Cover, Sprockets & Chain Removal

1. The timing gear is accessible with the engine in the car but unless the sump, and therefore the front axle are removed first, the sump gasket will have to be broken and a section replaced. This is not ideal but can be done with careful attention to the re-sealing of the timing case lower end to the sump, on replacement. It will be necessary to remove the radiator as described in Chapter 2.6., and the fan belt as described in Chapter 2.11. Then undo the four set screws at the front end of the sump which locate into the lower edge of the timing case. Then proceed as described from paragraph 2 onwards. (When drawing off the timing case cover, paragraph 7, it will be necessary to break the forward end of the sump gasket in the process).
2. First remove the large bolt which holds the fan belt driving pulley to the crankshaft. It will be necessary to prevent the crankshaft from turning by locking the flywheel with a bar in the starter ring teeth against one of the dowel pegs in the end of the crankcase (photo).
3. Another way is to block one of the crankshaft journals with a piece of wood against the side of the crankcase. With the engine in the car the pulley may also be removed. Put the car in gear while undoing the bolt.

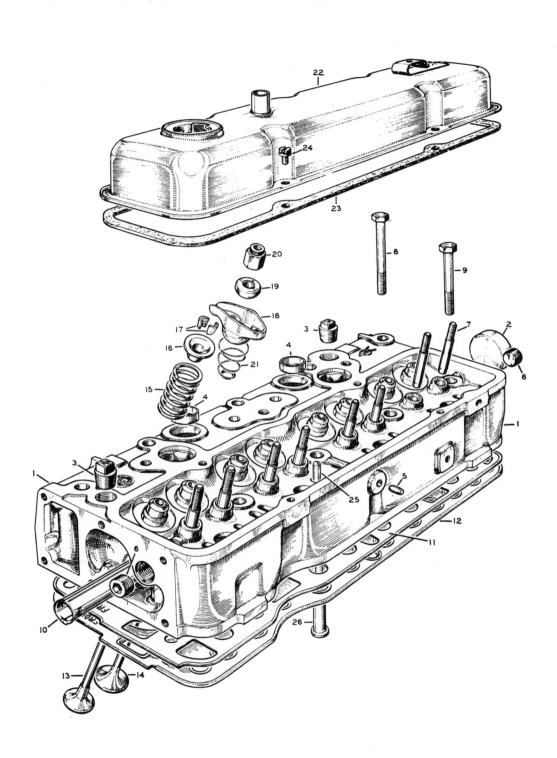

Fig.1.6. EXPLODED VIEW OF CYLINDER HEAD & COMPONENTS

1. Cylinder head
2. Core plug-water jacket
3. Blanking plug-water jacket
4. Core plug-water jacket
5. Plug-oilway
6. Plug-oilway
7. Rocker arm stud
8. Cylinder head bolt (long)
9. Cylinder head bolt (short)
10. Water distribution tube
11. Gasket - high compression
12. Gasket - low compression
13. Exhaust valve
14. Inlet valve
15. Valve spring
16. Valve collar
17. Collets.
18. Rocker arm
19. Rocker arm pivot
20. Rocker adjusting nut
21. Rocker support spring
22. Rocker cover
23. Rocker cover gasket
24. Rocker cover screw
25. Push rod
26. Tappet

4. Remove the spring washer and pulley washer. The pulley is keyed onto a straight shaft and should pull off easily. If not, lever it off with two screwdrivers at 180° to each other.

5. Take care not to damage either the pulley flange or the timing case cover which is made only of light alloy. Do not lose the woodruff key from the shaft—check that it fits tightly, and if not get another one, or make one from a piece of mild steel, that is a tight fit in the shaft and the keyway of the pulley boss.

6. Slacken the timing chain tensioner by turning the square headed screw clockwise as far as it will go to bring the pad right off the chain. On some later models the tensioner device adjusts automatically and is fitted independently of the cover.

7. Remove the bolts holding the timing case cover in place and draw it off.

8. Remove the bolt, lockwasher and plain washer from the camshaft timing sprocket. The sprocket may be prevented from turning by blocking one of the crankshaft journals against the crankcase with a piece of wood.

9. Both wheels and the chain may now be drawn off together—the sprockets are a push fit onto their respective shafts. Do not lose the woodruff keys, and if they are loose, check for fit. On models fitted with the automatic tensioning device this may now simply be removed from its mounting on the chain lubricating dowel peg. (See Section 33 for fuller details of this device).

17. Pistons, Connecting Rods & Big End Bearings — Removal

1. As it is necessary to remove the cylinder head and the sump from the engine in order to remove pistons and connecting rods, the removal of the engine is the logical thing to do first. With the engine on the bench and the cylinder head and sump removed, stand the block inverted (with crankshaft uppermost).

2. Each connecting rod and its bearing cap is matched, and held by two high tensile steel bolts. Before anything else, mark each connecting rod and cap with its cylinder number and relationship—preferably with the appropriate number of dabs of paint. Using punch or file marks may be satisfactory, but it has been known for tools to slip— or the marks even to cause metal fatigue in the connecting rod. Once marked, undo the bearing cap bolts using a good quality socket spanner. Lift off each bearing cap and put it in a safe place. Carefully turn the engine on its side. Each piston can now be pushed out from the block by its connecting rod. Note that if the pistons are standard there is a small notch in each which indicates the side of the piston towards the front of the engine. If there is no such notch, clean a small area on the front of each piston crown and place an indicative dab of paint. Do not use a punch or file marks on the pistons under any circumstances. The shell bearings in the connecting rods and caps can be removed simply by pressing the edge of the end opposite the notch in the shell and they will slide round to be lifted out.

18. Gudgeon Pins

The gudgeon pins float in the piston and are an interference fit in the connecting rods. If a connecting rod or piston requires a Vauxhall spares replacement it is necessary to buy the assembly. Any attempt to remove the pin will reduce the interference fit and may damage the rod or piston. Vauxhall spares do not supply the

items separately.

19. Piston Rings — Removal

Unless new rings are to be fitted for certain, care has to be taken that rings are not broken on removal. Starting with the top ring first (all rings are to be removed from the top of the piston) ease one end out of its groove and place a piece of steel band (shim, old feeler gauge blade, strip of cocoa tin!) behind it.

Then move the metal strip carefully round behind the ring, at the same time nudging the ring upwards so that it rests on the surface of the piston above until the whole ring is clear and can be slid off. With the second and third rings which must also come off the top, arrange the strip of metal to carry them over the other grooves.

Note where each ring has come from (pierce a piece of paper with each ring showing 'top 1', 'middle 1' etc.).

20. Flywheel — Removal

1. The flywheel can be removed with the engine in the car but it is not recommended, and the following procedures prevail when the engine has been lifted out.

2. Remove the clutch assembly (Chapter 5.6).

3. Remove the four bolts from the centre of the flywheel. There are no washers as the bolts are locked with a sealing compound.

4. Using a soft headed mallet tap the periphery of the flywheel progressively all round, gradually drawing it off the crankshaft flange and locating dowel. Do not allow it to assume a skew angle as the fit on the flange and dowel are at very close tolerances to maintain proper balance and concentricity with the crankshaft. When the flywheel is nearly off make sure it is well supported so that it does not drop. It is heavy.

21. Oil Pump — Removal

1. Remove the engine from the car and detach the sump.

2. Assuming that no dismantling of the camshaft and timing gear has taken place, set the crankshaft pulley pointer to the T.D.C. marker on the timing cover, (See Chapter 4.11), and ensure that the distributor rotor arm corresponds with the No.1 piston firing position. This will facilitate reassembly as the oil pump spindle also drives the distributor.

3. Remove the distributor (Chapter 4.7).

4. Disconnect the pump suction pipe support bracket by undoing the bolt holding it to the centre main bearing cap. Remove the two large bolts attaching the pump to the crankcase. Lift out the pump and gasket.

22. Camshaft — Removal

1. Remove the engine from the car.

2. Remove the sump, timing gear cover, timing chain and sprockets, oil pump and distributor.

3. Slacken all rocker arm nuts sufficiently to allow withdrawal of the pushrods.

4. Remove the fuel pump.

5. If the cylinder head has been removed stand the engine inverted—if not lie it on its right-hand side and rotate the camshaft several times to push the tappets out of the way.

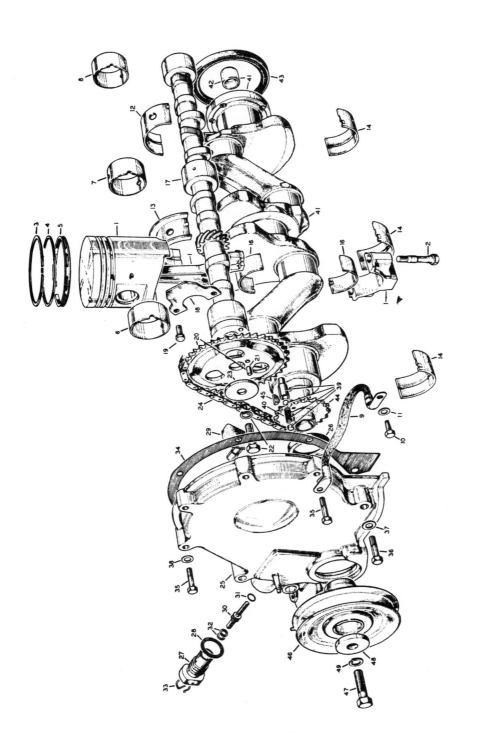

Fig.1.7. EXPLODED VIEW OF MOVING ENGINE COMPONENTS

1.	Piston	10.	Bolt	17.	Camshaft	25.	Timing gear cover	34.	Cover gasket	42.	Spigot bush
2.	Big end bearing cap bolt	11.	Washer	18.	Camshaft thrust plate	26.	Timing cover oil seal	35.	Cover bolt	43.	Crankshaft oil seal
3.	Top compression ring	12.	Main bearing shell upper—	19.	Thrust plate bolts	27.	Timing chain adjuster body	36.	Cover bolt	44.	Crankshaft timing sprocket
4.	Lower compression ring		front and rear	20.	Camshaft sprocket	28.	Fibre washer	37.	Washer	45.	Woodruff key
5.	Oil control ring	13.	Main bearing shell—upper	21.	Dowel	29.	Adjuster shoe-timing chain	38.	Washer	46.	Crankshaft pulley
6.	Camshaft bearing-front		centre	22.	Camshaft sprocket bolt	30.	Adjuster screw-timing chain	39.	Timing chain lubrication	47.	Pulley wheel bolt
7.	Camshaft bearing-centre	14.	Main bearing shells-		and washer	31.	Seal ring		assembly	48.	Washer
8.	Camshaft bearing-rear		lower	23.	Washer	32.	Seal rings	40.	Spring	49.	Lock washer
9.	Earthing strap	16.	Big end bearing shell	24.	Timing chain	33.	Lock spring	41.	Crankshaft		

25

6. Undo the two bolts retaining the thrust plate and slide the thrust plate out.

7. The camshaft can now be drawn out and care must be taken that it is manoeuvred past the tappets without damage to either the cams or the tappets. This will be easy if the engine is completely inverted. If, however, it is lying on its side with the tappets in such a position that they could fall out under their own weight, more care is necessary. In the event it would be advisable to prop the engine so that the tappets cannot fall out of their bores. Take care also not to damage the camshaft bearings with the edges of the cams as the shaft is withdrawn.

23. Tappets — Removal

1. With the camshaft removed, (Section 22) simply lift out the tappets and place them so that they can be returned similarly. A papier mache' egg box is a useful container for this (photo). (Note the pushrods through the cardboard in the background of the photo).

24. Crankshaft & Main Bearings — Removal

1. With the engine removed from the car, remove the sump, oil pump, timing chain and sprockets and flywheel. If the cylinder head is also removed so much the better as the engine can be stood firmly in an inverted position.

2. Remove the connecting rod bearing caps. This will already have been done if the pistons are removed.

3. Using a good quality socket wrench remove the two cap bolts from each of the three main bearing caps.

4. Lift off each cap carefully noting its position. Each one is different in shape however.

5. The bearing cap shells will probably come off with the caps, in which case they can be removed by pushing them round from the end opposite the notch and lifting them out.

6. Grip the crankshaft firmly at each end and lift it out. Put it somewhere safe where it cannot fall. Remove the shell bearings from the inner housings noting that the centre one has a flange on each side.

25. Engine Lubrication System — Description

1. A forced feed system of lubrication is used with oil circulated to all the engine bearing surfaces under pressure by a pump which draws oil from the sump under the crankcase. The oil is first pumped through a full flow oil filter (which means that all oil is passed through the filter. A by-pass oil filter is one through which only part of the oil in circulation passes).

2. From the filter, oil flows into a main oil gallery—which is cast integrally into the cylinder block. From this gallery, oil is fed via oilways in the block to the crankshaft main bearings and then from the main bearings along oilways in the crankshaft to the connecting rod bearings. From the same gallery, oilways carry the oil to the camshaft bearings.

3. From the centre camshaft bearing a further oilway passes oil to a gallery in the cylinder head. This gallery delivers oil through the hollow rocker mounting studs to lubricate the rocker pivots. The tappets are lubricated by oil returning from the rocker gear via the pushrods and is not under pressure. Once oil has passed through the bearings and out it finds its own way by gravity back to the sump.

If the filter gets blocked, oil will continue to flow because a pressure relief valve will open, permitting oil to circulate past the filter element. Similarly, any blockage in oilways (resulting in greatly increased pressure) will cause the oil pressure relief valve in the oil pump to operate, returning oil direct to the sump.

Oil pressure when hot is 35—45 lbs/sq.in. at 3,000 r.p.m. This pressure is measured after oil has passed through the filter. As the oil pressure warning light only comes on when the pressure is as low as 3—5 lbs/sq.in., it is most important that the filter element is regularly changed and the oil changed at the recommended intervals in order that the lubrication system remains clean.

Should the warning light ever come on when the engine is running at any speed above idling, stop at once and investigate — serious bearing and cylinder damage may otherwise result.

The crankcase is ventilated to prevent pressure building up from the action of the piston, and also to cause oil, and sometimes fuel, vapour to be carried away. Air enters via an oil wetted gauze filter at the dipstick hole and crankcase fumes are extracted via a pipe from the rocker cover into the air cleaner. From here it passes into the combustion chambers with the fuel/air mixture.

26. Oil Filter — Renewal of Element

1. Remove the filter casing as described in Section 9.4.

2. Clean out the interior of the bowl with paraffin ensuring that any sludge deposits are wiped out.

3. A new sealing ring will be supplied with the new element and this should be carefully fitted into the groove in the block. Do not stretch the ring by forcing one part into the groove and pressing the rest in afterwards, otherwise it will not seat properly — it will remain stretched. Get the whole ring into the groove at once and carefully bed it down with a small screwdriver, ensuring that it does not twist and jam across the groove. Put the new element in the bowl (photo), and place the bowl into the groove and screw up the centre bolt (this bolt is not detachable from the cover).

4. Before the cover is quite tight revolve it to ensure it is bedded into the sealing ring. Check the seating for leaks at the first opportunity by running the engine.

27. Engine Examination & Renovation — General

With the engine stripped down as described in the preceding sections, all parts should be thoroughly cleaned in preparation for examination. Details of what to look for are described in the following sections, together with instructions regarding the necessary repairs or renewals.

28. Crankshaft — Examination & Renovation

1. Examine all the crankpins and main bearing journals for signs of scoring or scratches. If all surfaces are undamaged check next that all the bearing journals are round. This can be done with a micrometer or calliper gauge, taking readings across the diameter at 6 or 7 points for each journal (photo). If you do not own or know how to use a micrometer, take the crankshaft to your local engineering works and ask them to 'mike it up' for you.

2. If the crankshaft is ridged or scored it must be reground. If the ovality exceeds .002 in. on measurement,

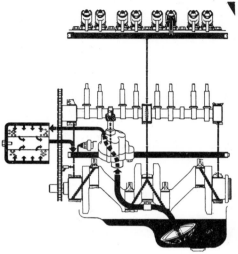

Fig.1.8. Descriptive drawing of lubrication system.

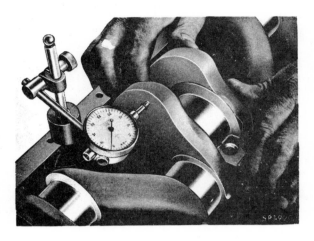

Fig.1.9. Showing measurement of crankshaft end float using a clock gauge micrometer.

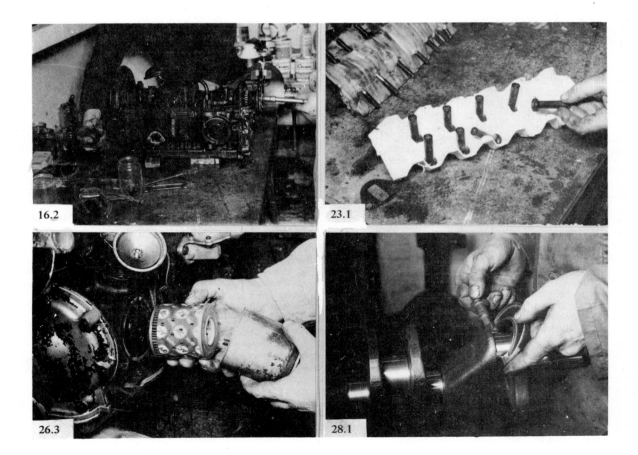

16.2

23.1

26.3

28.1

but there are no signs of scoring or scratching on the surfaces, regrinding may be necessary. It would be advisable to ask the advice of the engineering works to whom you would entrust the work of regrinding in such instances.

29. Big End (Connecting Rod) Bearings & Main Bearings - Examination & Renovation

1. Big end bearing failure is normally indicated by a pronounced knocking from the crankcase and a slight drop in oil pressure. Main bearing failure is normally accompanied by vibration, which can be quite severe at high engine speeds, and a more significant drop in oil pressure.
2. The shell bearing surfaces should be matt grey in colour with no sign of pitting or scoring.
3. Replacement shell bearings are supplied in a series of thicknesses dependent on the degree of regrinding that the crankshaft requires, which is done in multiples of .010 in. So depending on how much it is necessary to grind off, so bearing shells are supplied as '.010 in. undersize' and so on. The engineering works regrinding the crankshaft will normally supply the correct shells with the reground crank.
4. If an engine is removed for overhaul regularly it is worthwhile renewing big end bearings every 30,000 miles as a matter of course and main bearings every 50,000 miles. This will add many thousands of miles to the life of the engine before any regrinding of crankshafts is necessary. Make sure that bearing shells renewed are standard dimensions if the crankshaft has not been reground.

30. Cylinder Bores — Examination & Renovation

1. The bores must be checked for ovality, scoring, scratching and pitting. Starting from the top, look for a ridge where the top piston ring reaches the limit of its upward travel. The depth of this ridge will give a good indication of the degree of wear and can be checked with the engine in the car and the cylinder head removed. Other indications are excessive oil consumption and a smoky exhaust.
2. Measure the bore diameter across the block and just below any ridge. This can be done with an internal micrometer or a Mercer gauge. Compare this with the diameter of the bottom of the bore, which is not subject to wear. If no micrometer measuring instruments are available, use a piston from which the rings have been removed and measure the gap between it and the cylinder wall with a feeler gauge.
3. If the difference in bore diameters at top and bottom is .010 in. or more, then the cylinders need re-boring. If less than .010 inches, then the fitting of new and special rings to the pistons can cure the trouble.
4. If the cylinders have already been bored out to their maximum it is possible to have liners fitted. This situation will not often be encountered.

31. Pistons & Rings — Examination & Renovation

1. Examine the pistons (with the rings removed as described in Section 19) for signs of damage on the crown and around the top edge. If any of the piston rings have broken there could be quite noticeable damage to the grooves, in which case the piston must be renewed. Deep

scores in the piston walls also call for renewal. If the cylinders are being rebored new oversize pistons and rings will be needed anyway. If the cylinders do not need re-boring and the pistons are in good condition only the rings need to be checked.
2. To check the existing rings, place them in the cylinder bore and press each one down in turn to the bottom of the stroke. In this case a distance of 2½ in. from the top of the cylinder will be satisfactory. Use an inverted piston to press them down square. With a feeler gauge measure the gap for each ring which should be as given in the specifications at the beginning of this chapter. If the gap is too large, the rings will need renewal.
3. Check also that each ring gives a clearance in the piston groove according to specifications. If the gap is too great, new pistons and rings will be required if Vauxhall spares are used. However, independent specialist producers of pistons and rings can normally provide the rings required separately. If new Vauxhall pistons and rings are being obtained it will be necessary to have the ridge ground away from the top of each cylinder bore. If specialist oil control rings are being obtained from an independent supplier the ridge removal will not be necessary as the top rings will be stepped to provide the necessary clearance. If the top ring of a new set is not stepped it will hit the ridge made by the former ring and break.
4. If new pistons are obtained the rings will be included, so it must be emphasised that the top ring be stepped if fitted to an un-reground bore (or un-deridged bore).
5. The new rings should be placed in the bores as described in paragraph 2, and the gap checked. Any gaps which are too small should be increased by filing one end of the ring with a fine file. Be careful not to break the ring as they are brittle (and expensive). On no account make the gap less than specification. If the gap should close when under normal operating temperatures the ring will break.
6. The groove clearance of new rings in old pistons should be within the specified tolerances. If it is not enough, the rings could stick in the piston grooves causing loss of compression. The piston grooves in this case will need machining out to accept the new rings.

32. Camshaft & Camshaft Bearings — Examination & Renovation

1. With the camshaft removed, examine the bearings for signs of obvious wear and pitting. If there are signs, then the three bearings will need renewal. This is not a common requirement and to have to do so is indicative of severe engine neglect at some time. As special removal and replacement tools are necessary to do this work properly it is recommended that it is done by a 'specialist'. Check that the bearings are located properly so that the oilways from the bearing housings are not obstructed. Each camshaft bearing shell has a notch in the front edge on the side away from the crankshaft, as a position indicator.
2. The camshaft itself should show no marks on either the bearing journals or the profiles. If it does, it should be renewed. Check that the overall height of each cam from base to peak is within specification. If not, the camshaft should be renewed.
3. Examine the skew gear for signs of wear or damage. If this is badly worn it will mean renewing the camshaft.
4. The thrust plate (which also acts as the locating plate) should not be ridged or worn in any way. If it is, renew it.

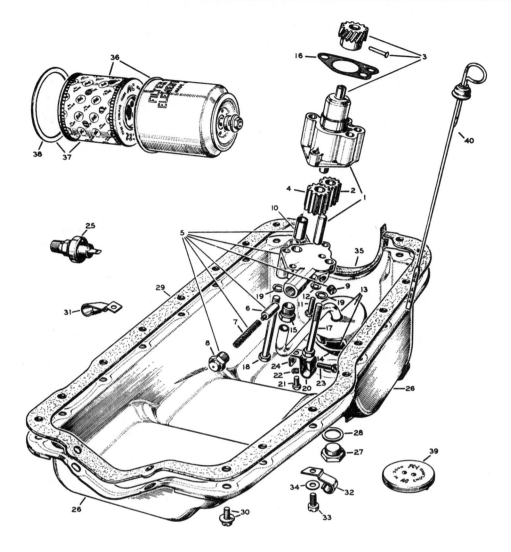

Fig.1.10. EXPLODED VIEW OF SUMP, OIL PUMP & FILTER ASSEMBLIES

1. Oil pump body
2. **Pump gears - driven**
3. **Pump drive gear and spindle**
4. **Pump gear - driving**
5. **Pump cover and relief valve assembly**
6. Pressure relief valve
7. Spring
8. Retaining plug
9. Plug
10. Reservoir tube
11. Bolt - cover to body
12. Washer
13. Strainer
14. Strainer gauze
15. Strainer pipe union
16. Pump to crankcase gasket
17. Pump mounting bolt
18. Pump mounting bolt
19. Washer
20. Clip
21. Bolt
22. Washer
23. Screw
24. Nut
25. Oil pressure switch
26. Sump
27. Drain plug
28. Drain plug washer
29. Sump gasket
30. Sump screw washer
31. Speedo cable clip
32. Clutch cable clip
33. Screw
34. Washer
35. Rear bearing cap to sump gasket
36. Filter element and bowl
37. Element and washer
38. Washer
39. Oil filler cap
40. Dipstick

38.3A

38.3(b)

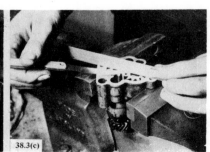
38.3(c)

33. Timing Chain, Sprockets & Tensioner — Examination & Renovation

1. Examine the teeth of both sprockets for wear. Each tooth is the shape of an inverted 'V' and if the driving (or driven) side is concave in shape, the tooth is worn and the sprocket should be replaced. The chain should also be replaced if the sprocket teeth are worn or if the tensioner adjustment is fully taken up. It is sensible practice to replace the chain anyway.
2. The tensioner is mounted in the timing case cover and consists of a screw which presses a shoe against the chain. If the shoe is badly ridged or worn it should be renewed.
3. Later production models are fitted with an automatic tensioning device mounted on the oiling stud (See Fig.1.13). It is held on the stud by the pressure of the timing chain cover against the rubber plug in the body of the unit. It is prevented from rotating by butting up to two extensions of the camshaft thrust plate which is also modified to suit. The principal is that the tensioner is spring loaded against the chain and as it moves out to take up slack, is locked by means of a piston with a spiral notched groove holding against a lug in the bore of the tensioner sleeve. (See Fig.1.14). Spares of the old model device are no longer made so it will be necessary to convert to the automatic device if renewing the assembly. In addition to the device itself a modified camshaft thrust plate and a sealing plug for the cover are included in the conversion kit.

34. Valve Rocker Arms & Pushrods — Examination & Renovation

1. Each rocker arm has three wearing surfaces, namely, the pushrod recess, the valve stem contact, and the centre pivot recess. If any of these surfaces appears severely grooved or worn the arm should be replaced. If only the valve stem contact area is worn it is possible to clean it up with a fine file.
2. If the rocker ball is pitted, or has flats worn in it this should also be replaced.
3. The nut is a self locking type on the stud. If it has been removed or adjusted many times the self locking ring may have become ineffective and the nut may be slack enough to turn involuntarily and alter the tappet clearance. If the tightening torque is less than the specified 3 lb/ft. minimum, new nuts should be fitted.
4. The rocker studs should be examined to ensure that the threads are undamaged and that the oil delivery hole in the side of the stud at the base of the thread is clear. Place a straight edge along the top of all the studs to ensure that none is standing higher than the rest. If any are, it means that they have come out of the head some distance. They should be removed and replaced with an oversize stud. As this involves reaming out the stud hole in the head you should seek professional advice and assistance to ensure that the new oversize stud is securely fitted at the correct angle.
5. Any pushrods which are bent should be renewed. On no account attempt to straighten them.

35. Tappets — Examination & Renovation

Examine the bearing surfaces of the tappets which lie on the camshaft. Any indentation in these surfaces or any cracks indicate serious wear and the tappets should be renewed. Thoroughly clean them out, removing all traces of sludge. It is most unlikely that the sides of the tappets will prove worn, but, if they are a very loose fit in their bores and can readily be rocked, they should be exchanged for new units. It is very unusual to find any wear in the tappets, and any wear present is likely to occur only at very high mileages, or in cases of neglect. If tappets are worn, examine the camshaft carefully as well.

36. Connecting Rods — Examination & Renovation

1. Examine the mating faces of the big end caps to see if they have ever been filed in a mistaken attempt to take up wear. If so, the offending rods must be renewed.
2. Check the alignment of the rods visually, and if all is not well, take the rods to your local Vauxhall agent for checking on a special jig.

37. Flywheel Starter Ring — Examination & Renovation

1. If the teeth on the flywheel starter ring are badly worn, or if some are missing, then it will be necessary to remove the ring and fit a new one.
2. Either split the ring with a cold chisel after making a cut with a hacksaw blade between two teeth, or use a soft headed hammer (not steel) to knock the ring off, striking it evenly and alternately, at equally spaced points. Take great care not to damage the flywheel during this process.
3. Clean and polish with emery cloth four evenly spaced areas on the outside face of the new starter ring.
4. Heat the ring evenly with a flame until the polished portions turn dark blue. Alternatively heat the ring in a bath of oil to a temperature of 200°C. (If a naked flame is used take careful fire precautions). Hold the ring at this temperature for five minutes and then quickly fit it to the flywheel so the chamfered portion of the teeth faces the gearbox side of the flywheel. Wipe all oil off the ring before fitting it.
5. The ring should be tapped gently down onto its register and left to cool naturally when the contraction of the metal on cooling will ensure that it is a secure and permanent fit. Great care must be taken not to overheat the ring, indicated by it turning light metallic blue, as if this happens the temper of the ring will be lost.

38. Oil Pump — Examination & Renovation

1. If the oil pump is worn it is best to purchase an exchange reconditioned unit, as to rebuild the oil pump is a job that calls for engineering shop facilities.
2. To check if the pump is still serviceable, first check if there is any slackness in the spindle bushes, and then remove the bottom cover held by two bolts.
3. Then check the two gears (the impellers) and the inside of the pump body for wear with the aid of a feeler gauge. Measure:— The backlash between the gearwheels (blade inserted between the sides of the teeth that are meshed together), [photo (a)] ; the gearwheels radial clearance (blade inserted between the end of the gearwheel teeth and the inside of the body), [photo (b)] ; the gearwheel end clearance (place a straight edge across the bottom flange of the pump body and measure with the feeler blades the gap between the straight edge and the sides of the gearwheel), [photo (c)]. The correct clearances are listed on page 13.
4. Fit a replacement pump if the clearances are incorrect.

39. Cylinder Head — Decarbonisation

1. This can be carried out with the engine either in or out of the car. With the cylinder head off, carefully remove with a wire brush and blunt scraper all traces of carbon deposits from the combustion spaces and the ports. The valve head stems and valve guides should also be freed from any carbon deposits. Wash the combustion spaces and ports down with petrol and scrape the cylinder head surface free of any foreign matter with the side of a steel rule, or a similar article.

2. Clean the pistons and top of the cylinder bores. If the pistons are still in the block, then it is essential that great care is taken to ensure that no carbon gets into the cylinder bores as this could scratch the cylinder walls or cause damage to the piston and rings. To ensure this does not happen, first turn the crankshaft so that two of the pistons are at the top of their bores. Stuff rag into the other two bores or seal them off with paper and masking tape. The waterways should also be covered with small pieces of masking tape to prevent particles of carbon entering the cooling system and damaging the water pump.

3. There are two schools of thought as to how much carbon should be removed from the piston crown. One school recommends that a ring of carbon should be left round the edge of the piston and on the cylinder bore wall as an aid to low oil consumption. Although this is probably true for early engines with worn bores, on later engines the thought of the second school can be applied i.e. that for effective decarbonisation all traces of carbon should be removed.

4. If all traces of carbon are to be removed, press a little grease into the gap between the cylinder walls and the two pistons which are to be worked on. With a blunt scraper carefully scrape away the carbon from the piston crown, taking great care not to scratch the aluminium. Also scrape away the carbon from the surrounding lip of the cylinder wall. When all carbon has been removed, scrape away the grease which will now be contaminated with carbon particles, taking care not to press any into the bores. To assist prevention of carbon build-up the piston crown can be polished with a metal polish such as Brasso. Remove the rags or masking tape from the other two cylinders and turn the crankshaft so that the two pistons which were at the bottom are now at the top. Place rag or masking tape in the cylinders which have been decarbonised and proceed as just described.

5. If a ring of carbon is going to be left round the piston then this can be helped by inserting an old piston ring into the top of the bore to rest on the piston and ensure that the carbon is not accidentally removed. Check that there are no particles of carbon in the cylinder bores. Decarbonising is now complete.

40. Valves, Valve Seats & Valve Springs — Examination & Renovation

1. Examine the heads of the valves for pitting and burning, especially the heads of the exhaust valves. The valve seatings should be examined at the same time. If the pitting on valve and seat is very slight, the marks can be removed by grinding the seats and valves together with coarse, and then fine, valve grinding paste.

2. Where bad pitting has occured to the valve seats it will be necessary to recut them and fit new valves. This latter job should be entrusted to the local Vauxhall agent or engineering works. In practice it is very seldom that the seats are so badly worn. Normally, it is the valve that is too badly worn for replacement, and the owner can easily purchase a new set of valves and match them to the seats by valve grinding.

3. Valve grinding is carried out as follows:- Smear a trace of coarse carborundum paste on the seat face and apply a suction grinder tool to the valve head. With a semi-rotary motion, grind the valve head to its seat, lifting the valve occasionally (photo) to redistribute the grinding paste. When a dull matt even surface finish is produced on both the valve seat and the valve, then wipe off the paste and repeat the process with fine carborundum paste, lifting and turning the valve to redistribute the paste as before. A light spring placed under the valve head will greatly ease this operation. When a smooth unbroken ring of light grey matt finish is produced, on both valve and valve seat faces, the grinding operation is complete.

4. Scrape away all carbon from the valve head and the valve stem. Carefully clean away every trace of grinding compound, taking great care to leave none in the ports or in the valve guides. Clean the valves and valve seats with a paraffin soaked rag, then with a clean rag, and finally, if an air line is available, blow the valves, valve guides and valve ports clean.

5. Check that all valve springs are intact. If any one is broken, all should be replaced. Check that the free height of the springs is within specifications also. If some springs are not within specification, replace them all. Springs suffer from fatigue and it is a good idea to replace them even if they look all right.

41. Engine Reassembly — General

1. To ensure maximum life with minimum trouble from a rebuilt engine, not only must everything be correctly assembled, but everything must be spotlessly clean, all the oilways must be clear, locking washers and spring washers must always be fitted where indicated and all bearing and other working surfaces must be thoroughly lubricated during assembly.

2. Before assembly begins renew any bolts or studs, the threads of which are in any way damaged, and whenever possible use new spring washers.

3. Apart from your normal tools, a supply of clean rag, an oil can filled with engine oil (an empty plastic detergent bottle thoroughly cleaned and washed out, will invariably do just as well), a new supply of assorted spring washers, a set of new gaskets, and preferably a torque spanner, should be collected together.

42. Crankshaft Replacement

1. Ensure that the crankcase is thoroughly clean and that all oilways are clear (photo). If possible blow the drillings out with compressed air.

2. It is best to take out the plug at each end of the main oil gallery and so clean out the oilways to the crankshaft bearing housings, and camshaft bearings. Replace the plugs using jointing compound to make an oil tight seal.

3. Treat the crankshaft in the same fashion and then inject engine oil into the crankshaft oilways.

4. If the old main bearing shells are to be replaced, (not to do so is a false economy unless they are virtually as new), fit the three upper halves of the main bearing shells to their locations in the crankcase, after wiping the locations clean (photo).

5. The centre upper shell bearing is flanged (photo). New bearings have over-thick flanges which must be reduced in order to permit the crankshaft to be replaced and fitted with the correct amount of endfloat, which is from .002 in. to .008 in. Endfloat, which is the amount a crankshaft can move endways, is measured between the centre bearing upper shell flange and the bearing surface on the web of the crankshaft, with the crankshaft moved to one extreme of its endfloat travel.

6. It will be necessary to reduce the shell bearing flange thickness by rubbing them down evenly on an engineers flat bed covered with fine emery cloth (photo). This is done progressively until a feeler blade of .002 in. thickness can be placed between the flange and the crankshaft web.

7. NOTE that at the back of each bearing is a tab which engages in locating grooves in either the crankcase or the main bearing cap housings.

8. If new bearings are being fitted, carefully clean away all traces of any protective grease or coating with which they may have been treated.

9. With the three upper bearing shells securely in place, wipe the lower bearing cap housings and fit the three lower shell bearings to their caps ensuring that the right shell goes into the right cap, if the old bearings are being refitted (photo).

10 Next install the new rear bearing oil seal. First lubricate the flange and oil seal lip with anti-scuffing paste and place the seal on the flange with the lip facing the centre of the crankshaft (photo). Make sure it is fitted squarely, that the lip is not turned back in any way and that the flange is completely free of burrs, scores or scratches, which will damage the seal and make it useless.

11 Check that the oil seal groove in the crankcase is completely free of old jointing compound and that the bearing cap faces throughout are similarly clean. Remove all traces of oil. When quite clean and dry apply 'Wellseal' jointing compound sparingly into the crankcase seal groove.

12 Thoroughly lubricate the main bearing shells with engine oil (photo A) and with the oil seal fitted, lower the crankshaft carefully into position (photo B). The weight of the crankshaft must be supported to ensure that the seal goes into the crankcase groove without damage or disturbance (photo C).

13 The main bearing caps with new shell bearings are next fitted in their respective positions, ensuring that the mating faces are perfectly clean to ensure perfect fitting. The rear bearing cap must have a head of Bostik 771 sealing compound applied along the register and chamfer on each side as shown in Fig.1.11. 'Wellseal' jointing compound should also be applied sparingly to the seal groove of this cap as was done in the seal groove of the crankcase.

14 The centre bearing cap should have the tapped hole, for the oil pump pipe support bracket bolt, on the camshaft side.

15 Oil all the threads and replace and tighten the bolts down to the specified torque of 58 lb/ft. (photo—centre bearing cap shows oil pipe bracket bolt position arrowed).

16 Any sealing compound which exudes from around the rear main bearing cap should be left where it is.

43. Pistons & Connecting Rods — Reassembly

1. As described in Section 18, the gudgeon pins and connecting rods are not supplied separately by Vauxhall so whenever the piston or connecting rod requires replacement the complete assembly must be purchased.

2. Specialised engineering works are able to fit new pistons to old connecting rods. Check locally to determine if this service is available.

44. Piston Ring Replacement

1. Ensure that the piston and piston rings have been inspected and renewed in accordance with the procedures described in Section 32.

2. Check that the ring grooves and oilways are completely clean.

3. Fit the rings over the top of the piston starting with the bottom oil control ring.

4. The ring may be spread with the fingers sufficiently to go around the piston, but it could be difficult getting the first ring past the other grooves. It is well worth spending a little time cutting a strip of thin tin plate from any handy can, say 1 inch wide and slightly shorter in length than the piston circumference. Place the ring round this and then slide the strip with the ring on it over the piston until the ring can be conveniently slipped off into its groove.

5. Follow in the same way with the other two rings— remembering that the ring with the cut-out step goes in the top groove with the step towards the top of the piston.

6. The words 'TOP' or 'BOTTOM' which may be marked on the rings indicate which way up the ring goes in its groove in the piston, i.e. the side marked 'TOP' should face the top of the piston, and does not mean that the ring concerned should necessarily go into the top groove.

45. Piston Replacement in Cylinder

1. The pistons, complete with connecting rods and new shell bearings (photo) can be fitted to the cylinder bores in the following sequence:—

2. With a wad of clean rag wipe the cylinder bores clean. If new rings are being fitted any surface oil 'glaze' on the walls should be removed by rubbing with a very fine abrasive. This can be a very fine emery cloth or a fine cutting paste as used for rubbing down paintwork. This enables new rings to bed into the cylinders properly which would otherwise be prevented or at least delayed for a long time. Make sure that all traces of abrasive are confined to the cylinder bores and are completely cleaned off before assembling the pistons into the cylinders. Then oil the pistons, rings, and cylinder bores generously with engine oil. Space the piston ring gaps equally around the piston.

3. The pistons, complete with connecting rods, are fitted to their bores from above.

4. As each piston is inserted into its bore ensure that it is the correct piston/connecting rod assembly for that particular bore and that the connecting rod is the right way round, and that the front of the piston (which is marked with a notch) is towards the front of the engine, (arrowed in photo).

5. The piston will only slide into the bore as far as the oil control ring. It is then necessary to compress the piston rings into a clamp (photo) and to gently tap the piston into the cylinder bore with a wooden or plastic hammer. If a proper piston ring clamp is not available then a suitable jubilee clip does the job very well.

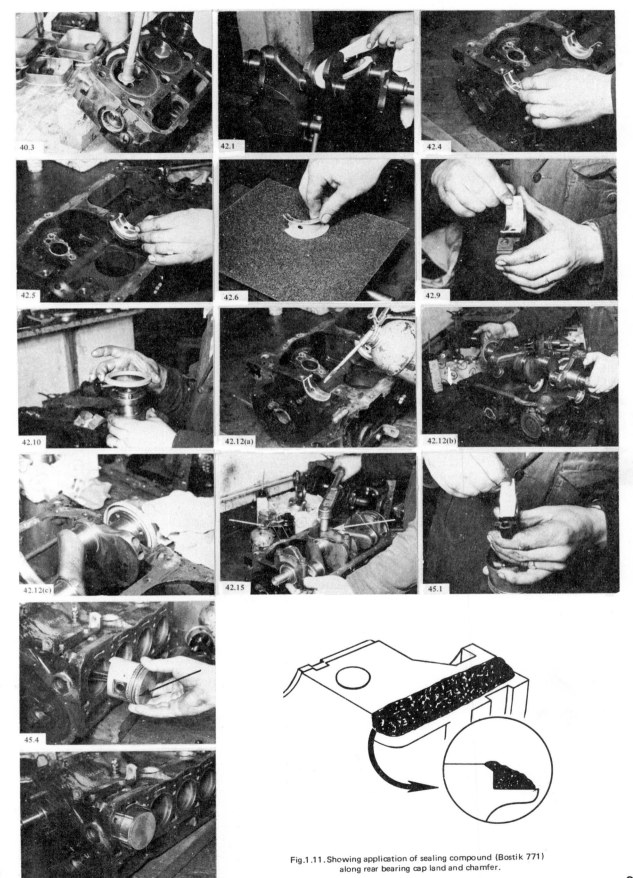

Fig.1.11. Showing application of sealing compound (Bostik 771)
along rear bearing cap land and chamfer.

6. If new pistons and rings are being fitted to a rebored block the clearances are very small and care has to be taken to make sure that no part of a piston ring catches the edge of the bore before being pressed down. They are very brittle and easily broken. For this reason it is acceptable practice to chamfer the lip of the cylinder very slightly to provide a lead for the rings into the cylinder. The chamfer should be at an angle of 45° and should not be cut back more than .010 in. If some form of hose clip is being used to compress the piston rings it may be found that the screw housing prevents the clip from lying exactly flush with the cylinder head. Here again watch carefully to ensure that no part of the ring slips from under the control of the clamp.

46. Connecting Rod to Crankshaft Reassembly

1. Wipe the connecting rod half of the big end bearing and the underside of the shell bearing, clean, and fit the shell bearing in position with its locating tongue engaged with the corresponding groove in the connecting rod (photo).
2. If the old bearings are nearly new and are being refitted, then ensure they are replaced in their correct locations on the correct rods.
3. Generously lubricate the crankpin journals with engine oil, and turn the crankshaft so that the crankpin is in the most advantageous position for the connecting rod to be drawn into it.
4. If not already done, wipe the connecting rod bearing cap and back of the shell bearing clean, and fit the shell bearing in position ensuring that the locating tongue at the back of the bearing engages with the locating groove in the connecting rod cap.
5. Make sure the cap fits the correct rod by checking the matching marks already made (photo).
6. Generously lubricate the shell bearing and offer up the connecting rod bearing cap to the connecting rod, (photo). Fit new big end bolts.
7. Fit the connecting rod bolts on oiled threads and tighten them down with a torque spanner to 25 lb/ft. (photo).
8. Oil the cylinder bores well for initial lubrication (photo).

47. Tappet / Camshaft Replacement

1. IMPORTANT. Replace the tappets in their respective bores before replacing the camshaft. They cannot be replaced afterwards. (Photos A and B).
2. Wipe the camshaft bearing journals clean and lubricate them generously with engine oil. Ensure the small oil hole in the centre of the camshaft is clear.
3. Insert the camshaft into the crankcase gently, taking care not to damage the camshaft bearings with the cams. (Photo).
4. Replace the camshaft locating plate (photo), and tighten down the two retaining bolts and washers.

48. Timing Sprockets, Timing Chain, Cover & Tensioner Replacement

1. This section describes the replacement procedure as part of the general overhaul of the engine and assumes that the engine is removed from the car. If, however, the timing gear has been removed with the engine in the car, the following additional points should be noted when refitting the timing case as described in paragraph 18. The front edge of the sump where the section of gasket between it and the timing case is fitted, must be thoroughly cleaned of all remaining traces of gasket and sealing compound. A new piece of gasket cut from either a whole new sump gasket or material of identical composition and thickness must be put into position using a sealing compound such as Hermetite or Wellseal. It must fit exactly, particularly where it joins in the angle between the sump and the front face of the engine block. The lower edge of the timing case must be similarly covered with sealing compound. When the timing case is refitted, the gap between the bottom of the timing case and the sump will be minimal and great care will be required to keep the piece of sump gasket in position. Replace the four set screws finger tight only, and finally tighten them when all the other procedures for refitting the timing case have been completed.
2. It is advisable to fit a new oil seal into the timing case, so first of all drive out the old one (photo).
3. Place the new seal in position with the lip facing the inside of the cover (photo).
4. Drive the seal home with a block of wood and a mallet (photo).
5. If a new chain has not been obtained as a complete unit, it may have been necessary to buy a length of chain and a connecting link. Having ensured that the total number of links, including the connector, is the same as on the old chain first join the two ends to the connector pin link (photo).
6. Place the link bar over the pins (photo).
7. Clip the spring (photo) so that both ends engage in the pin grooves fully.
8. IMPORTANT. When assembling the chain to the sprockets ensure that the closed end of the chain link clip leads in the direction of travel of the chain.
9. Note that the camshaft sprocket has a locating peg on the inner face which engages with a hole in the end of the camshaft (arrowed in photo).
10 Next assemble the chain to the two timing sprockets so that a straight line will pass through the centre of both wheels and the timing marks, with the timing marks facing each other (photo).
11 Next position the camshaft and the crankshaft so that the locating hole and key respectively are in the positions pointed out in the photo. This position will mean the minimum of fiddling when the sprockets and chain assembly is replaced in its correct position.
12 Holding the assembled timing sprockets and chain so that they cannot separate, place them on to the camshaft and crankshaft together so that the lug and keyway fit in their respective places (photo). Care is necessary to keep the sprockets in their relative positions in the chain as assembled in paragraph 10.
13 Replace the bolt and washer holding the camshaft sprocket in position, and locking the sprocket with a screwdriver, tighten the bolt (photo). DO NOT REVOLVE THE CRANKSHAFT DURING OR AFTER THIS — THE OIL PUMP INSTALLATION WILL THUS BE SIMPLIFIED.
14 If a new tensioner pad is being fitted, first partially screw in the main plug (photo) to the timing case.
15 Place the new pad, together with the adjusting screw (which should be screwed right down into the spindle of the pad) into the plug from the inside (photo). In the photo the oil seal has not yet been replaced in the groove of the pad spindle. Ensure that this is done with a new seal.
16 Tighten down the plug (photo) and ensure that the adjuster lock spring is properly located.

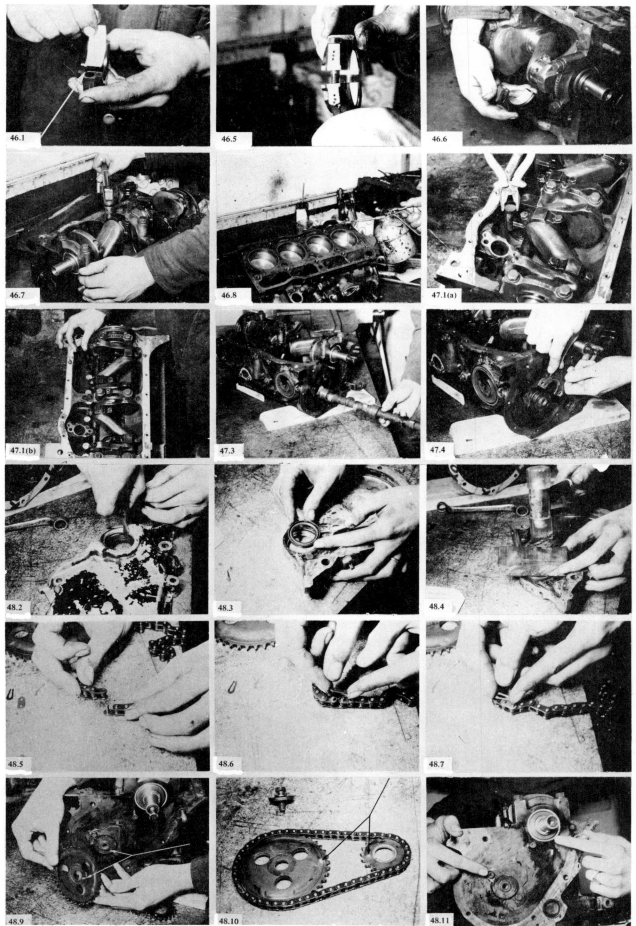

46.1

46.5

46.6

46.7

46.8

47.1(a)

47.1(b)

47.3

47.4

48.2

48.3

48.4

48.5

48.6

48.7

48.9

48.10

48.11

If the modified automatic tensioning device is to be fitted the procedures described in paragraph 21 should be followed.

17 On the face of the block, between the two timing sprockets, there is a protruding lug with a hole in it from which oil is fed to lubricate the timing chain. (It can be clearly seen in photo 48.12. On some early models (not this one illustrated), there is a vertical flat on the camshaft side. This locates on a lug cast into the inside of the timing case. This is to ensure that the oil hole faces in the proper direction, namely, towards the timing chain on a line 15° from the vertical. This hole position should be verified on later models as well.

18 With a new gasket fitted to the face of the block, lift the timing case into position (photo). Ensure the tensioner pad does not foul the chain, by seeing that the adjusting screw is turned fully clockwise.

19 Replace the mounting bolts, finger tight, and put the dynamo bracket on the stud before replacing the nut. (photo). In this photo the bracket is on the wrong way up. (The engine is upside down).

20 Temporarily replace the crankshaft pulley wheel on to the end of the crankshaft (photo), lining up the key in the shaft with the keyway in the pulley. This centralises the oil seal before the timing case bolts have been tightened up.

21 With the automatic tensioning device (See Section 33) compress the shoe into the body until it reaches the last notch on the piston where it will lock in position. The whole unit may then be placed in to position on the projecting dowel between the two timing sprockets. The top edge of the unit should abut the two extensions of the special camshaft thrust plate. When the chain and sprockets are reassembled the pad can be pressed in to release it from the notch in the piston. Spring pressure will then be applied to the chain.

22 Tighten down the cover bolts, and remove the pulley.

23 To adjust the tensioner, turn the square headed adjuster screw anti-clockwise until a firm resistance is felt and then back it off ½ turn. This adjustment must be re-checked later when the engine is running. A chatter indicates the tension is too slack and a whine, too tight.

49. Crankshaft Pulley Wheel — Replacement

1. With the timing cover located and bolted up as described in Section 48, paragraphs 19 and 20, fit the pulley on the crankshaft so that the key in the crankshaft fits in the pulley keyway. If there is any slackness of fit of the key in the shaft or the keyway, replace the key and clean up the slot or keyway as necessary.

2. Replace the large pulley washer followed by the lock washer and bolt. Hold the crankshaft steady with a wood block placed between the crankshaft web and the crankcase and tighten up the bolt (photo). If the engine is in the car, engage a gear to hold the crankshaft while the bolt is being tightened.

50. Oil Pump — Replacement

1. The oil pump spindle has an offset slot in the end of the impeller shaft which drives the distributor. It is therefore important that the drive gear is correctly meshed to the camshaft skew gear, otherwise the ignition timing will be incorrect.

2. If for any reason the drive gear has been removed from the oil pump spindle, make sure that the slot in the shaft is lined up with the gear teeth.

3. Next examine the pump, be it a new one or original, and ensure that the oilway drilling at the end of the body in the upper side of the spindle bush is clear. This oilway delivers oil for lubrication of the drive gear. Also check that the vent plug hole is clear.

4. Provided that the crankshaft has not been revolved since it was set at T.D.C. on No.1 compression (for pump removal), or since the valve timing gear was reassembled as described in Section xx the next paragraph may be ignored.

5. If the crankshaft has been turned it is necessary to ensure that the piston T.D.C. for No.1 is set on the compression stroke and not the exhaust stroke. To do this set No.1 piston at T.D.C. and examine the first two cams on the camshaft. If the lowest points on the cams are uppermost (meaning both valves would be closed), then T.D.C. No.1 is on compression which is what is required. If this is not the case turn the crankshaft through one revolution.

6. With the crankshaft (and therefore the camshaft) in the correct position, set the spindle of the oil pump so that the long side of the offset slot lines up with the holes in the body as shown in the photo.

7. Place a new gasket on the crankcase flange, put the mounting bolts through the pump body and line it up so that when installed it will not need any movement to line up the bolt holes (photo).

8. When replaced and viewed from the other end the slot should appear as shown in the photograph. The offset is to the rear and the slot is angled 14° anti-clockwise from a line at right angles (indicated in the photo by the steel rule) to the centre line of the crankshaft.

9. If the gear should be mistakenly meshed even one tooth out of position it will be quite obvious. In such cases remove the pump, re-align the spindle as described in paragraph 6, and replace and check it again.

10 Tighten down the holding bolts when the pump is correctly positioned (photo).

11 Replace the suction pipe and strainer and, before finally tightening the pipe union into the pump body, fix the mounting clip to the centre main bearing cap, (photo).

51. Sump — Replacement

1. Before replacing the sump, the timing case must be fitted. If the engine has undergone an overhaul to big end and main bearings check that all bearing caps have been properly tightened down, the oil pump replaced and that nothing that does not belong there has been left inside the crankcase.

2. Clean up, if not already done, the mating surfaces of the crankcase and the sump, and ensure that the outer groove in the rear main bearing cap is clean. Do NOT remove any of the sealer which may have exuded from the recent replacement of the bearing cap unless it has been left so long that it has gone completely hard.

3. Apply sealer (Bostik 771) to the ends of the groove (photo) in the bearing cap and apply a proprietary non-hardening jointing compound ('Hermetite'—Red) to the face of the crankcase.

4. Place the sump gasket in position (photo) ensuring the rear ends are firmly engaged in the groove and bedded in the sealing compound.

5. Apply a little more sealer and then place the cork strip gasket into the groove making sure that the chamfered ends face inwards overlapping the ends of the main sump gasket (photo). Make sure that an equal amount at each end overlaps the sump gasket ends.

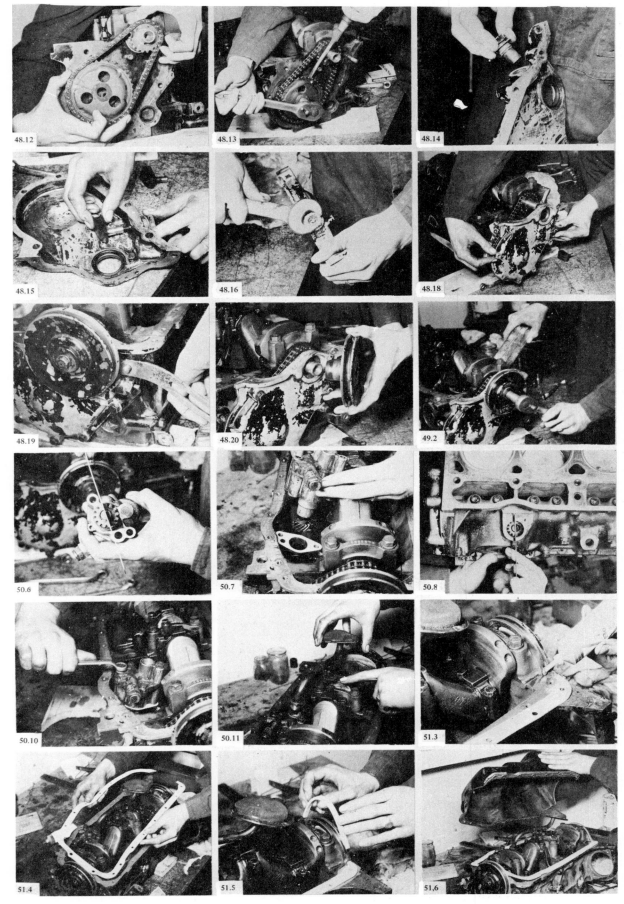

48.12

48.13

48.14

48.15

48.16

48.18

48.19

48.20

49.2

50.6

50.7

50.8

50.10

50.11

51.3

51.4

51.5

51.6

6. Replace the sump (photo) and when fitting ensure that the gaskets are not displaced. Some care is needed at the front where the sump gasket curves over the timing case.

7. Replace all the set screws and tighten the sump down evenly (photo).

52. Engine Mounting Brackets — Replacement

1. If the engine mounting brackets have been removed replace them now, ensuring that the bolts are treated with a suitable locking compound such as 'Loctite' (photo).

53. Flywheel — Replacement

1. If the starter ring gear needs renewal proceed as described in Section 40.

2. Usually the flywheel is such a close fit on the crankshaft flange that it is not possible to simply put it on and replace the bolts. The help of someone is almost imperative.

3. Note that there is a dowel peg on the crankshaft which locates in a hole in the flywheel (photo).

4. Offer up the flywheel to the crankshaft, hold it square and pick up the threads with the four mounting bolts. Then turn each bolt no more than ½ turn at a time and steadily draw the flywheel on.

5. When the flywheel is safely located on the shaft, remove the bolts and apply a small quantity of |Bostik 771 sealer to the centre only of each bolt thread. (This seals the holes in the crankshaft flange through which oil could otherwise seep, and also locks the bolts. The sealer is kept away from the end of the bolt to avoid the possibility of any falling inside the crankcase).

6. Replace the bolts and tighten them up evenly in rotation so that the flywheel is drawn on without slewing in any way. If this is not done carefully there is a possibility of damaging the flange and corresponding bore in the flywheel with resulting disturbance of the finely set balance.

7. Tighten up the bolts to the specified torque of 25 lb/ft. (photo). (Over-tightening can distort the mounting flange with serious consequences such as imbalance or the flywheel running out of true.)

8. See that the bush for the gearbox input shaft spigot is in good condition and in position in the end of the crankshaft (photo).

54. Valves & Valve Springs — Reassembly to Cylinder Head

1. Gather together all the new or reground valves and ensure that if the old valves are being replaced they will return into their original positions.

2. Ensure that all valves and springs are clean and free from carbon deposits and that the ports and valve guides in the cylinder head have no carbon dust or valve grinding paste left in them.

3. Starting at one end of the cylinder head take the appropriate valve, oil the stem and put it in the guide. Then put the screw head of the valve spring clamp over the valve head and place the valve spring over the other end of the valve stem (photo).

4. Then place the cap over the spring with the recessed part inside the coil of the spring (photo).

5. Place the end of the spring compressor over the cap and valve stem and screw up the clamp until the spring

is compressed past the groove in the valve stem. Then put a little grease round the groove (photo).

6. Place the two halves of the split collar (colletts) into the groove with the narrow ends pointing towards the spring. The grease will hold them in the groove (photo).

7. Release the clamp slowly and carefully, making sure that the colletts are not dislodged from the groove. When the clamp is fully released the top edges of the split collars should be in line with each other. It is quite good practice to give the top of each spring a smart tap with a soft mallet when assembly is complete to ensure that the colletts are properly settled.

55. Cylinder Head — Replacement

1. With the valves and springs reassembled examine the head to make sure that the mating face is perfectly clean and smooth and that no traces of gasket or other compounds are left. Any scores, grooves or burrs should be carefully cleaned up with a fine file.

2. Examine the face of the cylinder block in the same way as the head. Make sure also that the concave cups of the tappets are also clean and free from sludge.

3. The cylinder head gasket will be either a thin one of steel/asbestos, which is the standard high compression one, or a thicker copper and asbestos optional low compression one. Whichever gasket is used, Vauxhall recommend that it be smeared on both sides with 'Wellseal' jointing compound before assembly. Some people have different ideas and may use grease or nothing at all. Whatever jointing may be used it is imperative that it be smeared thinly and, more important, evenly. Any variation of thickness between the head and the block on reassembly is to be avoided at all costs.

4. Most head gaskets indicate which side is the top, but on the Viva there can be no confusion as it is not symmetrical, there being two distinctive shaped water jacket holes at the front end.

5. Place the gasket in position on the block and lower the head onto it (photo). Replace all the cylinder head bolts, (it will be obvious where the longer ones go, but in fact they are Nos.7,4,2,5 and 9 in Fig.1.4) and lightly tighten them.

6. Proceed with a torque wrench to tighten down the bolts ¼–½ turn at a time in the progressive order as indicated in Fig.1.4. (photo). This tightening sequence should continue until each bolt is down to a torque of 43 lb/ft. If, in the early stages any one bolt is obviously slacker than the rest it should be tightened equal to the others even if it may require a turn or so out of sequence. The whole point of the procedure is to keep the tightening stresses even over the whole head so that it goes down level and undistorted.

56. Valve Rocker Arms & Pushrods — Replacement

1. The rocker gear can be replaced with the head either on or off the engine. The only part of the procedure to watch is that the rocker nuts must not be screwed down too far or it will not be possible to replace the pushrods.

2. First place the washer over the rocker stud and then the light spring, with the narrower end down (photo).

3. Next put the rocker arm over the stud followed by the pivot ball (photo). Make sure that the spring fits snugly round the rocker arm centre section and that the two bearing surfaces of the interior of the arm and the ball face, are clear and lubricated with engine oil.

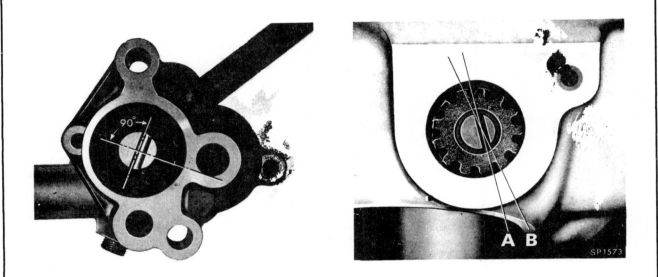

Fig.1.12. Showing position of oil pump drive slot prior to installation (left-hand picture) and position from above after installation (right-hand picture). Angle of slot may vary between A—B

4. Oil the stud thread with S.A.E.90 oil and fit the nut with the self locking collar uppermost (photo). Screw it down until the locking collar is on the stud.

5. Replace the pushrods through the head in the holes in line with each valve and rocker stud (photo). It is easy to drop the pushrods inadvertently and if they fall at an angle the lower end could get past the tappet and drop down into the crankcase. This would mean certain removal of the head and possible removal of the sump in order to retrieve it. It would be advisable therefore to push the top end through a small 'collar' of stiff cardboard or hold it in a bulldog clip so that it cannot drop through. When the lower end is felt to be firmly seated in the tappet recess the clip or collar may be removed.

6. Next screw down the stud nut so that the top of the pushrod engages in the recess in the rocker arm and approximately 1/8th inch of the stud protrudes above the top of each nut. It is as well to check the efficiency of the self locking ring at this stage by checking that at least 3 lb/ft. torque is needed to turn the nut. If it should be less the nuts could turn with vibration and should be renewed.

57. Valve Clearances — Adjustment

1. The valve clearances should be set by placing a .010 in. feeler gauge (exhaust valves) or a .006 in. feeler (inlet valves) between the valve stem and rocker arm and turning the nut until the clearance is correct (photo). This operation is carried out when each valve is closed, and the appropriate cam is at its lowest point. The initial settings can be made with the engine cold but recheck them when the engine is warm.

2. To ensure that each valve is in the correct position for checking the clearance, proceed as follows:

3. Set the crankshaft pulley marker to the T.D.C. pointer cast in the timing case (the upper one—see Chapter 4), and the distributor rotor at No.1 spark plug lead position.

4. If the engine is being reassembled after an overhaul it would be best to leave this job until it is back in the car. It will be easier to turn the engine over as needed.

5. With the No.1 piston in compression at T.D.C. both valves for that cylinder (Nos.1 and 2) may be set to their correct clearances as described in paragraph 1.

6. The firing order being 1,3,4,2, the crankshaft may then be rotated ½ revolution clockwise and No.3 piston will be at T.D.C. so that valve Nos. 5 and 6 may be adjusted. A further ½ revolution and No.4 piston is at T.D.C. for valves Nos.7 and 8 to be checked and finally the last half revolution presents No.2 piston at T.D.C. for valves Nos.3 and 4 to be checked. The table following shows the piston/valve relationship, and which are exhaust and inlet valves.

	Valve No.	Clearance	Piston No.
Exhaust	1	.010 in.	1
Inlet	2	.006 in.	1
Inlet	3	.006 in.	2
Exhaust	4	.010 in.	2
Exhaust	5	.010 in.	3
Inlet	6	.006 in.	3
Inlet	7	.006 in.	4
Exhaust	8	.010 in.	4

7. Another way of setting the valves to check the clearance is to do them in pairs, regardless of crankshaft setting. The table below shows the valves linked as pairs and when either one of a pair is fully open (valve spring compressed) the other is fully closed and the clearance may be checked.

Valve Fully Open	Check & Adjust
Valve No.8.	Valve No.1. ex.
Valve No.6.	Valve No.3. in.
Valve No.4.	Valve No.5. ex.
Valve No.7.	Valve No.2. in.
Valve No.1.	Valve No.8. ex.
Valve No.3.	Valve No.6. in.
Valve No.5.	Valve No.4. ex.
Valve No.2.	Valve No.7. in.

If the order of the left-hand column is followed the minimum amount of engine turning will be necessary.

58. Inlet Manifold — Replacement

1. Fit a new aluminium gasket (photo) so that it lines up with the ports in the top of the cylinder head.

2. Refit the manifold (photo) and replace the three bolts holding it down.

3. The centre one will need holding with pliers (photo) in order to place it easily into the centre locating hole (photo).

59. Exhaust Manifold — Replacement

1. If the engine has been removed from the car, and is being replaced with the gearbox, then the exhaust manifold may be refitted before the engine is replaced, provided that the starter motor is in position on the engine.

2. If the engine without the gearbox is being replaced, the exhaust manifold must not be fitted until after the engine is fixed back to the gearbox, because only then can the starter motor be replaced.

3. Place a new gasket in position (photo).

4. Replace the manifold (photo A) and when reconnecting the exhaust pipe fit a new gasket (photo B). Make sure that the inlet manifold brace is also refitted (photo 7.2.).

60. Final Engine Reassembly

1. All the components removed (see Section 10) should be replaced on the engine where possible before the engine is replaced in the car, as it is generally more easily done at bench level. One possible exception is the carburetter which is somewhat vulnerable and could be damaged when replacing the engine. The other exception is the exhaust manifold for the reasons discussed in Section 59. Even though the valve clearances have not been finally set, replace the rocker cover for protection. You need not fit the new gasket yet, as shown in the photo, as the cover will have to be removed once more.

61. Engine Replacement

Engine replacement is generally speaking a straight forward reversal of the removal sequence. The following hints and tips will however be found useful:

1. If the engine and gearbox have both been removed together it is best to replace them together. This will mean fitting the gearbox assembly to the engine on the

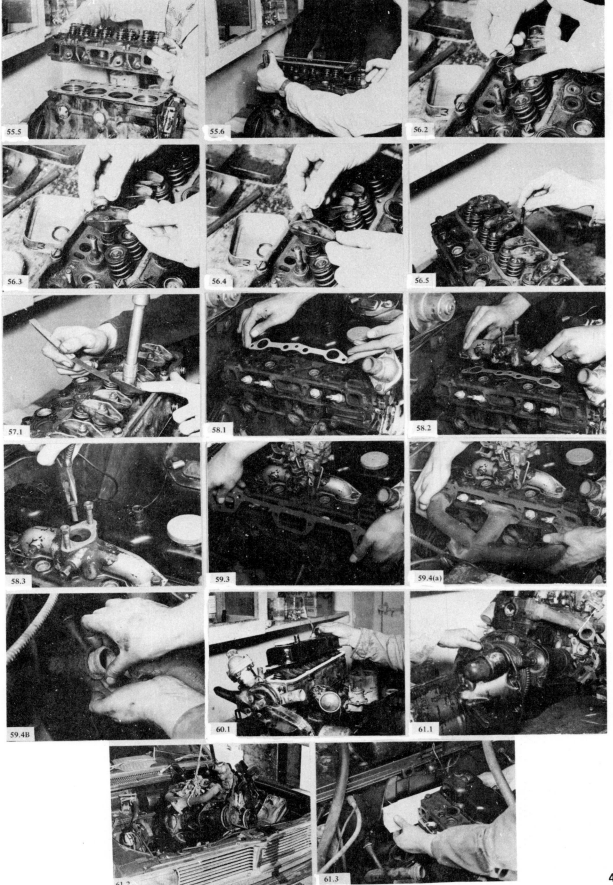

55.5

55.6

56.2

56.3

56.4

56.5

57.1

58.1

58.2

58.3

59.3

59.4(a)

59.4B

60.1

61.1

61.2

61.3

bench (photo) and will make the mating of the gearbox input shaft to the clutch that much easier (See Chapter 6.3.). It will also obviate the need to disconnect the propeller shaft which is necessary if the gearbox is removed and replaced separately from the engine. As the engine is lowered into the car the front of the propeller shaft must be fed into the rear of the gearbox by someone lying underneath the car.

2. The engine without the gearbox is shown being replaced in the photo. The exhaust manifold has been temporarily replaced as it provides a very useful sling attachment point. It will be removed when the engine is in position so that the starter motor may be replaced as mentioned in Section 59.

3. When the engine is being put back into the car make sure that it is watched every inch of the way to ensure that no pipes or wires get caught up or damaged. If, for any reason the engine will not go where you want it to, look and see why. Do not force anything. As soon as the engine is re-located on its forward mountings it must be supported at its rear end due to the fact that the gearbox is not yet installed. This can be done by placing a block of wood behind the cylinder head (photo).

4. If the engine is separated from the gearbox smear a little grease on the tip of the gearbox input shaft.

5. Always fit new oil and air cleaner elements after an overhaul.

6. The bonnet will need two pairs of hands to support it when refitting it (photo 6.2). Fix the bracket bolts and nuts just tight enough to hold it and then close the bonnet to ensure it is correctly lined up and central, before tightening them.

7. The following final check list should ensure that the engine starts safely and with the minimum of delay:

a) Fuel lines to pump and carburetter—connected and tightened.
b) Water hoses connected and clipped.
c) Radiator and engine drain taps closed.
d) Water system replenished.
e) Sump drain plug fitted and tight.
f) Oil in engine.
g) Oil in gearbox and level plug tight.
h) L.T. wires connected to distributor and coil.
i) Spark plugs tight.
j) Tappet clearances set correctly.
k) H.T. leads connected securely to distributor, spark plugs and coil.
l) Rotor arm replaced in distributor and pushed fully home.
m) Choke and throttle linkages connected.
n) Braided earthing cable, engine to frame reconnected.
o) Starter motor lead connected.
p) Fan belt fitted and correctly tensioned.
q) Dynamo leads connected.
r) Battery charged and leads connected to clean terminals.

62. Timing Chain Adjustment

1. When the engine is running listen for any unusual sounds coming from the timing case and adjust the chain as described in Section 48, paragraph 22. With the engine in the car it will be necessary to remove the fan belt and swing the dynamo to one side in order to get access to the adjusting screw. It is not necessary to replace the fan belt each time the engine is run to check the chain tension during adjustment. If the tensioner fitted is the modified self adjusting type this is of course unnecessary.

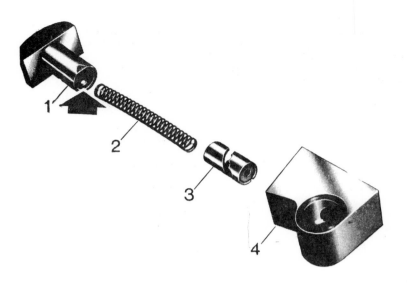

Fig.1.13. Showing installation of timing chain automatic tensioning fitment

Fig.1.14. TIMING CHAIN AUTOMATIC TENSIONER UNIT EXPLODED VIEW

1. Tensioner pad and sleeve   2. Spring.   3. Grooved piston   4. Body

Arrow indicates lug which engages in teeth of piston groove to prevent retraction of tensioner.

Symptom	Reason/s	Remedy
Engine will not turn over when starter switch is operated	Flat battery. Bad battery connections. Bad connections at solenoid switch and/or starter motor.	Check that battery is fully charged and that all connections are clean and tight.
	Starter motor jammed.	Turn the square headed end of the starter motor shaft with a spanner to free it. Where a pre-engaged starter is fitted rock the car back and forth with a gear engaged. If this does not free pinion remove starter.
	Defective solenoid.	Bridge the main terminals of the solenoid switch with a piece of heavy duty cable in order to operate the starter.
	Starter motor defective.	Remove and overhaul starter motor.
Engine turns over normally but fails to fire and run	No spark at plugs.	Check ignition system according to procedures given in Chapter 4.
	No fuel reaching engine.	Check fuel system according to procedures given in Chapter 3.
	Too much fuel reaching the engine (flooding).	Check the fuel system as above.
Engine starts but runs unevenly and misfires	Ignition and/or fuel system faults	Check the ignition and fuel systems as though the engine had failed to start.
	Incorrect valve clearances.	Check and reset clearances.
	Burnt out valves. Blown cylinder head gasket.	Remove cylinder head and examine and overhaul as necessary.
	Worn out piston rings. Worn cylinder bores.	Remove cylinder head and examine pistons and cylinder bores. Overhaul as necessary.
Lack of power	Ignition and/or fuel system faults.	Check the ignition and fuel systems for correct ignition timing and carburetter settings.
	Incorrect valve clearances	Check and reset the clearances.
	Burnt out valves. Blown cylinder head gasket.	Remove cylinder head and examine and overhaul as necessary.
	Worn out piston rings. Worn cylinder bores.	Remove cylinder head and examine pistons and cylinder bores. Overhaul as necessary.
Excessive oil consumption	Oil leaks from crankshaft rear oil seal, timing cover gasket and oil seal, rocker cover gasket, oil filter gasket, sump gasket, sump plug washer.	Identify source of leak and renew seal as appropriate.
	Worn piston rings or cylinder bores resulting in oil being burnt by engine. Smoky exhaust is an indication.	Fit new rings or rebore cylinders and fit new pistons, depending on degree of wear.
	Worn valve guides and/or defective valve stem seals. Smoke blowing out from the rocker cover vents is an indication.	Remove cylinder heads and recondition valve stem bores and valves and seals as necessary.
Excessive mechanical noise from engine	Wrong valve to rocker clearances.	Adjust valve clearances.
	Worn crankshaft bearings. Worn cylinders (piston slap).	Inspect and overhaul where necessary.
	Slack or worn timing chain and sprockets.	Adjust chain and/or inspect all timing mechanism.

NOTE: When investigating starting and uneven running faults do not be tempted into snap diagnosis. Start from the beginning of the check procedure and follow it through. It will take less time in the long run. Poor performance from an engine in terms of power and economy is not normally diagnosed quickly. In any event the ignition and fuel systems must be checked first before assuming any further investigation needs to be made.

Chapter 2/Cooling System

Contents

Specifications

Type of System	Pressurised, pump assisted circulation with thermostat temperature control

Capacity

Without heater...	10.4 pints
With heater...	11.4 pints

Radiator	Flow capacity is 5 gallons (Imp) in 22 seconds (maximum) with a constant 2 foot head through a 1¼ inch bore pipe. Leak test pressure is between 7 to 10 lbs/in^2 Filler cap valve opens at between 6¼ to 7¾ lbs/in^2
Fan Belt	V pulley drive. Tension permits depression of ½ inch between generator and fan pulleys under a 9 lb load

Thermostat

	Western Thomson (valve opens upwards)	A.C. (valve opens downwards)
Opening temperature...	85° — 89°C	80° — 84°C
Fully open temperature	102°C	98°C
Fully open lift from flange	.51 in. (min)	.48 in. (min)

Water Pump

Pulley flange fit on spindle	.0009 in. to .0026 interference
Rotor fit on spindle	.0004 in. to .0021 interference

1. General Description

The engine cooling water is circulated by a thermo-siphon, water pump assisted system, and the coolant is pressurised. This is both to prevent the loss of water down the overflow pipe with the radiator cap in position and to prevent premature boiling in adverse conditions.

The radiator cap is, in effect, a safety valve designed to lift at a pressure of 7 lbs sq.in. which means that the coolant can reach a temperature above 212°F (100°C) before it lifts the cap. It then boils off, steam escaping down the overflow pipe. When the temperature/pressure decreases the cap re-seats until the temperature/pressure builds up again.

It is therefore important to check that the radiator cap fitted is of the correct specification (the relief pressure is stamped on the top) and in good condition, and that the spring behind the sealing washer has not weakened. Most garages have a special machine in which radiator caps can be tested.

The system functions in the following fashion: Cold water in the bottom of the radiator circulates up the lower radiator hose to the water pump where it is pushed round the water passages in the cylinder block, helping to keep the cylinder bores and pistons cool.

The water then travels up into the cylinder head and circulates round the combustion spaces and valve seats absorbing more heat, and then when the engine is at its proper operating temperature, travels out of the cylinder head, past the open thermostat into the upper radiator hose and so into the radiator head tank.

The water travels down the radiator where it is rapidly cooled by the in-rush of cold air through the radiator core, which is created by both the fan and the motion of the car. The water, now cold, reaches the bottom of the radiator, whereupon the cycle is repeated.

When the engine is cold the thermostat (which is a valve which opens and closes according to the temperature of the water) maintains the circulation of the same water in the engine, excluding that in the radiator.

The cooling system comprises the radiator, top and bottom water hoses, heater hoses (if heater/demister fitted), the impeller water pump, (mounted on the front of the engine it carries the fan blades and is driven by the fan belt), the thermostat and the two drain taps.

Only when the correct minimum operating temperature has been reached, as shown in the specification, does the thermostat begin to open, allowing water to return to the radiator.

2. Routine Maintenance

1. Check the level of the water in the radiator once a week or more frequently if necessary, and top up with a soft water (rain water is excellent) as required.
2. Once every 6,000 miles check the fan belt for wear and correct tension and renew or adjust the belt as necessary. (See Section 11 for details).
3. Once every 12,000 miles unscrew the plug from the top of the water pump and press in by hand a little grease. Do not overgrease or the seal may be rendered inoperative. Replace the plug and screw down.

3. Cooling System — Draining

1. With the car on level ground drain the system as follows:—

2. If the engine is cold remove the filler cap from the radiator by turning the cap anti-clockwise. If the engine is hot having just been run, then turn the filler cap very slightly until the pressure in the system has had time to disperse. Use a rag over the cap to protect your hand from escaping steam. If, with the engine very hot, the cap is released suddenly, the drop in pressure can result in the water boiling. With the pressure released the cap can be removed.
3. If anti-freeze is in the radiator drain it into a clean bucket or bowl for re-use.
4. Open the two drain taps. The radiator drain tap is on the bottom radiator tank - see photo (A) - and the engine drain tap is halfway down the rear left-hand side of the cylinder block - see photo (B). A short length of rubber tubing over the radiator drain tap nozzle will assist draining the coolant into a container without splashing.
5. When the water has finished running, probe the drain tap orifices with a short piece of wire to dislodge any particles of rust or sediment which may be blocking the taps and preventing all the water draining out.
NOTE: Opening only the radiator tap will not drain the cylinder block.

4. Cooling System — Flushing

1. With time the cooling system will gradually lose its efficiency as the radiator becomes choked with rust scales, deposits from the water and other sediment. To clean the system out, remove the radiator cap and the drain tap and leave a hose running in the radiator cap orifice for ten to fifteen minutes.
2. In very bad cases the radiator should be reverse flushed. This can be done with the radiator in position. The cylinder block tap is closed and a hose placed over the open radiator drain tap. Water, under pressure, is then forced up through the radiator and out of the header tank filler orifice.
3. The hose is then removed and placed in the filler orifice and the radiator washed out in the usual fashion.

5. Cooling System — Filling

1. Close the two drain taps.
2. Fill the system slowly to ensure that air locks are minimised. If a heater is fitted it will be necessary to disconnect the outlet hose at the connector and fill up through the pipe to force air out of the heater battery. Chapter 12/23 gives details.
3. Do not fill the system higher than within ½ in. of the filler orifice. Overfilling will merely result in wastage, which is especially to be avoided when anti-freeze is in use.
4. Only use anti-freeze mixture with a glycerine or ethylene base.
5. Replace the filler cap and turn it firmly clockwise to lock it in position.

6. Radiator Removal, Inspection, Cleaning & Replacement

1. Drain the cooling system as described in Section 3.
2. Undo the clip which holds the top water hose to the thermostat outlet side of the water pump (see photo) and pull it off the pump.
3. Remove the hose from the heater (if fitted) where it joins the main bottom radiator hose. (See photo) and

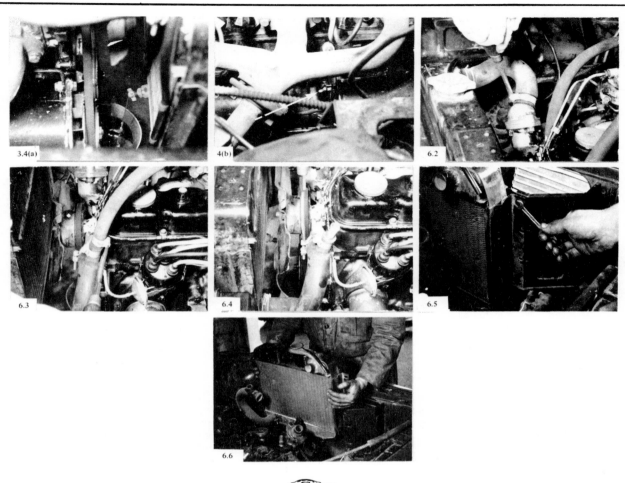

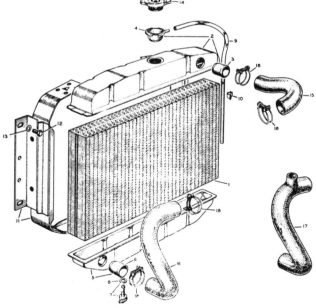

Fig.2.1. EXPLODED VIEW OF RADIATOR ASSEMBLY

1. Radiator core.	6. Outlet pipe	11. Mounting strap	16. Bottom hose
2. Header tank	7. Drain tap	12. Mounting bolt	17. Bottom hose (heater fitted)
3. Inlet pipe	8. Washer	13. Washer	18. Hose clips
4. Filler neck	9. Overflow pipe	14. Filler cap	
5. Lower tank	10. Clip	15. Top hose	

pull it off the connector.

4. Remove the clip securing the bottom hose to the input side of the water pump (see photo) and pull the hose from the pump.

5. Remove the four bolts (two each side) which hold the radiator to the bodyframe. (See photo).

6. Lift the radiator complete with hoses from the car. (See phcto).

7. With the radiator removed from the car any leaks can be soldered up or repaired with a substance such as 'Cataloy'. An unfortunate fault on some models is the fragile nature of the upper and lower radiator tank sections where the hose pipe unions are soldered in. With time they have been known to fracture due to the rocking motion of the flexibly mounted engine — or of course with rough handling when removing the flexible rubber hoses. If this occurs remove the radiator and re-solder the joint running in a reinforcing fillet of solder. This reduces the flexibility of the thin tank material at the joint.

Clean out the inside of the radiator by flushing as described in Section 4. When the radiator is out of the car it is well worthwhile to invert it for reverse flushing. Clean the exterior of the radiator by hosing down the matrix (honeycomb cooling material) with a strong water jet to clear away embedded dirt and insects which will impede the air flow.

8. If it is thought that the radiator may be partially blocked it is possible to test it. Five gallons of water poured through a 1¼ in. diameter pipe from a height of 2 feet above the filler cap should pass through the radiator in 22 seconds. If there are obvious indications of blockage a good proprietary chemical product such as 'Radflush' should be used to clear it.

9. Inspect the radiator hoses for cracks, internal or external perishing, and damage caused by overtightening of the securing clips. Replace the hoses as necessary. Examine the radiator hose securing clips and renew them if they are rusted or distorted. The drain taps should be renewed if leaking, but ensure the leak is not caused by a faulty washer behind the tap. If the tap is suspected try a new washer first to see if this clears the trouble.

10 Replacement is a straightforward reversal of the removal procedure.

7. Thermostat Removal, Testing & Replacement

1. To remove the thermostat, partially drain the cooling system (4 pints is enough), loosen the upper radiator hose at the thermostat elbow end and pull it off the elbow.

2. Unscrew the two set bolts and spring washers from the thermostat housing and lift the housing and paper gasket away. (See photo).

3. Remove the thermostat (photo) and suspend it by a piece of string in a saucepan of cold water together with a thermometer. Neither the thermostat nor the thermometer should touch the bottom of the saucepan, to ensure a false reading is not given.

4. Heat the water, stirring it gently with the thermometer to ensure temperature uniformity, and note when the thermostat begins to open. The temperature at which this should happen is given in the specifications on page 45.

5. Discard the thermostat if it opens too early. Continue heating the water until the thermostat is fully open. Then let it cool down naturally. If the thermostat will not open fully in boiling water, or does not close down as the water cools, then it must be exchanged for a new

one.

6. If the thermostat is stuck open when cold, this will be apparent when removing it from the housing.

7. Replacing the thermostat is a reversal of the removal procedure. Remember to use a new paper gasket between the thermostat housing elbow and the thermostat. Renew the thermostat elbow if it is badly eaten away.

8. Water Pump — Removal & Replacement

1. Partially drain the cooling system as described in Section 3.

2. Undo the clips which hold the hoses to the water pump and pull the hoses off.

3. Remove the fan belt (see Section 11).

4. Undo the 6 bolts which hold the pump body to the cylinder block. Lift the water pump away and remove the gasket.

5. Replacement is a straightforward reversal of the removal sequence (see photo). NOTE: The fan belt tension must be correct when all is reassembled. If the belt is too tight undue strain will be placed on the water pump and dynamo bearings, and if the belt is too loose it will slip and wear rapidly as well as giving rise to low electrical output from the dynamo.

9. Water Pump — Dismantling & Reassembly

All bracketed numbers refer to Fig.2.2.

1. Having removed the assembly from the engine complete with fan, remove the fan (17) and drive pulley (20) by unscrewing the four bolts and washers (18 and 19).

2. In order to get at the seal (4) the rotor (6) must be drawn off the shaft. There is no satisfactory way of doing this other than by using a puller — preferably one with two split claws so that the strain can be put onto the rotor astride the vanes which are the strongest part (Fig.2.4). If the rotor is a particularly tight fit any other way of attempting to remove it will probably break it.

3. With the rotor off, the seal (4) can be withdrawn. Examine the seal seat on the body of the pump for damage or pitting.

4. If the shaft/bearing assembly (2) needs to be renewed (due to excessive play in the bearings) it can now be removed. First lift out the locking ring (3) and then heat the body of the pump in water to 82°C (180°F). The shaft can then be drifted out complete with flange (5) at the flange end of the body. When out press or drift off the flange.

5. Reassembly sequence is in the reverse order but care must be taken to fit everything back in certain positions.

6. If the shaft assembly is being renewed, first of all press the flange on to the smaller end of the new shaft (identified by a groove close to the end, Fig.2.5).

7. Ensure that the flange boss is towards the end of the shaft and that the outer face of the flange is 3.46 in. (88 mm.) from the end of the body. (Fig.2.6).

8. Re-heat the pump body and install the shaft and bearing so that the groove in the bearing coincides with the groove in the body bore. Refit the locking ring.

9. Smear the face of the new seal with the recommended grease (and also around the body bore), and install the seal.

10 Press on the rotor (vanes inwards) so that the clearance between the flat face of the rotor and the pump body is .044 in. (1 mm). (Fig.2.5). Fit a new gasket when replacing the pump on the block.

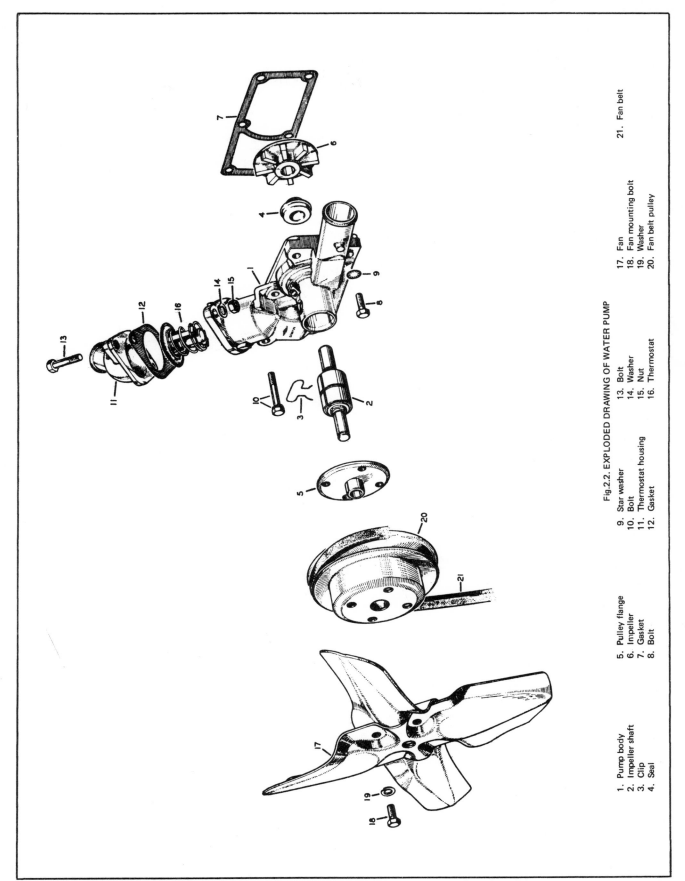

Fig.2.2. EXPLODED DRAWING OF WATER PUMP

1. Pump body
2. Impeller shaft
3. Clip
4. Seal
5. Pulley flange
6. Impeller
7. Gasket
8. Bolt
9. Star washer
10. Bolt
11. Thermostat housing
12. Gasket
13. Bolt
14. Washer
15. Nut
16. Thermostat
17. Fan
18. Fan mounting bolt
19. Washer
20. Fan belt pulley
21. Fan belt

10. Anti-Freeze Mixture

1. In circumstances where it is likely that the temperature will drop to below freezing it is essential that some of the water is drained and an adequate amount of ethylene glycol anti-freeze such as Bluecol added to the cooling system.

2. If Bluecol is not available any anti-freeze which conforms with specification B.S.3151 or B.S.3152 can be used. Never use an anti-freeze with an alcohol base as evaporation is too high.

3. Bluecol anti-freeze with an anti-corrosion additive can be left in the cooling system for up to two years, but after six months it is advisable to have the specific gravity of the coolant checked at your local garage, and thereafter once every three months during winter.

4. Given below are the recommended percentage of solution (by volume) and quantities for the Viva, to give frost protection at various temperature:-

% Solution	Quantity Pints/litres		Safe limit C°	F°	Complete Protection C°	F°
20	2¼	1.25	-13	8	- 8	17
25	2¾	1.50	-18	0	-11	12
30	3¼	1.80	-23	-10	-14	6
40	4¼	2.30	—	—	-23	-10
50	5¼	2.90	—	—	-35	-31

11. Fan Belt — Removal, Replacement & Adjustment

1. If the fan belt is worn or has stretched unduly it should be replaced. The most usual reason for replacement is breakage in service and every wise motorist will carry a spare always.

2. Even though the belt may have broken and fallen off, go through the removal routine which is first of all to loosen the two dynamo pivot bolts and the nut on the adjusting link (brace), (Fig.2.7) and push the dynamo towards the engine. Take the old belt off the three pulleys.

3. Put a new belt over the pulleys.

4. The dynamo must now be used as a tensioner in effect, by pulling it away from the engine and locking it in the required position. This can call for some sustained effort unless the pivot bolts are slackened only a little so that the dynamo is quite stiff to move. A lever between the dynamo and block can help and when the belt is tight lock up the brace nut and bolt first.

5. Check that the tension is such that at a point midway between the dynamo pulley and pump pulley, the deflection is ½ in. with a 9 lb. load on. (As far as you can push it with one finger). If in doubt it is better to be a little slack than tight. Only slipping will occur if it is too slack. If too tight, damage can be caused by excessive strain on the pulley bearings.

6. When the adjustment is right tighten all the dynamo mounting bolts.

7. With a new belt, check the tension 250 miles after fitting.

8. Periodic checking of the belt tension is necessary and there is no hard and fast rule as to the most suitable interval, because fan belts do not necessarily stretch or wear to a pre-determined schedule. Assuming most owners check their own oil and water regularly it is suggested as a good habit to check the fan belt tension every time the bonnet goes up. It takes only a second.

12. Water Temperature Gauge — Fault Diagnosis & Rectification

1. If no reading is shown on the electrically operated water temperature gauge when the engine is hot and the ignition switched on, either the gauge, the sender unit, or the wiring in between is at fault. Alternatively No.2 fuse may have blown.

2. Check the fuse and, if satisfactory, pull off the wire from the sender unit in the cylinder head. Connect a lead containing a 12 volt 6 watt bulb (this is essential to prevent damage to the water temperature gauge coils) between the end of the wire and a good earth.

3. Switch on the ignition and check if the gauge is working. The needle should rise to the 'H' (hot) or 130°C mark which indicates that the sender unit must be renewed. To do this simply undo it and fit a replacement item.

4. If the sender unit is apparently working correctly, check the gauge and, if necessary, replace it. Details of how to remove the gauge are given in Chapter 10.

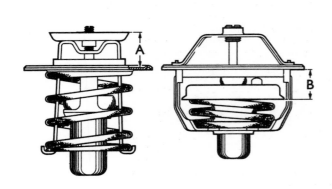

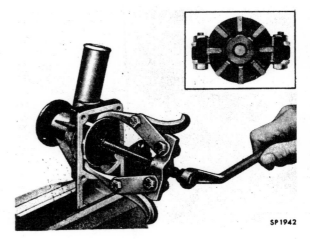

SP1942

Fig.2.3. CROSS SECTION OF TWO TYPES OF THERMOSTAT
FITTED

A .51 inch (fully open)   B .48 inch (fully open)

Fig.2.4. Photo showing water pump impeller being removed
from shaft with an extractor.

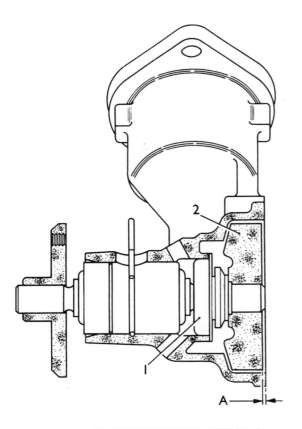

Fig.2.5. CROSS SECTION OF WATER PUMP

1   Shaft seal   2   Impeller

Dimension 'A' = .44 inches.

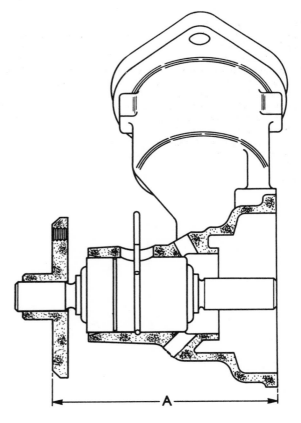

Fig.2.6. CROSS SECTION OF WATER PUMP
Dimension 'A' = 3.46 inches.

Fig.2.7. Illustration to show the bolts to be slackened in order to pivot the dynamo (upper) and the tensioner checking point of the fan belt (lower).

Fault Finding Chart — Cooling System

Symptom	Reason/s	Remedy
Loss of coolant	Leak in system	Examine all hoses, hose connections, drain taps and the radiator and heater for signs of leakage when the engine is cold, then when hot and under pressure. Tighten clips, renew hoses and repair radiator.
	Defective radiator pressure cap.	Examine cap for defective seal or spring and renew if necessary.
	Overheating causing rapid evaporation due to excessive pressure in system forcing vapour past radiator cap.	Check reasons for overheating.
	Blown cylinder head gasket causing excess pressure in cooling system forcing coolant past radiator cap overflow.	Remove cylinder head for examination
	Cracked block or head due to freezing.	Strip engine and examine. Repair as required.
Overheating	Insufficient coolant in system.	Top up.
	Water pump not turning properly due to slack fan belt.	Tighten fan belt.
	Kinked or collapsed water hoses causing restriction to circulation of coolant.	Renew hose as required.
	Faulty thermostat (not opening properly).	Fit new thermostat.
	Engine out of tune.	Check ignition setting and carburetter adjustments.
	Blocked radiator either internally or externally.	Flush out cooling system and clean out cooling fins.
	Cylinder head gaskets blown forcing coolant out of system.	Remove head and renew gasket.
	New engine not run-in.	Adjust engine speed until run-in.
Engine running too cool	Missing or faulty thermostat.	Fit new thermostat.

Chapter 3/Fuel System and Carburation

Contents

Specifications

Fuel Pump

Make and type	A.C. 'YD'
Delivery pressure	$2\frac{1}{2} - 3\frac{1}{2}$ lbs.in^2
Diaphragm spring load when compressed to ½ inch	4½ lbs. approx.

Carburetters - HB 22 Engines

	Solex B30 PSE 1-6		Zenith 30 1Z	
Make	Solex B30 PSE 1-6		Zenith 30 1Z	
Type	Fixed choke			
Air cleaner element	Gauze	Paper	Gauze	Paper
Element number	3109	3117	3119	3121
Choke	22 mm	22 mm	22 mm	22 mm
Main jet	100	102	100	102
Correction jet	175	180	180	180
Economy jet	55	55	60	55
Pilot jet...	50	50	50	50
Pump injector	50	50	50	50
Needle valve	1.6 mm	1.6 mm	1.6 mm	1.6 mm
Needle valve washer thickness	2.0 mm	2.0 mm	1.0 mm	1.0 mm
Fuel level	—	—	23 mm. below face of float chamber with float removed	
High altitude: Main jet - 5000 - 7000 ft	97.5	100	97.5	100
- 7000 - 10,000 ft..	95	97.5	95	97.5
- 10,000 - 15,000 ft	95	97.5	95	97.5
Correction jet - 5000 - 7000 ft	175	180	180	180
- 7000 - 10,000 ft..	175	180	180	180
- 10,000 - 15,000 ft	180	185	185	185

Carburetter - HB 23 Engines

Make	Zenith/Stromberg 150 CDS
Type	Variable choke
Metering needle	6N
Float level	Face of main body when carburetter is inverted and needle valve closed
High altitude	Consistently above 5000 ft. screw in jet adjuster one half turn

On later HB 23 engines improvements in performance may be achieved if the following specifications for the carburetter are used on carb. identification No.3350

Metering needle	5 BN
Air valve spring colour	Blue
Fast idle cam	5A

Cold start needle	F5
Needle valve	1.75 mm.
Needle valve washer thickness	1.6 mm.
Float position	With carburetter inverted and needle valve on seating highest point of float 16 mm. above face of body.
Jet adjuster nominal setting	2 turns down from a position flush with the bridge.

1. General Description

The fuel system consists of a seven gallon fuel tank mounted in the boot of the car; an AC, YD mechanical fuel pump bolted to the left-hand side of the cylinder block near the bellhousing, actuated by an eccentric on the camshaft and lever arm; and one of the following carburetters:- Solex B30 PSEI-6, Zenith 301Z or a Zenith/Stromberg 150 CD.
(The latter is fitted to '90' models only). Fuel is carried from the tank to the carburetter by two lengths of metal piping joined by a flexible hose and clipped to the left-hand longitudinal subframe member. An air filter of either oil wetted gauze or paper element type is fitted to the carburetter.

2. Routine Maintenance

1. Every summer and winter alter the accelerator pump stroke setting, (for procedure see Section 7.2. of this chapter).
2. Once every 6,000 miles, remove and clean the paper element and gauze filters as described in Section 3.
3. Oil the carburetter control linkages.
4. Clean the fuel pump filter. To clean the fuel pump filter, unscrew the fuel pump top cover centre bolt. Remove the top cover and with a needle, hook out the filter. Be careful not to break or enlarge the holes in the gauze.
5. Wash the filter in petrol, and if possible blow through it with compressed air. With a clean paint brush flick out any loose matter from inside the fuel pump body.
6. Inspect the top cover gasket, and if compressed or marked with a groove it should be replaced together with the centre bolt gasket.
7. Replace the filter, gasket and top cover, and tighten down the centre bolt. (Do not overtighten the bolt as it will distort the cover and possibly strip the fuel pump body threads).
8. Once every 12,000 miles renew the air filter paper element or foam element where fitted.
9. Clean wire type air filter element, for procedure see Section 3.
10 Renew the in-line fuel filter on later models, see Section 14.
11 Once every 24,000 miles it is beneficial to thoroughly clean the carburetter, (for procedure see Section 7 of this chapter).
12 Every 6,000 miles, for HB23 engines fitted with Stromberg carburetters, top up the damper oil as described in Section 9.

3. Air Filter Element — Removal & Servicing

1. Remove the air filter cover centre bolt. Remove the cover and the air filter, taking note of the position of the two gaskets.
2. To clean the filter element, proceed as follows:—
a) (Paper type). Lightly tap the end surfaces on a hard object and continue until dust and debris stop falling from the element. Do not try to brush, wash or use compressed air on a paper type of element.
b) (Gauze Type). Rinse in paraffin, blow out with an air pump or shake dry, dip element in clean engine oil and allow excess to drain off.
3. Thoroughly clean the interior of the air filter including the intake tube and base plate.
4. Ensure the gaskets are correctly positioned (paper element). Replace the element on the cover base and put the cover back in position so that the notch in the cover engages the lug on the base plate.

4. Solex Carburetters — Description

Only the early models of standard engine fitted to the HB series used the B30 PSEI-6 carburetter. It is a fixed choke design and incorporates an economy unit to correct fuel mixture at certain intermediate engine speeds. The principle of operation is as follows:- At full throttle opening with the choke flap open, the depression (low pressure) in the choke tube draws a fuel/air mixture from the main discharge beak.
This fuel/air mixture has been emulsified in the emulsion tube below the discharge beak. The fuel has reached the emulsion tube, via the reserve well, from the main jet in the float chamber.
When the engine is cold and the choke flap is closed the throttle flap is automatically slightly opened a pre-determined amount.
The choke tube depression draws principally on the discharge beak and therefore a very rich mixture reaches the engine, as air from the main air inlet has been closed off.
At idling speed, with the throttle shut, there is no depression at the main discharge beak. It is now concentrated at the idling discharge orifice on the engine side of the throttle flap. Fuel from the main reserve well is drawn via the pilot jet to this orifice, taking the requisite amount of air for the mixture through the pilot air bleed and by-pass orifice. The volume of the mixture supplied is controlled by the idling mixture control screw.
As soon as the throttle is opened further, the by-pass orifice is then also subject to depression, so instead of feeding air in one direction to the idling discharge orifice, it now delivers fuel/air mixture in the other direction until the throttle is open sufficiently for the main discharge beak to take over.
The economy unit augments the fuel flow from the main jet automatically through the economy jet when the choke tube depression is low. At cruising speeds, when the depression is high, a diaphragm operated valve shuts off the economy jet.
There is also an accelerator pump which delivers a metered jet of neat fuel into the choke tube whenever the accelerator pedal is operated quickly. This gives the richer mixture necessary for rapid acceleration. The fuel is drawn from the float chamber into the pump chamber via a non-return valve at the bottom of the float chamber. When the pump is operated quickly (i.e. sudden accelerator pedal operation) the pump release valve is forced shut under pressure and the

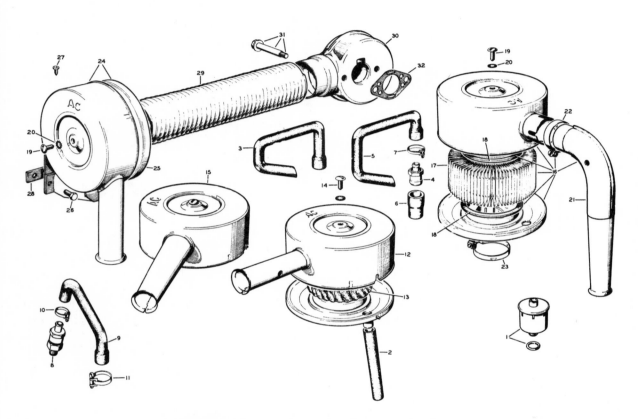

Fig.3.1. EXPLODED VIEWS OF DIFFERENT TYPES OF AIR FILTERS FITTED

1. Crankcase air breather/filter and washer
2. Rocker cover breather hose
3. Rocker cover breather hose (low temperature climate)
4. Ventilation valve HB22 engine
5. Breather hose - valve to carburetter. HB22 engine
6. Connector
7. Clip
8. Ventilator valve HB23 engine
9. Hose - HB23 engine
10. Clip
11. Clip
12. Air cleaner-mesh element
13. Mesh element
14. Screw
15. Air cleaner-paper element
16. Air cleaner and element-low temperature climates
17. Paper element
18. Rubber gasket
19. Screw
20. Star washer
21. Air inlet elbow
22. Clip
23. Clip
24. Air cleaner assembly HB23 engine
25. Bottom plate
26. Bolt
27. Screw
28. Bracket
29. Hose-cleaner to air chamber
30. Air chamber
31. Chamber mounting bolt
32. Gasket

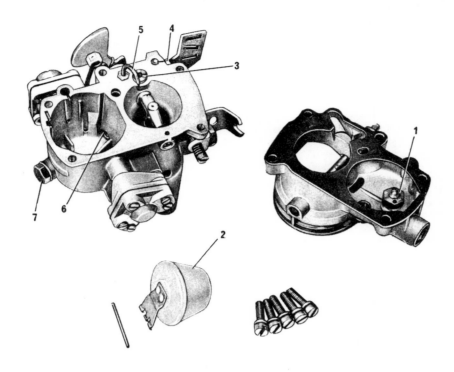

Fig.3.2. SOLEX B30 PSEI—6 CARBURETTER. GENERAL LAYOUT

1. Needle valve
2. Float
3. Correction jet and emulsion tube
4. Pilot jet air bleed
5. Pump injector
6. Main jet
7. Sealing plug

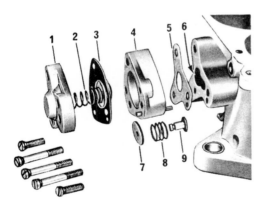

Fig.3.3. SOLEX & ZENITH CARBURETTERS — DETAIL OF ECONOMY UNIT

1 Cover
2 Spring
3 Diaphragm
4 Valve assembly
5 Gasket
6 Economy jet (in carburetter body)
7 Valve washer
8 Spring
9 Valve

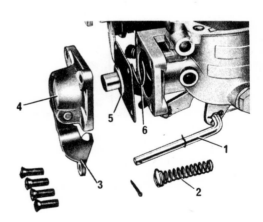

Fig.3.4. SOLEX & ZENITH CARBURETTERS — DETAIL OF ACCELERATOR PUMP

1 Control rod
2 Spring
3 Pump lever
4 Pump cover
5 Diaphragm
6 Diaphragm spring

fuel passes through the injector. If the pump is operated slowly, the pressure is insufficient to close the release valve, so fuel passes through it back to the float chamber rather than out of the injector.

5. Solex B30 PSEI-6 Carburetter — Removal, Dismantling & Reassembly

1. Slacken the clip holding the air filter unit to the carburetter air intake (photo).
2. Slacken the clip at the bottom of the hose connection from the filter to the rocker cover (arrowed in photo) and lift off the air filter unit complete.
3. Disconnect the throttle linkage by detaching the circlip and washer from the end of the control rod and moving the control rod out of the throttle lever (photo).
4. Slacken off the choke cable retaining bolt (photo), unclip the cable from the bracket (arrowed 1 in photo), and move the cable to one side.
5. Disconnect the fuel pipe from the carburetter by undoing the union into the float chamber cover (arrowed 2 in photo 5.4).
6. Remove the two nuts holding the carburetter to the inlet manifold. There is very little clearance above the manifold studs so the nuts should be undone together and the carburetter lifted, so that eventually the nuts will clear the tops of the studs. It is impossible to remove only one nut with the other tightened down. Remove the carburetter, heat block and gaskets from the manifold.
7. Dismantling. (All references to Fig.3.5). Remove the five screws (59) holding the float chamber cover (57) to the body (7). Unscrew the needle valve and packing washer (60,61), retain the washer, remove arm spindle (56) and lift out the needle valve actuating arm and float (55). Handle the float carefully as it is fragile.
8. Pull the pump injector and sealing ring (41,42) from the body and remove the spring and ball underneath from the drilling. Do not lose the ball. Unscrew the correction jet and emulsion tube (43), and pilot jet (15). Remove the sealing plug and washer (18,19) and unscrew the main jet and washer (16,17) through the orifice.
9. Disconnect the control rod and spring (24,25) from the pump lever. Undo the four screws (23) and remove the pump cover (22) diaphragm (21) and return spring (20).
10 To remove the economy unit undo the three long screws (54) and then the two short screws holding the sub-assembly together. Remove the cover (52), diaphragm spring (51) diaphragm (50), valve washer and spring (49,48), body and vacuum tube (44,46), gasket (45) and valve (47). The economy jet can then be unscrewed from the body.
11 Inspect the jets, needle valve, actuating arm and float top for excessive wear or damage, also the diaphragms for any signs of fatigue, or tears. Also shake the float to ensure it does not contain any petrol. NOTE: It is suggested that all jets, diaphragms, float needle valve actuating arm and needle valve are renewed. This may seem a needless expense, but it is obvious that a certain degree of wear will have taken place in all these components and this will lower performance and economy. Therefore the small outlay for these new parts will soon be recouped in lower running costs. Even if the other parts are not renewed the needle valve assembly certainly should be, as a worn needle valve will allow excessive fuel into the carburetter, making the mixture over-rich. This will not do the engine or your pocket any good!

12 The carburetter body and all components should be washed in clean petrol, and then blown dry. If an air jet is not available in any form, the parts can be wiped dry with a soft non-fluffy rag. Jets can be blown through by mouth to clear obstructions, or poked through with a nylon bristle. DO NOT scour the carburetter body or components with a wire brush of any variety, or poke through the jets with wire. The reason for this is that the carburetter is a precision instrument made of relatively soft metal i.e. (body - aluminium, jets - brass) and wire will scratch this material, possibly altering the performance of the carburetter.
13 Reassembly is a straightforward reversal of the dismantling procedure, but note the following points:-

a) New gaskets and sealing washers should be used. Note the normal thickness of the fibre washer under the needle valve is 1.0 mm.
b) When refitting the pump injector ensure that a sealing ring is fitted. Also when replacing the ball and spring in the drilling, ensure that the spring does not actually touch the ball and that its top (wide end) is just below the bottom of the hexagon recess.
c) Ensure that the economy jet is screwed into the carburetter body before refitting the economy unit.
d) The pump control rod and spring should be refitted to the appropriate hole in the pump lever, so that the large end of the spring contacts the lever.
f) The strangler flap return spring should be refitted in the centre notch of the spindle lever (see Fig.3.7).
g) Never use jointing compound on carburetter gaskets.

14 Before replacing the carburetter adjust the choke to throttle setting as follows: Close the throttle flap by unscrewing the throttle stop screw. Place a number 61 drill, or a 1.0 mm. piece of wire between the throttle flap and bore as shown in Fig.3.8. Hold the strangler cam against the stop pin and this will allow the strangler flap to be closed by the spindle spring. Loosen the swivel bolt and move the rod through it until the floating lever touches the pump rod lever. Retighten the swivel bolt and remove the drill or wire. The adjustment is now completed and the carburetter can be assembled to the manifold.

6. Solex B30 PSEI-6 Carburetter — Adjustment

1. Thoroughly clean the carburetter and manifold flanges and both sides of the insulating block.
2. Push one gasket over the manifold studs on to the flange, followed by the insulating block and the second gasket (photo a). Now replace the carburetter (photo b). Replace the two mounting washers and nuts together. It will be necessary to hold the carburetter up to the studs until the nuts can be caught onto the stud threads. Do not overtighten the nuts.
3. Reconnect the choke control, petrol pipe, vacuum pipe and the throttle controls. Retighten the bolts holding the throttle control rod, bush and retaining washer to the bulkhead.
4. Now check that the throttle flap opens fully when the pedal is depressed. If not, the throttle linkage can be adjusted as follows:
5. Disconnect the throttle return spring on the carburetter, and slacken the swivel screw securing the control rod to the relay lever (see Fig.3.9).
6. Get someone to depress the throttle pedal until it almost touches the carpet, and with the pedal in this position move the carburetter throttle lever until the throttle flap is fully open. Retighten the swivel screw,

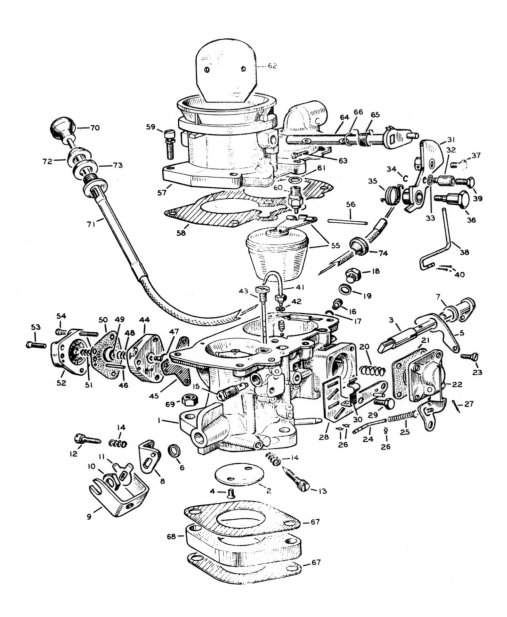

Fig.3.5. SOLEX B30 PSEI—6 & ZENITH 30IZ CARBURETTERS EXPLODED VIEW OF COMPONENTS

1. Body
2. Throttle flap
3. Throttle spindle and pump rod lever assembly
4. Throttle flap screw
5. Throttle floating lever
6. Distance washer
7. Distance washer
8. Throttle abutment plate
9. Throttle lever
10. Nut
11. Lockwasher
12. Throttle stop screw
13. Idling mixture volume control screw
14. Spring
15. Pilot jet
16. Main jet
17. Washer
18. Sealing plug

19. Washer
20. Diaphragm spring
21. Diaphragm
22. Pump cover
23. Pump cover screw
24. Control rod
25. Control rod spring
26. Rod circlips
27. Split pin
28. Strangler bracket
29. Bracket bolt
30. Cable clip
31. Choke cam assembly
32. Choke cable anchor lug
33. Washer
34. Circlip
35. Cam return spring
36. Cam pivot
37. Locking screw
38. Link rod

39. Choke cable locking screw
40. Split pins
41. Pump injector
42. Sealing ring
43. Emulsion tube and correction jet
44. Economy unit body
45. Gasket
46. Vacuum tube
47. Valve
48. Spring
49. Valve washer
50. Diaphragm
51. Spring
52. Economy unit cover
53. Screw
54. Screw
55. Float
56. Float spindle
57. Float chamber cover

58. Gasket
59. Cover screw
60. Needle valve
61. Washer
62. Choke flap
63. Flap screw
64. Flap spindle
65. Return spring
66. Washer
67. Gasket
68. Heat insulator
69. Carburetter mounting nut
70. Choke cable
71. Choke cable sleeve
72. Locking nut
73. Locking ring
74. Grommet

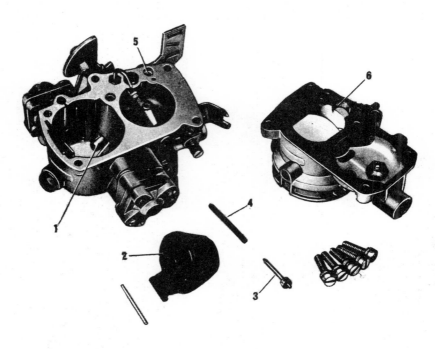

Fig.3.6. ZENITH 30 IZ CARBURETTER — GENERAL LAYOUT

1. Main jet
2. Float
3. Pilot jet
4. Filter
5. Pilot jet drilling
6. Pilot jet air bleed

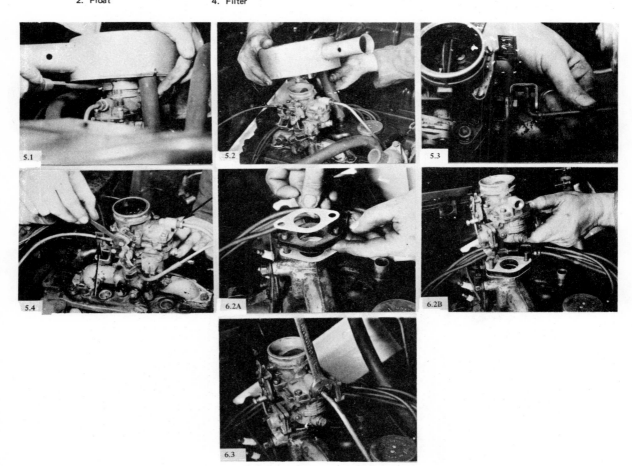

Fig.3.7. Illustration showing location of the choke flap return spring.

PUMP ROD LEVER

FLOATING LEVER

Fig.3.8. Adjusting the choke to throttle rod setting.

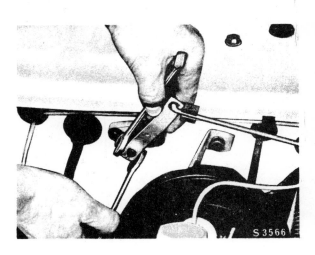

S 3566

Fig.3.9. Showing the setting of the accelerator control rod to the relay lever.

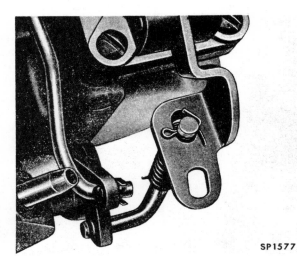

SP1577

Fig.3.10. Showing locating holes for summer and winter settings of the accelerator pump.

and the throttle control linkage should now be correctly adjusted.

7. Reconnect the throttle return spring on the carburetter.

8. Replace the air filter, not forgetting to replace the pipe between the air filter and rocker cover.

7. Solex B30 PSEI-6 Carburetter — Adjustment

1. The accelerator pump stroke is adjustable for summer and winter motoring. This adjustment allows a richer mixtu e during acceleration in the winter to compensate for the mixture's partial loss of vapourising ability and, in summer, lessens the delivery through the injector so preventing over richness.

2. In Fig.3.12 the pump stroke is set for cold weather motoring. To alter the setting for summer, remove the split pin, lift out the pump rod from the inner hole and place it in the outer one. Replace the split pin.

3. Slow running adjustment is set with the volume control screw. With the engine warm set the throttle stop screw to a fast idle speed. Then turn the volume control screw in whichever direction is necessary to obtain the fastest, smoothest tickover. Reduce the tickover speed with the throttle stop screw and, if necessary, make any further minor adjustments to maintain the smoothness of tickover using the volume control screw. It should be remembered that not only the carburetter is responsible for smooth idling. Distributor settings are also important and should be checked if the carburetter adjustment is insufficient. A full check against engine fault diagnosis, in Chapter One, may be necessary if a satisfactory tickover speed and smoothness cannot be obtained.

4. The level of the fuel in the float chamber is important in correct operation of the carburetter. Check first that the needle valve is in good condition (Section 5, paragraph 11).

5. When the carburetter is full of fuel remove the top cover. The fuel level should be 16 mm. below the top edge of the bowl with the float in place but with the valve actuating arm and spindle removed. This level check is virtually impossible visually and at best can be measured with only fair accuracy even with a lot of trouble. The following method is suggested as being one which will indicate any serious deviation from the operating level: Run the engine, switch off and disconnect the fuel supply pipe at the carburetter. Having removed the top cover, measure the position of the top of the float relative to the top edge of the float chamber. This can be done with reasonable accuracy using a straight edge. Then lift out the float carefully by gripping it with a piece of thin strip at each side. Find a transparent container, such as a jam jar, and put in enough petrol so that the float will float in it upright. Measure the height of the top of the float above the surface of the petrol. If this distance is, say, 20 mm. and the top of the float was 5 mm. above the float chamber, then the fuel level is 15 mm. below the top of the float chamber. To alter the level it will be necessary to increase or decrease the thickness of the washers behind the needle valve body, decreasing the thickness to raise the fuel level and vice versa. The only way to check adjustments is by replacing the carburetter cover and, having established what the free floating height of the float should be, proceeding by trial and error. Each time, the float chamber cover should be replaced, the fuel pipe connected and the engine run.

7a. Zenith 30 1Z Carburetter

1. The Zenith 30 1Z carburetter is almost identical to the Solex its appearance and all aspects of dismantling adjustment and assembly for the Solex apply to it. The following differences can be noted in the Zenith carburetter, with reference to Fig.3.6.

The main jet (1) protrudes into the float chamber. The float and arm (2) are a one piece plastic moulding. An extended pilot jet (3) shrouded in a filter (4) is located in a vertical drilling (5) in the body. The pilot jet air bleed (6) is located in the cover.

8. Stromberg 150 CD Carburetter — Description

All Viva 90 models are fitted with a single Stromberg 150 CD (constant depression) carburetter. It has a single horizontal variable choke and is quite different in principle of operation to the Solex.

Referring to Fig.3.12, it will be seen that the air intake (13) is choked by the cylindrical air valve (5) which can move vertically.

To the base of the air valve a tapered needle is fitted which runs in and out of a jet orifice (14) through which fuel can be drawn from the float chamber which is underneath the main body. Suction from the engine inlet manifold passes through a hole (18) in the base of the air valve (5) to the suction chamber (2). This suction acts on the diaphragm (3), to which the air valve and metering needle are attached, and raises them. This increases the air flow through the choke tube and the fuel flow through the jet (14) as the tapered needle withdraws. As the air valve rises so the concentration of suction through the valve hole (18) is reduced and the valve reaches a point of equilibrium, balanced against throttle opening and air valve height.

Sudden acceleration demands would apparently cause the air valve to rise sharply, thus tending to weaken the mixture. In fact the rise of the valve is damped by an oil controlled piston (17). Thus when the throttle (19) is opened suddenly the initial suction is concentrated at the fuel jet and the quantity of air let through to reduce the mixture richness to normal occurs slightly later as the piston rises. The taper of the metering needle is obviously the main controlling feature of the carburetter's performance and this controls the fuel/air mixture at all heights of the valve. At the same time the height of the air valve is nicely balanced, according to throttle opening, in conjunction with the metering needle. The jet itself is adjustable by raising or lowering, thus altering the position of the jet orifice in relation to the taper of the needle.

For cold starts the choke knob raises the valve metering needle by means of the starter bar (12) and only opens the throttle (19) a relatively small amount. This provides the required rich mixture. As with other types of variable choke carburetters the accelerator pedal should not be depressed for cold starts as this will open the throttle flap and effectively weaken the mixture by causing the air valve to rise too high. On some later types the cold start arrangement was changed and instead of lifting the jet needle the choke control operated a rotating disc which progressively allowed more fuel to be fed direct to the choke tube direct from the float chamber.

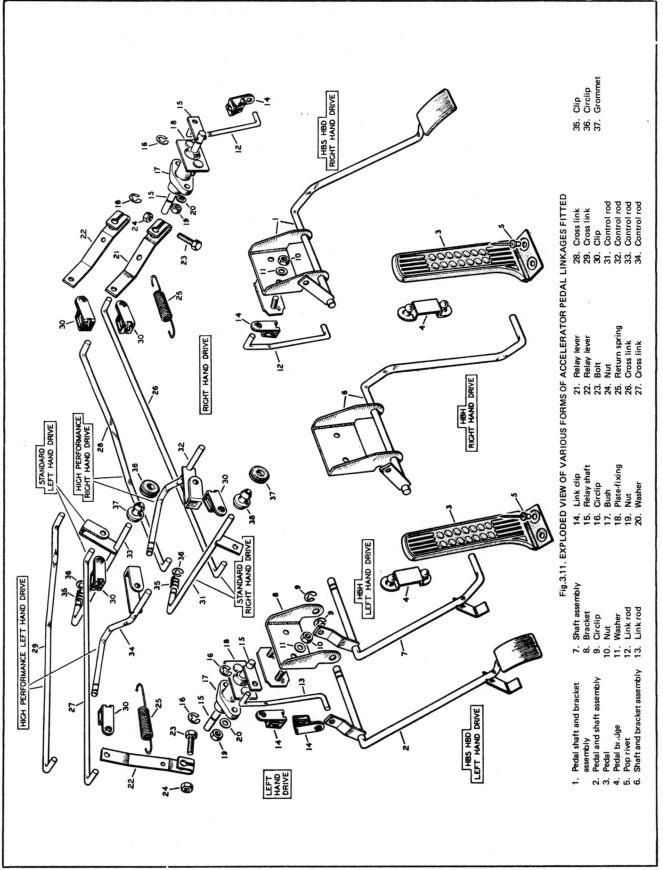

Fig.3.11. EXPLODED VIEW OF VARIOUS FORMS OF ACCELERATOR PEDAL LINKAGES FITTED

1. Pedal shaft and bracket
   assembly
2. Pedal and shaft assembly
3. Pedal
4. Pedal bridge
5. Pop rivet
6. Shaft and bracket assembly
7. Shaft assembly
8. Bracket
9. Circlip
10. Nut
11. Washer
12. Link rod
13. Link rod
14. Link clip
15. Relay shaft
16. Circlip
17. Bush
18. Plate-fixing
19. Nut
20. Washer
21. Relay lever
22. Relay lever
23. Bolt
24. Nut
25. Return spring
26. Cross link
27. Cross link
28. Cross link
29. Cross link
30. Clip
31. Control rod
32. Control rod
33. Control rod
34. Control rod
35. Clip
36. Circlip
37. Grommet

9. Stromberg 150 CD Carburetter — Adjustments

1. As there is no separate idling jet, the mixture for all conditions is supplied by the main jet and variable choke. Thus the strength of the mixture throughout the range depends on the height of the jet in the carburetter body and when the idling mixture is correct, the mixture will be correct throughout the range. A slotted nut (9) at the base of the carburetter increases or decreases the strength of the mixture. Turning the nut clockwise raises the jet and weakens the mixture. Turning the jet anti-clockwise enriches the mixture. The idling speed is controlled by the throttle stop screw.

2. To adjust a stromberg 150 CD carburetter from scratch, run the engine until it is at its normal working temperature and then remove the air cleaner. Insert a 0.002 in. feeler gauge between the air valve and carburetter body and screw in the jet adjusting screw (9) until it touches the air valve (5). The feeler should now be withdrawn and the adjuster unscrewed three complete revolutions. This will give an approximate setting. Start the engine and adjust the throttle stop screw so that the engine runs fairly slowly and smoothly (about 750 r.p.m.) without vibrating excessively on its mountings. To get the engine to run smoothly at this speed it may be necessary to turn the jet adjuster nut a small amount in either direction.

3. To test if the correct setting has been found, lift the air valve piston 1/32 in. with the lifting pin (4). This is a very small amount and care should be taken to lift the piston only fractionally. If the engine speed increases and stays so then the mixture is too rich. If it hesitates or stalls it is too weak. Re-adjust the jet adjusting nut and recheck. All is correct when the engine speed rises momentarily and then drops when the air valve is lifted the specified 1/32 inch. Make sure that the air valve damper is correctly filled with engine oil. With the plunger and air filter removed, the level should be ¼ inch below the top of the air valve guide. Lift the air valve with a finger through the air intake during the topping up operation. (See Fig.3.13).

4. Replace the air cleaner.

10. Stromberg 150 CD Carburetter — Float Chamber Fuel Level Setting

1. Take off the air cleaner and then remove the carburetter from the engine.

2. Slacken the jet bush retainer (8) and undo the screws which hold the float chamber to the base of the carburetter. Remove the float chamber.

3. Turn the carburetter body upside down and accurately measure the highest point of the floats which should be ¾ in. above the flange normally adjacent to the float chamber (See Fig.3.14). During this operation ensure that the needle is against its seating. To reset the level, carefully bend the tag which bears against the end of the needle.

4. When replacing the float chamber, ensure that the head of the fulcrum pin is adjacent to the stop in the casting (See Fig.3.16).

5. Re-centre the jet after replacing the float chamber, (Section 11).

11. Stromberg 150 CD Carburetter — Dismantling — Reassembly

1. Take off the air cleaner, disconnect the choke and accelerator controls at the carburetter, also the vacuum advance and retard pipe, and undo the nuts and spring washers holding the carburetter in place. Remove the carburetter.

2. All figures in brackets refer to Fig.3.15. With the carburetter on the bench, undo and remove the damper cap and plunger (3). Then undo the four screws (2) which hold the suction chamber cover (1) in place and lift off the cover.

3. The air valve (9) complete with needle (27) and diaphragm (10) is then lifted out. Handle the assembly with the greatest of care as it is very easy to knock the needle out of true.

4. The bottom of the float chamber (55) is removed by undoing the five screws (57,58) and the spring, and flat washers which hold it in place. Take out the pin (62) and remove the float assembly (61).

5. If wished, the needle (27) may be removed from the air valve (10) by undoing the grub screw (11) (see Fig.3.15)

6. To remove the diaphragm (10) from the piston, simply undo the four screws and washers (12) which hold the diaphragm retaining ring (11) in place.

7. The jet (14) and associated parts are removed after the jet locking nut has been undone.

8. On reassembly there are several points which should be noted particularly. The first is that if fitting a new needle to the piston ensure it has the same markings as the old stamped on it, and fit it so that the needle shoulder is perfectly flush with the base of the piston. This can be done by placing a metal ruler across the base of the valve and pulling the needle out until it abuts the rule.

9. Thoroughly clean the piston and its cylinder in paraffin and when replacing the jet centralise it as described in paragraphs 10 to 12.

10 Refit the jet and associated parts, lift the piston and tighten the jet assembly.

11 Turn the mixture adjusting nut clockwise until the tip of the jet just stands proud into the choke tube. Now loosen the jet bush retainer about one turn so as to free the bush (18).

12 Allow the piston to fall. As it descends the needle will enter the orifice and automatically centralise it. With the needle still in the orifice tighten the jet assembly slowly, frequently raising and dropping the piston ¼ in. to ensure the orifice bush has not moved. Finally check that the piston drops freely without hesitation and hits the bridge with a soft metallic sound.

13 Make sure that the holes in the diaphragm line up with the screw holes in the piston and retaining ring, and that the diaphragm is correctly positioned. Reassembly is otherwise a straightforward reversal of the dismantling sequence.

14 Fig.3.18 shows the cold start device which may be fitted to some later models. The 2-position stop (1) can be set to control the maximum amount to which the unit may rotate. With the cross-pin in the slot the device may rotate to its full extent, but this is not usually needed unless the temperature drops below −18°C. The fast idle cam (3) operates against the throttle lever via an adjusting screw (4) which may be set to ensure a suitably fast idling speed under cold start situations.

12. Fuel Tank Removal & Replacement

1. Remove the battery from the car as a safety measure, also ensure there are no open flames in the vicinity. DO NOT smoke during removal and replacement of the tank.

2. The tank outlet pipe is on the front of the tank and should be disconnected by removing the clip and pulling off the flexible pipe connection (Fig.3.19). If the

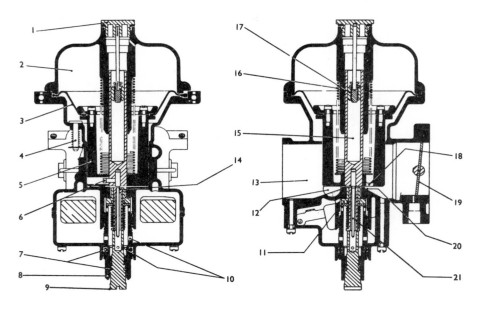

Fig.3.12. DIAGRAMMATIC SECTIONED VIEW OF THE STROMBERG 150 CD CARBURETTER

1. Hydraulic damper cap
2. Suction chamber
3. Diaphragm
4. Air valve lifting pin
5. Air valve
6. Needle locking screw
7. Sealing rings
8. Jet bush retainer
9. Jet adjuster
10. Drillings to jet
11. Jet bush
12. Starter bar
13. Air intake
14. Jet
15. Air valve guide
16. Air valve return spring
17. Hydraulic damper
18. Drilling to suction chamber
19. Throttle flap
20. Choke bridge
21. Metering needle

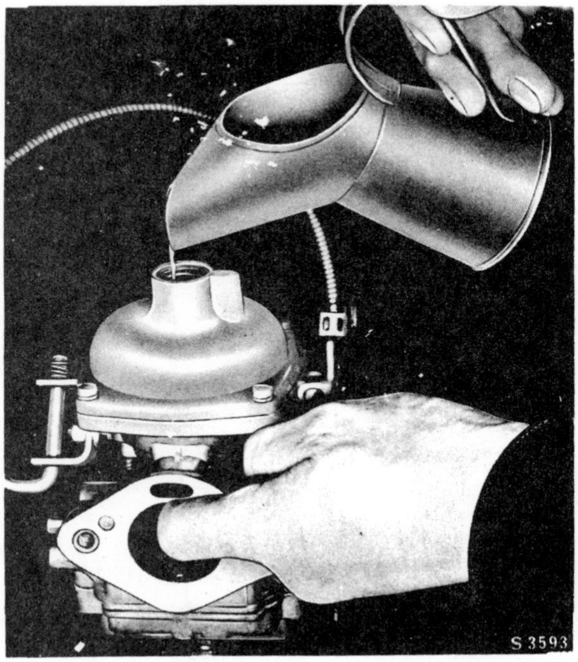

Fig.3.13. Showing how the air valve of a Stromberg carburetter is lifted whilst topping up the damper oil level.

Fig.3.14. Stromberg 150 CD carburetter — float setting dimension 'A' should be ¾ inch (19 mm).

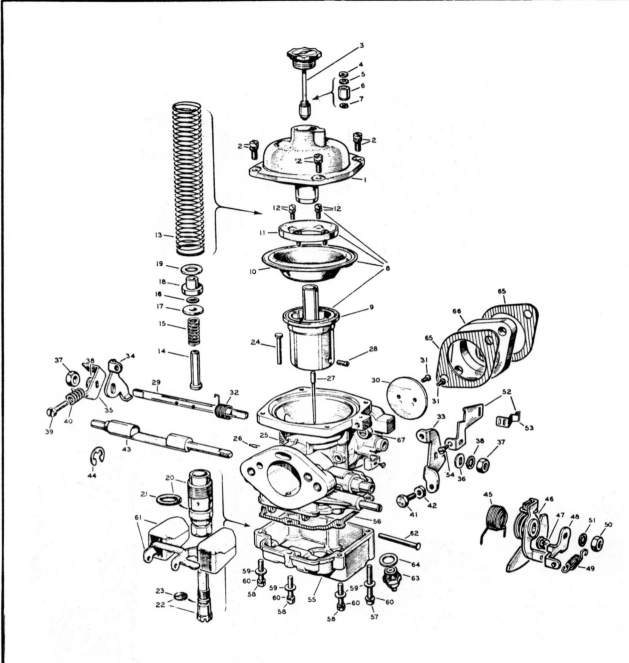

Fig.3.15. STROMBERG 150 CD CARBURETTER EXPLODED DRAWING

1. Suction chamber cover
2. Cover screws
3. Hydraulic damper
4. Washer
5. Retaining ring
6. Bush
7. Retaining ring
8. Air valve and diaphragm assembly
9. Air valve
10. Diaphragm
11. Retaining ring
12. Screw and washer
13. Air valve return spring
14. Jet
15. Jet spring
16. 'O' ring

17. Washer
18. Jet bush
19. Washer
20. Jet retainer
21. 'O' ring
22. Adjusting screw
23. 'O' ring
24. Air valve lifting pin
25. Lifting pin spring
26. Clip
27. Metering needle
28. Needle locking screw
29. Throttle spindle
30. Throttle flap
31. Flap screws
32. Throttle return spring
33. Fast idle lever

34. Throttle stop
35. Throttle lever
36. Spacing washer
37. Nut
38. Lock washer
39. Throttle stop screw
40. Spring
41. Fast idle screw
42. Lock nut
43. Starter bar
44. Circlip
45. Spring - starter bar
46. Choke lever cam
47. Swivel screw
48. Choke lever
49. Return spring
50. Nut

51. Lock washer
52. Choke cable bracket
53. Cable clip
54. Bracket screw
55. Float chamber
56. Gasket
57. Float chamber screw (long)
58. Float chamber screw (short)
59. Plain washer
60. Spring washer
61. Float and arm assembly
62. Float hinge pin
63. Needle valve assembly
64. Washer
65. Carburetter gasket
66. Heat insulator
67. Nut

Fig.3.16. Stromberg 150 CD carburetter — arrows show how head of float hinge pin locates against lug in cover.

Fig.3.17. Stromberg 150 CD carburetter — slackening locking screw to remove jet needle.

Fig.3.18. STROMBERG 150 CDS CARBURETTER FITTED WITH MODIFIED COLD START DEVICE

1 Limit stop (2 position)   3 Fast idle cam
2 Disc spindle   4 Throttle fast idle adjustment
                                   screw.

tank is to be drained this should be done now by attaching a longer piece of pipe to the outlet and siphoning the contents out.

3. From inside the boot lift the floor mat, and the tank mounting screws are accessible. Before lifting the tank out, disconnect the lead from the gauge sender unit. Take care not to strain the filler neck when manoeuvring it through the grommet in the body.

4. Replacement is a reversal of the removal procedure but the flange should be sealed with a suitable compound to prevent water coming up into the luggage compartment.

5. Repairs to the fuel tank to stop leaks are best carried out using resin adhesives and hardeners as supplied in most accessory shops. In cases of repairs being done to large holes, fibre glass mats or perforated zinc sheet may be required to give area support. If any soldering, welding or brazing is contemplated, the tank must be steamed out to remove any traces of petroleum vapour. It is dangerous to use naked flames on a fuel tank without this, even though it may have been lying empty for a considerable period.

13. Fuel Pump — Removal

1. Disconnect the two fuel lines from the pump and make sure that the line from the fuel tank (photo) is blocked by clamping or plugging it.

2. Undo the two retaining nuts holding the pump to the engine. The forward nut is not very accessible and will require a box spanner in order to remove it.

3. Lift the pump away from the mounting studs and lift away the insulating block also.

14. Fuel Pump — Dismantling

1. Remove the top cover securing screw and lift off the cover and filter screen. Do not lose the nylon spacer collar round the screw between the cover and the screen. This ensures that the screen is held down in position.

2. Mark the relationship between centre and base sections of the pump body and then remove the five securing screws and lift off the centre section.

3. To release the diaphragm, depress the centre and turn it 90°. This will release the diaphragm pull rod from the stirrup in the operating link. Lift out the seal and seal retainer.

4. Do not remove the rocker arm and pivot pin from the body base unless there are signs of excessive wear— in which case it would probably be more economical to obtain an exchange pump.

5. To remove the valve assemblies from the body centre section they must be prised out carefully past the stakes which locate them. Remove the sealing ring fitted behind each valve.

15. Fuel Pump — Inspection, Reassembly & Replacement

1. Examine the diaphragm for signs of splitting or cracking and renew it if in any doubt.

2. If the valves are suspected of malfunctioning, replace them.

3. The filter screen should be intact with no signs of enlarged holes or broken strands.

4. Renew the oil seal.

5. Clean up the recesses where the valves have been

staked into the body to ensure that when replaced the valves will seat neatly.

6. To refit the valves fit new gaskets first and then press them carefully home, preferably with a tube that will locate round their rims. If this is not available press round each rim with a non-metallic article, a little at a time so that they bed down square. Then stake the body in six positions round each valve to hold them in position (Fig.3.20).

7. To refit the diaphragm first put a new oil seal followed by the retainer into the body base. Put the diaphragm pull rod through the seal and the groove in the rocker arm link. Then turn the diaphragm anti-clockwise 90° so that it lines up with the screw holes and the lug on the body aligns with the tab on the diaphragm (Fig.3.21)

8. Move the rocker arm until the diaphragm is level with the body flanges and hold the arm in this position. Reassemble the two halves of the pump ensuring that the previously made marks on the flanges are adjacent to each other.

9. Insert the five screws and lock washers and tighten them down finger tight.

10 Move the rocker arm up and down several times to centralise the diaphragm, and then with the arm held down, tighten the screws securely in a diagonal sequence.

11 Replace the gauze filter in position. Fit the cover sealing ring, fit the cover, and insert the bolt with the fibre washer under its head. Do not over-tighten the bolt but ensure that it is tight enough to prevent any leaks.

12 Fuel pump replacement is a straightforward reversal of the removal procedure. However note the following points:—

a) The fuel pump should be assembled to the engine block with new gaskets.

b) Ensure that the pump operating arm is resting on the camshaft, and not under it.

c) Do not over-tighten the pump retaining nuts.

d) Test that the pump is working, by disconnecting the pipe feed at the carburetter, holding a container under it and getting someone to turn the engine. The fuel should spurt out in intermittent jets.

16. Fuel Gauge Sender Unit — Fault Finding

1. If the fuel gauge does not work correctly the fault is either in the sender unit in the fuel tank, the gauge in the instrument panel or the wiring.

2. To check the sender unit first disconnect the green/black wire from the unit at the connector on the tank. With the ignition on, the gauge should read 'full'. With the same lead connected to earth the gauge should read 'empty'. If BOTH of these situations are correct then the fault (if any) lies in the sender unit.

3. If the gauge does not read full with the wire disconnected from the sender unit, the wire should then also be disconnected from the gauge unit (having removed the instrument panel as described in Chapter 10). If the gauge now reads 'full' then the fault lies in the wire from the gauge to the sender unit.

4. If not, the gauge is faulty and should be replaced. (For details see Chapter 10).

5. With the wire disconnected from the sender unit and earthed, if the gauge reads anything other than empty, check the rest of the circuit as described in Chapter 10.

6. To remove the sender unit, first remove the boot floor cover and disconnect the lead from the sender. The six screws should be removed and the unit can

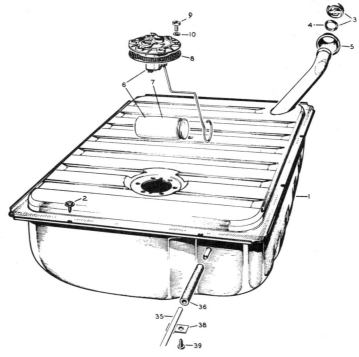

Fig.3.19. FUEL TANK & COMPONENTS

1. Tank	5. Grommet	9. Screw	38. Pipe clip
2. Securing screw	6. Gauge sender unit	10. Lock washer	39. Screw
3. Filler cap	7. Float	35. Outlet pipe to pump	
4. Washer	8. Sealing ring	36. Flexible connector	

Fig.3.21. Indicating how the diaphragm tab lines up with the fuel pump body.

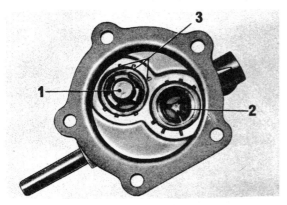

Fig.3.20. VIEW OF FUEL PUMP NON-RETURN VALVES

1 Inlet valve   3 Staking
2 Outlet valve

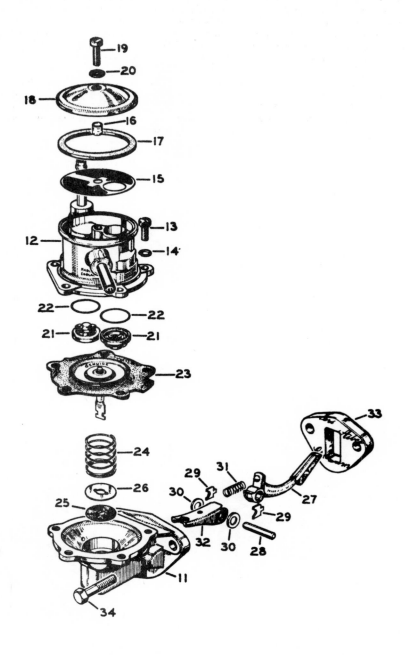

Fig.3.22. EXPLODED DRAWING OF AC Y.D. FUEL PUMP

11 Body base	17. Cover sealing ring	23. Diaphragm	29. Rocker pin retainer
12 Body centre	18. Cover	24. Spring	30. Spacer washer
13 Body screw	19. Cover screw	25. Oil seal	31. Spring
14 Washer	20. Washer	26. Seal retainer	32. Link
15 Filter screen	21. Valve	27. Rocker arm	33. Insulator
16 Spacer collar	22. Sealing ring	28. Rocker pin	34. Mounting bolt

then be lifted out together with the float.

7. Replacement is a straightforward reversal of the removal procedure. Fit a new gasket and position it so that the terminal blade points to the front of the car. After the wire is connected bend the terminal blade down flush with the tank.

17. Exhaust System

1. The exhaust system incorporates two silencers and is supported at the front where it bolts to the manifold; and underneath by two flexible hangars. One supports the rear silencer and the other tail pipe. (See Fig. 3.23).

2. If any one section of the system needs replacement it is often easiest and (in the long run) cheapest to replace the whole lot.

3. Make sure that the attitude and clearance of the front silencer is as shown in Fig.3.24., and always fit a new manifold to pipe gasket.

4. On HB23 engines, with twin outlet pipes from the manifold, the centre two nuts should be tightened up first.

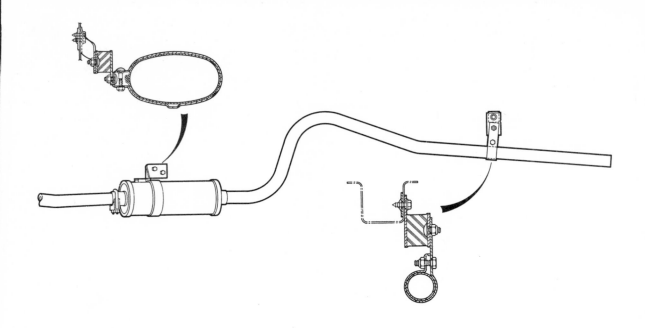

Fig.3.23. Position and cross section of exhaust system flexible hangars.

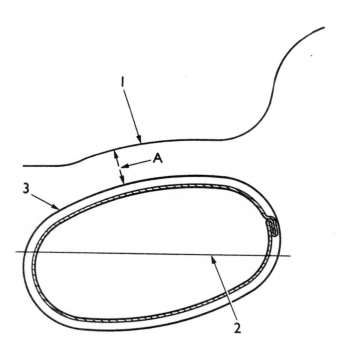

Fig.3.24. POSITION OF FRONT SILENCER RELATIVE TO UNDERBODY
1. Underbody. 2. Horizontal. 3. Front silencer.
'A' dimension 1.00 to 1.25 inches.

Fault Finding Chart — Fuel System & Carburation

Unsatisfactory engine performance and excessive fuel consumption are not necessarily the fault of the fuel system or carburetter. In fact they more commonly occur as a result of ignition and timing faults. Before acting on the following it is necessary to check the ignition system first. Even though a fault may lie in the fuel system it will be difficult to trace unless the ignition is correct. The faults below, therefore, assume that this has been attended to first (where appropriate).

Symptom	Reason/s	Remedy
Smell of petrol when engine is stopped	Leaking fuel lines or unions.	Repair or renew as necessary.
	Leaking fuel tank.	Fill fuel tank to capacity and examine carefully at seams, unions and filler pipe connections. Repair as necessary.
Smell of petrol when engine is idling	Leaking fuel line unions between pump and carburetter.	Check line and unions and tighten or repair.
	Overflow of fuel from float chamber due to wrong level setting or ineffective needle valve or punctured float.	Check fuel level setting and condition of float and needle valve and renew if necessary.
Excessive fuel consumption for reasons not covered by leaks or float chamber faults	Worn jets (Solex and Zenith).	Renew jets.
	Over-rich jet setting (Stromberg).	Adjust jet.
	Sticking strangler flap (Solex, Zenith)	Check correct movement of strangler flap.
Difficult starting, uneven running, lack of power, cutting out.	One or more jets. Blocked or restricted.	Dismantle and clean out float chamber and jets.
	Fuel pump not delivering sufficient fuel.	Check pump delivery and clean or repair as required.
	Air valve piston not operating correctly (Stromberg).	Dismantle and examine. Clean and repair as required.

Chapter 4/Ignition System

Contents

Specifications

Sparking Plugs

Standard	AC 42 x L5
Electrode gap	.028 to .032 in.
H.T. leads - Suppressor type	4000 - 8000 ohms resistance per foot

Coil

Make	AC-Delco
Current consumption..	.78 amps at 1000 r.p.m. (distributor)
Primary coil resistance	1.3 − 1.5 ohms at 20°C
Resistor coil resistance	2 ohms at 20°C

Distributor

Make	Delco-Remy D202
Rotation	Anti-clockwise
Firing sequence	1, 3, 4, 2
Contacts points gap - new	.022 in.
- used	.020 in.
Contact spring arm tension	17 − 21 ozs.
Cam dwell angle	35° − 37°
Points breaker plate rotation load...	10 − 16 ozs.
Mainshaft - diameter	.4895 in. to .4900 in.
- clearance in bushes..	.0003 in. to .0013 in.
- endfloat - initial..	.002 in. to .005 in.
- maximum	.010 in.
Upper thrust washer thickness	.029 in. to .033 in.
Lower thrust washer thickness...	.062 in. to .066 in.

Ignition Timing

Static advance - HB 22 - low compression	9° B.T.D.C.
- high compression	4½°B.T.D.C.
HB 23 engine	4½°B.T.D.C.
Maximum vacuum advance	15° (Crankshaft)
Maximum centrifugal advance	33° (Crankshaft)

Vacuum advance range   ... ...

Vacuum (Hg.)	Distributor Advance°
5	0 − 1½°
7	1 − 4½°
9	3½ − 7½°
11+	5½ − 7½°

Centrifugal advance range   ... ...

Crankshaft r.p.m.	Crankshaft advance°
800	0 − 3½
1200	5 − 10
1600	11½ − 16½
2000	17½ − 23
2400	19½ − 25
2800	21½ − 27

Crankshaft r.p.m.	Crankshaft advance^o
3200	23½ — 29
3600	26 — 31
4000+	28 — 33

HB 23 engines - later models have a different distributor (Part No.7953579) calling for different settings viz:—

Static advance ... ... 9° B.T.D.C.

Vacuum advance range ... ...

Vacuum (Hg.)	Advance distributor^o
2	0
4	0 — 5
6	5¼ — 7¾
8	7½ — 9½
10+	9 — 11

1. General Description

In order that the engine can run correctly it is necessary for an electrical spark to ignite the fuel/air mixture in the combustion chamber at exactly the right moment in relation to engine speed and load. The ignition system is based on feeding low tension voltage from the battery to the coil where it is converted to high tension voltage. The high tension voltage is powerful enough to jump the sparking plug gap in the cylinders many times a second under high compression pressures, providing that the system is in good condition and that all adjustments are correct.

The ignition system is divided into two circuits. The low tension circuit and the high tension circuit.

The low tension (sometimes known as the primary) circuit consists of the battery, lead to the control box, lead to the ignition switch, lead from the ignition switch to the low tension or primary coil windings (terminal SW), and the lead from the low tension coil windings (coil terminal CB) to the contact breaker points and condenser in the distributor.

The high tension circuit consists of the high tension or secondary coil windings, the heavy ignition lead from the centre of the coil to the centre of the distributor cap, the rotor arm, and the sparking plug leads and sparking plugs.

The system functions in the following manner. Low tension voltage is changed in the coil into high tension voltage by the opening and closing of the contact breaker points in the low tension circuit. High tension voltage is then fed via the carbon brush in the centre of the distributor cap to the rotor arm of the distributor.

The rotor arm revolves anti-clockwise at half engine speed inside the distributor cap, and each time it comes in line with one of the four metal segments in the cap, which are connected to the sparking plug leads, the opening and closing of the contact breaker points causes the high tension voltage to build up, jump the gap from the rotor arm to the appropriate metal segment and so via the sparking plug lead to the sparking plug, where it finally jumps the spark plug gap before going to earth.

The ignition is advanced and retarded automatically, to ensure the spark occurs at just the right instant for the particular load at the prevailing engine speed.

The ignition advance is controlled both mechanically and by a vacuum operated system. The mechanical governor mechanism comprises two lead weights, which move out from the distributor shaft as the engine speed rises, due to centrifugal force. As they move outwards they rotate the cam relative to the distributor shaft, and so advance the spark. The weights are held in position by two light springs and it is the tension of the springs which is largely responsible for correct spark advancement.

The vacuum control consists of a diaphragm, one side of which is connected via a small bore tube to the carburetter, and the other side to the contact breaker plate. Depression in the inlet manifold and carburetter, which varies with engine speed and throttle opening, causes the diaphragm to move, so moving the contact breaker plate, and advancing or retarding the spark. A fine degree of control is achieved by a spring in the vacuum assembly.

2. Routine Maintenance

1. Once every 6,000 miles remove the sparking plugs, clean them, and reset the gap as described in Section 12, paragraphs 7 to 10.
2. At intervals of 12,000 miles remove the distributor cap and lubricate the distributor as described in Section 6.
3. Check the condition of the contact breaker points, clean and regap them, and if necessary fit a new set. Check the static timing and the distributor advance and retard mechanism (See Sections 3, 4 and 11).
4. Inspect the ignition leads for cracks and signs of perishing and replace as necessary. Ensure the ends of the leads are firmly attached to the plug clips and ensure the clips fit tightly over the heads of the plugs.

3. Contact Breaker Adjustment

1. To adjust the contact breaker points to the correct gap, first pull off the two clips securing the distributor cap to the distributor body, and lift away the cap. Clean the cap inside and out with a dry cloth. It is unlikely that the four segments will be badly burned or scored, but if they are, the cap will have to be renewed.
2. Check the carbon brush located in the top of the cap to make sure that it is not broken or missing.
3. Gently prise the contact breaker points open to examine the condition of their faces. If they are rough, pitted or dirty, it will be necessary to remove them for resurfacing, or for replacement points to be fitted.
4. Presuming the points are satisfactory, or that they have been cleaned and replaced, measure the gap between the points by turning the engine over until the contact breaker arm is on the peak of one of the four cam lobes.
5. A 0.020 inch feeler gauge should now just fit between the points.
6. If the gap varies from this amount, slacken the contact plate securing screw, (photo - arrowed).
7. Adjust the contact gap by inserting a screwdriver in

the nick in the side of the fixed plate and lever it in the required direction, (see photo).

8. Replace the rotor arm and distributor cap and clip the spring blade cap retainer into place.

4. Contact Breaker Points — Removing & Replacing

1. Remove the distributor cap, (see photo).
2. Remove the rotor arm by pulling it straight up. Do not pull it by the contact spring (see photo). If it is tight lever it carefully from underneath with a screwdriver.
3. Remove the contact points holding screw.
4. Pull the condenser lead clip and coil lead clip from the nylon lug holding the end of the moving contact spring.
5. Lift the complete contact set assembly off the pivot pin of the mounting plate.
6. If the condition of the points is not too bad they can be reconditioned by rubbing the contacts clean with fine emery cloth or a fine carborundum stone. It is important that the faces are rubbed flat and parallel to each other so that there will be complete face to face contact when the points are closed. One of the points will be pitted and the other will have deposits on it.
7. It is necessary to completely remove the built-up deposits, but not necessary to rub the pitted point right down to the stage where all the pitting has disappeared, though obviously if this is done it will prolong the time before the operation of refacing the points has to be repeated.
8. Thoroughly clean the points before refitting them. Locate the fixed contact plate over the base of the pivot pin and then fix the moving contact into position so that the end of the spring fits over the centre boss of the nylon lug. (photo A). Replace the fixing screw. Press in the condenser and coil lead tags to the nylon lug behind the spring. When complete the assembly should appear as in photo (C).
9. Adjust the gap as described in Section 3.

5. Condenser Removal, Testing & Replacement

1. The purpose of the condenser, (sometimes known as capacitor) is to ensure that when the contact breaker points open there is no sparking across them which would waste voltage and cause wear.
2. The condenser is fitted in parallel with the contact breaker points. If it develops a short circuit, it will cause ignition failure as the points will be prevented from interrupting the low tension circuit.
3. If the engine becomes very difficult to start or begins to miss after several miles running and the breaker points show signs of excessive burning, then the condition of the condenser must be suspect. A further test can be made by separating the points by hand with the ignition switched on. If this is accompanied by a flash it is indicative that the condenser has failed.
4. Without special test equipment the only sure way to diagnose condenser trouble is to replace a suspected unit with a new one and note if there is any improvement.
5. To remove the condenser from the distributor, remove the distributor cap and the rotor arm.
6. Pull out the condenser lead clip from the nylon lug where it fits behind the spring.
7. Undo the mounting bracket screw and remove the condenser.
8. Replacement is simply a reversal of the removal pro-

cess. Take particular care that the condenser lead does not short circuit against any portion of the breaker plate.

6. Distributor Lubrication

1. Once every 12,000 miles thoroughly lubricate and grease the distributor. Take great care not to use too much lubricant, as any excess that finds its way onto the contact breaker points could cause burning and misfiring.
2. Remove the distributor cap and pull off the rotor arm. With an oil can inject five drops of Castrolite or similar onto the felt pad in the centre of the cam spindle. (The pad is exposed when the rotor arm is lifted off).
3. Inject 5 c.c. (about a teaspoonful or two long squirts from an oil can) of Castrolite or similar through the hole in the plate marked by an arrow and the word 'OIL'. This lubricates the mechanical advance and retard mechanism and the main spindle bush.
4. Smear the thinnest trace of grease over the vertical faces of the distributor cam, taking great care that no grease reaches the contact breaker points.
5. Replace the rotor arm taking care not to push down the spring loaded contact in the centre of the arm, and refit the distributor cap.

7. Distributor Removal & Replacement

1. To remove the distributor complete with cap from the engine, begin by pulling the plug lead terminals off the four sparking plugs. Free the H.T. lead from the centre of the coil to the centre of the distributor by undoing the lead retaining cap from the coil.
2. Pull off the pipe holding the vacuum tube to the distributor vacuum advance and retard take off pipe.
3. Disconnect the low tension wire from the coil.
4. Undo and remove the bolt which holds the distributor clamp plate to the crankcase and lift out the distributor (photo).
5. NOTE: If it is not wished to disturb the timing then under no circumstances should the clamp pinch bolt, which secures the distributor in its relative position in the clamp, be loosened. Providing the distributor is removed without the clamp being loosened from the distributor body, the timing will not be lost.
6. Replacement is a reversal of the above process. When putting the distributor into position, line up the offset tongue of the spindle with the offset slot in the drive shaft. The correct timing will be automatically obtained provided the clamp plate has not been touched. If it is moved, retime the ignition as described in Section 11.

8. Distributor Dismantling

1. The only time when the distributor should be dismantled is when it is wished to recondition it, and certain parts should always be discarded as a matter of course. Ensure that these parts, described in the following text, are available before taking the distributor down.
2. With the distributor removed from the car and on the bench, remove the distributor cap and lift off the rotor arm. If very tight, lever it off gently with a screwdriver.
3. Remove the points from the distributor as described

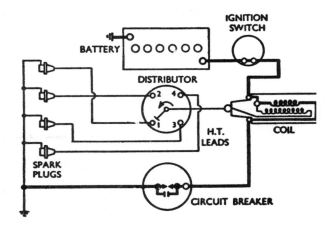

Fig.4.1. The ignition system. The primary circuit is indicated by the heavier lines.

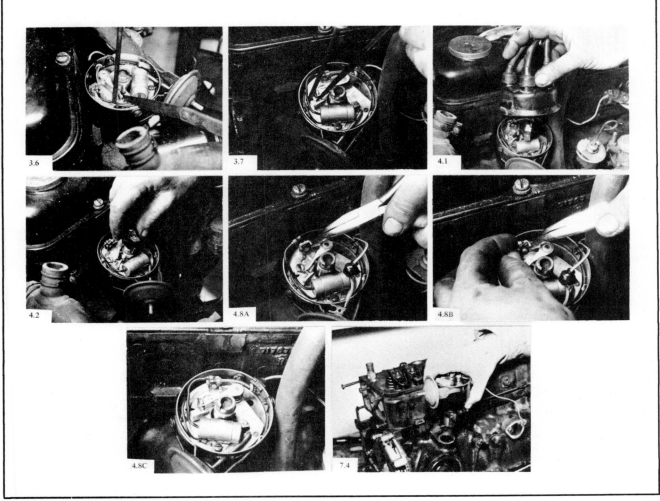

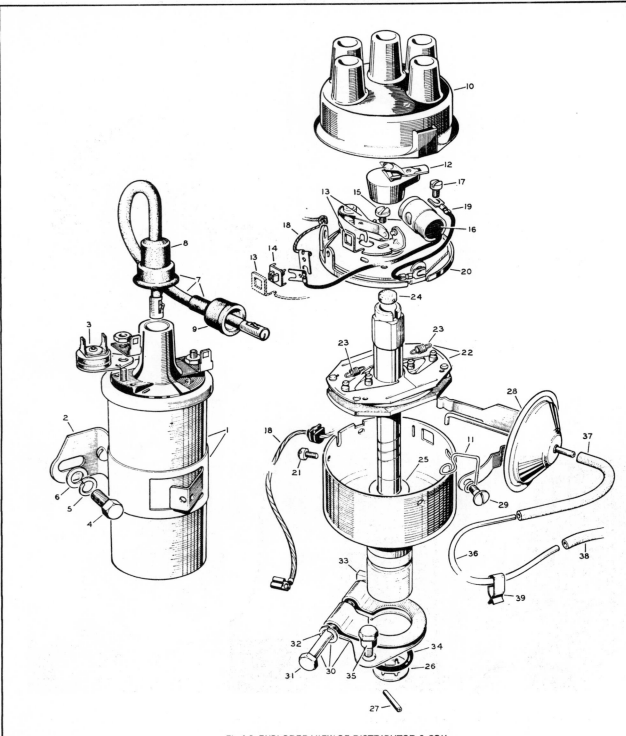

Fig.4.2. EXPLODED VIEW OF DISTRIBUTOR & COIL

1. Coil
2. Mounting bracket
3. Resistor
4. Mounting bolt
5. Lock washer
6. Plain washer
7. H.T.lead
8. Grommet
9. Grommet
10 Distributor cap
11 Clip

12. Rotor arm
13. Contact points assembly
14. Nylon terminal lug
15. Fixed contact mounting screw
16. Condenser
17. Earth wire screw
18. L.T.lead from coil
19. Earth wire
20. Contact breaker plate
21. Plate securing screw

22. Main shaft and balance weight assembly
23. Balance weight spring
24. Lubricating feet
25. Upper washer
26. Retaining washer
27. Locating pin
28. Vacuum advance unit
29. Vacuum unit fixing screw
30. Clamping ring assembly
31. Clamping bolt

32. Spring washer
33. Nut
34. Oil seal ring
35. Locating bolt
36. Vacuum pipe
37. Flexible connector pipe
38. Flexible pipe to manifold
39. Clip

Fig.4.3. The rotor arm spring contact. The setting 'A' should be .30—.35 inch (7—8½ mm).

Fig.4.4. Distributor mainshaft showing identification number 30.5°

Fig.4.5. IGNITION STATIC TIMING SETTING WITH NO.1 COMING UP TO T.D.C.

1 Crankshaft pulley pointer   3   T.D.C. marker
2 9° BTDC marker

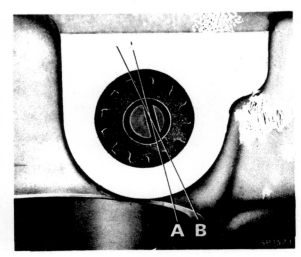

Fig.4.6. Showing position of distributor drive shaft slot with No.1 piston at T.D.C. lines A and B indicate permitted variance.

in Section 4.

4. Carefully remove the vacuum unit assembly after undoing the two screws from the side of the distributor body which also serves to partially hold the contact breaker plate in place. Undo the third plate retaining screw and lift out the plate assembly and the condenser.

5. With a fine nosed punch remove the retaining pin from the bottom end of the distributor mainshaft.

6. Take the tagged washer off the mainshaft.

7. Pull the mainshaft out of the housing and throw away the thrust washers and the advance weight springs.

8. Undo the clamp bolt and remove the clamp and oil seal ring from the shank of the housing.

9. Distributor Inspection & Repair

1. Check the points as described in Section 3. Check the distributor cap for signs of tracking indicated by a thin black line between the segments. Replace the cap if any signs of tracking are found.

2. If the metal portion of the rotor arm is badly burned or loose, renew the arm. If slightly burnt clean the arm with a fine file. Check that the rotor contact spring setting is between .30 to .35 in. as shown in Fig.4.3.

3. Check that the carbon brush is intact in the centre of the distributor cover.

4. Examine the fit of the breaker plate on the bearing plate and also check the breaker arm pivot for looseness or wear and renew as necessary.

5. Examine the balance weights and pivot pins for wear, and renew the weights or cam assembly if a degree of wear is found.

6. Examine the length of the balance weight springs and compare them with new springs. If they have stretched they must be renewed. It is almost inevitable that they will have stretched and it is best to fit new springs as a matter of course.

7. Check that the mainshaft is not a slack fit in the housing bushes. If it is, the points gap setting will fluctuate according to the degree of slackness. Replace the bushes and also the shaft if the old one is still slack.

8. The diaphragm should be checked visually for proper operation when the engine is running.

10. Distributor Reassembly

1. Reassembly is a straightforward reversal of the dismantling process, but there are several points which should be noted.

2. Lubricate with S.A.E.20 engine oil the balance weights and other parts of the mechanical advance mechanism, the cam, the mainshaft, and the felts, during assembly.

3. Always use a new upper and lower thrust washer and check the mainshaft endfloat between the bottom thrust washer and the housing with a feeler gauge. The dimension should be between .002 and .005 in. where using new thrust washers (.010 inch if not).

4. If a new mainshaft is being fitted check that it is of the correct type as they can vary between the same type of distributor. The figure '30.5' stamped on the underside of the centrifugal advance mechanism plate indicates that the correct type is being used. (See Fig.4.4). It will also be necessary to drill the end of the shaft to accept a new pin using a No.30 drill. To do this replace the shaft into the distributor body with the upper thrust washer in place, and put the tabbed retaining washer on the

end of the shaft. If you are not too sure of your ability to drill the shaft accurately in order to obtain the specified end float, then it is always better to err on the side of a little too much endfloat which can be taken up with additional spacer washers. Be sure to drill the hole exactly at right angles to the shaft axis and through the shaft centre line. It is not important about its radial position relative to the tongue on the end of the shaft.

5. Finally set the contact breaker gap to the specified clearance.

11. Ignition Timing

1. If the clamp plate pinch bolt has been loosened and moved on the distributor, or the engine turned with the distributor removed, the following procedure should be followed.

2. The correct engine position for static timing is 4½° B.T.D.C. for HB22 high compression, and HB23 engines. For the optional low compression HB22 engine, the static timing is 9° B.T.D.C. These positions are found by turning the engine so that the pointer on the crankshaft pulley wheel is set between the two markers on the timing case (4½° B.T.D.C.) or to the lower one (9° B.T.D.C.). See Fig.4.5.

3. Check the slot in the distributor drive shaft (inside the mounting hole in the crankcase). The slot offset should be towards the rear (see Fig.4.6). If it is not towards the rear (but directly opposite) then rotate the engine one more complete revolution and it will be in the correct position.

4. Position the mainshaft of the distributor so that the tongue lines up with the slot in the drive. (As a check, if the rotor arm is now fitted to the distributor, the contact should be in a position to line up with the segment in the distributor cap attached to No.1 plug lead).

5. Loosen the distributor clamp bolt and tighten the fixing bolt which holds the clamp to the engine.

6. Now turn the distributor body clockwise until the contact points are just about to open. This can be accurately gauged if a 12 volt 6 watt bulb is wired in parallel with the contact points. Switch on the ignition and when the points open the bulb should light.

7. Tighten the distributor clamp bolt.

8. If a stroboscopic light is used for a final static ignition timing check, remove the lead from No.1 plug and then connect the strobe, one wire to the plug and the other to the plug lead. With the engine idling as slowly as possible shine the strobe light on to the timing case marker when the pulley pointer should appear stationary between the two timing case markers (4½° advance) or on the lower marker (9° advance).

9. If the engine speed is increased, then the effect of the vacuum and centrifugal advance controls can be seen and in fact, measured to some extent, in so far as the distance between the two crankcase timing markers represents 9° of crankshaft revolution.

12. Sparking Plugs & Leads

1. The correct functioning of the sparking plugs is vital for the correct running and efficiency of the engine. The plugs fitted as standard are listed in the specification page.

2. At intervals of 6,000 miles the plugs should be removed, examined, cleaned and, if worn excessively, replaced. The condition of the sparking plug will also tell much about the overall condition of the engine.

Measuring plug gap. A feeler gauge of the correct size (see ignition system specifications) should have a slight 'drag' when slid between the electrodes. Adjust gap if necessary

Adjusting plug gap. The plug gap is adjusted by bending the earth electrode inwards, or outwards, as necessary until the correct clearance is obtained. Note the use of the correct tool

Normal. Grey-brown deposits lightly coated core nose. Gap increasing by around 0.001 in (0.025 mm) per 1000 miles (1600 km). Plugs ideally suited to engine and engine in good condition

Carbon fouling. Dry, black, sooty deposits. Will cause weak spark and eventually misfire. Fault: over-rich fuel mixture. Check: carburettor mixture settings, float level and jet sizes; choke operation and cleanliness of air filter. Plugs can be re-used after cleaning

Oil fouling. Wet, oily deposits. Will cause weak spark and eventually misfire. Fault: worn bores/piston rings or valve guides; sometimes occurs (temporarily) during running-in period. Plugs can be re-used after thorough cleaning

Overheating. Electrodes have glazed appearance, core nose very white - few deposits. Fault: plug overheating. Check: plug value, ignition timing, fuel octane rating (too low) and fuel mixture (too weak). Discard plugs and cure fault immediately

Electrode damage. Electrodes burned away; core nose has burned, glazed appearance. Fault: initial pre-ignition. Check: for 'Overheating' but may be more severe. Discard plugs and remedy fault before piston or valve damage occurs

Split core nose (may appear initially as a crack). Damage is self-evident, but cracks will only show after cleaning. Fault: pre-ignition or wrong gap-setting technique. Check: ignition timing, cooling system, fuel octane rating (too low) and fuel mixture (too weak). Discard plugs, rectify fault immediately

3. If the insulator nose of the sparking plug is clean and white, with no deposits, this is indicative of a weak mixture, or too hot a plug. (A hot plug transfers heat away from the electrode slowly — a cold plug transfers it away quickly).

4. If the tip and insulator nose is covered with hard black looking deposits, then this is indicative that the mixture is too rich. Should the plug be black and oily, then it is likely that the engine is fairly worn, as well as the mixture being too rich.

5. If the insulator nose is covered with light tan to greyish brown deposits, then the mixture is correct and it is likely that the engine is in good condition.

6. If there are any traces of long brown tapering stains on the outside of the white portion of the plug, then the plug will have to be renewed, as this shows that there is a faulty joint between the plug body and the insulator, and compression is being allowed to leak away.

7. Plugs should be cleaned by a sand blasting machine, which will free them from carbon more thoroughly than cleaning by hand. The machine will also test the condition of the plugs under compression. Any plug that fails to spark at the recommended pressure should be renewed.

8. The sparking plug gap is of considerable importance, as, if it is too large or too small the size of the spark and its efficiency will be seriously imparied. The sparking plug gap should be set to 0.030 in. for the best results.

9. To set it, measure the gap with a feeler gauge, and then bend open, or close, the outer plug electrode until the correct gap is achieved. The centre electrode should never be bent as this may crack the insulation and cause plug failure, if nothing worse.

10 When replacing the plugs, remember to use new plug washers, and replace the leads from the distributor in the correct firing order, which is 1,3,4,2, No.1 cylinder being the one nearest the radiator.

11 The plug leads require no routine attention other than being kept clean and wiped over regularly. At intervals of 6,000 miles, however, pull each lead off the plug in turn and pull them from the distributor cap. Water can seep down into these joints giving rise to a white corrosive deposit which must be carefully removed from the brass washer at the end of each cable, through which the ignition wires pass.

13. Ignition System Faults — Symptoms & Remedies

1. By far the majority of breakdown and running troubles are caused by faults in the ignition system either in the low tension or high tension circuits.

2. There are two main symptoms indicating ignition faults. Either the engine will not start or fire, or the engine is difficult to start and misfires. If it is a regular misfire, i.e. the engine is only running on two or three cylinders, the fault is almost sure to be in the secondary, or high tension, circuit. If the misfiring is intermittent. the fault could be in either the high or low tension circuits. If the car stops suddenly, or will not start at all, it is likely that the fault is in the low tension circuit. Loss of power and overheating, apart from faulty carburation settings, are normally due to faults in the distributor, or incorrect ignition timing.

3. If the engine fails to start and the car was running normally when it was last used, first check there is fuel in the petrol tank. If the engine turns over normally on the starter motor and the battery is evidently well charged, then the fault may be in either the high or low tension circuits. First check the H.T. circuit. NOTE: If

the battery is known to be fully charged; the ignition light comes on, and the starter motor fails to turn the engine CHECK THE TIGHTNESS OF THE LEADS ON THE BATTERY TERMINALS and also the secureness of the earth lead to its CONNECTION TO THE BODY. It is quite common for the leads to have worked loose, even if they look and feel secure. If one of the battery terminal posts gets very hot when trying to work the starter motor this is a sure indication of a faulty connection to that terminal.

4. One of the commonest reasons for bad starting is wet or damp sparking plug leads and distributor. Remove the distributor cap. If condensation is visible internally, dry the cap with a rag and also wipe over the leads. Replace the cap.

5. If the engine still fails to start, check that current is reaching the plugs, by disconnecting each plug lead in turn at the sparking plug end, and hold the end of the cable about 3/16th inch away from the cylinder block. Spin the engine on the starter motor.

6. Sparking between the end of the cable and the block should be fairly strong with a regular blue spark. (Hold the lead with rubber to avoid electric shocks). If current is reaching the plugs, then remove them and clean and regap them to 0.025 in. The engine should now start.

7. If there is no spark at the plug leads take off the H.T. lead from the centre of the distributor cap and hold it to the block as before. Spin the engine on the starter once more. A rapid succession of blue sparks between the end of the lead and the block indicate that the coil is in order and that the distributor cap is cracked, the rotor arm faulty, or the carbon brush in the top of the distributor cap is not making good contact with the spring on the rotor arm. Possibly the points are in bad condition. Clean and reset them as described in this chapter section 3, paragraphs 4 — 8.

8. If there are no sparks from the end of the lead from the coil, check the connections at the coil end of the lead. If it is in order start checking the low tension circuit.

9. Use a 12v voltmeter on a 12v bulb and two lengths of wire. With the ignition switch on and the points open test between the low tension wire to the coil (it is marked S.W. or +) and earth. No reading indicates a break in the supply from the ignition switch. Check the connections at the switch to see if any are loose. Refit them and the engine should run. A reading shows a faulty coil or condenser, or broken lead between the coil and the distributor.

10 Take the condenser wire off the points assembly and with the points open, test between the moving point and earth. If there is now a reading, then the fault is in the condenser. Fit a new one and the fault is cleared.

11 With no reading from the moving point to earth, take a reading between earth and the CB or - terminal of the coil. A reading here shows a broken wire which will need to be replaced between the coil and distributor. No reading confirms that the coil has failed and must be replaced, after which the engine will run once more. Remember to refit the condenser wire to the points assembly. For these tests it is sufficient to separate the points with a piece of dry paper while testing with the points open.

12 The Viva is fitted with a device which boosts the output from the coil when the starter is operated, and battery voltage tends to drop due to the load placed upon it. Quite simply, the coil is rated for a continuous 6 volt supply. As the vehicle system is 12 volt a resistor is fitted into the L.T. supply to the coil so that under normal running conditions the coil only receives a 6 volt

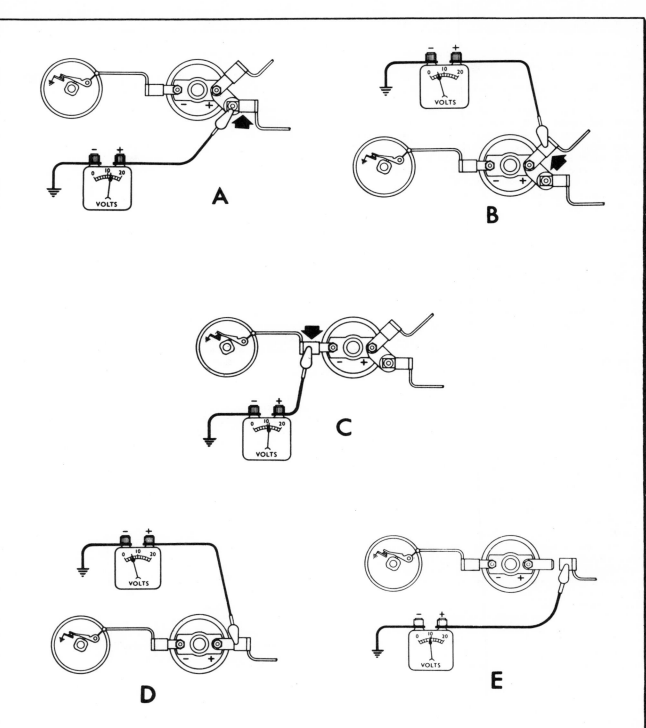

Fig.4.7. DIAGRAM SHOWING CONNECTIONS FOR THREE STAGE TESTING OF PRIMARY CIRCUIT TO COIL

A. To check running supply to coil (prior to resistor).
B. To check running supply to coil from resistor and start feed.
C. To check condition of coil primary windings.
D. Later models — to check supply to coil from resistor.
E. Later models — to check supply to coil at starting.

supply. However, when the starter is operated the system voltage drops. This is usual. In addition to the normal L.T. feed to the coil therefore an additional feed is taken from the starter solenoid switch direct to the coil This feed only operates when the solenoid starter terminals are closed, i.e. when the starter is turning. Consequently, for the brief time when the voltage drops from 12 to about 8 volts, 8 volts is fed direct to the 6 volt coil providing a temporary starting boost.

Certain checks are necessary to ensure that:—
a) The starter feed is functioning properly — otherwise only about 2 volts would reach the coil on starting.
b) The resistor is in good order — otherwise 12 volts or no volts may reach the 6 volt coil.

Test procedures — Fig.4.7A shows connection with a voltmeter, ignition on and points closed. A reading of 11½ to 12 volts indicates that the battery voltage is reaching the resistor under running conditions. If not, check that other items on the ignition circuit are working (fuel gauge). If they are the wire from the coil resistor back to the switch is at fault. If not, the feed to the ignition switch from the multi-socket connector, and further back if necessary, must be traced through.

Fig.4.7B shows the connection to check the resistor— ignition switched on and points closed. The reading should be 5—6 volts. If the starter motor is operated with this connection still made, the voltmeter should jump to about 8 volts to show that the start feed is working properly. If not the wire or solenoid switch are faulty.

Fig.4.7C shows the connection to check that the coil primary windings are in order. With ignition switched on and points open the voltage should be 11½ to 12 volts. If not the coil primary windings are deteriorating or defunct and the coil should be renewed.

On some later models the resistor may not be mounted on the coil terminal but incorporated in the wiring harness — particularly where an alternator instead of a generator is used. In such cases a simple wire only leads to the '+' terminal of the coil even though the 'start feed' function still obtains.

Fig.4.7A shows the connection to be made to check the running supply which should be 5—6 volts. This is the same as the first test for Fig.4.7B.

Fig.4.7E shows the start feed check connections — the test being the same as the second one described for Fig.4.7B.

Should indications be that the resistance in the wiring harness is faulty the whole harness may need replacement as this particular resistance wire is not supplied or serviced separately. However, if the wiring harness is removed and the wires separated a competent electrician might suceed in fitting a new resistance wire according to the specifications shown on the wiring diagram on page 190 (Chapter 10).

14. Misfiring — Diagnosis & Remedies

1. If the engine misfires regularly run it at a fast idling speed. Pull off each of the plug caps in turn and listen to the note of the engine. Hold the plug cap in a dry cloth or with a rubber glove as additional protection against a shock from the H.T. supply.
2. No difference in engine running will be noticed when the lead from the defective circuit is removed. Removing the lead from one of the good cylinders will accentuate the misfire.
3. Remove the plug lead from the end of the defective plug and hold it about 3/16th inch away from the block. Restart the engine. If the sparking is fairly strong and regular the fault must lie in the sparking plug.
4. The plug may be loose, the insulation may be cracked, or the points may have burnt away giving too wide a gap for the spark to jump. Worse still, one of the points may have broken off. Either renew the plug, or clean it, reset the gap, and then test it.
5. If there is no spark at the end of the plug lead, or if it is weak and intermittent, check the ignition lead from the distributor to the plug. If the insulation is cracked or perished, renew the lead. Check the connections at the distributor cap.
6. If there is still no spark, examine the distributor cap carefully for tracking. This can be recognised by a very thin black line running between two or more electrodes, or between an electrode and some other part of the distributor. These lines are paths which now conduct electricity across the cap thus letting it run to earth. The only answer is a new distributor cap.
7. Apart from the ignition timing being incorrect, other causes of misfiring have already been dealt with under the section dealing with the failure of the engine to start. To recap - these are that:-

a) The coil may be faulty giving an intermittent misfire.
b) There may be a damaged wire or loose connection in the low tension circuit.
c) The condenser may be short circuiting.
d) There may be a mechanical fault in the distributor (Broken driving spindle or contact breaker spring).

8. If the ignition timing is too far retarded, it should be noted that the engine will tend to overheat, and there will be a quite noticeable drop in power. If the engine is overheating and the power is down, and the ignition timing is correct, then the carburetter should be checked, as it is likely that this is where the fault lies.

Chapter 5/Clutch and Actuating Mechanism

Contents

Specifications

Make	Borg & Beck
Type	Diaphragm spring
Diameter	6¼ inch
Operating fork free travel	¼ in. between fork and cable adjusting nut

Torque Wrench Setting

Clutch cover to flywheel bolts	14 lb/ft. - dry threads

1. General Description

The clutch consists of an integral pressure plate and diaphragm spring assembly with a single dry plate friction disc between the pressure plate assembly and the flywheel.

The bellhousing on the gearbox encloses the whole unit but only the top half of the bellhousing bolts to the engine. Consequently there is a semi-circular steel plate bolted to the lower half of the bellhousing to act as a cover.

The clutch is operated mechanically by a Bowden cable direct from the clutch pedal. This actuates a clutch release lever and thrust bearing, the lever pivoting on a ball pin inside the bellhousing and projecting through an aperture in the bellhousing opposite to the pin. Adjustment of free play is effected by a threaded ball joint at the end of the cable where it is attached to the clutch operating lever.

2. Routine Maintenance

1. The clutch cable should not be lubricated.
2. The ball end of the cable where it bears in the clutch operating lever should be oiled periodically with engine oil.
3. The free play in the clutch pedal cannot be accurately determined from the pedal because of the cable method of operation. It is therefore necessary to check the gap between the ball on the cable end and the mating face of the operating lever. The gap should be ¼ in. when the cable is pulled tight through the lever hole from the bottom end of the cable. Make sure that the clutch operating lever is correctly held back by the return spring when checking the gap.
4. The gap can be adjusted by undoing the locknut on

the threaded end of the cable and turning the ball ended nut as required. Lock the nut up again after adjustment.

3. Clutch Cable — Removal & Replacement

1. Slacken the locknut at the clutch operating lever end of the cable [see photo, arrow (a)] and remove it and the adjusting ball nut completely from the thread. Remove the sump screw which holds the cable clip locating the outer cable to the side of the engine where the sump joins the crankcase. Then draw the cable through the hole in the bellhousing, [see photo, arrow (b)].

2. Remove the parcel shelf.
3. Withdraw the insulator panel covering the pedal mounting assembly.
4. Pull the clip off the end of the pedal shaft and then draw it to one side far enough to allow the pedal arm to drop down. The end of the cable may then be detached by removing the clevis pin.

5. Unscrew the outer cable locknut and remove the washer.
6. The cable assembly may then be drawn out through the bulkhead. Note the washer fitted on the engine compartment side also.
7. Replacement of the cable is an exact reversal of the removal procedure.

8. If there are signs that the pedal shaft bushes are worn this is a good opportunity to renew them. They can easily be prised out of their locations if the pedal shaft is fully withdrawn. New ones are simply pressed into position.
9. Reset the clutch fork free travel as described in Section 2.

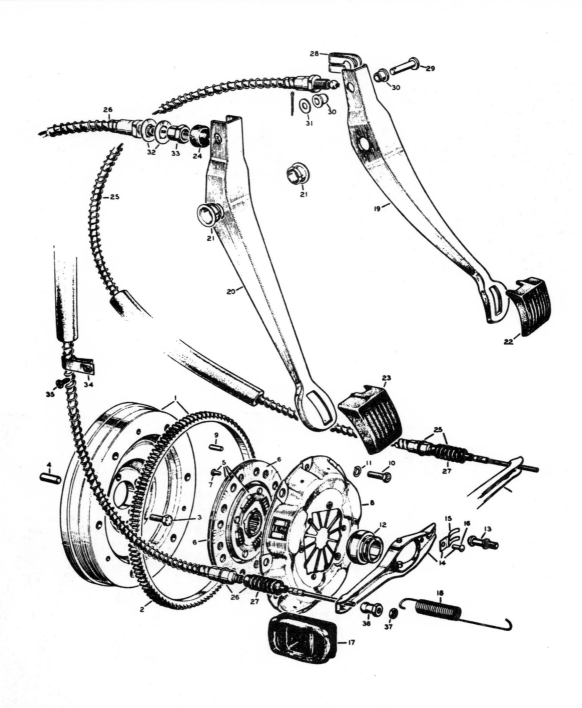

Fig.5.1. EXPLODED DRAWING OF THE CLUTCH & COMPONENTS

1. Flywheel & starter ring
2. Ring gear
3. Flywheel mounting bolt
4. Flywheel locating dowel peg
5. Clutch friction disc assembly
6. Friction lining
7. Rivet
8. Clutch pressure plate

   and cover
9. Clutch cover locating pegs
10. Clutch cover bolt
11. Spring washer
12. Thrust release bearing
13. Operating lever pivot pin
14. Clutch lever assembly
15. Retaining spring
16. Rivet
17. Lever aperture cover

18. Return spring
19. Pedal R.H.D.
20. Pedal L.H.D.
21. Pedal shaft bushes
22. Pedal rubber R.H.D.
23. Pedal rubber L.H.D.
24. Pedal stop rubber
25. Cable (R.H.D) assembly
26. Cable (L.H.D) assembly
27. Rubber boot

28. Clevis
29. Clevis pin
30. Bush
31. Washer
32. Washer
33. Anchor nut
34. Clip
35. Screw
36. Adjuster nut
37. Lock nut

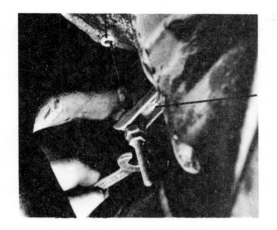

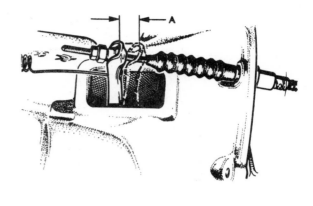

Fig.5.2. Diagram to show measurement ('A') of clutch fork free travel which should be ¼ inch.

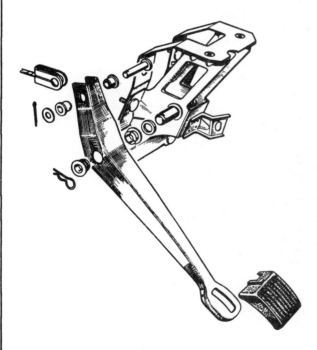

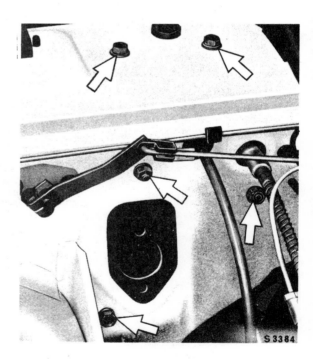

Fig.5.3. Explanatory drawing of clutch pedal relative to pedal mounting brackets.

Fig.5.4. Figure showing five nuts and bolts securing the clutch (and brake) pedal mounting bracket.

4. Clutch Pedal Shaft Assembly — Removal & Replacement

1. If it is necessary to carry out extensive repairs on the clutch pedal mounting shaft and brackets, the easiest way is to remove the whole unit from the car first.
2. Disconnect the clutch fork end of the cable as described in Section 3, and unclip it from the engine also.
3. Remove the parcel shelf and insulator panel from round the pedals.
4. Disconnect the hydraulic pipe from the brake master cylinder as described in Chapter 9/12.
5. Undo the five nuts and bolts (See Fig.5.4, arrowed). which hold the pedal support bracket to the body panel. The whole assembly, with pedals, master cylinder, and clutch cable can then be taken out from inside the car.
6. Replacement is a reversal of the removal procedure. Bleed the hydraulic brake system (Chapter 9), and adjust the clutch pedal free travel after reassembly.
NOTE: The three lower stud holes holding the mounting bracket to the bulkhead should be sealed with some suitable strip to prevent possible rattles.

5. Clutch Pedal Support Brackets Assembly, Examination & Repair

1. Remove the assembly as described in the previous section.
2. Examine the pedal shaft and bushes, clevis pins and pedal arm bush housings for signs of sloppiness and wear. Renew all defective parts as required.

6. Clutch Assembly — Removal & Inspection

1. Remove the gearbox — (See Chapter 6 'Gearbox Removal').
2. Mark the position of the clutch cover relative to the flywheel (see photo).
3. Slacken off the bolts holding the cover to the flywheel in a diagonal sequence, undoing each bolt a little at a time. This keeps the pressure even all round the diaphragm spring and prevents distortion. When all the pressure is released on the bolts remove them, lift the cover off the dowel pegs and take it off together with the friction disc which is between it and the flywheel.
4. Examine the diaphragm spring for signs of distortion or fracture.
5. Examine the pressure plate for signs of scoring or abnormal wear.
6. If either the spring or the plate is defective it will be necessary to replace the complete assembly with an exchange unit. The assembly can only be taken to pieces with special equipment and in any case individual parts of the assembly are not obtainable as regular spares. NOTE: Some later models could be fitted with the Laycock clutch assembly. On these versions the diaphragm spring, driving plate and pressure plate can be separated as they are simply held together by a large retaining ring and no rivets are used. See Fig.5.6. The relative position of the three items should be marked. The retaining ring and anti-rattle springs can then be detached and the assembly comes apart. On assembly the pressure points should be greased sparingly with a heavy lubricant. Castrol MS3. Make sure the retaining ring is replaced with the flat sections under the pressure

plate lugs and the curved sections against the edge of the diaphragm spring.
7. Examine the friction disc for indications of uneven wear and scoring of the friction surfaces. Contamination by oil will also show as hard and blackened areas which can cause defective operation. If the clearance between the heads of the securing rivets and the face of the friction lining material is less than .025 inches it would be worthwhile to fit a new disc also. Around the hub of the friction disc are four springs acting as shock absorbers between the hub and the friction area. These should be intact and tightly in position.
8. The face of the flywheel should be examined for signs of scoring or uneven wear and if necessary it will have to be renewed and replaced or reconditioned. See Chapter 1, Section 20, for details of flywheel removal.

7. Clutch Assembly Replacement — Engine Removed From Car

1. Replacement of the clutch cover and friction plate is the reverse of the removal procedure but not quite so straightforward, as the following paragraphs will indicate.
2. If the clutch assembly has been removed from the engine with the engine out of the car, it is a relatively easy matter to line up the hub of the friction disc with the centre of the cover and flywheel. The cover and friction plate are replaced onto the flywheel with the holes in the cover fitting over the three dowels on the flywheel. The friction plate is supported with a finger while this is being done (see Fig.5.7).
3. Note that the friction plate is mounted with the longer hub of the boss towards the flywheel (see photo).
4. Replace the cover mounting bolts finger tight sufficiently to just grip the friction plate. Then set the friction plate in position by moving it with a screwdriver in its hub so that the hub is exactly concentric with the centre of the flywheel and the cover assembly. (See photo).
5. Tighten up the cover bolts one turn at a time in a diagonal sequence to maintain an even pressure. Final torque setting should be 14 lb/ft. with clean dry bolt threads.

8. Clutch Assembly Replacement — Engine in Car

1. The procedure to be followed is exactly as described in Section 7, but it is not possible to line up the friction plate hub visually.
2. If possible use a spare gearbox input shaft as a positioning jig. With the clutch cover and friction plate in position, but not clamped in any way with the bolts, put the spare shaft into the centre of the assembly so that the nose of the spigot is located in the flywheel centre bushing. Then tighten up all the mounting bolts as described in Section 7, Paragraph 5 and remove the shaft.
3. If, as is quite likely, no spare shaft is readily available, it is essential to obtain an alternative. The diameter of the bore of the flywheel bush is a few thou. less than .6 inches, and the internal diameter of the splined disc hub is fractionally more. It is strongly recommended that a metal shaft or wooden dowel as near as possible to .6 inches diameter is obtained to use as a jig to line up the disc hub. There is also a service tool No.S.E.768 which is designed to do the job.
4. Failing all the suggestions in the previous two paragraphs then resort will have to be made to the use of a smaller rod, such as a plug spanner tommy bar which

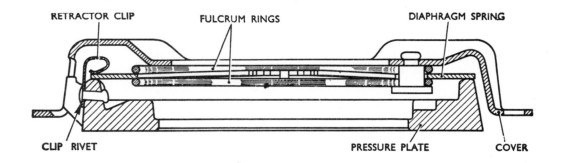

RETRACTOR CLIP   FULCRUM RINGS   DIAPHRAGM SPRING

CLIP RIVET   PRESSURE PLATE   COVER

Fig.5.5. Cross section of clutch pressure plate assembly

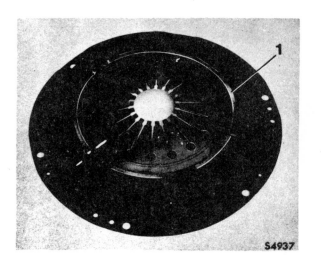

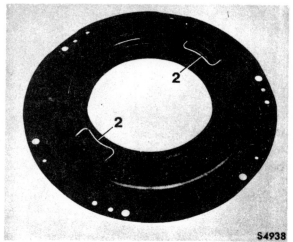

Fig.5.6. Laycock clutch cover, which can be dismantled after removing the retaining ring (1) and anti-rattle springs (2)

can be run around the edge of the respective bores which need lining up. Or use a finger to try and judge the concentricity.

5. Replace the gearbox as described in Chapter 6 'Gearbox Replacement', and reconnect and adjust the clutch operating cable as described in Section 3.

9. Clutch Actuating Lever & Thrust Release Bearing — Removal, Inspection & Replacement

1. Remove the gearbox as described in Chapter 6, 'Gearbox Removal'.

2. Move the lever sideways so that the end over the ball pivot pin is freed by springing back the retaining clip.

3. The lever jaw pins can then be disengaged from the groove in the thrust release bearing and the lever taken off over the end of the input shaft.

4. The clutch release bearing may then be taken off the input shaft.

5. Inspect the pivot pin ball for signs of wear and flats. If necessary it can be removed by driving it out of the bellhousing with a drift. A new one can be driven in with a soft headed hammer.

6. If the release bearing is obviously worn and is noisy it should be replaced. Do not clean the release bearing in any oil solvent liquid as the ball races have been pre-packed with grease and such cleaning would wash it out.

7. Replace the operating lever and release bearing in the reverse order of dismantling. Note that the grooved side of the thrust bearing goes towards the gearbox.

8. Ensure also that the spring retaining clip on the end of the lever fastens securely over the mushroom head of the ball pivot pin.

9. Replace the gearbox as described in Chapter 6, 'Gearbox Replacement'.

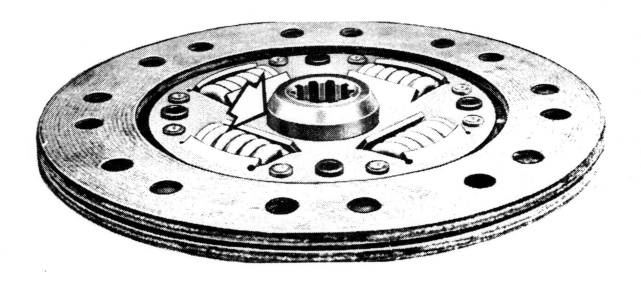

Fig.5.7. Clutch friction disc showing long boss of hub (arrowed) which goes towards the flywheel.

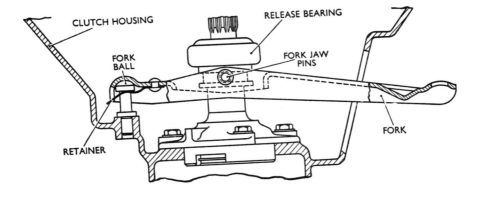

Fig.5.8. Cross section of clutch release mechanism

Fault Finding Chart — Clutch & Actuating Mechanism

Symptom	Reason/s	Remedy
Judder when taking up drive	Loose engine or gearbox mountings or over flexible mountings.	Check and tighten all mounting bolts and replace any 'soft' or broken mountings.
	Badly worn friction surfaces or friction plate contaminated with oil carbon deposit.	Remove clutch assembly and replace parts as required. Rectify any oil leakage points which may have caused contamination.
	Worn splines in the friction plate hub or on the gearbox input shaft.	Renew friction plate and/or input shaft.
	Badly worn bush in flywheel centre for input shaft spigot.	Renew bush in flywheel.
Clutch spin (or failure to disengage) so that gears cannot be engaged.	Clutch actuating cable clearance from fork too great.	Adjust clearance.
	Clutch friction disc sticking to pressure surface because of oil contamination (usually apparent after standing idle for some length of time)	As temporary remedy engage top gear, apply handbrakes, depress clutch and start engine. (If very badly stuck engine will not turn). When running rev up engine and slip clutch until disengagement is normally possible. Renew friction plate at earliest opportunity.
	Damaged or misaligned pressure plate assembly.	Replace pressure plate assembly.
Clutch slip — (increase in engine speed does not result in increase in car speed- especially on hills).	Clutch actuating cable clearance from fork too little resulting in partially disengaged clutch at all times.	Adjust clearance.
	Clutch friction surfaces worn out (beyond further adjustment of operating cable) or clutch surfaces oil soaked.	Replace friction plate and remedy source of oil leakage.

Chapter 6/Gearbox

Contents

Specifications

General

Number of gears	4 forward, 1 reverse
Type	Helical constant mesh, with straight cut reverse gear. Synchromesh on all forward speeds.
Oil capacity	9 pint (Imp.)

Ratios:-		Gearbox	Overall 3.89:1 axle	Overall 4.12:1 axle
First		3.765 : 1	14.64 : 1	15.53 : 1
Second		2.213 : 1	8.61 : 1	9.13 : 1
Third...		1.404 : 1	5.46 : 1	5.79 : 1
Fourth		1 : 1	3.89 : 1	4.12 : 1
Reverse		3.707 : 1	14.42 : 1	15.29 : 1

Mainshaft & Bearings

Mainshaft diameter - first gear	.8917 to .8923 in.
First gear bore fit...	.0014 to .0028 in. clearance
Mainshaft diameter - second and third gears...	1.0994 to 1.100 in.
Second and thrid gears bore fit..	.0014 to .0028 in. clearance
Synchro hub: circlip thicknesses available	.061 in. to .072 in. in four stages - each clip covering .003 in.
Speedo drive gear circlip: thicknesses available	.059 in. to .075 in. in six stages - each clip covering .003 in.

Laygear & Layshaft

Overall length	6.021 in. to 6.023 in.
End float	.005 in. to .017 in.
Thrust washer thickness...	.0615 in. to .0635 in.

Reverse Gear

Idler pinion shaft diameter	.5521 in. to .5528 in.
Idler pinion fit on shaft	.0022 in. to .0039 in. clearance
Clearance between rear face of reverse gear pinion & casing..	.002 in. to .012 in.

Rear Extension Cover

Sliding sleeve diameter	1.1240 in. to 1.1250 in.
Sleeve clearance in bush...	.0015 in. to .004 in.

Gear Lever

Clearance between selector shaft and change lever...	.002 in. to .012 in.

Speedometer Driven Gears Available

Axle ratio	Tyre size	No. of teeth
9 : 35	5.20 x 12	14
	5.50 x 12	12
	6.20 x 12	15
8 : 33	5.20 x 13	15
	5.50 x 12	16
	6.20 x 12	16

1. General Description

A four forward speed all synchromesh gearbox is fitted and is the same on all HB series models. Any optional final drive ratios are made with a different rear axle ratio only, and this applies to the HB23 engine cars as standard.

The gearchange is a standard remote control on the floor and a single selector rod operates directly to two selector forks and a reverse striking lever with an ingenious one piece collar device which locates and holds the forks through all gear changing operations.

All forward gears are helically cut, constant mesh and gear engagement is by sliding hubs and cones engaging dogs on each mainshaft gear.

The laygear (supported at each end on needle roller bearings) runs on a stationary shaft. The reverse gear is straight cut and is part of the 1st/2nd speed synchro hub. The reverse idler gear runs on its own shaft without bushing or bearing.

All bearings and hub locations are made by circlips in grooves and the stationary shafts by interference fit steel balls in depressions on the shafts and cut-outs in the casing. There are no set screws, grub screws, keys or pins used anywhere inside the gearbox. There is no oil drain plug. Provision is made for level checking and topping up.

2. Routine Maintenance

The manufacturers state that periodic draining and refilling is unnecessary. Checks for levels should be made every 6,000 miles or immediately there are signs of drips on your garage drip tray or floor. Whilst no failures due to lack of new oil have come to the notice of the publisher it is suggested that investment in a pint of fresh SAE 90 gear oil whenever the gearbox or propeller shaft is removed would be a safe and modest investment.

3. Gearbox — Removal & Replacement

1. Jack up the front of the car and support it properly on stands in the same way as for engine removal (Chapter 1.6).
2. If the engine is not being removed together with the gearbox, jack up the rear of the car also and support it on stands and remove the propeller shaft as described in Chapter 7.
3. From inside the car unscrew the gear lever knob, and remove the rubber grommet round the lever. Another rubber cover will now be visible and this shrouds a metal cap (somewhat similar to the cap on an ordinary 1 gallon oil tin!) which is then unscrewed. On later models this retaining cap is peened into a hole in the extension housing thread to prevent it unscrewing inadvertently. Do not puncture this cap in any way when removing or replacing it. The gear lever, cap, spring and retaining plate can then all be lifted from the selector rod extension tube.
4. Undo the nut in the centre of the crossmember supporting the gearbox and remove it together with the washer. (See photo).
5. Disconnect the speedometer drive cable from the lower R.H. side of the gearbox rear extension cover by undoing the knurled nut which holds it in place.
6. Disconnect the clutch actuating cable (for details see Chapter 5).

7. Support the gearbox just forward of the crossmember using a jack and then remove the crossmember holding bolts, two at each end (see photo) and remove the crossmember,
8. Remove all bolts holding the gearbox casing to the engine (still supporting the gearbox on the jack) as described in Chapter 1 — 'Engine Removal.'
9. Gently lower the jack, at the same time supporting the gearbox.
10 With very little effort it can now be drawn off the dowels on the engine block and, still being supported, the gearbox input shaft pinion disengaged from the clutch assembly.
11 It will be necessary to tilt the gearbox down at the tail end. At first the engine will tilt also on its mountings until the valve rocker cover comes up against the bulkhead. By this point the gearbox should be almost completely clear. It is very important that no strain in any direction is imparted to the input shaft as it could be damaged, as could the clutch assembly.
12 If the gearbox is to be taken out of the car together with the engine, it is necessary only to carry out the requirements of paragraphs 1,3,4,5 and 6 in this section and in addition provide a support for the front end of the propeller shaft when it is released from the back of the gearbox, when the gearbox is taken away with the engine.
13 Remember to pause a minute or two after the propeller shaft is disengaged and catch the oil which will drain out of the gearbox mainshaft rear cover as the front of the engine tilts up.
14 Replacement is a direct reversal of the removal procedure, having made sure that the clutch assembly is suitably lined up to accept the gearbox input shaft (See Chapter 5 — Clutch Assembly Replacement). Some juggling may be needed but at all costs avoid forcing in any way.
15 Once the gearbox is bolted up to the engine (which is firmly fixed to its forward mountings) there is no real need for support at the gearbox for the short time before the crossmember is replaced to support it.

4. Gearbox — Dismantling

1. Place the complete unit on a firm bench or table and ensure that you have the following tools (in addition to the normal range of spanners etc) available:—

a) Good quality circlip pliers, 2 pairs — 1 expanding and 1 contracting.
b) Copper headed mallet, at least 2 lb.
c) Drifts, steel 3/8 inch and brass 3/8 inch.
d) Small containers for needle rollers.
e) Engineer's vice mounted on firm bench.
f) Method of heating, such as blow lamp or butagas stove.

Any attempt to dismantle the gearbox without the foregoing is not necessarily impossible, but will certainly be very difficult and inconvenient, resulting in possible injury or damage.

Read the whole of this section before starting work.
2. Remove the top cover holding bolts and lift off the cover (photo).
3. This will release the detent spring (arrow 'A' in photo) which can be lifted out. There will probably be some oil left inside the casing so it is wise to invert the gearbox over a bowl.
4. When this is done the ball (see photo) under the detent spring will drop out and so will the interlock

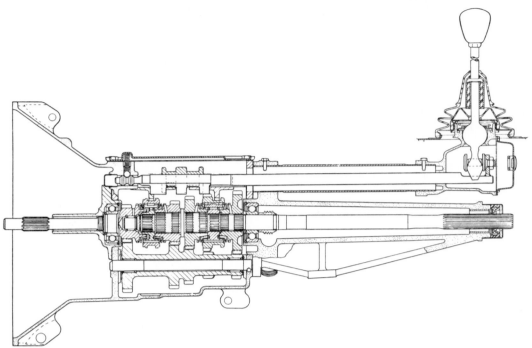

Fig.6.1. Cross section drawing of assembled gearbox and change mechanism

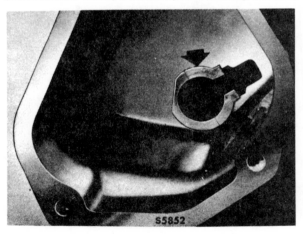

Fig.6.2. Nylon bush (arrowed) fitted in later models to support rear of selector shaft

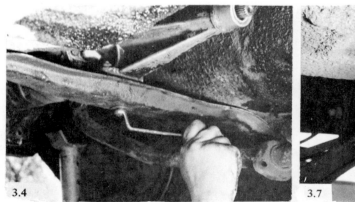

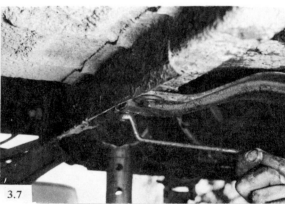

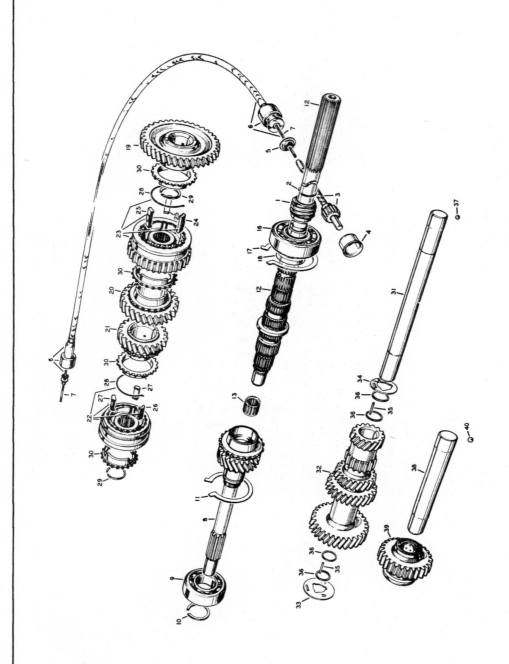

Fig.6.3. EXPLODED VIEW OF GEARBOX MAINSHAFT ASSEMBLY, LAYSHAFT & LAYGEAR, REVERSE SHAFT & GEAR

1.	Speedometer drive gear	7.	Cable inner	16.	Mainshaft bearing	22.	3rd/4th gear synchro hub	29.	Circlip	36.	Keep ring
2.	Circlip	8.	Input shaft	17.	Circlip-bearing to	23.	1st/2nd gear synchro hub	30.	Synchro ring	37.	Locating ball
3.	Speedometer cable	9.	Input shaft bearing		housing	24.	Blocker bar (sliding key)	31.	Layshaft	38.	Reverse idler pinion shaft
	assembly	10.	Circlip-bearing to shaft	18.	Spacer	25.	Blocker bar	32.	Lay gear	39.	Reverse idler gear
4.	Plug	11.	Circlip-bearing to housing	19.	1st gear	26.	Blocker bar	33.	Thrust washer	40.	Locating ball
5.	Sealing ring	12.	Main shaft	20.	2nd gear	27.	Blocker bar	34.	Thrust washer		
6.	Cable assembly	13.	Mainshaft spigot bearing	21.	3rd gear	28.	Retaining spring	35.	Needle roller		

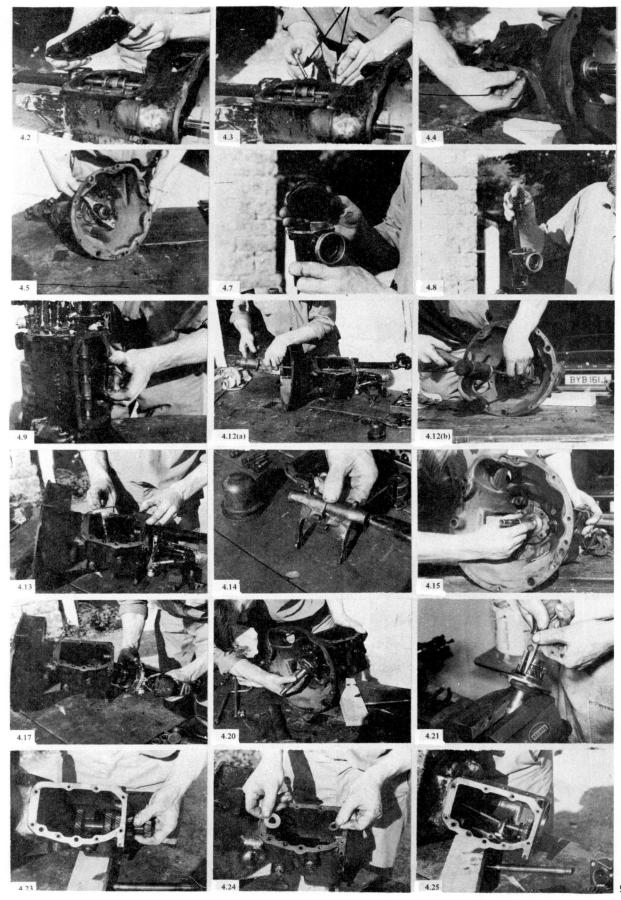

4.2

4.3

4.4

4.5

4.7

4.8

4.9

4.12(a)

4.12(b)

4.13

4.14

4.15

4.17

4.20

4.21

4.23

4.24

4.25

collar retaining pin (arrow 'B' in photo 4.3). Retrieve these items and keep in a jar.

5. Whilst the oil is draining into the bowl, the clutch actuating fork can be removed (see photo), if not already done, by drawing the inner end off the fork ball and then drawing the whole assembly out of the bell-housing over the splined end of the input shaft.

6. Remove the rubber cover from the bellhousing which shrouds the starter motor pinion.

7. Remove the end cover from the remote control selector rod housing by undoing the retaining bolts (see photo).

8. The selector rod can now be drawn out, (photo) twisting it to avoid obstructions at the gearbox end. On later models a nylon bush in the housing supports the tail end of the selector rod. (See Fig.6.2.). There is only just sufficient room at the end to draw the key part through, so do not try and free it through too quickly.

9. The interlock collar can now be lifted straight out of the main gearbox casing (photo).

10 The mainshaft extension rear cover is now released (but not removed) by unscrewing the six bolts holding it in position. Three of these bolts are larger than the other three, but it is quite obvious where they go from the position of the shoulders in the casting.

11 The rear cover can now be rotated so that the small hole in its periphery can be lined up with the end of the selector fork mounting rod.

12 Using a brass drift, this rod can now be driven out from the front of the casing. (See photos A and B).

13 The selector forks themselves can now be lifted out (see photo).

14 Note that the selector forks are different. In the photo the 1st and 2nd gear selector fork which is at the rear of the gearbox is on the right.

15 Remove the four front cover bolts (inside the bell-housing) and draw the cover and input shaft forward together as far as they will go (photo). This will increase the clearance at the end of the mainshaft where it fits into the input shaft.

16 Fourth speed should now be engaged by pushing the 3rd/4th speed clutch to the extremity of the mainshaft. Withdraw the mainshaft until the end spigot is clear of the input shaft. If there is a clatter of falling needle rollers at this juncture do not worry, they can be picked out of the casing later.

17 Now that the mainshaft is clear of the input shaft, it can be tipped so that the 3rd and 4th speed clutch clears the layshaft gears and the whole unit drawn out. (photo).

18 When removed, detach the synchronising ring and spacer from the end of the shaft so that they do not inadvertently fall to the ground.

19 Now collect up the needle rollers and keep ring from the gearbox and in the counter bore of the input shaft. There should be twenty-two of them.

20 The input shaft assembly can now be removed. This consists of the front cover, bearing and shaft and is held into the casing by a circlip on the inside. Remove this circlip and then tap the shaft with a soft metal hammer and the cover, bearing and shaft will come out (photo).

21 By removing the other circlip the bearing can be taken off the shaft for replacement (photo).

22 The layshaft can now be removed by drifting it out from the front of the casing. It is located at the rear end by a steel ball which locks it into the casing. This prevents the shaft from moving longitudinally and also from rotating.

23 With the layshaft out the laygear can be removed by lifting it up and out through the rear of the casing (photo). Keep it horizontal so that the needle rollers at each end can be collected rather than scattered all over the place. Each set of needle rollers also has a spacer ring.

24 Two thrust washers will have dropped down when the laygear is removed. These are of different sizes to suit each end of the laygear. They each have dimpled oil reservoirs on one side (photo), (next to the laygear) and a locating lug on the other side which fits into a recess in the casing.

25 The only remaining items are the reverse idler gear and shaft. Ideally the reverse idler rod is drawn out with a special tool. However it can be drifted out with a suitably long steel drift from inside the casing. It will need to be driven at an angle (photo) so the nose of the drift will need careful and firm location and a smart strike with a reasonably heavy mallet is necessary. Here again there is a locating ball at the rear of the shaft to prevent it from both revolving and moving axially.

26 The reverse idler gear is then removed (photo).

27 With the reverse gear and shaft removed, the reverse selector arm can be lifted off its fulcrum pin (photo).

28 The fulcrum pin is eccentric and held in position by a lock nut. This can be slackened and the pin removed from the casing in which it is a push fit (photo).

29 The gearbox is now completely stripped out from its casing.

30 Clean out the interior thoroughly and check for dropped needle rollers.

31 The mainshaft is dismantled next. The assembly should first of all be held horizontally in a vice by the selector rod extension tube. This is made of sheet steel so be careful not to crush or distort its shape. Have the speedometer drive spindle facing towards you and with a brass drift drive it smartly through (photo). There is a press fit cap opposite which will come out with it.

32 Remove the paper gasket from the face of the rear cover and retain it, if undamaged. It may be refitted, although it would be as well to get a new one.

33 Now remove the circlip retaining the bearing into the cover (photo).

34 The mainshaft can next be drifted out of the cover. The bearing which retains it in place is an interference fit. Heat the housing with a gas burner, or similar, for several minutes. Make sure that someone's hand supports the mainshaft as it comes out (photo). Removal is easy if the housing has been heated.

35 Remove the cover from the vice and then grip the mainshaft in the vice at an angle, with the 3rd and 4th gear hub uppermost.

36 Remove the circlip around the shaft (photo).

37 The hub and third speed gear behind it should all pull off quite easily (photo). Sometimes however, there can be a slight burr on the circlip groove which necessitates a few light mallet taps to assist their removal, or even a screwdriver behind the third gear wheel for leverage.

38 Nothing more can be removed from this end of the shaft which should now be turned round in the vice so that the longer end faces upwards in preparation for the next steps.

39 The next item to remove is the speedometer driving gear from the end of the shaft. First remove the circlip around the shaft (photo).

40 More often than not this drive gear and the bearing behind it is a very tight fit and causes more difficulty than anything else on the mainshaft. Gather together two pieces of flat bar or two flat spanners, slightly thinner than the gap between the bearing and the 1st

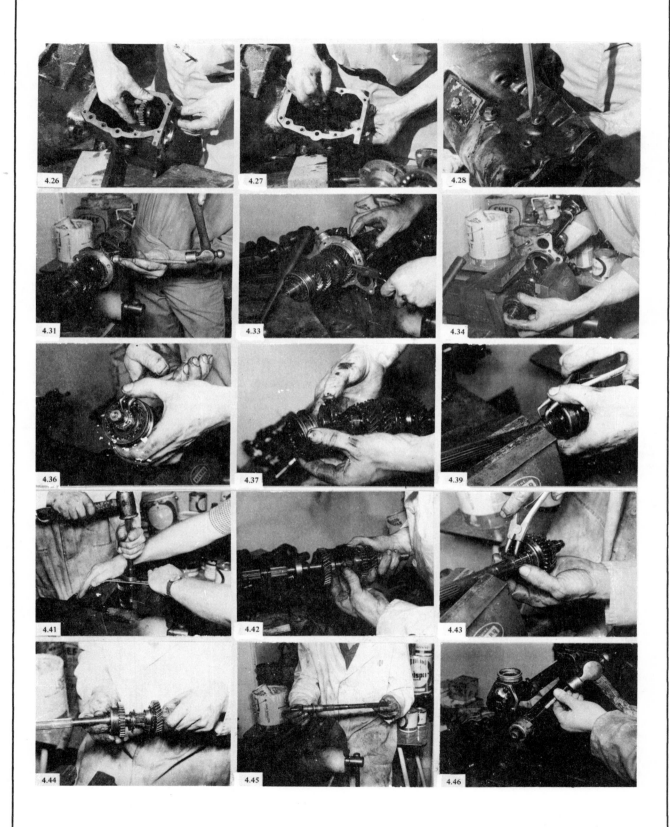

4.26

4.27

4.28

4.31

4.33

4.34

4.36

4.37

4.39

4.41

4.42

4.43

4.44

4.45

4.46

speed gear. The circlip between the bearing and the gear should be removed and drawn off over the bearing.

41 The two pieces of flat bar or spanners, one each side of the shaft behind the bearing, are now placed across the vice jaws so that the mainshaft is suspended below them clear of any obstruction (photo). If the end of the shaft is now struck hard with a copper mallet some progress will be made, albeit slow. Two people are essential for this job as the flat bars across the vice need steadying. The man who does the striking must be confident with the mallet as half-hearted strikes will not serve. On no account support the shaft with the bars behind the 1st speed gear. Although hard, these gears are brittle and any shock force would probably shatter, or at least crack, them. If you feel that the speedo drive gear will never come off, then you would be well advised to get a local garage to do it for you. Any badly applied leverage or mishits could be very expensive indeed.

42 Assuming all went well with removal of the speedo gear the thrust washer, 1st gear and synchroniser ring can be drawn off (photo).

43 Remove the final circlip from around the shaft (photo).

44 The 1st and 2nd gear hub and reverse gear, followed by second gear, can be drawn off (photo), after a little tapping, if necessary.

45 The mainshaft is now completely dismantled (photo).

46 The oil seal in the rear cover around the propeller shaft can be removed by getting a bite with a sharp edge into the soft cover of the oil seal cap and driving it off (photo).

5. Gearbox Inspection

1. It is assumed that the gearbox has been dismantled for reasons of excessive noise, lack of synchromesh on certain gears or for failure to stay in gear. If anything more drastic than this (total failure, seizure or gear case cracked) it would be better to leave well alone and look for a replacement, either secondhand or exchange unit).

2. Examine all gears for excessively worn, chipped or damaged teeth. Any such gears should be replaced.

3. Check all synchromesh cones for wear on the bearing surfaces, which normally have clearly machined oil reservoir lines in them. If these are smooth or obviously uneven, replacement is essential. Also, when the cones are put together - as they would be when in operation - there should be no rock. This would signify ovality, or lack of concentricity. One of the most satisfactory ways of checking is by comparing the fit of a new cone on the hub with the old one. If the teeth of the ring are obviously worn or damaged (causing engagement difficulties) they should be renewed.

4. All ball race bearings should be checked for chatter. It is advisable to replace these anyway even though they may not appear too badly worn.

5. Circlips which in this particular gearbox are all important in locating bearings, gears and hubs should also be checked to ensure that they are undistorted and undamaged. In any case a selection of new circlips of varying thicknesses should be obtained to compensate for variations in new components fitted, or wear in old ones. The specifications indicate what is available.

6. The thrust washers at the ends of the laygear should also be replaced, as they will almost certainly have worn if the gearbox is of any age.

7. Needle roller bearings between the input shaft and mainshaft and in the laygear are usually found in good order, but if in any doubt replace the needles as necessary.

8. The sliding hubs themselves are also subject to wear and where the fault has been failure of any gear to remain engaged or actual difficulty in engagement then the hub is one of the likely suspects. It is possible to examine the internal splines without dismantling. The ends of the splines are machined in such a way as to form a 'keystone' effect on engagement with the corresponding mainshaft gear (See Fig.6.4 and 6.5). Do not confuse this with wear. Check also that the blocker bars (sliding keys) are not sloppy and move freely. (See Fig. 6.6). If there is any rock or backlash between the inner and outer sections of the hub, the whole assembly should be renewed, particularly if there has been a complaint of jumping out of gear.

6. Gearbox Reassembly

1. Start by reassembling the mainshaft.

2. Place the 2nd gear wheel onto the longer end of the mainshaft with the helical cut part towards the centre of the shaft (see photo).

3. Next follows a synchro ring and the reverse gear/1st and 2nd synchro hub assembly. (See photo).

4. It is important not to let the hub and gear assembly come to pieces, so if it is a tight fit on the splines of the shaft use a tube so that the centre of the hub may be tapped on to the shaft (see photo). It is obviously impossible to tap the outer gear part and keep the hub together.

5. When the hub and synchro ring are up together, ensure that the sliding keys (blocker bars) mate with the corresponding cut-outs in the synchro ring (see photo - the pencil points to the bar and cut-out).

6. The retaining circlip is fitted next and must be selected from the range of thicknesses available so that endfloat at the hub is eliminated (see photo).

7. Fit another synchro ring, so that the cut-outs mate with the other ends of the blocker bars (sliding keys) in the hub and then follow with 1st gear, cone towards the synchro ring of course (see photo). Place the main bearing circlip over the shaft (see paragraph 17).

8. Next fit the thrust washer and bearing over the shaft (see photo).

9. To drive the bearing onto the shaft it is again necessary to select a piece of tube which will go round the shaft and onto the inner race of the bearing so that it may be driven on (see photo). Ensure that the end of the shaft rests on something soft to avoid damage.

10 Fit the speedometer drive gear over the shaft with the long boss towards the bearing. Then put the shaft between the soft jaws of a vice (two pieces of 'L' shaped lead are sufficiently soft) so that the jaws support the shoulder of the gear hub but do not grip the shaft. Then drive the shaft downwards with a soft headed mallet until the speedometer drive butts against the bearing (see photo).

11 Select and fit a circlip that will take up the clearance between the outer side of the groove and the gear. (See photo).

12 Turning to the other end of the shaft, fit 3rd gear and a synchro ring right up to the shoulder on the shaft (see photo).

13 Fit the 3rd and 4th speed hub assembly ensuring it goes on the proper way round, which is with the larger hub of the boss towards the end of the shaft. The narrow groove in the outside also is towards the end of the shaft (see photo). Ensure that the blocker bars in the hub engage in the synchro ring cut-outs.

14 Select a circlip which will take up the endfloat

Fig.6.4. Synchro hub outer ring showing 'keystone' design teeth (inset).

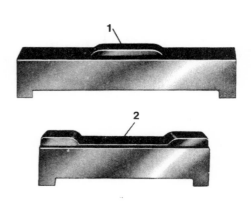

Fig.6.5. Blocker bars (sliding keys) of synchro hubs showing pips (1st/2nd depression (3rd/4th gear hub—2) subject to wear.

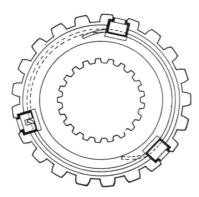

Fig.6.6. Cross section drawing of assembled hub showing blocker bars and retaining springs.

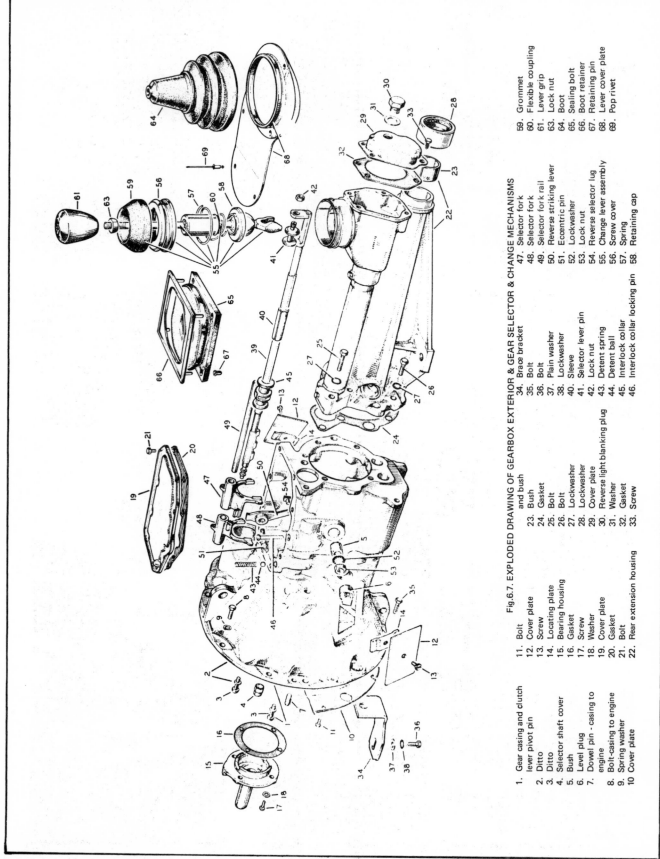

Fig.6.7. EXPLODED DRAWING OF GEARBOX EXTERIOR & GEAR SELECTOR & CHANGE MECHANISMS

1. Gear casing and clutch lever pivot pin	11. Bolt	34. Brace bracket and bush
2. Ditto	12. Cover plate	35. Bolt
3. Ditto	13. Screw	36. Bolt
4. Selector shaft cover	14. Locating plate	37. Plain washer
5. Bush	15. Bearing housing	38. Lockwasher
6. Level plug	16. Gasket	40. Sleeve
7. Dowel pin - casing to engine	17. Screw	41. Selector lever pin
8. Bolt-casing to engine	18. Washer	42. Lock nut
9. Spring washer	19. Cover plate	43. Detent spring
10 Cover plate	20. Gasket	44. Detent ball
	21. Bolt	45. Interlock collar
	22. Rear extension housing	46. Interlock collar locking pin
	23. Bush	47. Selector fork
	24. Gasket	48. Selector fork
	25. Bolt	49. Selector fork rail
	26. Bolt	50. Reverse striking lever
	27. Lockwasher	51. Eccentric pin
	28. Screw	52. Lockwasher
	29. Cover plate	53. Lock nut
	30. Reverse light blanking plug	54. Reverse selector lug
	31. Washer	55. Change lever assembly
	32. Gasket	56. Screw cover
	33. Screw	57. Spring
		58. Retaining cap
		59. Grommet
		60. Flexible coupling
		61. Lever grip
		63. Lock nut
		64. Boot
		65. Sealing bolt
		66. Boot retainer
		67. Retaining pin
		68. Lever cover plate
		69. Pop rivet

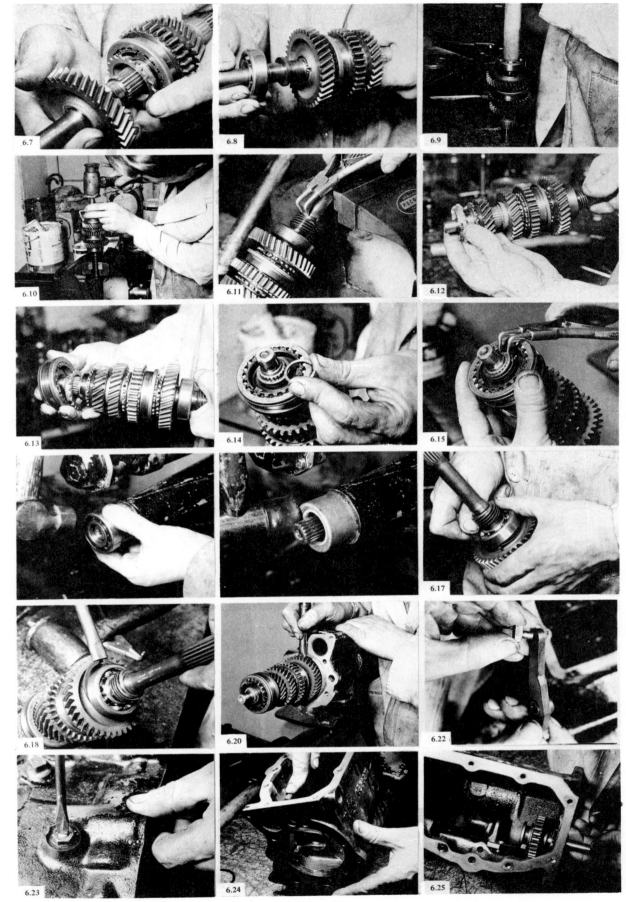

6.7

6.8

6.9

6.10

6.11

6.12

6.13

6.14

6.15

6.17

6.18

6.20

6.22

6.23

6.24

6.25

between hub and groove and try it first (see photo).

15 When selected, fit the circlip in the groove (see photo). The mainshaft assembly is now complete.

16 To fit a new extension cover oil seal drive it in using something like an old bearing to spread the driving force. (Photo A). When nearly home it can be tapped with a soft headed mallet to finish off (photo B). Soak the felt ring with engine oil. (On later models no felt ring was incorporated. On these the seal lip should be coated with an anti-scuffing paste before the propeller shaft is re-fitted).

17 The mainshaft is next installed in the rear housing and if you have forgotten to place the circlip over the shaft after 1st gear (paragraph 7) you should put it behind the bearing now, spreading it a little to get it over (see photo).

18 To install the mainshaft in the cover is a tricky operation and the procedure detailed hereafter is the only way to do it. First of all find a suitable piece of soft metal pipe at least 6 inches long and approximately ¼—3/8th inch inside diameter and flatten one end in a vice in such a way as to hold closed the main bearing retaining circlip. (See photo).

19 Mount the rear extension cover in a vice with the selector rod tube uppermost and start warming it up gently and generally with a blow lamp, butane gas lamp or similar. This is essential to ease the pressing of the bearing into the housing. Do NOT overheat, merely warm it up so that it is still just comfortable to touch.

20 When the casing is sufficiently warm, insert the mainshaft assembly and tap it in with a soft headed hammer until the circlip and its improvised holding pipe are up against the cover in the cut-away portion of the bearing housing (see photo).

21 The circlip is then released so that it can be located in its groove after the bearing is driven fully home. Make sure that before it is released it will be held inside the bearing housing!

22 Returning to the main gearbox casing, fit the reverse selector lug into the reverse gear selector arm on the side opposite to the boss (see photo).

23 Fit the reverse gear selector arm pivot pin (which is eccentric) so that the two punch marks are uppermost in relation to the gear casing. (See Fig.6.11 and photo), and tighten the lock nut.

24 Place the reverse selector lever on the pivot pin so that the boss side goes on first, leaving the selector ring at the bottom, facing inwards (see photo).

25 Put the reverse idler gear into the box so that the selector lug locates in the groove and the groove side of the gear is towards the front of the casing. Holding the gear in position, push the plain end of the reverse idler gear shaft through the housing and gear (see photo).

26 Drive the shaft fully home so that the locating ball on the end of the shaft is in position in the cut-away part in the casing (see photo).

27 In theory, one should now check the clearance between the idler gear and the rear of the casing, and adjust it. As this entails assembling the rear cover temporarily, it is recommended that the setting be made when the gearbox is assembled by actually operating the reverse gear in the normal manner.

28 Place a spacer in each end of the laygear and, using clean grease in the bore, assemble the needles for the laygear bearings, ensuring that there are twenty-five at each end. (See photo). Place the outer spacers in after them with a little grease to hold them in place.

29 Next put the laygear thrust washers in position by locating each one so that the small lug engages with the groove in the casing. The larger washer goes at the front

of the gearbox. Hold them in position with a smear of grease (see photo).

30 Take the laygear and, with care, lower it into the casing with the larger end towards the front of the casing. Be careful not to dislodge the thrust washers or the needle rollers and spacers in the laygear (photo).

31 It is not possible to replace the layshaft yet because the input shaft has to be put back first. Otherwise with the layshaft in position the fourth gear driving dogs will not get past the large laygear at the front end.

32 Take the input shaft and, if a new bearing is to be fitted, drive it on with a piece of pipe around the shaft and on to the inner bearing race (see photo).

33 Refit the circlip retaining the bearing (see photo).

34 Place the circlip, to hold the bearing in the housing over the shaft and put the shaft into the front housing (photo).

35 Hold the circlip with pliers, tap the bearing into the housing until the circlip can be released, and then ensure that it locates properly into the groove in the bearing housing. (See photo).

36 With a smear of grease place the needle rollers into the counterbore of the input shaft (see photo). Then compress the keep ring and slide it inside them halfway along their length (it will hold the rollers securely whilst the mainshaft is being assembled into the gear casing and it will push to the back of the counterbore when the two shafts are put together). On later models the needle rollers are assembled in a cage (see Fig.6.8), so this part of the reassembly is simplified. Then replace the spacer ring over the nose of the mainshaft spigot.

37 Fit a new gasket to the front cover flange (see photo).

38 Put the input shaft assembly into the front of the casing, but do not replace the bolts yet.

39 Next introduce the plain end of the layshaft into the hole in the rear of the casing and, with care, raise the laygear so that the layshaft may be pushed into it without disturbing the bearings or thrust washers. When the shaft is nearly home ensure that the ball in the shaft is lined up with the recess in the casing and drive the shaft home with a soft hammer (see photo).

40 Fit a new gasket to the rear cover flange of the mainshaft. Now draw the input shaft assembly forwards (out) as far as it will go, (you will see now why the layshaft could not go in first) and place a synchro ring over the end of the gear. Then carefully draw the 3rd/4th speed hub towards the forward end of the mainshaft as far as possible without pulling it right off. This is so that when you introduce the mainshaft assembly into the casing at an angle you will just be able to clear the 3rd speed laygear (see photo).

41 Locate the spigot of the mainshaft into the needle roller bearings in the input shaft. Line up the slots in the synchro ring with the blocker bars (sliding keys) of the 3rd/4th speed hub and mate the two shafts together fully (see photo).

42 Install the 3rd/4th speed selector fork so that it rests in the groove of the 3rd/4th speed hub (see photo).

43 Install the 1st/2nd speed selector fork so that it sits in the groove of the 1st/2nd speed hub.

44 In order to fit the selector fork rod, rotate the rear cover until the hole in the cover lines up with the bearing holes for the rod in the casing. The rod is fractionally larger (about 2 thou.) at one end, so place the smaller end into the casing first (see photo). Run the rod through the mounting holes in the forks and drive it fully home with a brass drift.

45 Match up the rear cover to the gearbox casing and replace and tighten all bolts evenly. (see photo).

46 Next go to the input shaft bearing front cover and

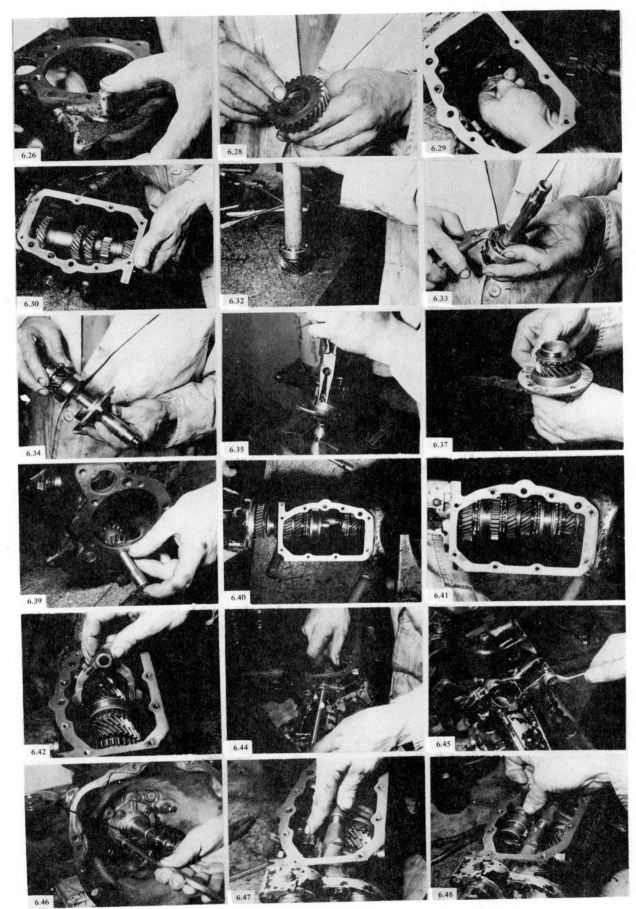

position it so that the small oil drain hole in the cover is at the bottom. Replace the bolts with new copper washers and tighten up (see photo).

47 With both end covers now bolted up check that all shafts rotate freely. If they do not, slacken off the front cover and then the rear cover until they do. Then take everything out and check all circlips and spacers for correct location. Line up the end of the reverse gear selector lever with the lug on the 1st/2nd speed selector fork. (See photo).

48 Replace the interlock collar so that the large peripheral grooves rest over the jaws on the selector forks and the longitudinal slot in the collar faces into the centre of the gearbox (see photo).

49 Insert the selector rod, key end first, into the end of the remote lever extension tube. (See photo).

50 Pass it through the interlock collar so that the key flanges pass through the slot in the collar and the end locates in the hole in the front of the casing (see photo).

51 Turn the interlock collar so that the groove in the centre section is lined up to accept the collar retaining pin through the hole in the casing (see photo).

52 Replace the detent ball and spring into the hole in the casing (see photo).

53 Fit a new gasket and replace the top cover ensuring that the detent spring locates properly in the dimple in the cover (see photo). Replace four bolts, one at each corner of the cover, for the moment.

54 Refit the gear lever as it came out, with the longer lug on the lever fork to the left. (See photo).

55 Now engage and disengage all gears including reverse. Any difficulty with reverse may be due to the setting of the eccentric pivot pin mentioned in paragraph 23. Any difficulty with the selection and disengagement of the forward speeds could be due to the setting of the eccentric pin on the selector shaft. (See Fig.6.9). With 1st speed gear engaged, the gap between the reverse stop on the lever (i.e. the long lug) and the rod should be between 2 and 12 thou. Adjust, if necessary, by unlocking the nut and turning the eccentric pin with a screwdriver.

56 Select neutral, remove the gear lever, and replace the extension tube end cover with a new gasket.

57 Replace the remainder of the top cover retaining bolts.

58 Replace the speedometer drive by returning the spindle so that the gear enters the casing last on the left-hand side. Replace the locating cup in the hole, having first smeared the sides and lip with sealing compound. Reassembly is now complete.

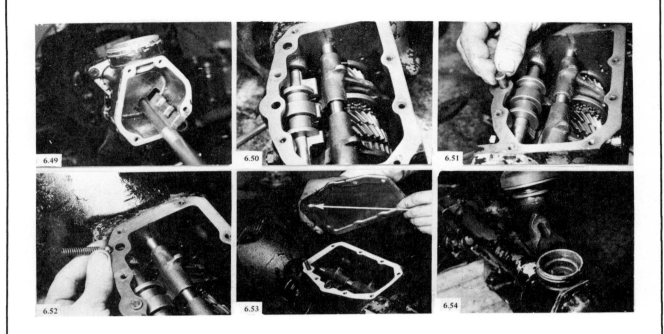

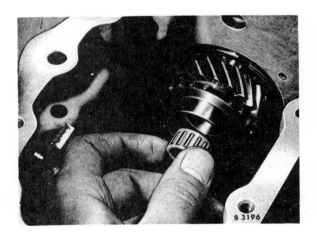

Fig.6.8. Showing fitting of the caged roller bearing into the input shaft bore.

Fig.6.9. Setting the selector rod to eccentric pin clearance for the reverse stop with a feeler gauge.

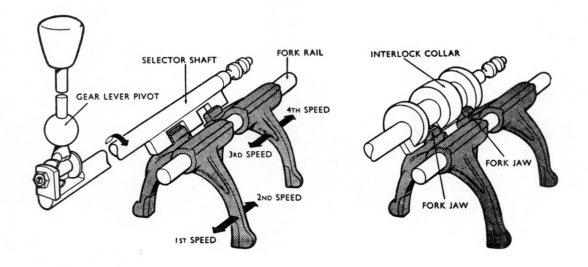

Fig.6.10. Diagrammatic drawing of gear selector operation

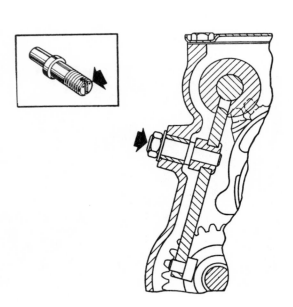

Fig.6.11. Showing the position of the reverse striking lever pivot pin and punch mark to indicate the highpoint of the eccentric.

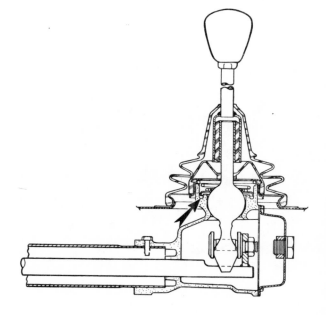

Fig.6.12. Cross section of gear change lever assembly to show recess (arrowed) to be packed with grease on assembly.

Fault Finding Chart — Gearbox

Symptom	Reason/s	Remedy
Ineffective synchromesh	Worn baulk rings or synchro hubs.	Dismantle and renew.
Jumps out of one or more gears (on drive or over-run)	Weak detent springs or worn selector forks or worn gears.	Dismantle and renew
Noisy, rough, whining and vibration.	Worn bearings and/or laygear thrust washers (initially) resulting in extended wear generally due to play and backlash	Dismantle and renew.
Noisy and difficult engagement of gears	Clutch fault.	Examine clutch operation.

NOTE: It is sometimes difficult to decide whether it is worthwhile removing and dismantling the gearbox for a fault which may be nothing more than a minor irritant. Gearboxes which howl, or where the synchromesh can be 'beaten' by a quick gear change, may continue to perform for a long time in this state. A worn gearbox usually needs a complete rebuild to eliminate noise because the various gears, if re-aligned on new bearings will continue to howl when different wearing surfaces are presented to each other.

The decision to overhaul therefore, must be considered with regard to time and money available, relative to the degree of noise or malfunction that the driver has to suffer.

Chapter 7/Propeller Shaft and Universal Joints

Contents

Specifications

Propeller Shaft

Make	Hardy Spicer or B.R.D.
Type	Tubular

Universal Joints

Make	Hardy Spicer or B.R.D.
Type	Needle roller - sealed lubrication
Number of rollers per bearing	34
Sliding sleeve diameter	1.1240 to 1.1250 in.

1. General Description

The drive from the gearbox to the rear axle is via the propeller shaft which is in fact a tube. Due to the variety of angles caused by the up and down motion of the rear axle in relation to the gearbox, universal joints are fitted to each end of the shaft to convey the drive through the constantly varying angles. As the movement also increases and decreases the distance between the rear axle and the gearbox, the forward end of the propeller shaft is a splined sleeve which is a sliding fit over the rear of the gearbox splined mainshaft. The splined sleeve runs in an oil seal in the gearbox mainshaft rear cover, and is supported with the mainshaft on the gearbox rear bearing. The splines are lubricated by oil in the rear cover coming from the gearbox.

The universal joints each comprise a four way trunnion, or 'spider', each leg of which runs in a needle roller bearing race, pre-packed with grease and fitted into the bearing journal yokes of the sliding sleeve and propeller shaft and flange.

2. Routine Maintenance

No lubrication of the universal joints is required as they are pre-packed with grease on assembly. The sliding sleeve of the forward end of the propeller shaft is lubricated from the gearbox. It is recommended that periodic inspection is carried out, however, whenever the car may be undergoing service, to check for any slackness in the universal bearings or at the flange bolts at the rear.

3. Propeller Shaft - Removal, Inspection & Replacement

1. Jack up the rear of the car and support it on stands.

2. The rear of the shaft is connected to the rear axle pinion by a flange held by four nuts and bolts. Mark the position of both flanges relative to each other, and then undo the bolts (photo).
3. Move the propeller shaft forward to disengage it from the pinion flange and then lower it to the ground.
4. Draw the other end of the propeller shaft, that is the splined sleeve, out of the rear of the gearbox extension cover, and the shaft is then clear for removal (photo).
5. Place a receptacle under the gearbox rear cover opening to catch any oil which will certainly come out if the gearbox is tilted.
6. If the propeller shaft is removed for inspection, first examine the bore and counterbore of the two flanges which mate at the rear. If they are damaged in any way, or a slack fit, it could mean that the propeller shaft is running off centre at the flange and causing vibration in the drive. If nothing obvious is wrong, and the universal joints are in good order, it is permissible to reconnect the flanges with one turned through 180° relative to the other. This may stop the vibration.
7. The replacement of the shaft is a reversal of the removal procedure. Ensure that the sliding sleeve is inserted into the gearbox end cover with care, and is perfectly clean, so as not to cause damage to, or failure of, the oil seal in the cover.
8. The flanges should be mated according to the position marks (unless a 180° turn is being done as mentioned in paragraph 6).
9. The four bolts should be fitted with the heads towards the universal joint.

4. Universal Joints — Inspection, Removal & Replacement

1. Preliminary inspection of the universal joints can be carried out with the propeller shaft on the car.
2. Grasp each side of the universal joint, and with a

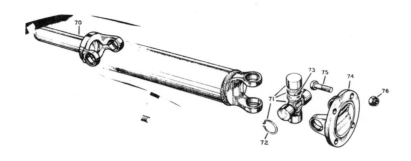

Fig.7.1. EXPLODED VIEW OF PROPELLER SHAFT COMPONENTS

70 Sleeve yoke	72. Circlip	74. Yoke flange	flange
71 Journal bearings	73. Seal	75. Bolt - flange to pinion	76. Self locking nut

3.2

3.4

twisting action determine whether there is any play or slackness in the Joint. Also try an up and down rocking motion for the same purpose. If there is any sign whatsoever of play, the joints need replacement.

3. Remove the propeller shaft as described in the previous section.

4. Clean away all dirt from the ends of the bearings on the yokes so that the circlips may be removed using a pair of contracting circlip pliers. If they are very tight, tap the end of the bearing race (inside the circlip) with a drift and hammer to relieve the pressure.

5. Once the circlips are removed, tap the universal joints at the yoke with a soft hammer and the bearings and races will come out of the housing (Fig.7.3), and can be removed easily.

6. If they are obstinate they can be gripped in a self locking wrench for final removal provided they are to be replaced.

7. Once the bearings are removed from each opposite journal the trunnion can be easily disengaged.

8. Replacement of the new trunnions and needle rollers and races is a reversal of the removal procedure.

9. Keep the grease seals on the inner ends of each trunnion as dry as possible.

10 Place the needles in each race and fill the race 1/3rd full with grease prior to placing it over the trunnion, and tap each one home with a brass drift. Any grease exuding from the further bearing journal after three have been fitted should be renewed before fitting the fourth race.

11 Replace the circlips ensuring they seat neatly in the retaining grooves.

12 In cases of extreme wear or neglect, it is conceivable that the bearing housings in the propeller shaft, sliding sleeve or rear flange have worn so much that the bearing races are a slack fit in them. In such cases it will be necessary to replace the item affected as well. Check also that the sliding sleeve splines are in good condition and not a sloppy fit in the gearbox mainshaft.

13 Replace the propeller shaft as described in Section 3.

5. Universal Joint Renewal -- Some Later Models

1. On some cars the universal joint bearings are not held in position by circlips, but by staking the edge of the yoke over the retaining disc. (See Fig.7.3). If you have the misfortune to own a car with this arrangement, which needs universal joint renewal, you may find it necessary to renew the propeller shaft as well. Without proper press equipment it will be virtually impossible to stake any new needle roller bearing assemblies tightly into position.

Fig.7.2. Striking the yoke to free the bearing journal.

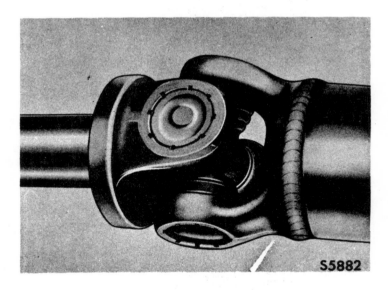

Fig.7.3. Showing universal joint bearings held by staking rather than circlips.

Chapter 8/Rear Axle

Contents

Specifications

Type ... ... Hypoid - Semi floating with overhung mounted pinion

Ratio
HB 22 engine ... ... 8/33 (4.125 : 1)
HB 23 engine ... ... 9/35 (3.89 : 1)

Oil Capacity ... ... 1.8 pints (Imperial)
Type ... ... SAE 90 E.P.

Half Shafts
Permissible run-out on bearing land ... ... .002 in. maximum
Permissible run-out on flange face... .. .. .005 in. maximum

Pinion
Bearing pre-load - new ... ... 4 — 7 lb/in.
      - used ... ... 2 — 4 lb/in.
Rear bearing - spacer thickness available ... ... .059 in. and .060 in.
      - shim thickness available ... ... .003 in.

Differential
Side bearing pre-load - new ... ... 4 lb.
      - used... ... ... 1¼ lb.
Pinion fit on shaft.. ... ... .0015 in. to .0060 in. clearance
Pinion bore .. .. .5528 in. to .5567 in.
Pinion thrust washer thickness... ... ... .016 in. to .019 in.
Pinion shaft diameter.. ... ... .5507 in. to .5513 in.
Side gear spacer thicknesses available... ... ... .019 in. to .033 in.
      in seven stages overlapping by .001
Differential case run-out permissible ... ... .001 maximum
Side bearing shims available... ... ... .003 in.
Side bearing spacers available ... ... .122 and .123 inches

Crown Wheel
Run-out permissible ... ... .002 in. maximum
Backlash between pinion and crown wheel ... ... .006 in. to .008 in.

Torque Wrench Settings
Differential side bearing cap bolts... ... ... 24 lb/ft.
Crown wheel to casing bolts.. ... ... 36 lb/ft.
Half shaft bearing retainer plate nuts ... ... 18 lb/ft.
Coupling flange nut ... ... 75 lb/ft.
Coupling flange to propeller shaft flange bolts ... ... 18 lb/ft.
(ALL THREADS DRY)

1. General Description

The rear axle is of the semi-floating type with a hypoid final drive, the pinion is overhung and contained in an extension to the axle housing which is supported by a crossmember.

The rear axle casing assembly is located to the rear body members by means of four arms, two each side. Two of these are longitudinal and two diagonal, and their attachment points consist of steel bolts in rubber mounting bushes to hangers which are an integral part of the axle casing.

To control pinion to side gear backlash, thrust washers are used against spherical faces on the differential pinions and graded spacers are assembled to the side gears. The whole crown wheel and pinion unit is supported in the axle housing by two taper roller bearings secured by caps and bolts. The pinion runs in two pre-loaded taper roller bearings. The pinion is held in correct location to the crown wheel by spacers and shims between the front face of the rear bearing outer race and the abutment face in the axle housing.

An oil seal is pressed into the end of the pinion housing and operates directly on the pinion.

2. Routine Maintenance

1. Every 12,000 miles remove the combined oil level and filler plug (all dirt should be cleared away from the immediate area of the plug before removing) located in the axle casing rear cover, and top up with an S.A.E.90 gear oil such as Castrol Hypoy. Wait a few minutes before replacing the plug, to allow any excess oil to drain out. This excess oil could find it's way into the axle tubes, and eventually on to the rear brake linings, rendering them ineffectual. The vehicle should be unladen for this procedure.
2. Every 24,000 miles drain the oil when hot. As no drain plug is fitted, undo the bolts holding the rear cover and prise it away from the axle casing sufficiently for the oil to drain out. Refill the axle with 1.8 pints of the recommended lubricant. This is not a factory recommended task, as there will have been no deterioration in the condition of the oil. However, the oil will have become contaminated with minute particles of metal and this suspended metal is obviously conducive to early failure of the axle. For this reason the author prefers to change the oil once every two years, or 24,000 miles, whichever comes sooner, rather than leave it in place for the life of the car.

3. Rear Axle — Removal & Replacement

1. Remove the hub caps and loosen the wheel nuts.
2. Raise and support the rear of the vehicle body, and remove the wheels. The easiest way to do this is to jack the car under the centre of the differential unit.
3. When it is sufficiently high, stands should be placed under the longitudinal lower suspension arms (see Fig.8.3).
4. The front wheels should be chocked also to prevent any inadvertent movement. Under no circumstances should makeshift supports be used when doing work of this nature under the car.
5. Next, mark and disconnect the propeller shaft at the pinion flange as described in Chapter 7.3.
6. When the shaft is disconnected tie it in position to one side rather than lower it which would possibly impose a strain and cause damage to the gearbox extension housing bush and oil seal. If wished, the propeller shaft may be removed from the gearbox (see Chapter 7). Oil will not drain out of the gearbox provided the rear of the car is several inches higher than the front.
7. Disconnect the handbrake cable clevis pins from the brake shoe levers, having first slackened off the handbrake cable. For details refer to Chapter 9.
8. Disconnect the lower end of the flexible hydraulic fluid pipe where it is attached to a bracket on the rear axle.
9. Detach the lower end of each rear telescopic damper from the axle bracket by removing the two nuts and driving out the stud and bushes. For details see Chapter 11.
10 Remove the nuts and bolts from the longitudinal radius arm rear mountings on the axle and then do the same with the diagonal arms where they locate to the brackets on the top of the differential casing.
11 The whole axle assembly is now free and by pushing the hydraulic dampers out of the way it can be drawn out straight back from under the car.

4. Halfshafts — Removal & Replacement

1. Remove the hub caps, and loosen the wheel nuts.
2. Raise and support the side of the axle from which the halfshaft will be removed. Remove the wheel. NOTE: If both halfshafts are to be removed and the vehicle is raised level, drain off the axle oil as in Section 2.2 of this chapter. If this is not done when the halfshafts are withdrawn oil will run out over the brake linings.
3. Release the handbrake. Undo the bolts which hold the brake drum to the halfshaft flange and remove the drum.
4. Remove the nuts securing the halfshaft bearing retaining plate. This must be done through one of the holes in the halfshaft flange (Fig.8.4). As each bolt is undone and removed, the flange must be rotated through 90° to the next bolt. Take care not to lose the four lock washers.
5. The shaft can now be withdrawn and inspected.
6. Carefully inspect the differential engagement splines for wear, and also the bearing and oil seal. If the oil seal shows any signs of failure it should be replaced. If the oil seal is to be replaced, the bearing will also have to be renewed because the oil seal is integral with the bearing.
7. Replacement of the halfshaft is a straightforward reversal of the removal procedure. However, before replacement ensure that the oil drain hole in the brake backplate is clear, coat the halfshaft, from bearing and bearing circumference oil seal to splines, with oil. Also coat with oil the bearing bore in the axle halfshaft tube; this will allow easy replacement. The bearing retainer plate nuts should be tightened to 18 lb/ft. with clean dry threads. Remember to adjust the brakes as described in Chapter 9.3.

5. Halfshaft Outer Bearings & Oil Seals — Removal & Replacement

If it is decided, after inspection, to replace the bearing and oil seal the procedure is as follows:
1. Slacken the bearing retainer ring by nicking it with a chisel. The retainer and bearing can be removed as one. As you will probably not have the correct Vauxhall pullers to remove the bearing, and the bearing is to be discarded, the following method of removal can be employed:—

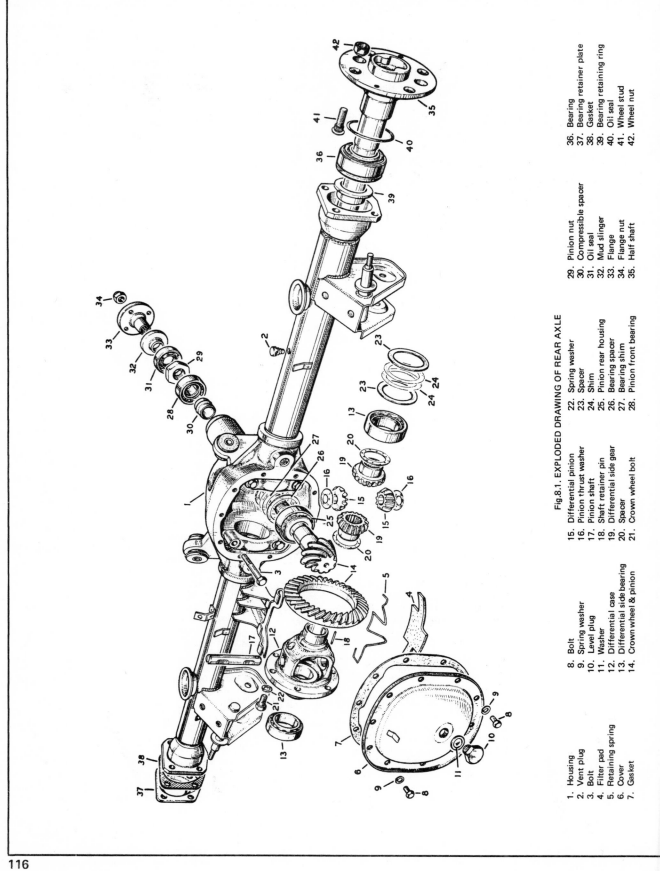

Fig.8.1. EXPLODED DRAWING OF REAR AXLE

1.	Housing	8.	Bolt	15.	Differential pinion
2.	Vent plug	9.	Spring washer	16.	Pinion thrust washer
3.	Bolt	10.	Level plug	17.	Pinion shaft
4.	Filter pad	11.	Washer	18.	Shaft retainer pin
5.	Retaining spring	12.	Differential case	19.	Differential side gear
6.	Cover	13.	Differential side bearing	20.	Spacer
7.	Gasket	14.	Crown wheel & pinion	21.	Crown wheel bolt

22.	Spring washer	29.	Pinion nut	36.	Bearing
23.	Spacer	30.	Compressible spacer	37.	Bearing retainer plate
24.	Shim	31.	Oil seal	38.	Gasket
25.	Pinion rear housing	32.	Mud slinger	39.	Bearing retaining ring
26.	Bearing spacer	33.	Flange	40.	Oil seal
27.	Bearing shim	34.	Flange nut	41.	Wheel stud
28.	Pinion front bearing	35.	Half shaft	42.	Wheel nut

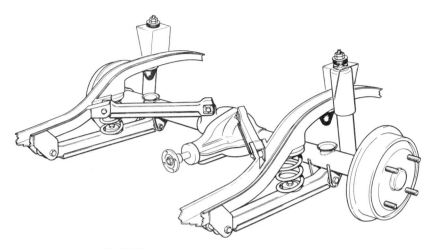

Fig.8.2. Drawing to show rear axle location to rear suspension.

Fig.8.3. Showing car supported on rear longitudinal suspension arms and exhaust moved and tied to one side.

Fig.8.4. Removal of half shaft bearing retaining flange bolts through the half shaft flange with a socket wrench.

a) Clamp the bearing in a vice so that the halfshaft is parallel with the jaws.

b) Now using a hide hammer or mallet on the splined end of the halfshaft drive it back through the bearing and retainer. NOTE: A piece of wood MUST be interposed between the hammer and halfshaft.

2. Oil the new bearing journal and push the bearing down the halfshaft as far as it will go by hand. Ensure that the integral oil seal is facing towards the splines. Now drive the bearing right home against the shaft shoulder using a piece of steel tubing of a suitable length and diameter. Note that the tubing must only contact the bearing inner race, not the bearings, oil seal or outer race.

4. The bearing retainer can be driven home by the same method as the bearing, ensuring that retaining ring collar faces the bearing.

5. Halfshaft replacement is described in Section 4, paragraph 7 of this chapter.

6. Pinion Oil Seal — Removal & Replacement

If oil is leaking from the axle casing where the pinion emerges it will mean that the oil seal needs renewal.

1. Raise the car, support it on stands and disconnect the propeller shaft as described earlier in this chapter, under Section 3.

2. The pinion flange nut will now be exposed and, where it is staked into the slot in the pinion, should be tapped back.

3. In order to hold the flange when undoing the nut it will be necessary to make up a piece of flat bar with two holes at one end which can be bolted to the flange. This can then be held firm while the socket wrench turns the nut which is, initially, a very tight fit.

4. Before pulling the flange off the pinion splines mark the positions of flange to pinion so that it may be replaced in the same position.

5. Next prise the mud slinger disc off the end of the shaft which will expose the oil seal.

6. The oil seal may then be literally dug out of the housing with a pointed punch and a hammer (see Fig.8.10)

7. A new seal should be installed with the lip facing into the casing. Oil the seal lip and the pinion first and then carefully tap it home until it butts up to the bore face in the casing. It may assist in fitting the seal square if a piece of pipe, which will fit over the pinion, is used to drive it home.

8. Replace the mud slinger so that its forward face is 3.70 in from the end of the pinion   (see Fig.8.9, Dimension A).

9. Replace the pinion flange to the pinion ensuring the location marks made line up. Then fit the flange nut and tighten it to the specified torque of 75 lb/ft. This will require use of the tool described in paragraph 3 once more.

10 Finally, stake the nut rim into the pinion slot and reconnect the propeller shaft.

7. Pinion, Hypoid Gear & Differential

1. This chapter has so far shown how to replace bearings and oil seals for the halfshafts and the pinion oil seal, as these are considered to be within the average owner-drivers competence and facilities. We do not recommend that owners go into the more complex problems of pinion to crown wheel settings, differential gear settings, differential side bearing replacement, or pinion bearing

replacement.

2. If, however, an owner feels he has the requisite tools and competence we give the procedures to be followed. We shall refer to the special tools needed as it is not considered either sensible to attempt, or feasible to carry out, this work without them.

3. Remove the rear axle from the car and the halfshafts from the axle as described in Sections 3 and 4.

4. Remove the rear cover plate from the axle casing and drain the oil if not already done.

5. Remove the bolts holding the differential side bearing caps and when removing the caps note the marks on the right-hand cap and the casting to prevent inadvertent mixing up on replacement.

6. Place a bar under one of the differential case bolts and lever the casing assembly and crown wheel out of the housing.

7. Carefully remove the spacers and shims from each side of the housing and keep the bearing inner races on the bench noting which side they are from.

8. Remove the pinion flange (See Section 6).

9. Remove the pinion mud slinger and oil seal.

10 Remove the pinion nut using a holding tool (Z.8307) the special wrench (Z.8534).

11 Tap out the pinion and remove the front inner bearing, bearing washer and compressible spacer.

12 Press the outer races of the pinion bearings from the housing using the removers as shown in Fig.8.6.

13 Press the pinion rear bearing inner race from the shaft.

14 Dismantle the hypoid gear and differential by first removing the hypoid gear from the differential casing by removing the bolts. Tap the gear off from alternate sides using a soft mallet.

15 Punch out the pin which locates the differential pinion shaft, and remove the shaft.

16 The pinion can be lifted out with the hemispherical shaped thrust washers followed by the side gears and spacers.

17 If the side bearings are to be replaced, draw them off the differential case using a puller.

18 When new races are fitted ensure that they are pressed fully home to the shoulder on the casing (using installer Z.8552).

19 Fit a new filter pad in the axle housing.

20 Examine the pinion shaft for wear at the oil seal land. If badly worn, a new pinion (and therefore crown wheel as well) will be required. If only lightly scored clean up the shaft with very fine emery cloth.

21 To reset the differential pinions and side gears in the differential casing, first dip all the components in oil to ensure initial lubrication when first put back into use.

22 Replace the pinions together with new thrust washers and the side gears, each with a selected spacer.

23 Replace the pinion gear shaft, lining up the locating pin hole in the casing, but do not replace the retaining pin yet.

24 With a feeler gauge behind opposite sides of the side-gear spacers, check the clearance between each of them and the case, which should be .006 in. with no gear backlash evident.

25 Increase or decrease the spacer thickness accordingly. Spacers are available in seven thicknesses with a total range from .019 — .033 inch inclusive. It is permissible for the spacers used on each side to be of different thicknesses if necessary. When tolerances are correct fit a new shaft retaining pin and punch the end flush with the casing. As a final check the gears should turn by hand with the half-shafts inserted in the side gears.

26 Install the hypoid gear to the differential case by first warming the gear evenly (on a hot plate). It is

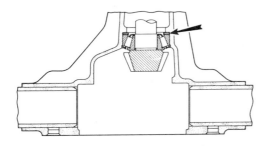

Fig.8.5. Drawing showing position of pinion rear bearing spacers and shims (arrowed) which control pinion position.

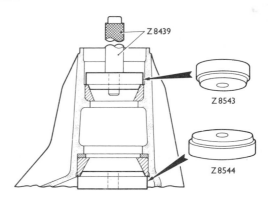

Fig.8.6. Drawing showing positioning of special installing tools for re-fitting pinion bearing outer races.

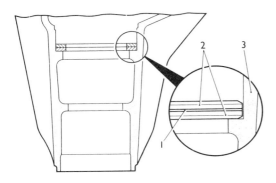

Fig.8.7. Drawing to show detail of arrangement of pinion rear bearing spacers (2) and shims (1) in the axle housing (3).

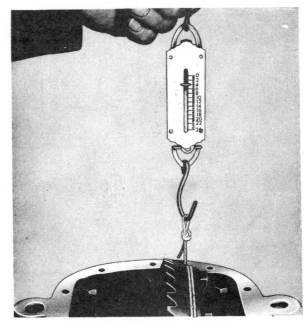

Fig.8.8. Using a spring scale to check pre-loading of differential side bearings.

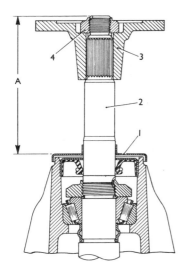

Fig.8.9. CROSS SECTION OF PINION HOUSING AND FLANGE
Dimension 'A' = 3.70 inch

1 Mud slinger   3 Flange
2 Pinion   4 Flange nut

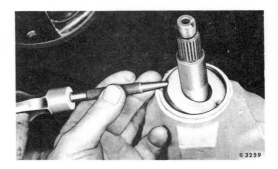

Fig.8.10. Removing the pinion oil seal from the casing using a pointed punch.

best also to make up two guide studs that can be screwed into two opposite bolt holes in the gear. These will ensure that the register on the case fits into the gear, first time, squarely. Draw the gear on with the mounting bolts and new lock washers and tighten to specified torque.

27 The lateral location of the differential case and hypoid gear assembly in the axle casing is controlled by spacers and shims. These also determine the side bearing pre-load and are available in two thicknesses of spacer, viz. .050 in. and .051 in. and shims of .003 in. These cover from .100 in. upwards, therefore, in steps of .001 in., using two spacers for each bearing and the requisite shims.

28 Replace the differential case in the housing complete with side bearings, and then select four spacers and the appropriate number of shims which will remove all the endfloat between the bearing outer races and the ends of the axle housing tubes.

29 Remove the differential casing once more and then divide the spacers and shims equally into two lots, i.e. two spacers for each side with the necessary shims. Fit one lot on one side of the housing, ensuring that any shims are sandwiched between the spacers and that the spacer chamfers are facing outwards (see Fig.8.7).

30 Add one extra shim of .003 in. to the second lot, arranging them in the same way, and placing these at the other end of the axle housing, fit the casing back into the housing once more. Some pressure will be needed to force the assembly in and care must be taken to ensure the side bearings do not tilt and jam.

31 Tap the axle housing lightly near the bearings and rotate the assembly so that the bearings will settle properly. Then replace the bearing caps in the correct sides and tighten the bolts to the specified torque.

32 The pre-load on the bearings can now be checked by measuring the torque resistance at the periphery of the crown wheel. This is simply done by tying a piece of string around the crown wheel and measuring the turning resistance with a spring balance. (See Fig.8.8). If the reading is outside the specifications, then the unit must be removed and the shim thicknesses adjusted accordingly.

33 Check that the run-out of the hypoid gear rear face does not exceed .002 in. on a clock gauge micrometer. If it does, it indicates that dirt or burrs may have affected it when being re-assembled to the differential case.

34 Once the differential has been satisfactorily fitted and checked remove it once more, keeping the shims and spacers carefully for final assembly on their respective sides.

35 The pinion fitting is somewhat more complex and there are four factors which determine the initial selection of pinion spacers and shims to control the pinion/crown wheel mesh. These are:—

a) The pinion bearing correction — being the variance from the maximum of .8445 in. of the thickness of the pinion rear bearing - is determined by measuring the actual thickness of the rear pinion bearing on a special jig plate, with a micrometer.

b) The pinion meshing correction — being the variance from standard required in production assembly — is stamped on the nose of the pinion in single figures representing thousandths of an inch.

c) The designed basic spacer thickness — being the standard spacer used in production assembly of .1230 in.

d) The axle housing correction — being the deviation from the nominal depth of the bearing abutment face in

relation to the centre line of the crown wheel axis. This figure is stamped on the axle housing rear face at the top - the single figure representing thousandths of an inch.

36 The calculation of the pinion spacer/shims required is best indicated using an example:—

Pinion rear bearing maximum thickness.	.8445 in.
Pinion rear bearing actual thickness.	.8410 in.
Difference (pinion bearing correction).	.0035 in.
Axle housing correction '3'	.0030 in.
Pinion meshing correction '5'	.0050 in.
Basic spacer thickness.	.1230 in.
Total spacer thickness required.	.1345 in.

Spacers are available in thicknesses of .059 in. and .060 in. and shims in a thickness of .003 in. In this case, therefore, one could select:—

2 spacers (.060)	.1200	OR	1 spacer	.0600
5 shims (.003)	.0150		1 spacer	.0590
			5 shims (.003)	.0150
Total	.1350			.1340

It is better to select the larger thickness as this will reduce backlash fractionally, rather than increase it.

37 Having checked each shim and spacer with a micrometer the shims should be sandwiched between the spacers as before (see Fig.8.7) and placed on the pinion rear bearing abutment face in the axle housing.

38 The pinion rear bearing outer race should then be pressed firmly into place in the housing using installer No.Z8544 as shown in Fig.8.6 followed by the front bearing outer race using installer Z8543.

39 Having fitted the pinion rear bearing inner race to the shaft with installer Z8553, then fit a new compressible spacer and bearing washer over the shaft. Place the shaft into the axle housing.

40 Next place the front bearing inner race over the shaft and, whilst supporting the end of the pinion, tap it home on the shaft using installer Z8537.

41 All is now set to apply the pinion bearing pre-load. Using a new pinion nut lubricated with rear axle oil, tighten it until a positive resistance is felt, indicating that all endfloat is taken up between the front bearing inner race, bearing washer and compressible spacer.

42 Using a torque pre-load gauge fitted to the pinion shaft the pinion nut should now be tightened gradually, (compressing the spacer as it does so) until the pre-load reading is within specification.

43 If the pre-load is exceeded it will be necessary to fit a new compressible spacer and start again.

44 The differential case/crown wheel assembly together with the selected shims should now be installed in the axle housing as previously described in paragraphs 30 and 31. If there is an odd number of shims the greater number should be put between the right-hand pair of spacers.

45 Check the backlash between crown wheel and pinion. If incorrect, then the shims can be moved from one side to the other, (fitting them always between the spacers) until it is correct. On no account alter the total number of shims and spacers originally selected, or the side bearing pre-load will be altered.

46 With the backlash correct, according to specification, the bearing caps can be replaced and tightened down to specified torque, after which backlash needs to be rechecked.

47 A final test for correct pinion/crown wheel location can be carried out by applying a load to the crown wheel and driving it by turning the pinion so that marks

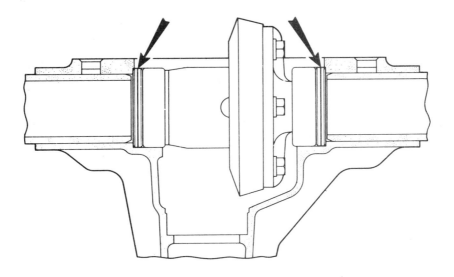

Fig.8.11. Showing location of shims and spacers (arrowed) used in setting the differential side bearing pre-load.

Fig.8.12. Crown wheel and pinion meshing marks. 'A'—correct. 'B'—Pinion too far out. 'C'—Pinion too far in.

will be made on the teeth. Use engineers blue to emphasise the marks if necessary.

48 If the pinion is too far out (i.e. too far away from the crown wheel) the marks will be on the peaks of the crown wheel teeth, whereas if the pinion is too far in,

they will be in the valleys (see Fig.8.12).

49 Stake the nut into the pinion shaft slots and install the new oil seal, pinion shaft extension, extension shaft bearing and coupling flange as described in Section 6.

Chapter 9/Braking System

Contents

Specifications

Type - Girling ... ... Hydraulically operated disc or drum brakes at the front and drum at the rear with a cable operated handbrake to the rear wheels only.

Hydraulic Fluid ... ... Girling crimson brake and clutch fluid

Brake Drums
Internal diameter... ... ... 8.000 in. to 8.005 in.
Maximum internal diameter... ... ... 8.062 in.
Maximum run-out of front drums from hubs ... ... .002 in.
Maximum run-out of rear drums from half shafts ... ... .004 in.

Disc Brakes
Disc thickness ... ... .375 in. to .380 in.
Maximum run-out ... ... .004 in.
Friction pad minimum thickness ... ... .12 ins.

Torque Wrench Settings
Front brake flange plate to steering knuckle nuts ... ... 25 lb/ft.
Rear brake flange plate to rear axle nuts... ... ... 12 lb/ft.
Disc calliper to steering knuckle bolts.. ... ... 33 lb/ft.
(ALL DRY THREADS)

1. General Description

The Standard and DeLuxe models of the Viva HB are fitted with hydraulically operated internally expanding drum brakes on all wheels. The drums are 8 inches in diameter and equipped with two leading shoes on the front wheels, and one leading and one trailing shoe on the rear wheels. The pedal operated hydraulic master cylinder is located behind the brake pedal in the pedal mounting bracket, and it has an integral fluid reservoir which protrudes through the bulkhead into the engine compartment. Each of the front wheels has two fixed single ended cylinders, one operating each shoe. Each rear wheel has one hydraulic cylinder, single ended but floating, operating the trailing and leading end of both shoes in each drum. On the 90 and SL90 models disc

brakes are fitted to the front wheels, and the hydraulic pressure to all wheels is boosted by a vacuum—servo unit interposed in the system between the master cylinder and the wheel cylinders. A secondary fluid reservoir is fitted to the master cylinder on these models to cope with the increased fluid capacity of the system. The master cylinder also has a larger diameter bore. Disc brakes are optional extras on the Standard and DeLuxe models.

The parking or emergency brakes are mechanically operated to the rear wheels only, by a hand operated lever mounted on the floor between the front seats. The lever is connected to the rear wheel brake shoes by a stranded steel cable, which can be adjusted, and operating links in the rear wheel drums. All drum brakes are equipped with adjusters to the shoes which bring them nearer to the drums when the linings of the shoes start to

123

wear down. On front wheels with drum brakes these adjusters are the cam type, one to each shoe, and the rear wheels have the conical ended screw type, one adjuster serving both shoes in each rear drum. None of the brake shoes is pivoted on a fixed arc, each end being located in a groove in the cylinders and adjuster assemblies. By this means all shoes are automatically self centring on the drums when applied. Disc brake pads are automatically adjusted to the discs by the hydraulic systems.

The basic principles of operation of the hydraulic brake system are as follows:—

The brake pedal, when depressed, operates the plunger of a pump containing hydraulic fluid (the master cylinder) and forces this fluid along small diameter pipes, both rigid and flexible, to a series of small cylinders located at each wheel. The hydraulic fluid pressure at these cylinders (wheel cylinders) forces their pistons outwards. These pistons are connected to the ends of the brake shoes which are then forced against the drums, thereby applying the brakes. When the brake pedal is released, the shoes are drawn off the drums by springs which link the pairs of shoes together inside each wheel drum.

With disc brakes the conventional drum is replaced by a disc, against each side of which pads of friction material are forced by hydraulic pressure from a calliper—rather like gripping a gramophone record between a thumb and fore finger.

As the pads wear, so the hydraulic piston which forces them against the disc advances further towards the disc and obviates the need for adjustment. There is no return spring of any sort for the brake pads so that when the hydraulic pressure is relieved, the fractional reverse movement of the pistons relieves the pads sufficiently to clear the disc surfaces. This automatic adjustment is the reason why an additional reservoir of hydraulic fluid is required. The rear wheel brakes and handbrake on models fitted with front disc brakes are identical to those fitted on standard models.

In addition to the disc brakes where fitted, a vacuum-servo unit is installed. This unit uses the vacuum of the inlet manifold of the engine to operate what is, in effect, another pump to apply pressure to the hydraulic system. This reduces the pressure required on the conventional brake pedal when operating the brakes.

2. Routine Maintenance — Drum & Disc Brakes

1. Every 3,000 miles clean the cap and top of the master cylinder reservoir, remove the cap and check the level of the fluid which should be ¼ in. (6 mm) below the top, for both drum and disc brake systems. If necessary top up the reservoir with clean fluid of the correct specification (Castrol/Girling Crimson). On no account use any other specification or fluid, or serious risk of damage and failure of the system could result.
2. If the reservoir level has dropped significantly—or requires frequent topping up - then there must be a leak in the system which does not normally consume fluid. This must be investigated.
3. Every 2—3,000 miles the drum brakes will need adjustment to compensate for wear on the shoes. This is apparent when the travel, or depression of the brake pedal becomes excessive, in order to apply the brakes.
4. The handbrake cable linkage requires oiling periodically at the guides and clevises. Due to natural stretch in the cables it will become necessary to adjust this also from time to time in order that the movement of the handbrake lever is adequate to apply the necessary degree of braking force.

5. Disc brakes being self adjusting, it will be necessary to inspect the pads at regular intervals of not more than 2,000 miles. Do not expect them to last much more than 10,000 miles.
6. If they are less than .125 in. (3 mm) thick they must be replaced.

7. If you have just acquired a Viva it is strongly recommended that all brake drums, brake shoes, discs and pads are removed as necessary and inspected for condition and wear. Even though they may be working prefectly they could be nearing the end of their useful life and it is as well to know this straight away. Similarly, the hydraulic cylinders and pipes, and connections should be carefully examined for signs of fluid leaks, and if any are apparent, action to rectify them should be taken immediately. It should be remembered that the compulsory vehicle safety tests for cars over three years of age, which the earlier production models of HB Vivas, pay particular attention to brake condition. Braking efficiency is also measured with special instruments. If they are not satisfactory your vehicle will not be allowed on the road as it will be considered unsafe.

3. Adjustment — Drum Brakes

1. If the pedal travel becomes noticably excessive before the brakes operate, and presuming that the pedal pressure is still firm and hard when pressure is applied, then the brake shoes need adjustment. This will be necessary on average about every 2—3,000 miles.
2. Adjust the front wheels first. Jack up the car so that one front wheel is just clear of the ground and spins freely.
3. Behind the brake backplate are two square headed adjusters, one at the top and the other at the bottom of the backplate. Turn the top one clockwise (see Fig.9.1), (using a square headed ring spanner preferably, to prevent burring of the screw head), until the shoe is locked tight on the drum. Then release the adjuster in the opposite direction for two notches (which can be felt when turning it). Spin the wheel to ensure the shoe is not binding on the drum. Repeat this process with the lower adjusting screw.

4. Lower the wheel to the ground and repeat the full adjustment process for the other front wheel.
5. Release the handbrake, block the front wheels and jack up the rear wheels in turn. The single adjuster also has a square head and is located at the bottom of the brake flange and towards the rear of the car. Turn the adjuster clockwise until the brake shoes lock the wheel, then reverse it two notches as for the front wheel adjusters. Turn the wheel to ensure that the shoes are not binding on the drum. The rear wheels will not spin quite so freely as the front ones because the differential gear and propeller shaft will be revolving with it, so do not confuse this turning resistance with brake drag. Repeat the adjustment process with the other rear wheel.

6. It is often possible that a little shoe rubbing can be detected even after the adjusters have been slackened off the required two notches. Provided the degree of drag in such instances is negligible, ignore it. The shoes will bed down into their new positions on the drums after a mile or two. If there is serious binding after the adjusters have been slackened off two or more notches it will be necessary to remove the drum and examine the shoes and drums further. (See Section 5).

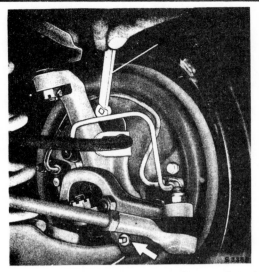

Fig.9.1. Adjustment of front brake shoes. Bottom adjuster is arrowed (Girling).

Fig.9.2. Removing the rear brake shoes. (Girling).

Fig.9.3. Correct assembly of front shoes and springs to the back plate. (Girling).

Fig.9.4. Removing the front brake shoes. (Girling).

Fig.9.5. Lockheed front drum brake showing correct assembly of shoes and springs.

Fig.9.6. Correct assembly of rear brake shoes and springs to the back plate. (Girling).

4. Adjustment — Disc Brakes

1. Disc brakes are fitted to the front wheels only and do not require adjustment.
2. Drum brakes are fitted to the rear wheels of all cars fitted with front disc brakes and adjustment should be carried out in accordance with Section 3, paragraphs 5 and 6 when the symptoms as described in Section 3, paragraph 1, are evident.

5. Drum Brakes — Removal, Inspection & Replacement of Drums & Shoes

1. If the brakes are inefficient, or the pedal travel excessive and the hydraulic system is showing no signs of leaks, first try adjusting the brakes. If little or no improvement results it will be necessary to examine the drums and shoes.
2. It is possible to attend to each wheel individually, so start with the front and remove the hub cap and slacken the wheel nuts. Then jack up the car and remove the nuts and wheel.
3. Next undo the two locating bolts which position the drum on the front hub (photo). (The purpose of these bolts is to hold the drum tight in position when the wheel is off. The full load of the braking force applied to the drum is carried by the four wheel studs and the drum is only fully clamped when the wheel is on).
4. Now draw the drum off the studs. A light tap around the periphery with a soft mallet will help to start it moving if it tends to stick at the roots of the studs.
5. It is also possible that the drum, although loose on the studs, is restricted by the shoes inside from coming off. In this case slacken off the adjuster screws (Section 3), until the drum can be removed (photo).
6. Examine the friction surface on the interior of the drum (arrow, photo 5.5). Normally this should be completely smooth and bright. Remove any dust with a dry cloth and examine the surface for any score marks or blemishes. Very light hairline scores running around the surface area are not serious but indicate that the shoes may be wearing out, or heavy grit and dirt have got into the drum at some time. If there are signs of deep scoring the drum needs reconditioning or replacement. As reconditioning will probably cost as much as a new drum, and certainly more than a good second hand one (obtained from car breakers without difficulty), it is not recommended. In theory a drum should not be renewed without replacing the front hub assembly also, but in practice the variations of concentricity which may occur with matched drums do not significantly affect the braking efficiency unless you are particularly unfortunate and have hub and drum tolerances at the extreme limits.
7. Examine the brake shoes for signs of oil contamination, deep scoring, or overall wear of the friction material. Deep scoring will be immediately apparent and will relate to any scoring in the drum. Oil contamination is evident where there are hard black shiny patches on the linings caused by the heat generated in braking which carbonises any oil that may have reached them. As a temporary measure, these areas can be rasped down but it is far better to replace the shoes. Normal wear can be judged by the depth of the rivet heads from the surface of the linings. If this is .025 in. (.65 mm) or less, the shoes should be renewed.
8. To remove the brake shoes, first of all slacken the two cam adjusters (front brakes) or cone adjuster (rear

brakes) anti-clockwise until the contracting movement of the shoes (pulled inwards by the springs) ceases. On the rear brakes only, each shoe is held by a locating pin and spring in the centre of each shoe. With a pair of pliers turn the slotted washer on the pin so that it comes off the end of the pin. The spring and pin can then be removed.
9. Continuing with the rear brakes, release one of the shoes from the adjuster by levering it away with a screwdriver (Fig.9.2). Once this spring tension is released it will be quite easy to remove the shoes and springs.
10 With the front brakes it is much simpler to remove the front wheel hubs before trying to remove the shoes, as the return springs are hooked into the backplate. Shoe replacement is virtually impossible with the hubs fitted, so much time will be saved in the long run by turning to Chapter 11, and removing the hubs as detailed there. Some cars however, are fitted with Lockheed brakes and on these the retractor springs are between the shoes rather than from the shoes to the backplate. It is possible to remove and replace these without removing the hub.
11 With the hub removed, release the trailing end of a shoe from a cylinder slot (Fig.9.4) with a screwdriver. Both shoes can then be easily lifted off. As soon as any shoes are removed make sure that the hydraulic cylinder pistons are prevented from coming out of the cylinders. This can be done by tying wire or even string around the slots to hold the pistons in.
12 Replacement of the shoes is a direct reversal of the removal procedure paying special attention to the following:—

a) Ensure that the shoes and springs for the front brakes are reassembled exactly as shown in Fig.9.3. (Girling) or Fig.9.5 (Lockheed).
b) Reassemble the rear brake shoes exactly as indicated in Fig.9.6 (Girling). The spring next to the hydraulic cylinder should have the smallest number of coils towards the piston end of the cylinder. Ensure the cylinder slides freely in its slot in the backplate. Lockheed rear brakes, fitted to some cars should be re-assembled as shown in Fig.9.7. Note that Lockheed rear brake shoes are actuated by a double ended cylinder with two pistons. The shorter coil of the longer spring should be hooked into the hole near the parking brake lever.
c) Handle the brake shoes with clean hands. Even a small oil or grease deposit could affect their performance.
d) Apply a thin film of grease (Duckhams KG20 Keenol) to the backplates where the edges of the shoes rub against them.
e) If any shoe requires replacement it means that all shoes at the front or all shoes at the rear (i.e. a minimum of four shoes) must be replaced together. Anything less can only lead to dangerous braking characteristics and uneconomical wear. Front and rear shoes are not interchangeable, except on those cars fitted with Lockheed brakes.

13 Replace the drums to the wheels from which they came and screw up the locating bolts.
14 Adjust the brakes as described in Section 3, and road test as soon as possible.

6. Handbrake Adjustment

1. Assuming that the rear brake shoes have been adjusted in accordance with Section 3, the handbrake should be fully on when five or six clicks of the ratchet have been

Fig.9.7. Lockheed rear drum brake showing correct assembly of shoes and springs

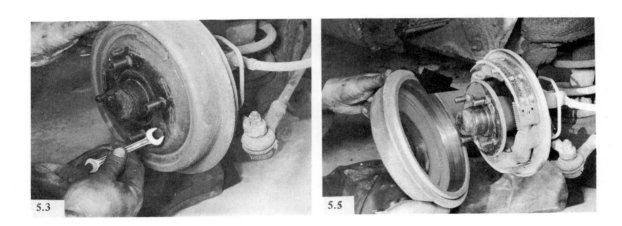

5.3

5.5

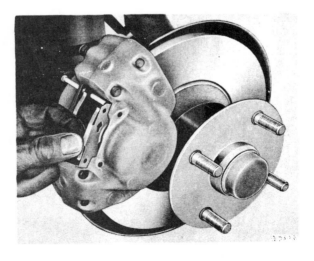

Fig.9.8. Removal of shims and disc brake pads.

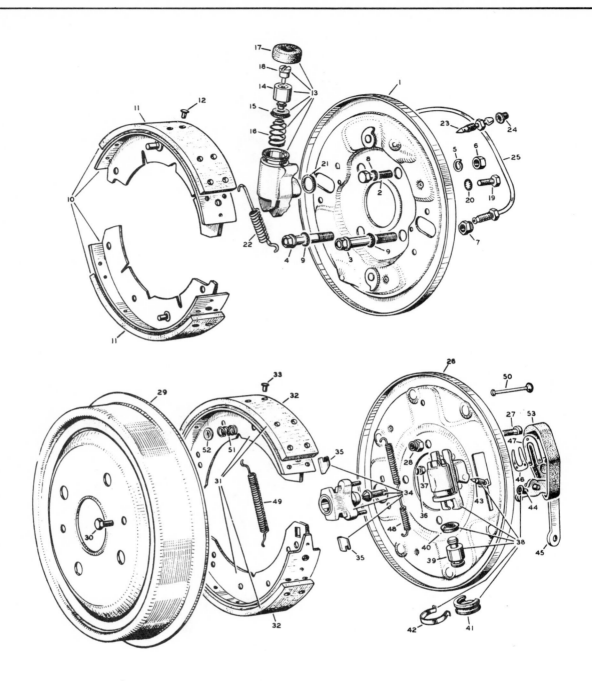

Fig.9.9. EXPLODED DRAWING OF FRONT DRUM BRAKE COMPONENTS (TOP) AND REAR BRAKE COMPONENTS (BOTTOM) GIRLING

1. Backplate
2. Bolt - backplate to steering) knuckle)
3. Bolt long - backplate to) steering knuckle)
4. Bolt long - backplate to) steering knuckle)
5. Washer & nut, top bolts
6. Washer & nut, top bolts
7. Nut
8. Lockwashers
9. Lockwashers
10 Shoe & lining assembly (front)
11 Lining

12. Rivet
13. Slave cylinder assembly
14. Piston
15. Seal
16. Spring
17. Dust excluder
18. Excluder clip
19. Bolt and washer,)
20. cylinder fixing.)
21. Sealing ring
22. Shoe return spring
23. Bleeder screw
24. Dust excluder
25. Front wheel hydrau.pipe

26. Back plate
27. Bolt-flange to axle
28. Nut
29. Drum (front & rear)
30. Drum locating screw
31. Brake shoe assembly - (rear)
32. Lining
33. Rivet
34. Adjuster assembly - rear
35. Adjuster tappets
36. Washer and nut, adjuster)
37. fixing.)
38. Cylinder assembly (rear)
39. Piston

40. Seal
41. Dust cap
42. Clip
43. Bleed screw
44. Dust excluder
45. Brake lever
46. Spring plate - cylinder
47. Retaining plate-cylinder
48. Return spring - shoes
49. Spring - shoe adjuster
50. Shoe securing pin
51. Spring - securing pin
52. Cup washer - slotted
53. Dust excluder

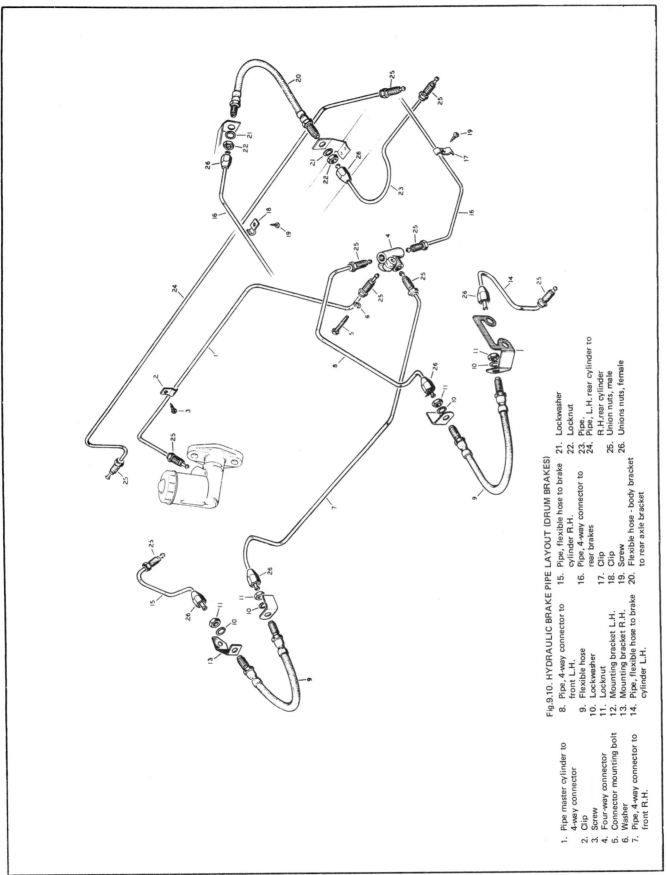

Fig.9.10. HYDRAULIC BRAKE PIPE LAYOUT (DRUM BRAKES)

1. Pipe master cylinder to 4-way connector
2. Clip
3. Screw
4. Four-way connector
5. Connector mounting bolt
6. Washer
7. Pipe, 4-way connector to front R.H.
8. Pipe, 4-way connector to front L.H.
9. Flexible hose
10. Lockwasher
11. Locknut
12. Mounting bracket L.H.
13. Mounting bracket R.H.
14. Pipe, flexible hose to brake cylinder L.H.
15. Pipe, flexible hose to brake cylinder R.H.
16. Pipe, 4-way connector to rear brakes
17. Clip
18. Clip
19. Screw
20. Flexible hose - body bracket to rear axle bracket
21. Lockwasher
22. Locknut
23. Pipe, L.H.rear cylinder to R.H.rear cylinder
24. Pipe, R.H.rear cylinder
25. Union nuts, male
26. Unions nuts, female

pulled on. If more than this, then the cable adjuster lock nut should be slackened and the adjuster screwed up until the desired condition is achieved. Tighten the lock nut. There is only one adjuster, as the cable is a single loop with the ends at each wheel and the point of the loop on a sliding bridle at the handbrake lever. If the cable has stretched so much that the adjustment is fully taken up, it is possible to take up more by selecting an alternative pin hole at the brake lever clevis. (Item 14 in Fig.9.11).

7. Disc Brakes — Removal, Inspection & Replacement of Pads

1. The thickness of the pads can be visually checked by jacking up the car and removing each front wheel, when the pads can be seen between the disc and calliper body. If the thickness of the friction material is less than .125 inches (3 mm) they must be replaced. Sometimes the pads wear unevenly, but if one of a pair is under specification thickness, the pair should be renewed. As a general rule pads on both front wheels should be renewed even if only one needs it. Some cars are fitted with Lockheed disc brakes which can be identified by the fact that only the heads of the two attaching bolts are visible - unlike the Girling callipers where four bolt heads can be seen. The thickness of the pad friction material on Lockheed disc pads should not be less than .06 inch (1.5 mm).
2. Remove the fluid reservoir cap and siphon out some fluid — say ¼ in. down. This will prevent the fluid overflowing when the level rises as the pistons are pushed back for fitting new pads.
3. To remove the pads, first pull the clips off the retaining pins and withdraw the pins.
4. Apply pressure to the faces of the old pads with the fingers, so pressing the pistons behind them back into the calliper. Then lift out the pads and shims from the calliper body (Fig.9.8).
5. Refit new pads and new shims also if the old ones show signs of distortion or deterioration. Make sure the shims are fitted with the arrow shaped hole in the top edge pointing in the direction of forward disc rotation.
6. Replace the locating pins and clips.
7. Depress the brake pedal two or three times to position the pistons and pads once more, and top up the fluid reservoir to the specified level.

8. Drum & Disc Brakes — Hydraulic Pipes, Rigid & Flexible — Inspection, Removal & Replacement

1. Periodically, and certainly well before the next M.O.T. test is due, all brake pipes, pipe connections and unions should be completely and carefully examined. Fig.9.10. and 9.27 show what pipes and unions there are in the systems.
2. First examine for signs of leakage where the pipe unions occur. Then examine the flexible hoses for signs of chafing and fraying and, of course, leakage. This is only a preliminary part of the flexible hose inspection, as exterior condition does not necessarily indicate their interior condition which will be considered later in the chapter.
3. The steel pipes must be examined equally carefully. They must be cleaned off and examined for any signs of dents, or other percussive damage and rust and corrosion. Rust and corrosion should be scraped off and if the depth of pitting in the pipes is significant, they

will need replacement. This is particularly likely in those areas underneath the car body and along the rear axle where the pipes are exposed to the full force of road and weather conditions.
4. If any section of pipe is to be taken off, first of all remove the fluid reservoir cap and line it with a piece of polythene film to make it air tight, and replace it. This will minimise the amount of fluid dripping out of the system, when pipes are removed, by preventing the replacement of fluid by air in the reservoir.
5. Rigid pipe removal is usually quite straightforward. The unions at each end are undone and the pipe and union pulled out and the centre sections of the pipe removed from the body clips where necessary. Underneath the car, exposed unions can sometimes be very tight. As one can use only an open ended spanner and the unions are not large, burring of the flats is not uncommon when attempting to undo them. For this reason a self locking grip wrench (mole) is often the only way to remove a stubborn union.
6. Flexible hoses are always mounted at both ends in a rigid bracket attached to the body or a sub-assembly. To remove them it is necessary first of all to uscrew the pipe unions of the rigid pipes which go into them. Then, with a spanner on the hexagonal end of the flexible pipe union, the locknut and washer on the other side of the mounting bracket need to be removed. Here again exposure to the elements often tends to seize the locknut and in this case the use of penetrating oil or 'Plus-gas' is necessary. The mounting brackets, particularly on the bodyframe, are not very heavy gauge and care must be taken not to wrench them off. A self-grip wrench is often of use here as well. Use it on the pipe union in this instance as one is able to get a ring spanner on the locknut.
7. With the flexible hose removed, examine the internal bore. If it is blown through first, it should be possible to see through it. Any specks of rubber which come out, or signs of restriction in the bore, mean that the inner lining is breaking up and the pipe must be replaced.
8. Rigid pipes which need replacement can usually be purchased at any local garage where they have the pipe, unions and special tools to make them up. All they need to know is the total length of the pipe, and the type of flare used at each end with the union. This is very important as one can have a flare and a mushroom on the same pipe.
9. Replacement of pipes is a straightforward reversal of the removal procedure. If the rigid pipes have been made up it is best to get all the sets (or bends) in them before trying to install them. Also if there are any acute bends, ask your supplier to put these in for you on a tube bender. Otherwise you may kink the pipe and thereby restrict the bore area and fluid flow.
10 With the pipes replaced, remove the polythene film from the reservoir cap (paragraph 4), and bleed the system as described in Section 16. It is not necessary always to bleed at all four wheels. It depends which pipe has been removed. Obviously if the main one from the master cylinder is removed, air could have reached any line from the later distribution of pipes. If, however a flexible hose at a front wheel is replaced, only that wheel needs to be bled.

9. Drum Brakes — Hydraulic Wheel Cylinders, Inspection & Repair

1. If it is suspected that one or more wheel cylinders is malfunctioning, jack up the suspect wheel and remove the brake drum (See Section 5).

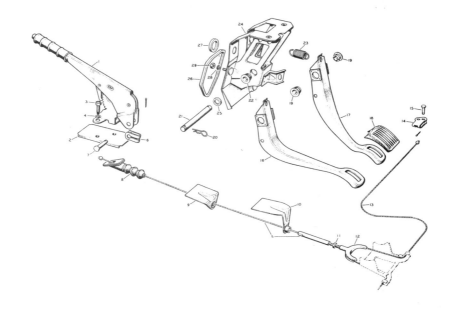

Fig.9.11. EXPLODED DRAWING OF HANDBRAKE LINKAGE, FOOTBRAKE PEDAL & MOUNTING BRACKET

1.	Lever	9.	Guide plate - front	17.	Brake pedal L.H.D.	25. Spacer
2.	Mounting plate	10.	Guide plate - rear	18.	Pedal rubber	26. Gasket
3.	Screw	11.	Locknut	19.	Pedal bush	27. Gasket
4.	Washer	12.	Yoke	20.	Clip - pedal shaft	28. Spring washer
5.	Cable assembly-front	13.	Cable assembly-rear	21.	Pedal shaft	29. Nut
6.	Clevis	14.	Clevis	22.	Shaft bush	
7.	Clevis pin	15.	Clevis pin	23.	Return spring	
8.	Boot	16.	Brake pedal R.H.D.	24.	Mounting bracket	

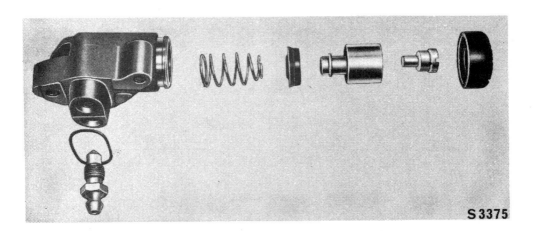

S 3375

Fig.9.12. Exploded picture of front brake cylinder

2. Inspect for signs of fluid leakage around the wheel cylinder, and if there are any, proceed with instructions at paragraph 4.

3. Next get someone to very gently press the brake pedal a small distance. On rear brakes watch the wheel cylinder to see that the piston moves out a little. On no account allow it to come right out or you will have to reassemble it and bleed the system. Then release the pedal and ensure that the shoe springs force the piston back. On front brakes, block the shoe on each cylinder in turn with a piece of wood and see that the other one moves in and out as the pedal is depressed and released. Do not let the piston move too far out.

4. A wheel cylinder where there is leaking fluid or which does not move at all (i.e. with a seized piston) will have to be fitted with new seals at least.

5. Remove the brake shoes as described in Section 5, and seal the fluid reservoir cap as described in Section 8, paragraph 4.

6. Remove the rubber dust cover and clip from the end of the cylinder, and draw out the piston, on the inner end of which a seal will be fitted. On front brake cylinders only draw out the spring behind the piston.

7. If the piston is seized in the cylinder it may be very difficult to remove, in which case it may be quicker in the long run to remove the cylinder from the wheel. (See paragraph 14—20).

8. Examine the bores of the wheel cylinders. Any sign of scoring or ridging in the walls where the piston seal travels means that the cylinder should be replaced.

9. If the cylinder is in good condition it will be necessary to replace only the seal on the piston. Pull the old one off and carefully fit a new one over the long boss of the piston, engaging it over the raised rim. The lip of the seal must face away from the centre of the piston.

10 Clean out the interior of the cylinder with a dry cloth and ensure the piston is quite clean. Then use a little rubber grease (as specified only) and lubricate the piston seal before replacing the spring (front only) and piston in the cylinder. Be careful not to damage or turn over the seal lip on replacement.

11 If the old seal shows signs of swelling and deterioration, rather than just wear on the lip, it indicates that the hydraulic fluid in the system may have been contaminated. In such cases all the fluid must be removed from the system and all seals replaced including those in the master cylinder. Flexible hose should be checked too.

12 Replace the shoe guide clip (front) and dust cover.

13 Replace brake shoes and drums (Section 5), remove the fluid reservoir cap seal (paragraph 5), and bleed the hydraulic system (Section 16).

14 If the cylinders are to be replaced, unscrew the unions of the hydraulic pipes on the brake backplate.

15 On front brakes, undo the two cylinder fixing bolts and washers and remove the cylinder and sealing ring. Replace the cylinder with a new sealing ring. Continue reassembly as from paragraph 9, using new piston seals always.

16 On rear brake cylinders, undo the pipe union behind the backplate and also remove the bleed screw.

17 Disconnect the handbrake cable from the lever by removing the clevis pin and then remove the dust cover.

18 Using a small screwdriver or spike, prise off the cylinder retaining plate followed by the spring plate, (Fig.9.14).

19 Lift out the cylinder assembly. Replacement is a reversal of the removal procedure. Continue reassembly as from paragraph 9, using new piston seals always.

20 Bleed the system (Section 16).

10. Disc Brakes — Calliper Removal, Inspection & Replacement

1. If the calliper pistons are suspected of malfunctioning jack up the car and remove the relevant wheel.

2. Examine for signs of fluid leaks and if these are apparent it will be necessary to remove the calliper and proceed as described from paragraph 4 onwards.

3. If there are no signs of leaking get someone to depress the brake pedal and watch how the two disc pads come up to the disc. One may move very slowly or not at all, in which case it will be necessary to remove the calliper and proceed further.

4. Remove disc pads and shims as described in Section 7.

5. Seal the reservoir cap as described in Section 8, paragraph 4.

6. Undo the hydraulic pipe union from the body of the calliper and draw back the pipe.

7. Undo the two bolts holding the calliper to the steering knuckle plate. Do NOT undo the bolts which clamp the two halves of the calliper together.

8. Lift the calliper off the disc.

9. Clean the exterior of the calliper assembly and then ease each rubber piston cover out of the grooves in the piston and the calliper body, and remove them.

10 It may be possible to pull the pistons out of their bores, but if not, it will be necessary to blow them out with pressure from an air pump hose attached to the hydraulic fluid inlet port. Support one piston while the other is blown out and then block the empty cylinder with a cloth while the other comes out. If one piston moves very slowly remove this one before the other. If one piston does not move at all it will have seized in the cylinder. Use a hydraulic cleaning fluid or methylated spirits to soak it for some time in an attempt to free it. If harsher measures are needed try to confine any damage to the piston, and not the calliper body.

11 With the pistons removed, the fluid seal rings may be eased out of the piston grooves with a small screwdriver. Make sure that the piston and groove are not damaged. Examine the bores and pistons for signs of scoring or scuffing. If severe, it is unlikely that a proper fluid seal will be possible and a new calliper assembly may be required. The part of the piston on the pad side of the seal groove may be cleaned up with steel wool if necessary. Take care to leave no traces of steel wool anywhere. Clean the cylinder bores also, using hydraulic cleaning fluid if possible, or methylated spirits otherwise.

12 Reassembly is an exact reversal of the dismantling process, taking care with the following in particular:

13 Ensure that the new fluid seal is seated properly in its groove.

14 The calliper mounting bolts have a nylon locking insert in the threads. If this is the third time of removal, then the bolts should be renewed. Tighten the bolts to the specified torque of 33 lb/ft. Replace the pads, as described in Section 7, remove the reservoir cap seal and bleed the system.

15 Some cars are fitted with disc brakes made by Lockheed. These are basically the same in operating principle. Two particular items to be noted on reassembly are the piston dust seal and the piston itself. The grooved rubber dust seal is located in a recess in the mouth of the cylinder bore and is kept there by a retaining ring. The piston has a cut-away portion on its outer edge, and this must face down and rearwards as shown in Fig.9.17) when the piston is pressed back into the cylinder. Care must be taken when re-fitting the dust seal and retainer to ensure that they go in

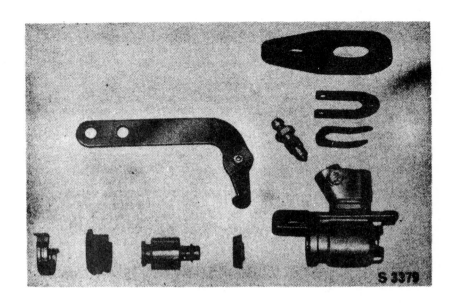

Fig.9.13. Exploded view of rear brake cylinder.

Fig. 9.14. Removal of the rear brake cylinder securing plate (1) after which the spring plate (2) may be removed

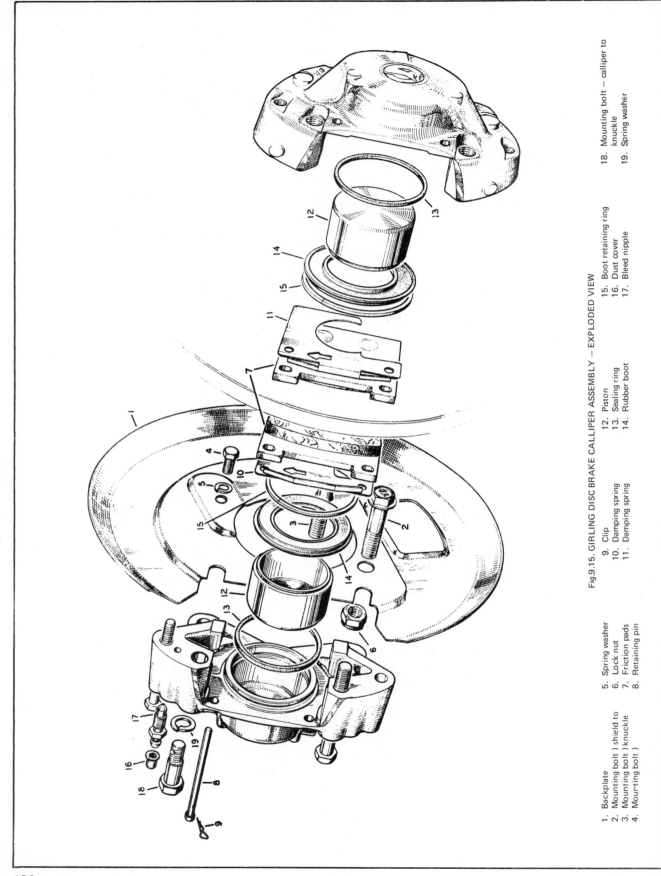

Fig.9.15. GIRLING DISC BRAKE CALLIPER ASSEMBLY – EXPLODED VIEW

1. Backplate
2. Mounting bolt) shield to knuckle
3. Mounting bolt) knuckle
4. Mounting bolt)

5. Spring washer
6. Lock nut
7. Friction pads
8. Retaining pin

9. Clip
10. Damping spring
11. Damping spring

12. Piston
13. Sealing ring
14. Rubber boot

15. Boot retaining ring
16. Dust cover
17. Bleed nipple

18. Mounting bolt – calliper to knuckle
19. Spring washer

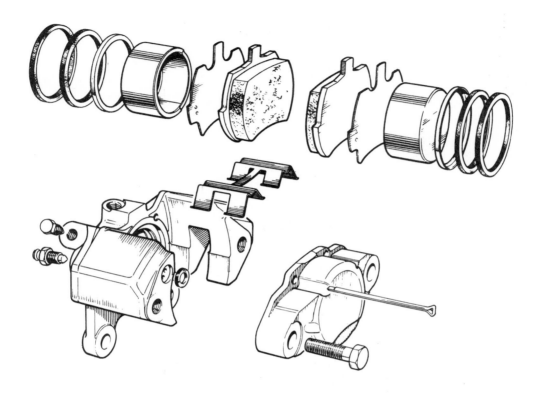

Fig.9.16. Lockheed disc brake calliper assembly exploded view.

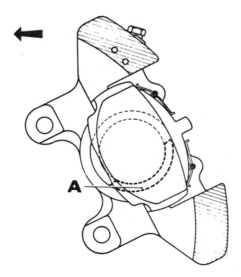

Fig.9.17. Drawing to show position of cutaway ('A') in Lockheed disc brake piston relative to calliper. Arrow points to front of car.

square and undistorted.

11. Disc Brakes, Disc Run-Out Check

1. If the disc does not run true then it will tend to push the disc pads aside and force the pistons further into the calliper. This will increase the brake pedal travel necessary to apply the brakes, apart from impairing brake efficiency and the life of the pads.

2. To check the disc run-out (trueness), jack up the car and remove the wheel. Ensure the hub bearing has no free float in it.

3. Set a clock gauge micrometer on a firm stand up to a friction face of the disc near the outside edge so that a reading above .004 inch is registered on the gauge.

4. Spin the hub and if the gauge registers more than ± .004 inch the disc is warped and needs replacement.

12. Drum & Disc Brakes — Hydraulic Master Cylinder

1. Unless there are obvious signs of leakage any defects in the master cylinder are usually the last to be detected in a hydraulic system.

2. Before assuming that a fault in the system is in the master cylinder, the pipes and wheel cylinders should all be checked and examined as described in Sections 8,9 and 10.

3. To remove the master cylinder, first disconnect the pipe at the four-way connector which comes from it. (See Fig.9.10). On disc brake models detach the pipe from the servo unit (Fig.9.27).

4. Drain the master cylinder by pumping the brake pedal and collect the fluid at the end of the disconnected pipe. Then remove the pipe by undoing the union at the master cylinder end.

5. Remove the clevis pin from the brake pedal which attaches the pushrod from the master cylinder.

6. Remove the bolts and nuts which hold the master cylinder to the pedal support bracket and lift it out.

7. To dismantle the cylinder, first ease off the rubber dust cover from the end of the cylinder to expose the circlip.

8. Unclip the circlip from inside the end of the cylinder body and withdraw the pushrod, circlip, retaining washer and dust cover, all together.

9. The piston and valve assembly should now be taken out, or shaken out. If it sticks, try forcing air through the outlet port of the cylinder.

10 To remove the spring from the piston, prise up the tab on the spring retainer which engages in a shoulder on the end of the piston. The spring, spring retainer and valve assembly can then be detached from the piston.

11 To remove the valve stem from the spring retainer, compress the spring and move the stem out of the slotted hole in the retainer.

12 Withdraw the valve stem from the valve spacer, taking care not to damage or lose the spring shim washer.

13 Remove the gland seal from the piston and the valve seal from the valve stem.

14 Clean all parts in hydraulic cleaning fluid or methylated spirits and examine the cylinder bore for signs of ridges and scores. If in doubt, renew the cylinder.

15 Both rubber seals should be renewed. Assemble the valve seal, shim washer and spacer to the stem as shown in Fig.9.18.

16 Fit a new gland seal with the lip towards the piston spigot as shown in Fig.9.19.

17 Assemble the valve stem to the spring and retainer,

and then locate the retainer over the piston spigot.

18 Press the retainer tab into the piston recess.

19 Smear the outer end of the piston and the cylinder mouth with the special grease usually provided with the new seals (no other is to be used except castor oil based rubber grease) and insert the piston and valve assembly into the cylinder bore with care.

20 Replace the pushrod assembly and engage the circlip in the cylinder mouth recess fully. Replace the dust cover.

21 The cylinder is replaced on the car in the reverse order of removal. Ensure that the brake pedal clevis pin is installed with the head between the clutch and brake pedals and that the bushes engage the clevis on the pushrod.

22 Reconnect the hydraulic pipe and bleed the system as detailed in Section 16.

13. Tandem Master Cylinders

1. Some left-hand drive cars are fitted with dual braking systems and this is provided by a tandem master cylinder. Should the hydraulic system fail on either the front or rear brakes, it means that the car may still be halted as the pressure in each system is independent of the other.

2. Two types of tandem cylinder are fitted, namely Girling or Teves. Fig.9.22 gives a cross section and exploded view of the Girling cylinder. In order to remove the plungers for renewal of seals the reservoir must first be unbolted from the flange housing the tip valve and swung to one side. Do not try and remove the reservoir as it is held in its other location by a captive circlip in the body, and can only be detached with the possibility of damage. Once the tip valve retaining plug is removed the valve should be lifted out. The primary and secondary plungers may be removed after taking out the retaining circlip in the cylinder bore. In order to dismantle the secondary plunger assembly, the spring must be compressed in vice jaws to enable the retainer tag to be detached from the plunger. Similarly the spring must be compressed for reassembly.

3. The tip valve retainer plug must be tightened on reassembly to a torque of 38 lb/ft.

4. Fig.9.20 gives a cross section of the Teves cylinder which operates on the same principles as the Girling in a slightly different fashion.

5. To renew the plunger seals, first pull off the reservoir and remove the stop plug in the cylinder body between the two inlet ports. Then the two pistons may be drawn out after removing the retaining circlip inside the cylinder. The primary plunger components are separated by removing the screw in the end to which the spring is fitted. Note carefully the order in which the parts are assembled.

5. When renewing the seals, note that the two front seals of both plungers are the same as each other, but different from the two rear seals of the secondary plunger. They must not be mixed up. The rear seal on the primary plunger is different again. Fig.9.25 indicates how the different seals are arranged.

6. On cars fitted with tandem master cylinders a brake pressure warning lamp indicator is also installed. This will immediately indicate the loss of pressure in either half of the system when it occurs. Basically, the unit is a common piston held in position between opposing pressures in a cylinder. If there is any pressure difference the piston will move to one side, operate a plunger switch and light the warning lamp. The piston is in fact in two parts — the longer section incorporating the switch operating groove, and when dismantling, each

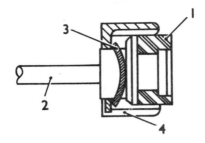

Fig.9.18. CROSS SECTION OF MASTER CYLINDER VALVE
STEM AND SEAL ASSEMBLY

1 Seal   3 Spring shim washer
2 Stem   4 Valve spacer

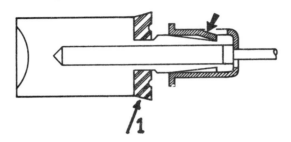

Fig.9.19. CROSS SECTION OF PISTON AND SPRING RE-
TAINER TAB (ARROWED) IS PUSHED INTO THE PLUNGER
RECESS

1 Piston seal

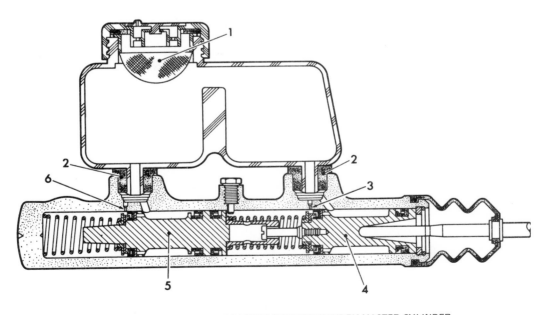

Fig.9.20. CROSS-SECTIONAL DRAWING OF TEVES TANDEM MASTER CYLINDER

1. Fluid filter screen   3. Compensating port (rear)   5. Secondary plunger   6. Compensating port (front)
2. Reservoir sealing plugs   4. Primary plunger

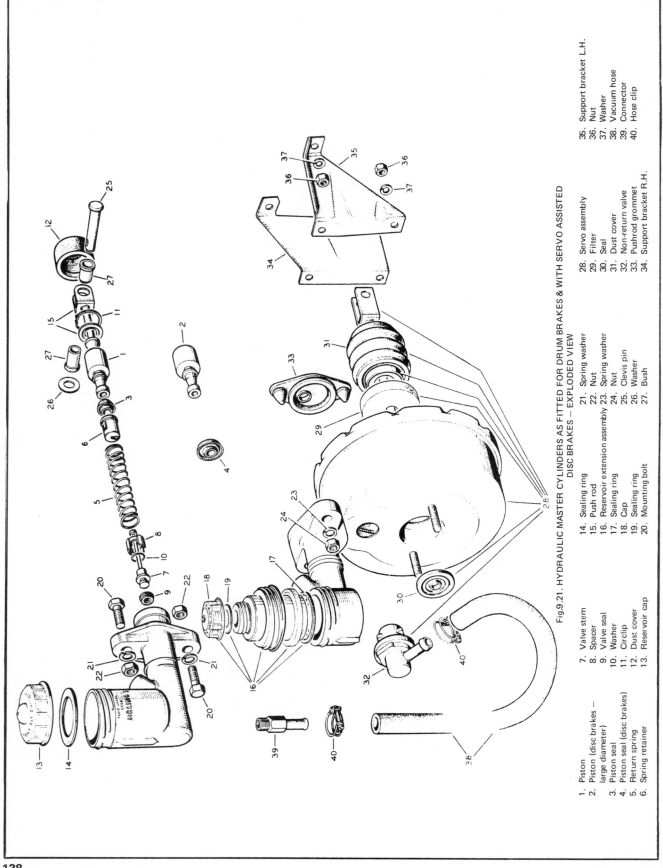

Fig.9.21. HYDRAULIC MASTER CYLINDERS AS FITTED FOR DRUM BRAKES & WITH SERVO ASSISTED DISC BRAKES — EXPLODED VIEW

1. Piston
2. Piston (disc brakes — large diameter)
3. Piston seal
4. Piston seal (disc brakes)
5. Return spring
6. Spring retainer
7. Valve stem
8. Spacer
9. Valve seal
10. Washer
11. Circlip
12. Dust cover
13. Reservoir cap
14. Sealing ring
15. Push rod
16. Reservoir extension assembly
17. Sealing ring
18. Cap
19. Sealing ring
20. Mounting bolt
21. Spring washer
22. Nut
23. Spring washer
24. Nut
25. Clevis pin
26. Washer
27. Bush
28. Servo assembly
29. Filter
30. Seal
31. Dust cover
32. Non-return valve
33. Pushrod grommet
34. Support bracket R.H.
35. Support bracket L.H.
36. Nut
37. Washer
38. Vacuum hose
39. Connector
40. Hose clip

138

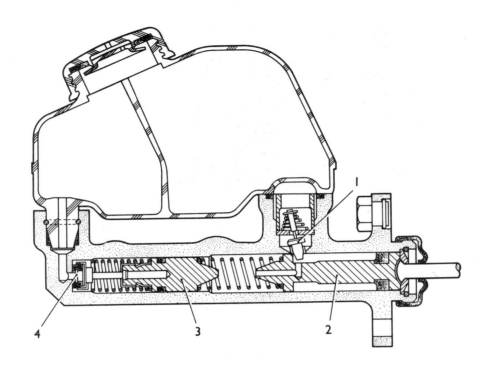

Fig.9.22. CROSS-SECTIONAL & EXPLODED DRAWINGS OF GIRLING TANDEM MASTER CYLINDER

1. Tip valve   2. Primary plunger   3. Secondary plunger   4. Centre valve

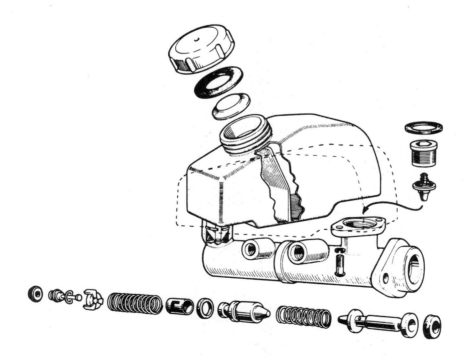

part should be removed from its arm end of the cylinder. If this is not done the seals could be damaged when passing the switch orifice. In order to centralise the piston on reassembly, it will be necessary to bleed first the front and then rear brakes until the warning light goes out when the plunger is in the central position. For obvious reasons it is not spring loaded, being maintained in balance by the equal pressure of the front and rear hydraulic systems.

14. Vacuum Servo Unit — General Description

1. The vacuum servo unit is incorporated with a master cylinder and, unlike the earlier HA series of Viva is operated directly from the brake pedal. It acts on all four wheels. When the pedal is depressed, suction from the induction manifold of the engine is applied to the piston inside the large cylindrical bowl of the servo unit. The piston then moves a plunger attached to its centre applying additional pressure to the hydraulic master cylinder piston. If the servo unit should fail to operate, hydraulic pressure from the foot pedal is still applied to the system but, of course, the pedal pressure required will be more than it would be if the servo was functioning. With the development of modern assembly line techniques the servo unit is no longer put together in a way that permits servicing or repair to it. If it fails it must be renewed as a complete assembly.

15. Vacuum Servo — Maintenance

1. In addition to normal hydraulic brake maintenance as described in Section 2, the servo unit is equipped with a replacement air filter. The air filter is situated at the rear of the unit and is in the form of a disc round the pushrod. Pull the rubber dust cover away from the servo body and then the filter retainer out of the housing. The filter element may be cut in order to remove it and it is permissible to cut the new one in order to fit it over the pushrod. Replace the retainer and ensure the dust cover engages properly in the retaining flange.

16. Vacuum Servo — Examination, Removal & Replacement

1. The manifold suction pipe is fitted with a non-return valve where it connects with the servo unit (Fig.9.24). If any back pressure from the manifold occured it could enter the servo unit and damage it. The non-return valve may be removed by turning it anti-clockwise one quarter of a turn and lifting it out. When fitting a new valve always renew the 'O' sealing ring behind it. On later models the non-return valve is retained by a rubber grommet and is replaced by twisting and pushing it fully home.

2. The correct operation of the servo unit also depends on the movement of the pushrod. When correct, the nose of the pushrod should protrude between .095 - .100 in. beyond the front face of the servo shell (Fig.9.23). This may be checked by first removing the master cylinder from the servo shell. Seal the cap of the fluid reservoir to prevent loss, disconnect the hydraulic pipe union and remove the two mounting nuts and washers. The pushrod sealing ring should be removed also after detaching the master cylinder. The protrusion of the pushrod as mentioned above should be measured with vacuum in the system — in other words with the engine running on tickover and the brakes 'off'. If the measurement is incorrect the servo unit needs renewal.

3. With the master cylinder detached as described in the previous paragraph, examine and renew the pushrod sealing ring if signs of deterioration are apparent.

4. To remove the servo unit, first remove the hydraulic master cylinder as described in paragraph 3, and disconnect the vacuum pipe from the non-return valve union. Remove the clevis pin attaching the pushrod to the brake pedal. Remove the nuts securing the servo body shell to the car. The whole unit may then be withdrawn. When replacing the servo, which is a direct reversal of the removal procedure, make sure that the pushrod grommet rubber pegs are properly engaged in the holes in the pedal support bracket.

17. Hydraulic System — Bleeding

1. The system should need bleeding only when some part of the system has been dismantled which would allow air into the fluid circuit, or if the reservoir level has been allowed to drop so far that air has entered the master cylinder. If the vehicle has been standing unused for any length of time it is possible also that air bubbles may have developed in the system due to the air absorbing nature of hydraulic fluid. Bleed nipples are found on each of the front wheels and on the rear right wheel only. The line from the four-way connector goes through the left-hand rear cylinder on route to the right rear cylinder.

2. Ensure that a supply of clean non-aerated fluid of the correct specification is to hand in order to replenish the reservoir during the bleeding process. It is advisable, if not essential, to have someone available to help, as one person has to pump the brake pedal while the other attends to each wheel. The reservoir level has also to be continuously watched and replenished. Fluid bled out should not be re-used. A clean glass jar and a 9—12 in. length of 1/8th inch internal diameter rubber tube that will fit tightly over the bleed nipples is also required.

3. The order of bleeding the wheels is to start with the longest line first, which in the Viva is the right rear, followed by right front and left front, for drum brakes.

4. For disc brakes, the engine must not be running and the pedal should be operated three or four times to make sure that there is no residual vacuum in the servo unit. The order of bleeding should be right front, left front, right rear. The lengths of the runs to the front wheels are no greater, but the fluid capacity of the disc calliper cylinders is much larger.

5. Make sure the bleed nipple is clean and put a small quantity of fluid in the bottom of the jar. Fit the tube onto the nipple and place the other end in the jar under the surface of the fluid. Keep it under the surface throughout the bleeding operation.

6. Unscrew the bleed screw ½ turn and get your assistant to depress and release the brake pedal in short sharp bursts when you direct him. Short sharp jabs are better because they will force any air bubbles along the line with the fluid rather than pump the fluid past them. It is not essential to remove all the air first time. If the whole system has to be bled, attend to each wheel for three or four complete pedal strokes and then repeat the process. On the second time around operate the pedal sharply in the same way until no bubbles come out of the pipe into the jar. With the brake pedal in the fully depressed position the bleed screw should be tightened. Do not forget to keep the reservoir topped up

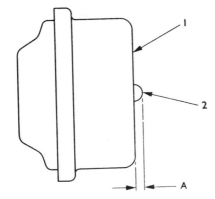

Fig.9.23. VACUUM SERVO UNIT. CORRECT POSITION OF PUSHROD — ENGINE RUNNING, BRAKES OFF

1 Servo shell   2 Pushrod

Dimension 'A' to be .095—.100 in.(2.3—2.5 mm)

Fig.9.24. Servo unit non-return valve. Cross section of type fitted to later models.

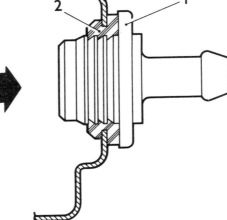

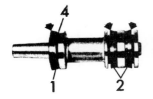
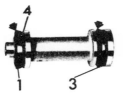

Fig.9.25. TEVES TANDEM MASTER CYLINDER. ARRANGEMENT OF PLUNGER SEALS

1 Front seal—primary and secondary plungers
2 Rear seals—secondary plunger
3 Rear seal—primary plunger
4 Front seal backing washers

Fig.9.26. BRAKE PRESSURE FAILURE WARNING DEVICE CROSS SECTION (TANDEM MASTER CYLINDERS ONLY)

1 Short piston
2 Long piston with actuating recess
3 Switch plunger

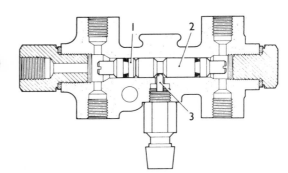

throughout.

7. When all wheels have been bled satisfactorily re-adjust the shoes (Section 3).

8. If the reason for bleeding has been a repair to a pipe or cylinder AFTER the four-way connector, then it should be normally necessary to bleed only the wheel of the line in question — PROVIDED that no fluid has been allowed to drain out of the disconnected line. If in any doubt bleed the whole system.

9. Depress the brake pedal which should offer a firm resistance with no trace of 'sponginess'. The pedal should not continue to go down under sustained pressure. If it does there is a leak, or the master cylinder seals are worn out.

---

18. Brake Pedal — Removal & Replacement

1. If for any reason (such as worn out bushes) the brake pedal needs to be removed, follow the procedures as described for the clutch pedal in Chapter 5, Section 4.

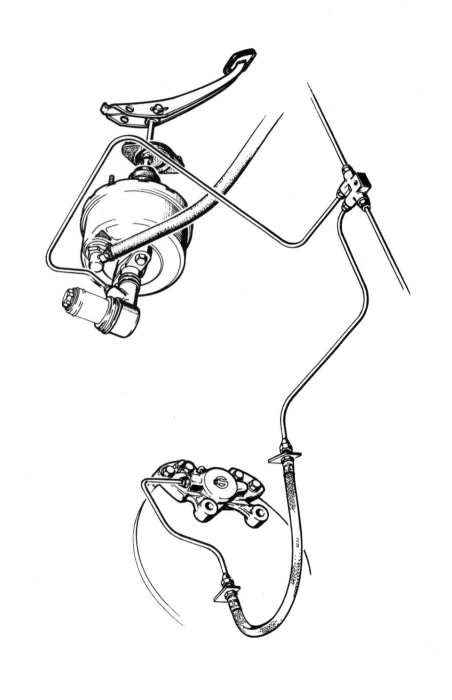

Fig.9.27. Drawing to show incorporation of brake servo unit into disc brake system.

Before diagnosing faults from the following chart, check that any braking irregularities are not caused by: —

1. Uneven and incorrect tyre pressures.
2. Incorrect 'mix' of radial and cross-ply tyres.
3. Wear in the steering mechanism.
4. Defects in the suspension and dampers.
5. Misalignment of the body frame.

NOTE: For vehicles fitted with disc brakes at the front the references in the chart to front wheel shoe adjustments do not apply. The causes referring to hydraulic system faults or wear to the friction material of the linings still apply however. Disc pads also come in different material and references to variations are also relevant.

Symptoms	Reason/s	Remedy
Pedal travels a long way before the brakes operate.	Brake shoes set too far from the drums.	Adjust the brake shoes to the drums.
Stopping ability poor, even though pedal pressure is firm.	Linings and/or drums badly worn or scored.	Dismantle, inspect and renew as required.
	One or more wheel hydraulic cylinders seized, resulting in some brake shoes not pressing against the drums (or pads against discs).	Dismantle and inspect wheel cylinders. Renew as necessary.
	Brake linings contaminated with oil.	Renew linings and repair source of oil contamination.
	Wrong type of linings fitted (too hard)	Verify type of material which is correct for the car and fit it.
	Brake shoes wrongly assembled.	Check for correct assembly.
	Servo unit not functioning (disc brakes)	Check and repair as necessary.
Car veers to one side when the brakes are applied.	Brake pads or linings on one side are contaminated with oil.	Renew pads or linings and stop oil leak.
	Hydraulic wheel cylinder(s) on one side partially or fully seized.	Inspect wheel cylinders for correct operation and renew as necessary.
	A mixture of lining materials fitted between sides.	Standardize on types of linings fitted.
	Unequal wear between sides caused by partially seized wheel cylinders.	Check wheel cylinders and renew linings and drums as required.
Pedal feels spongy when the brakes are applied.	Air is present in the hydraulic system.	Bleed the hydraulic system and check for any signs of leakage.
Pedal feels springy when the brakes are applied.	Brake linings not bedded into the drums (after fitting new ones).	Allow time for new linings to bed in after which it will certainly be necessary to adjust the shoes to the drums as pedal travel will have increased.
	Master cylinder or brake backplate mounting bolts loose.	Re-tighten mounting bolts.
	Severe wear in brake drums causing distortion when brakes are applied.	Renew drums and linings.
Pedal travels right down with little or no resistance and brakes are virtually non-operative.	Leak in hydraulic system resulting in lack of pressure for operating wheel cylinders.	Examine the whole of the hydraulic system and locate and repair source of leaks. Test after repairing each and every leak source.
	If no signs of leakage are apparent the master cylinder internal seals are failing to sustain pressure.	Overhaul master cylinder. If indications are that seals have failed for reasons other than wear all the wheel cylinder seals should be checked also and the system completely replenished with the correct fluid.
Binding, juddering overheating.	One or a combination of causes given in the foregoing sections.	Complete and systematic inspection of the whole braking system.

Chapter 10/Electrical System

Contents

Specifications

Battery

Standard	Exide 6 VTA7 BR or Lucas BH7/9A
	32 amp. hours at 20 hr. rate
Heavy duty	Exide VTM 11 BR
	53 amp. hours at 20 hr. rate
Earth..	Negative

Generator

Type...	Lucas C40 or C40/1
Output	22 amps. 2250 r.p.m. at 13.5 volts
Cut in speed	1450 r.p.m. at 13 volts
Field coil resistance	6 ohms.
Fabricated commutator undercut depth	.03 in. maximum
Moulded commutator undercut	NIL
Fabricated commutator minimum diameter...	1.385 in.
Moulded commutator minimum diameter	1.430 in.
Brush length minimum	.28 in.
Brush spring tension	30 oz. new brushes
	13 oz. at minimum brush length
Drive belt tension...	½ inch midway between fan and generator pulleys with load of 9 lbs.

Starter Motor

Type	Lucas M35G/1
Brush length minimum	.30 in.
Brush spring tension	34 — 46 oz. new brushes
	25 oz. minimum length
Minimum commutator diameter	1.28 in.
Free running current...	45 amps at 9,500 — 11,000 r.p.m
Lock torque.	10 lb/ft. at 420 — 440 amps
	7.8 — 7.4 volts

Type	Lucas M35J/PR
Brush length	.38 in. (9.5 mm) minimum
Spring pressure on brushes	At .06 in. (1.5 mm) protrusion -- 28 oz. (790 gms)
Minimum commutator thickness	.080 in. (2 mm)
Armature shaft end float..	.010 in. (.25 mm) maximum
Free running current...	65 amps at 8000 — 10,000 r.p.m.
Lock torque	7 lb/ft. at 350 — 375 amps

Type	Lucas M35K/PE
Brush length	.38 (9.5 mm) minimum
Spring pressure on brushes	At .06 in. (1.5 mm) protrusion - 28 ozs. (790 gms)
Minimum commutator thickness	.080 in. (2 mm)
Armature shaft end float	.010 maximum
Free running current...	70 amps at 8000 — 11,500 r.p.m.
Lock torque	8 lb/ft. at 350 — 400 amps

Voltage & Current Regulator (Dynamo)

Type	Lucas RB 340
Swamp resistor	53 - 57 ohms. between tag ends prior to assembly
	13.25 to 14.25 ohms. between centre tag and controller
	base after assembly
Field resistance	55 - 65 ohms.
Voltage regulator - shunt winding resistance	10.8 - 11.8 ohms. at 20°C
- open circuit settings	at 2000 r.p.m. engine speed

Air Pump	Volts
10°C	14.9 - 15.5
20°C	14.7 - 15.3
30°C	14.5 - 15.1
40°C	14.3 - 14.9
armature to core gap .056 to .060 in.	

Cut-out relay - shunt winding resistance	9.5 - 10.5 ohms.
- cut-in voltage	12.6 - 13.4 volts
- reverse current	8 amps maximum
- armature to core gap	.035 in. to .045 in.
- moving contact follow through	contacts just touching with gap of .015 in. between armature and core
Current regulator - load setting	21 - 23 amps
- armature to core gap...	.056 in. to .060 in.

Alternators

Type	Lucas 10 AC	11 AC
Voltage	12	12
Output	35 amps	45 amps
Field resistance (± 5%)	3.5 ohms	3.7 ohms
Brushes - minimum length	0.16 in.	0.16 in.

Regulator type..	4 TR
Voltage setting..	13.9 — 14.3 volts

Relay - Type	6 RA
Warning lamp contact type	3 A.W.

Type	Lucas 15 ACR	17 ACR
Voltage	12	12
Output	28 amps	36 amps
Field resistance (± 5%)	4.3 ohms	4.16 ohms
Brushes - minimum length	0.20 in.	0.20 in.
Brush spring pressure...	7 - 10 oz.	7 - 10 oz.
Regulator (incorporated)	8 TR	

Windscreen Wiper Motors

Type...	Delco 258
Normal running current consumption..	2.5 amps, warm
Drive to wheel boxes...	Crank and cross-shaft
Armature shaft clearance in bushes	.002 in. max.
Cross-shaft clearance in bushes	.003 in. max.
Stall torque at crank	5 lb/ft.
Later type — permanent magnet	
Cross-shaft end float	.001 — .013 in. (.025 - .325 mm)
Wormwheel end float..	.002 in. (.05 mm) maximum
High speed running current (warm)	2 amps after 5 — 10 minutes
Low speed running current (warm)	1.2 amps after 5 — 10 minutes

Fuses

A fuse block is mounted in the engine compartment on the bulkhead behind the dash panel and contains four 35 amp fuses and provision for 2 spares

Fuse No.1 protects:	Windscreen wiper, cigarette lighter, radio and fog/spot lamps
Fuse No.2 protects:	Fuel gauge, ignition and oil warning lamps, stop lamp, direction indicator lamps, heater motor, temperature gauge and reversing lamps.
Fuse No.3 protects:	Headlamp flashers, horn, interior lamp, map reading and parking lamps.
Fuse No.4 protects:	Instrument lamps, number plate lamps, tail lamps, boot interior lamp and cigarette lighter lamp.

Bulbs

Headlamps	60/50 watt - bayonet fitting L.H. dip (U.K.)
	45/40 watt - clip fitting R.H. dip (Europe)
Side number plate, and boot interior lamps	6 watt - miniature centre contact
Tail/stop lamp...	6/21 watt - small bayonet cap
Direction indicator lamps	21 watt - single centre contact
Interior dome	6 watt - festoon
Direction indicator, main beam indicator, ignition and oil warning and instrument lamps	2.2 watt - miniature Edison screw

Flasher Unit

Frequency	75 — 100 flashes per minute

Torque Wrench Settings

Alternator through bolts..	47 lbs/inches
Alternator rectifier securing nut	37 lbs/inches

1. General Description

1. The electrical system is of the 12-volt type and the major components comprise: A 12-volt battery with the negative terminal earthed. A large warning label is put near the battery mounting to indicate this ('Negative Ground') as damage could result if the connection was incorrectly made or if certain electrical parts were fitted which did not also conform to this; a voltage regulator and cut-out; a Lucas dynamo or alternator which is fitted to the front left-hand side of the engine and is driven by the fan belt from the crankshaft pulley wheel; and a starter motor which is fitted to the clutch bell-housing on the right-hand side of the engine.

2. The 12-volt battery supplies a steady amount of current for the ignition, lighting, and other electrical circuits, and provides a reserve of electricity when the current consumed by the electrical equipment exceeds that being produced by the dynamo or alternator.

3. The dynamo is of the two brush type and works in conjunction with the voltage regulator and cut-out. The dynamo is cooled by a multi-bladed fan mounted behind the dynamo pulley, and blows air through cooling holes

in the dynamo end brackets. The output from the dynamo is controlled by the voltage regulator which ensures a high output if the battery is in a low state of charge or the demands from the electrical equipment high, and a low output if the battery is fully charged and there is little demand from the electrical equipment.

4. The C40/L dynamo fitted to certain models differs little from the C40 type but has a higher output. The physical differences between the two dynamos are that the C40/L unit has a smaller fan pulley wheel; an improved output fan; no oil retainer ring on the front bracket; differently rated springs and brushes; and some C40 commutators are of the moulded type. Later models of the Viva HB were fitted with alternators. Four different types were used, early units being the Lucas 10AC or 11AC in conjunction with a 4TR regulator, 6RA relay and 3AW warning lamp control. Later on, the 15ACR or 17ACR (heavy duty) units were used which incorporated the regulator and control in the body of the alternator. On some cars the AC-Delco 28 and 35 amp units may be used as alternatives.

2. Battery — Removal & Replacement

1. Disconnect the negative (earth) lead from the battery terminal post and then the positive lead similarly. The leads are held by either a clamp, which necessitates slackening the clamp bolt and nut, or by a screw driven through an all enclosing shroud. (Photo).

2. Remove the battery clamp and carefully lift the battery out of its compartment. Hold the battery vertical to ensure that none of the electrolyte is spilled (see photo).

3. Replacement is a direct reversal of this procedure. NOTE' Replace the positive lead before the earth (negative) lead and smear the terminals with petroleum jelly (vaseline) to prevent corrosion. NEVER use an ordinary grease as applied to other parts of the car.

3. Battery — Maintenance & Inspection

1. Normal weekly battery maintenance consists of checking the electrolyte level of each cell to ensure that the separators are covered by ¼ in. of electrolyte. If the level has fallen, top up the battery using distilled water only. Do not overfill. If a battery is overfilled or any electrolyte spilled, immediately wipe away the excess as electrolyte attacks and corrodes any metal it comes into contact with very rapidly.

2. As well as keeping the terminals clean and covered with petroleum jelly, the top of the battery, and especially the top of the cells, should be kept clean and dry. This helps prevent corrosion and ensures that the battery does not become partially discharged by leakage through dampness and dirt.

3. Once every three months, remove the battery and inspect the battery securing bolts, the battery clamp plate, tray and battery leads for corrosion (white fluffy deposits on the metal which are brittle to touch). If any corrosion is found, clean off the deposits with ammonia and paint over the clean metal with an anti-rust/anti-acid paint.

4. At the same time inspect the battery case for cracks. If a crack is found, clean and plug it with one of the proprietary compounds marketed by firms, such as Holts, for this purpose. If leakage through the crack has been excessive then it will be necessary to refill the appropriate cell with fresh electrolyte as detailed later. Cracks are frequently caused to the top of the battery cases by pouring in distilled water in the middle of winter AFTER instead of BEFORE a run. This gives the water no chance to mix with the electrolyte and so the former freezes and splits the battery case.

5. If topping up the battery becomes excessive and the case has been inspected for cracks that could cause leakage, but none are found, the battery is being over-charged and the voltage regulator will have to be checked and reset.

6. With the battery on the bench at the three monthly interval check, measure its specific gravity with a hydrometer to determine the state of charge and condition of the electrolyte. There should be very little variation between the different cells and if a variation in excess of 0.025 is present it will be due to either:-

a) Loss of electrolyte from the battery at some time caused by spillage or a leak, resulting in a drop in the specific gravity of the electrolyte when the deficiency was replaced with distilled water instead of fresh electrolyte.

b) An internal short circuit caused by buckling of the plates or a similar malady pointing to the likelihood of total battery failure in the near future.

7. The specific gravity of the electrolyte for fully charged conditions at the electrolyte temperature indicated, is listed in Table A. The specific gravity of a fully discharged battery at different temperatures of the electrolyte is given in Table B.

Table A
Specific Gravity — Battery fully charged

1.268 at 100°F or 38°C electrolyte temperature
1.272 at 90°F or 32°C electrolyte temperature
1.276 at 80°F or 27°C electrolyte temperature
1.280 at 70°F or 21°C electrolyte temperature
1.284 at 60°F or 16°C electrolyte temperature
1.288 at 50°F or 10°C electrolyte temperature
1.292 at 40°F or   4°C electrolyte temperature
1.296 at 30°F or -1.5°C electrolyte temperature

Table B
Specific Gravity — Battery fully discharged

1.098 at 100°F or 38°C electrolyte temperature
1.102 at 90°F or 32°C electrolyte temperature
1.106 at 80°F or 27°C electrolyte temperature
1.110 at 70°F or 21°C electrolyte temperature
1.114 at 60°F or 16°C electrolyte temperature
1.118 at 50°F or 10°C electrolyte temperature
1.122 at 40°F or   4°C electrolyte temperature
1.126 at 30°F or -1.5°C electrolyte temperature

4. Electrolyte Replenishment

1. If the battery is in a fully charged state and one of the cells maintains a specific gravity reading which is 0.025 or more lower than the others, and a check of each cell has been made with a voltage meter to check for short circuits (a four to seven second test should give a steady reading of between 1.2 to 1.8 volts), then it is likely that electrolyte has been lost from the cell with the low reading at some time.

2. Top the cell up with a solution of 1 part suphuric acid to 2.5 parts of water. If the cell is already fully topped up draw some electrolyte out of it with a pipette.

3. When mixing the sulphuric acid and water NEVER ADD WATER TO SULPHURIC ACID-always pour the acid slowly onto the water in a glass container. IF WATER IS ADDED TO SULPHURIC ACID IT WILL EXPLODE.

4. Continue to top up the cell with the freshly made electrolyte and then recharge the battery and check the hydrometer readings.

5. Battery Charging

1. In winter time when heavy demand is placed upon the battery, such as when starting from cold, and much electrical equipment is continually in use, it is a good idea occasionally to have the battery fully charged from an external source at the rate of 3.5 to 4 amps.

2. Continue to charge the battery at this rate until no further rise in specific gravity is noted over a four hour period.

3. Alternatively, a trickle charger, charging at the rate of 1.5 amps can be safely used overnight.

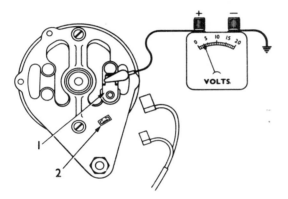

Fig.10.1. SHOWING CONNECTION OF VOLTMETER FOR OUTPUT TEST OF DYNAMO

1. Output (D) terminal   2. Field (F) terminal

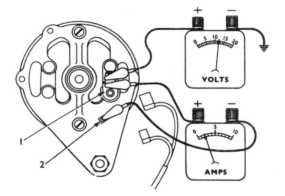

Fig.10.2. SHOWING CONNECTIONS OF VOLTMETER AND AMMETER FOR TEST OF FIELD CIRCUIT OF DYNAMO

1. Output (D) terminal   2. Field (F) terminal

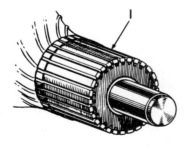

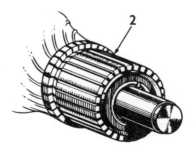

Fig.10.3. Diagram showing dynamo armature with (1) moulded commutator and (2) fabricated commutator.

4. Specially rapid 'boost' charges which are claimed to restore the power of the battery in 1 to 2 hours are most dangerous as they can cause serious damage to the battery plates through over-heating.

5. While charging the battery note that the temperature of the electrolyte should never exceed 100°F.

6. Dynamo — Routine Maintenance

1. Routine maintenance consists of checking the tension of the fan belt, and lubricating the dynamo rear bearing once every 6,000 miles.

2. The fan belt should be tight enough to ensure no slip between the belt and the dynamo pulley. If a shrieking noise comes from the engine when the unit is accelerated rapidly, it is likely that it is the fan belt slipping. On the other hand, the belt must not be too taut or the bearings will wear rapidly and cause dynamo failure or bearing seizure. Ideally ½ in. of total free movement should be available at the fan belt, midway between the fan and the dynamo pulley.

3. To adjust the fan belt tension, slightly slacken the three dynamo retaining bolts, and swing the dynamo on the upper two bolts outwards to increase the tension, and inwards to lower it.

4. It is best to leave the bolts fairly tight so that considerable effort has to be used to move the dynamo, otherwise it is difficult to get the correct setting. If the dynamo is being moved outwards to increase the tension and the bolts have only been slackened a little, a long spanner acting as a lever placed behind the dynamo with the lower end resting against the block, works very well in moving the dynamo outwards. Retighten the dynamo bolts and check that the dynamo pulley is correctly aligned with the fan belt.

5. Lubrication on the dynamo consists of inserting three drops of S.A.E.30 engine oil in the small oil hole in the centre of the commutator end bracket. This lubricates the rear bearing. The front bearing is pre-packed with grease and requires no attention.

7. Dynamo — Testing in Position

1. If, with the engine running, no charge comes from the dynamo, or the charge is very low, first check that the fan belt is in place and is not slipping. Then check that the leads from the control box to the dynamo are firmly attached and that one has not come loose from its terminal.

2. The lead from the 'D' terminal on the dynamo should be connected to the 'D' terminal on the control box, and similarly the 'F' terminals on the dynamo and control box should also be connected together. Check that this is so and that the leads have not been incorrectly fitted.

3. Make sure none of the electrical equipment (such as the lights or radio) is on, and then pull the leads off the dynamo terminals marked 'D' and 'F'.

4. Using a voltmeter (rated up to 20 volts) connect the positive lead to the output 'D' terminal of the generator and the negative lead to earth (see Fig.10.1). With the engine running at approximately 1500 r.p.m. there should be a reading of 2–4 volts.

5. If there is no reading a possible cause may be a lack of residual magnetism in the field coil pole shoes. To rectify this, flash a lead from the battery positive terminal to the field (F) terminal on the dynamo. If there is still no reading then check the brushes and brush connections.

6. If the output reading is satisfactory it will be necessary to check the field circuit. With the voltmeter still connected as before connect in addition an ammeter with its negative lead to the field (F) terminal and its positive lead to the 'D' terminal of the dynamo (see Fig.10.2).

7. Run the engine and increase the revolutions slowly until the voltmeter reads 12 volts. The ammeter should then read approximately 2 amps. It is also advisable to check this again when the generator has reached normal running temperature (after about fifteen minutes).

8. If the dynamo tests are satisfactory, any failure to charge the battery must be due to a break in the wiring or a fault in the voltage control/regulator unit.

8. Dynamo — Removal & Replacement

1. Slacken the two dynamo retaining bolts, and the bolt on the sliding link, and move the dynamo in towards the engine so that the fan belt can be removed.

2. Disconnect the two leads from the dynamo terminals.

3. Remove the sliding link bolt, and remove the two upper bolts. The dynamo is then free to be lifted away from the engine.

4. Replacement is a reversal of the above procedure. Do not finally tighten the retaining bolts and the bolt on the sliding link until the fan belt has been tensioned correctly. (See Chapter 2.11. for details).

9. Dynamo — Dismantling & Inspection

1. Mount the dynamo in a vice and unscrew and remove the two through bolts from the commutator end bracket. (See photo).

2. The end bracket may now be pulled off the armature. Take care not to damage or break the field coil wire attached to the smaller of the two terminal connectors. This connector will draw out of the end plate. Note also that there is a raised pip in the end plate which engages in a small recess in the dynamo casing. This ensures that the end plate is correctly lined up when replaced. (See photo).

3. Lift the two brush springs and draw the brushes out of the brush holders (arrowed).

4. Measure the brushes and, if worn down to 9/32 in. or less, unscrew the screws holding the brush leads to the end bracket. Take off the brushes complete with leads. Old and new brushes are compared in the photograph.

5. Then pull the drive end bracket complete with armature out of the casing.

6. Check the condition of the ball bearing in the drive end plate by firmly holding the plate and noting if there is visible side movement of the armature shaft in relation to the end plate. If play is present, the armature assembly must be separated from the end plate. If the bearing is sound there is no need to carry out the work described in the following two paragraphs.

7. Hold the armature in one hand (mount it carefully in a vice if preferred) and undo the nut holding the pulley wheel and fan in place. Pull off the pulley wheel and fan.

8. Next remove the woodruff key (arrowed) from its slot in the armature shaft and also the bearing locating ring.

9. Place the drive end bracket across the open jaws of a vice with the armature downwards and gently tap the armature shaft from the bearing in the end plate with the aid of a suitable drift. Support the armature so that it does not fall to the ground.

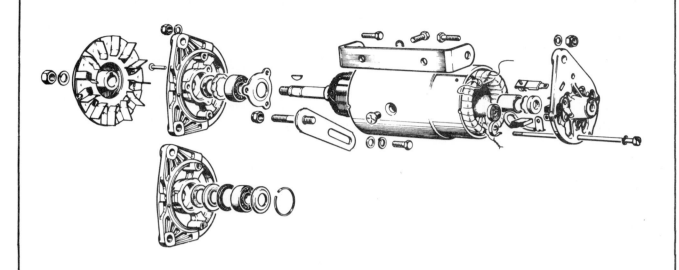

Fig.10.4. Dynamo — exploded view showing alternative ball bearing retaining methods in the end cover (plate and rivets or spacer and circlip).

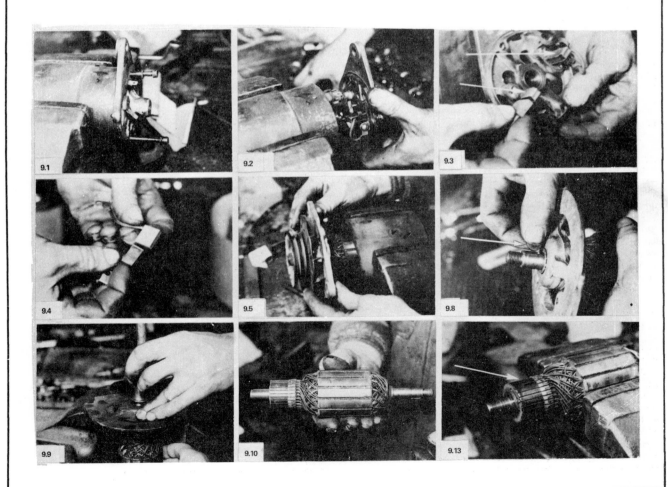

10 Carefully inspect the armature and check it for open or short circuited windings. It is a good indication of an open circuited armature when the commutator segments are burnt. If the armature has short circuited the commutator segments will be very badly burnt, and the overheated armature windings badly discoloured. If open or short circuits are suspected substitute the suspect armature with a new one.

11 Check the resistance of the field coils. To do this, connect an ohmmeter between the field terminal and the yoke and note the reading on the ohmmeter which should be about 6 ohms. If the ohmmeter reading is infinity this indicates an open circuit in the field winding. If the ohmmeter reading is below 5 ohms this indicates that one of the field coils is faulty and must be replaced.

12 Field coil replacement involves the use of a wheel operated screwdriver, a soldering iron, caulking and riveting and this operation is considered to be beyond the scope of most owners. Therefore, if the field coils are at fault either purchase a rebuilt dynamo, or take the casing to a Vauxhall dealer or electrical engineering works for new field coils to be fitted.

13 Next check the condition of the commutator (arrowed). If it is dirty and blackened, as shown, clean it with a petrol dampened rag. If the commutator is in good condition the surface will be smooth and quite free from pits or burnt areas, and the insulated segments clearly defined.

14 If, after the commutator has been cleaned, pits and burnt spots are still present, wrap a strip of glass paper round the commutator taking great care to move the commutator ¼ of a turn every ten rubs till it is thoroughly clean.

15 In extreme cases of wear the commutator can be mounted in a lathe and with the lathe turning at high speed, a very fine cut may be taken off the commutator. Then polish the commutator with glass paper. If the commutator has worn so that the insulators between the segments are level with the top of the segments, then undercut the insulators to a depth of 1/32 in. (.8 mm). This applies to fabricated commutators only. Do NOT undercut moulded commutators. (See Fig.10.3). The best tool to use for this purpose is half a hacksaw blade ground to a thickness of the insulator, and with the handle end of the blade covered in insulating tape to make it comfortable to hold. For the sort of finish the surface of the commutator should have when finished. (see photo).

16 Check the bush bearing (arrowed) in the commutator end bracket for wear, by noting if the armature spindle rocks when placed in it. If worn, it must be renewed.

17 The bush bearing can be removed by a suitable extractor or by screwing a 5/8 in. tap four or five times into the bush. The tap complete with bush is then pulled out of the end bracket.

18 NOTE: The bush bearing is made of a porous bronze material which needs to be saturated in engine oil before use. Oil can be forced through it, before installation, by blocking one end with a thumb, filling it with oil and squeezing it through the material by forcing a finger in at the other end. Otherwise, soak it in oil for several hours. If the oil is hot it will saturate the material more quickly.

19 Carefully fit the new bush into the end plate, pressing it in until the end of the bearing is flush with the inner side of the end plate. If available, press the bush in with a smooth shouldered mandrel the same diameter as the armature shaft.

10. Dynamo — Repair & Reassembly

1. To renew the ball bearing fitted to the drive end bracket, drill out the rivets which hold the bearing retainer plate to the end bracket and lift off the plate. On later models the bearing is held by a circlip which is quite simply removed to release the bearing from the end plate.

2. Press out the bearing from the end bracket and remove the corrugated and felt washers from the bearing housing.

3. Thoroughly clean the bearing housing and the new bearing, and pack with high melting point grease.

4. Place the felt washer and corrugated washer, in that order, in the end bracket bearing housing. On later models when the bearing is retained by a circlip there are a felt ring, retaining washer and pressure ring to be fitted in the housing before the bearing.

5. Then fit the new bearing as shown.

6. Gently tap the bearing into place with the aid of a suitable drift.

7. Replace the bearing plate and fit three new rivets (or fit the collar and circlip).

8. Open up the rivets with the aid of a suitable cold chisel.

9. Finally peen over the open end of the rivets with the aid of a ball hammer as illustrated.

10 Refit the drive end bracket to the armature shaft. Do not try and force the bracket on but. with the aid of a suitable socket abutting the bearing, tap the bearing on gently, so pulling the end bracket down with it.

11 Slide the spacer up the shaft and refit the woodruff key.

12 Replace the fan and pulley wheel and then fit the spring washer and nut and tighten the latter. The drive bracket end of the dynamo is now fully assembled as shown.

13 If the brushes are little worn and are to be used again then ensure that they are placed in the same holders from which they were removed. When refitting brushes, either new or old, check that they move freely in their holders. If either brush sticks, clean with a petrol moistened rag and if still stiff, lightly polish the sides of the brush with a very fine file until the brush moves quite freely in its holder.

14 Tighten the two retaining screws and washers which hold the wire leads to the brushes in place.

15 It is far easier to slip the end piece with brushes over the commutator if the brushes are raised in their holders, as shown, and held in this position by the pressure of the springs resting against their flanks (arrowed).

16 Refit the armature to the casing and then the commutator end plate, and screw up the two through bolts.

17 Finally, hook the ends of the two springs off the flanks of the brushes and onto their heads so that the brushes are forced down into contact with the armature.

11. Alternators — General Description

Alternators are becoming more common as a replacement for the dynamo because they provide a higher output for lower weight and are able to cope with the full electrical loads at low revolutions.

Basically the alternator, as its name implies, generates alternating current rather than direct current. This current is rectified (by diodes) into direct current so that it can be stored by the battery. The transistorized regulators are self limiting in current output so they

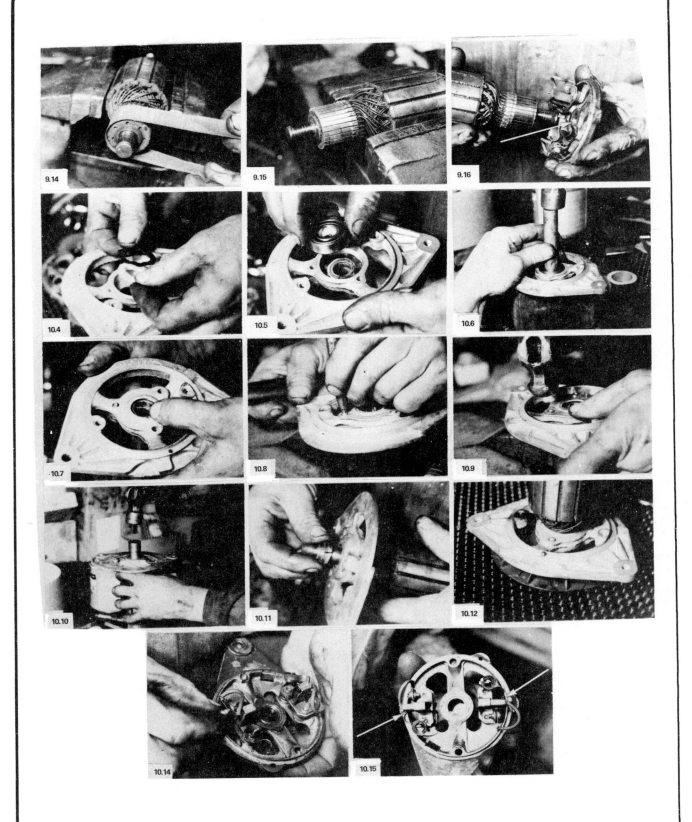

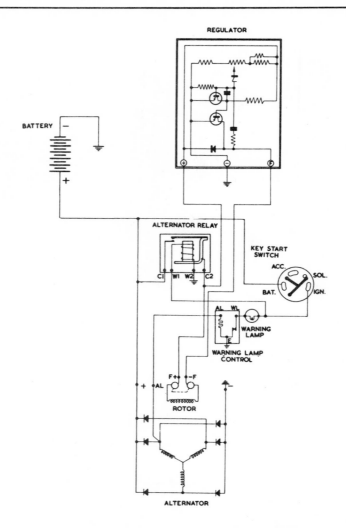

Fig.10.5. Lucas 10AC and 11AC alternator systems circuit diagram.

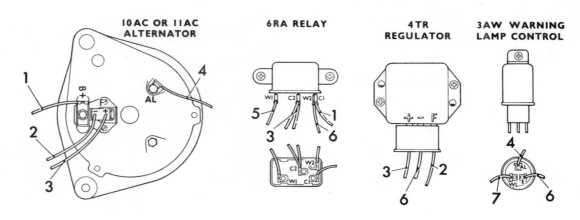

Fig.10.6. LUCAS 10AC & 11AC ALTERNATOR SYSTEMS TERMINAL CONNECTIONS

1. Brown
2. Brown/Green
3. Brown/White
4. Brown/Purple
5. White
6. Black
7. Brown/Yellow

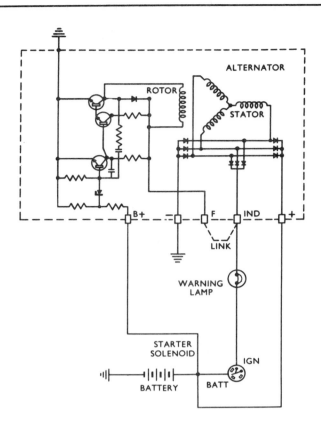

Fig.10.8. Lucas 15ACR and 17ACR alternator systems circuit diagram.

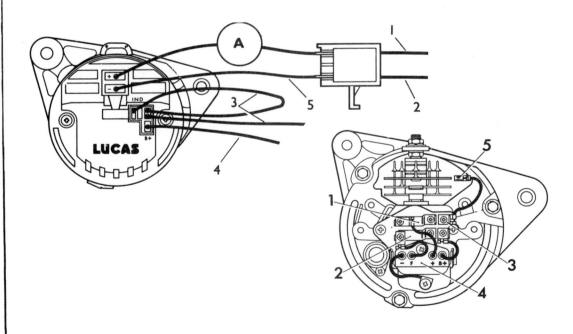

Fig.10.7. LUCAS 15ACR & 17ACR ALTERNATOR SYSTEMS TERMINAL CONNECTIONS

A1. Brown 65/.012	A4. Brown 14/.012	B2. Inner contact strip	B5. Field diode heat sink
A2. Black	A5. Slave wire	B3. Indicator terminal	wire (Yellow)
A3. Brown/Yellow	B1. Outer contact strip	B4. 8TR regulator	

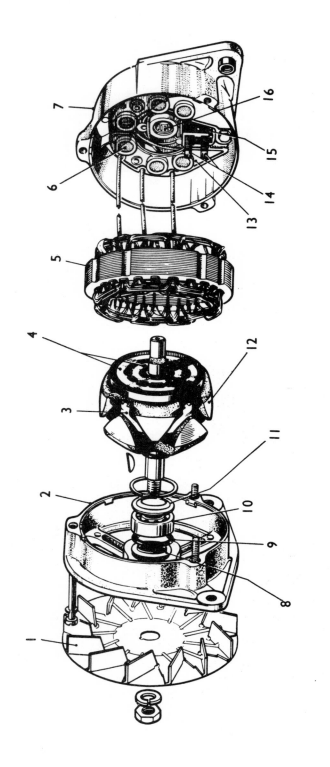

Fig.10.9. LUCAS 10AC & 11AC ALTERNATORS – EXPLODED DRAWING

1. Fan	4. Slip rings	7. Slip ring end cover	10. Bearing	13. Diode heat sink	16. Needle roller bearing
2. Drive end cover	5. Stator	8. 'O' ring retainer washer	11. Bearing retaining plate	14. Brushes	
3. Rotor field windings	6. Diodes	9. 'O' ring oil seal	12. Rotor	15. Brush holder	

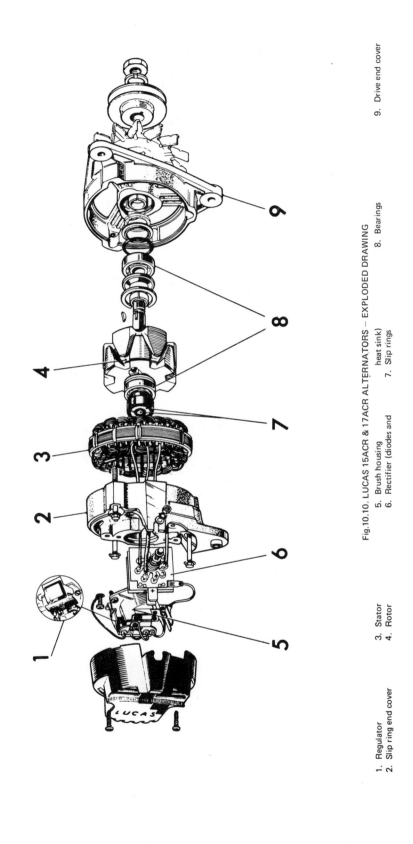

Fig.10.10. LUCAS 15ACR & 17ACR ALTERNATORS – EXPLODED DRAWING

1. Regulator
2. Slip ring end cover
3. Stator
4. Rotor
5. Brush housing
6. Rectifier (diodes and heat sink)
7. Slip rings
8. Bearings
9. Drive end cover

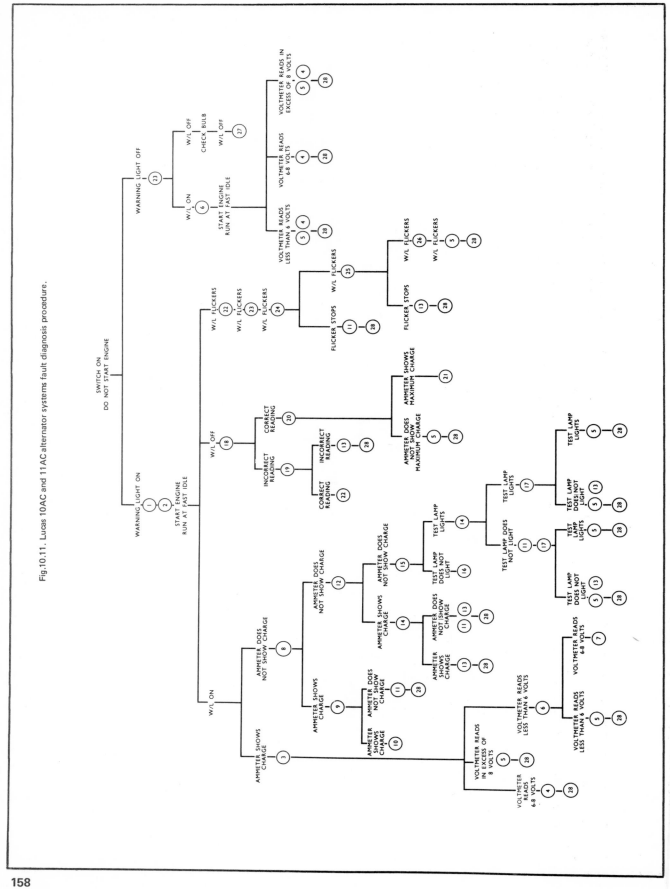

Fig.10.11. Lucas 10AC and 11AC alternator systems fault diagnosis procedure.

1. Check fan belt(s) for tension and condition.

2. Disconnect battery ground terminal. Disconnect wire (brown) from alternator positive terminal and connect ammeter between wire and terminal. Reinstall battery terminal.

3. Remove warning lamp control three-way connector and connect voltmeter between 'AL' wire (brown/purple) and ground.

4. Install new warning lamp control.

5. Install new or repair alternator.

6. Connect voltmeter between alternator 'AL' and ground.

7. Check wire (brown/purple) between alternator 'AL' and warning lamp control 'AL' for continuity.

8. Disconnect 'C1' wire (brown) and 'C2' wire (brown/white) from relay and join together.

9. Reconnect 'C1' wire (brown) and 'C2' wire (brown/white) to relay and check 'W2' terminal to ground.

10. Check all relay connections for cleanliness and security.

11. Install new relay.

12. With 'C1' and 'C2' relay wires joined together, remove three-way connector from regulator and bridge ground wire (black) and field wire (brown/green) in connector.

13. Install new regulator.

14. Reconnect wires to 'C1' and 'C2' terminals on relay.

15. Remove field double connector from alternator and connect test lamp between terminals of connector.

16. Check field wires and connections between: starter solenoid and relay 'C1' (brown); relay 'C2' and regulator positive and alternator 'F' positive (brown/white); regulator 'F' terminal and alternator 'F' negative (brown/green); regulator negative terminal to ground (black).

17. Reconnect three-way connector to regulator.

18. Connect voltmeter between battery positive and negative terminals, switch on lights and increase engine speed to approximately 1500 rpm. Voltmeter should read 13.9 to 14.3 volts.

19. Disconnect voltmeter from between battery positive and negative terminals: connect voltmeter between regulator positive terminal and ground.

20. Remove three-way connector from regulator and bridge field wire (brown/green) and negative wire (black) in regulator connector; increase engine speed.

21. If fan belt(s) tension and condition are satisfactory, a faulty battery or an overloaded system is indicated. A comparison should be made between electrical loading and alternator output. (10AC: 35 amp; 11AC: 45 amp).

22. Clean connections 'C1' and 'C2' on relay: clean positive and negative connections on regulator and regulator ground connections: clean battery posts and terminals.

23. Remove warning lamp control three-way connector and bridge ground wire (black) and 'WL' wire (brown/yellow) in connector.

24. Bridge 'C1' and 'C2' terminals on relay.

25. Remove bridge from between 'C1' and 'C2' terminals on relay and link regulator 'F' and negative wires.

26. Check warning lamp bulb. Check bulb-holder for loose connection.

27. Check continuity of warning lamp circuit, i.e. battery to warning lamp (green): warning lamp to warning lamp control 'WL' (brown/yellow): warning lamp control 'E' terminal to ground (black).

28. Check that charging system operates satisfactorily by connecting voltmeter across battery terminals and ammeter in series with alternator output circuit. Impose approximate 35 amp (10AC) or 45 amp (11AC) load on battery, start engine and increase engine speed until ammeter reads maximum charge (35 amp and 45 amp respectively). Remove load from battery. Ammeter needle should then drop slowly back to show trickle charge. Voltmeter should show 13.9 to 14.3 volts.

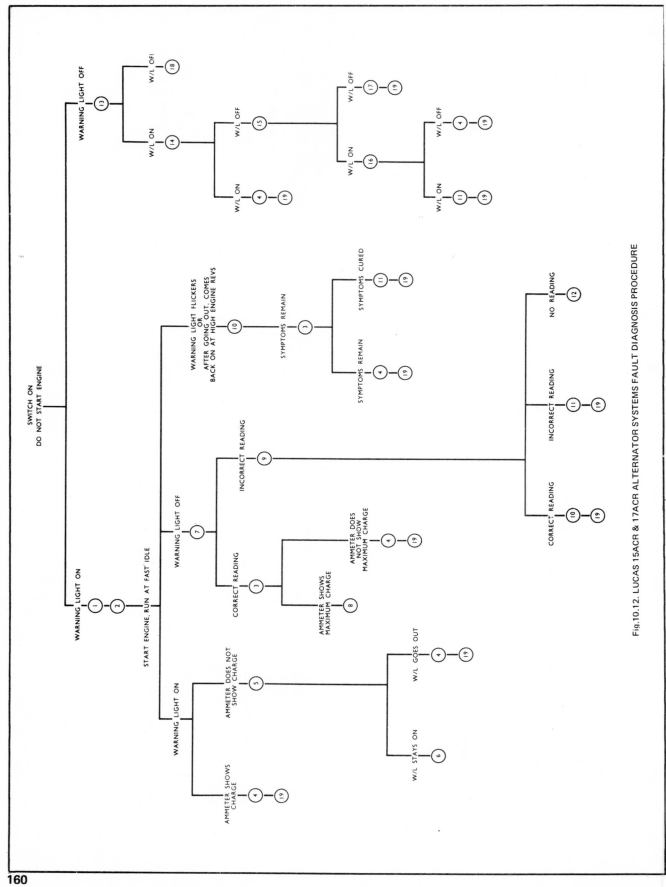

Fig.10,12. LUCAS 15ACR & 17ACR ALTERNATOR SYSTEMS FAULT DIAGNOSIS PROCEDURE

1. Check fan belt(s) for tension and condition.

2. Disconnect main output connector and auxiliary connector. Install slave wire with a male Lucar terminal and a female Lucar terminal between alternator negative terminal and socket. Connect ammeter between alternator positive terminal and socket removed from this terminal. Reconnect auxiliary connector. See illustration on page 39.

3. Remove rear cover from alternator. Reinstall auxiliary connector, slave and ammeter wires. Bridge outer brush contact strip to ground. Adjust engine speed to give maximum output.

4. Install new or repair alternator.

5. Remove connector from field and sensing terminals (IND and B+). 'Switch On' but do not start engine.

6. Check for short circuit in wire between alternator indicator terminal and warning light bulb.

7. Connect voltmeter between battery positive and negative terminals; increase speed to approximately 1500 rpm. Voltmeter should read 14.1 to 14.5 volts, ammeter reading 7.5 amp maximum. Higher amperage which would probably give lower voltage readings could indicate need to recharge battery before continuing with test.

8. If fan belt tension and condition are satisfactory, faulty battery or overloaded system is indicated. Comparison should be made between electrical loading and alternator output. 15ACR: 28 amp. 17ACR: 36 amp.

9. Remove voltmeter from battery and connect it between battery sensing terminal on alternator (B+) and ground (this should be done without moving socket connector by inserting a probe in rear of connector to contact Lucas female blade terminal of brown 14/.012 wire).

10. Check battery terminals, ground strap connections, and wiring between battery and alternator for poor connection and resistive circuits.

11. Install new 8TR regulator.

12. Check wire from alternator B+ to starter solenoid for continuity.

13. Remove connector from alternator indicator socket and bridge double wires (brown/yellow 9/.012) in connector to ground.

14. Remove rear cover from alternator, reinstall socket connectors. Disconnect yellow wire from field diode heat sink.

15. Reconnect yellow wire to field diode heat sink. Connect slave wire between outer brush contact strip and ground.

16. Disconnect slave wire from outer brush contact strip and connect between inner brush contact strip and ground.

17. Check connecting wire between indicator and field terminals in socket connector for continuity.

18. Check warning lamp bulb. Check bulb-holder for loose connection. Check wire (brown/yellow) between alternator indicator terminal, warning lamp bulb and key-start switch for continuity. Note: warning lamp bulb must be 12 volt 2.2 watt.

19. Check that charging system operates satisfactorily by connecting voltmeter across battery terminals and ammeter in series with alternator output circuit. Impose approximate 28 amp (15ACR) or 36 amp (17ACR) load on battery, start engine and increase engine speed until ammeter reads maximum charge, 28 amp and 36 amp respectively. Remove load from battery. Ammeter should then drop slowly back to show trickle charge. Voltmeter should show 14.1 to 14.5 volts.

control only the voltage. The relays and warning lamp controls are fitted only to the earlier 10AC and 11AC systems.

Apart from the renewal of the rotor slip ring brushes and rotor shaft bearings, there are no other parts which need periodic inspection. All other items are sealed assemblies and must be replaced if indications are that they are faulty.

12. Alternators — Safety Precautions

If there are indications that the charging system is malfunctioning in any way, care must be taken to diagnose faults properly, otherwise damage of a serious and expensive nature may occur to parts which are in fact quite serviceable.

The following basic requirements must be observed at all times therefore, if damage is to be prevented.
1. ALL alternator systems use a NEGATIVE earth. Even the simple mistake of connecting a battery the wrong way round could burn out the alternator diodes in a few seconds.
2. Before disconnecting any wires in the system the engine and ignition circuits should be switched off. This will minimise accidental short circuits.
3. The alternator must NEVER be run with the output wire disconnected.
4. Always disconnect the battery from the car's electrical system if an outside charging source is being used.
5. Do not use test wire connections that could move accidentally and short circuit against nearby terminals. Short circuits will not blow fuses — they will blow diodes or transistors.
6. Always disconnect the battery cables and alternator output wires before any electric welding work is done on the car body.

13. Lucas 10AC & 11AC Alternator Systems — Fault Diagnosis

1. It is essential that when a fault occurs the correct procedure is followed to diagnose it. If it is not, the likelihood of damage is high. The safety precautions as described in Section 12 should always be observed
2. No proper diagnosis is possible without an ammeter (0—100 amps range) a voltmeter (0—50 volts range) and a test lamp (12v 6 watt) being available. If you are unable to acquire these then leave the circuit checking to a competent electrician.
3. Check the obvious first, i.e. battery, battery terminals, fan belt tension and disconnected wires.
4. Follow the line of diagnosis as shown in Fig.10.11, and the accompanying table.

14. Lucas 15ACR or 17ACR Alternator Systems — Fault Diagnosis

1. Paragraphs 1—3 in the previous section apply. Thereafter follow the line of diagnosis as shown in Fig.10.12.

15. Alternators — Dismantling & Inspection

1. If tests indicate that the alternator is faulty it is possible that the slip ring brushes and slip rings may be the cause. In this case the remedy is simple on the 10AC and 11AC units.

2. After removing the fan and pulley nut, the through bolts may be removed. Mark the position of the end covers relative to the stator and withdraw the drive end cover and rotor together. The brushes may be checked for length and the slip rings cleaned up with fine glass paper.
3. 15ACR and 17ACR alternators require the unsoldering of the stator connections to get at the brushes and slip ring and this is not recommended. If the diodes to which they are attached are overheated they could be damaged.
4. Although, therefore, there is the possibility of an owner successfully rectifying a fault on the 10/11 AC types we do not recommend dismantling as a general principle, as more damage could be caused to the system — not just the alternator if a mistake is made.
5. When an alternator is diagnosed as unserviceable it should only be as a result of a thorough check of the complete system. If this is not done a new unit could be completely ruined immediately following installation if something is also at fault elsewhere.

16. Starter Motor M35 G/1 — General Description

The starter motor is mounted on the right-hand lower side of the engine end plate, and is held in position by two bolts. The motor is of the four field coil, four pole piece type, and utilises four spring-loaded commutator brushes. Two of these brushes are earthed, and the other two are insulated and attached to the field coil ends.

17. Starter Motor M35 G/1 — Testing in the Car

1. If the starter motor fails to operate then check the condition of the battery by turning on the headlamps. If they glow brightly for several seconds and then gradually dim, the battery is in an uncharged condition.
2. If the headlamps glow brightly and it is obvious that the battery is in good condition then check the tightness of the battery wiring connections (and in particular the earth lead from the battery terminal to its connection on the bodyframe). Check the tightness of the connections at the relay switch and at the starter motor.
3. If the starter motor still fails to turn the fault lies in the wiring, the solenoid switch or the motor itself. The following procedure will determine where the fault lies.
4. Connect a voltmeter (or 12 volt bulb) to the terminal to which the white/red wire is connected (Fig.10.13). If there is no reading (12 volts) when the starter switch is operated, there is a fault in the starter switch or white/red wire.
5. If there is a reading on the previous test, disconnect the white/red lead and connect an Ammeter as shown in Fig.10.14. When the starter switch is operated there should be a 4 to 6 amp reading. If not the solenoid switch needs renewal.
6. If previous two tests are favourable connect voltmeter (or 12 volt bulb) to the two main terminals as shown in Fig.10.15. A 12 volt reading should be obtained (without touching the starter switch). If the starter switch is operated the reading should fall to zero (bulb goes out). If it does not the solenoid switch needs renewal.
7. If the previous three tests are favourable then any fault must lie with the starter motor itself.
8. The remaining terminal on the solenoid switch, to which the white/blue lead is attached, is the cold start feed to the coil which directs current to the coil only when the solenoid is operating. It can be tested by

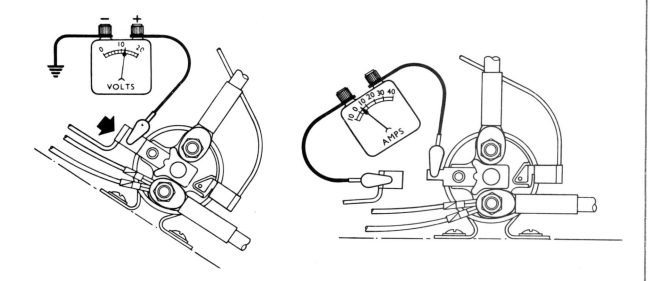

Fig.10.13. Connection of voltmeter to solenoid starter switch for testing.

Fig.10.14. Connection of Ammeter to solenoid starter switch for testing

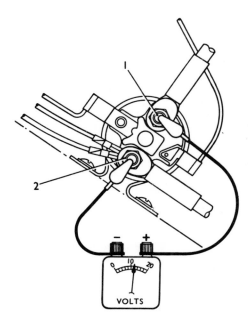

Fig.10.15. Connection of voltmeter across solenoid starter switch terminals for testing.

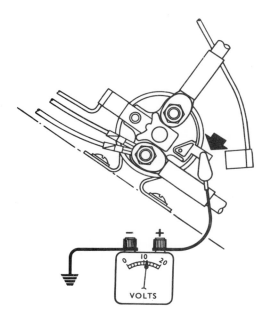

Fig.10.16. Connection of voltmeter to solenoid starter switch for testing coil cold start connection.

connecting a voltmeter (or 12v bulb) to the terminal, after disconnecting the lead, as shown in Fig.10.16. When the starter is operated there should be a 12v reading (bulb lights). If not there must be a fault in the internal solenoid connection, but this will not prevent the engine from starting provided the normal ignition connections are correct. (See Chapter 4). In very cold weather, however, difficulty may be experienced.

9. NOTE: When a new or reconditioned engine has been fitted it will be initially very stiff to turn. This could result in a very rapid discharge of the battery and slow turning of the engine before the engine has been successfully started. It is always advisable to have an additional battery available (in someone elses car perhaps) with a pair of jumper leads so that the extra power is available when it is really needed.

10 If the starter motor is the faulty item it must be removed from the car for inspection. Make sure that it is not merely jammed. This can be ascertained by putting a spanner on the square end of the shaft which protrudes. If it turns easily the starter is free. Otherwise use the spanner to turn the shaft in either direction until it is completely free.

18. Starter Motor M35 G/1 — Removal & Replacement

1. Disconnect the battery earth lead from the negative terminal. Obtain a new exhaust pipe/manifold flange gasket.

2. Remove the two nuts securing the exhaust pipe to the exhaust manifold flange (see Chapter 1 for details of removal).

3. Remove the six bolts holding the exhaust manifold to the cylinder head. One of the two centre bolts secures a bracing strap which is connected to the inlet manifold also. Slacken the nut on the inlet manifold stud holding the stay and push it to one side. (See Chapter 1.7 for details).

4. With care, the exhaust manifold can now be lifted out clear and the manifold gaskets should be removed undamaged.

5. Remove the cable from the starter solenoid terminal. (See photo).

6. Remove the two bolts and lockwashers securing the starter motor to the clutch housing and lift out the starter (see photo).

7. Replacement is the reverse procedure of removal paying attention to the correct replacement of the exhaust manifold gasket. The exhaust pipe flange gasket should always be renewed (see Chapter 1 for details of exhaust replacement). When all has been reassembled check the exhaust manifold nuts for tightness when the engine has cooled after having been run to reach its normal operating temperature.

19. Starter Motor M35 G/1 — Dismantling & Reassembly

1. With the starter motor on the bench, loosen the screw on the cover band and slip the cover band off. With a piece of wire bent into the shape of a hook, lift back each of the brush springs in turn and check the movement of the brushes in their holders by pulling on the flexible connectors. If the brushes are so worn that their faces do not rest against the commutator, or if the ends of the brush leads are exposed on their working face, they must be renewed.

2. If any of the brushes tend to stick in their holders then wash them with a petrol moistened cloth and, if necessary, lightly polish the sides of the brush with a very fine file, until the brushes move quite freely in their holders.

3. If the surface of the commutator is dirty or blackened, clean it with a petrol dampened rag. Secure the starter motor in a vice and check it by connecting a heavy gauge cable between the starter motor terminal and a 12-volt battery.

4. Connect the cable from the other battery terminal to earth in the starter motor body. If the motor turns at high speed it is in good order.

5. If the starter motor still fails to function or if it is wished to renew the brushes, then it is necessary to further dismantle the motor.

6. Lift the brush springs with the wire hook and lift all four brushes out of their holders one at a time.

7. Remove the terminal nuts and washers from the terminal post on the commutator end bracket.

8. Unscrew the two through bolts which hold the end plates together and pull off the commutator end bracket. Also remove the driving end bracket which will come away complete with the armature.

9. At this stage if the brushes are to be renewed, their flexible connectors must be unsoldered and the connectors of new brushes soldered in their place. Check that the new brushes move freely in their holders as detailed above. If cleaning the commutator with petrol fails to remove all the burnt areas and spots, then wrap a piece of glass paper round the commutator and rotate the armature.

10 If the commutator is very badly worn, remove the drive gear as detailed in the following section. Then mount the armature in a lathe and, with the lathe turning at high speed, take a very fine cut out of the commutator and finish the surface by polishing with glass paper. DO NOT UNDERCUT THE MICA INSULATORS BETWEEN THE COMMUTATOR SEGMENTS.

11 With the starter motor dismantled, test the four field coils for an open circuit. Connect a 12-volt battery with a 12-volt bulb in one of the leads between the field terminal post and the tapping point of the field coils to which the brushes are connected. An open circuit is proved by the bulb not lighting.

12 If the bulb lights, it does not necessarily mean that the field coils are in order, as there is a possibility that one of the coils will be earthing to the starter yoke or pole shoes. To check this, remove the lead from the brush connector and place it against a clean portion of the starter yoke. If the bulb lights, the field coils are earthing. Replacement of the field coils calls for the use of a wheel operated screwdriver, a soldering iron, caulking and riveting operations and is beyond the scope of the majority of owners. The starter yoke should be taken to a reputable electrical engineering works for new field coils to be fitted. Alternatively, purchase an exchange Lucas starter motor.

13 If the armature is damaged this will be evident after visual inspection. Look for signs of burning, discolouration, and for conductors that have lifted away from the commutator. Reassembly is a straightforward reversal of the dismantling procedure.

20. Starter Motor Drive M35 G/1 — General Description

1. The starter motor drive is of the outboard type. When the starter motor is operated the pinion moves into contact with the flywheel gear ring by moving in towards the starter motor.

2. If the engine kicks back, or the pinion fails to engage

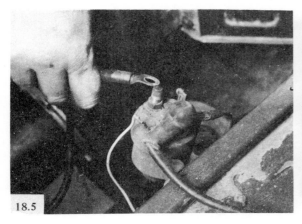

18.5

18.6

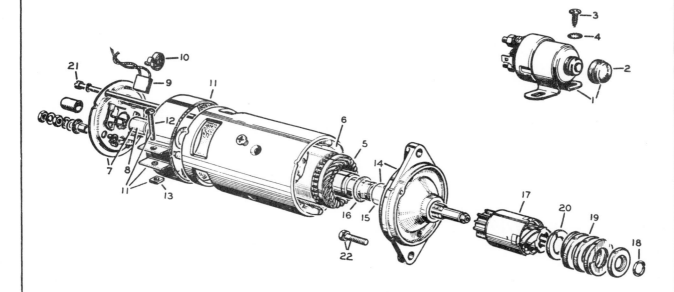

Fig.10.17. STARTER MOTOR & SOLENOID SWITCH EXPLODED VIEW

1. Switch & cover assembly	7. Commutator end cover	13. Captive nut	19. Spring
2. Rubber dust cover	8. Bush	14. Driven end cover	20. Spacer
3. Mounting screw	9. Brush	15. Bush	21. Through bolt
4. Washer	10. Spring	16. Spacer	22. Mounting bolt
5. Armature	11. Window cover	17. Starter drive gear	23. Dust shield
6. Feild coils	12. Screw	18. Circlip	

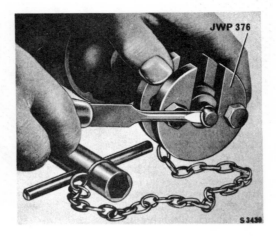

Fig.10.18. Removal of starter motor drive using special compressor tool.

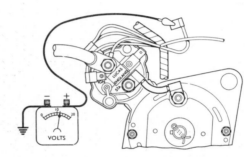

Fig.10.19. Diagram showing connection of voltmeter to check feed to pre-engaged starter solenoid.

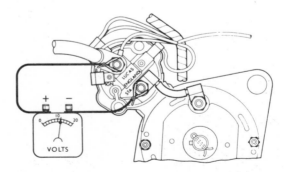

Fig.10.20. Diagram showing connection of voltmeter to check operation of solenoid switch main contacts.

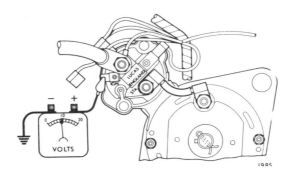

Fig.10.21. Diagram showing connection of voltmeter to check start feed to coil.

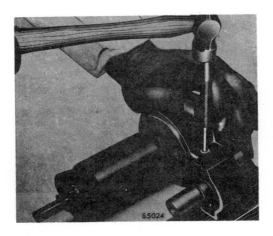

Fig.10.22. Pre-engaged starters. Driving out engagement lev·
pivot pin to separate drive end cover from armature.

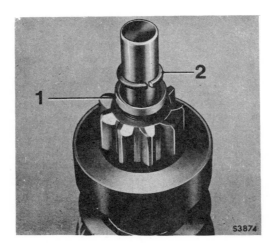

Fig.10.23. PRE-ENGAGED STARTERS — REMOVAL OF
DRIVING PINION ASSEMBLY

1. Thrust collar   2. Circlip

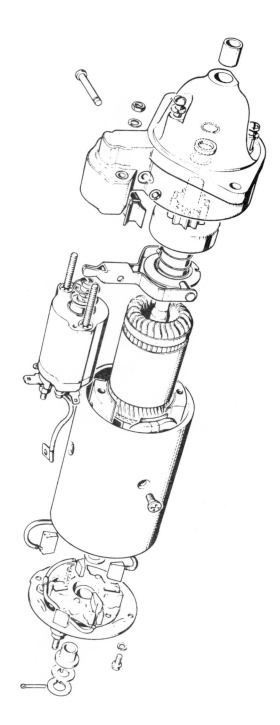

Fig.10.24. Starter Motor M35J/PE – Exploded View.

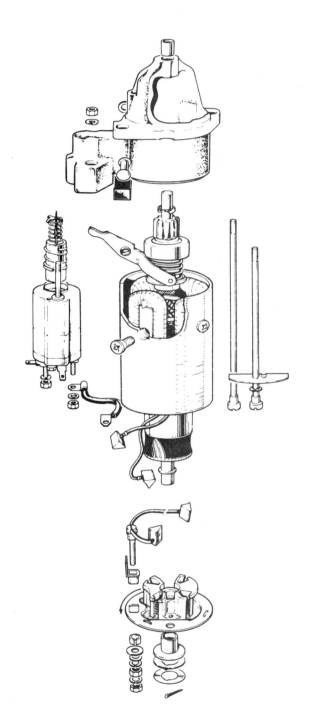

Fig.10.25. Starter Motor M35K/PE – Exploded View.

with the flywheel gear ring when the starter motor is actuated no undue strain is placed on the armature shaft, as the pinion sleeve disengages from the pinion and turns independently.

21. Starter Motor Drive M35 G/1 — Removal & Replacement

1. It is essential to obtain a press or clamp which can safely compress the heavy spring at the end of the shaft. Fig.10.18 shows the official tool (JWP 376) used by Vauxhall agents for this, but if one possesses a vice and a little ingenuity it can be done in other ways. As soon as the pressure is taken off the circlip it can be removed with a screwdriver. Then release the pressure on the spring.
2. Remove the spring collar and spring.
3. Slide the remaining parts with a rotary action off the armature shaft.
4. Reassembly is a straightforward reversal of the above procedure. NOTE: It is most important that the drive gear is completely free from oil, grease and dirt. With the drive gear removed, clean all the parts thoroughly in paraffin. UNDER NO CIRCUMSTANCES OIL THE DRIVE COMPONENTS. Lubrication of the drive components could easily cause the pinion to stick.

22. Starter Motor Bushes M35 G/1 — Inspection, Removal & Replacement

1. With the starter motor stripped down check the condition of the bushes. They should be renewed when they are sufficiently worn to allow visible side movement of the armature shaft.
2. The old bushes are simply driven out with a suitable drift and the new bushes inserted by the same method. As the bearings are of the phosphor bronze type it is essential that they are properly saturated with engine oil before fitting. (See Section 9.18 for details).

23. Starter Motors — M35J/M35K/PE — General Description

Some later Vivas are fitted with pre-engaged type starters. The M35K/PE models is a heavier duty version of the M35J/PE and the only difference is that the ends are held by long through bolts (as opposed to separate short bolts at each end) and the field winding is a four coil copper strip compared to a continuous aluminium strip on the other. Both have end face commutators and four wedge section brushes. The drive pinion engagement is by means of a solenoid actuator and starter switch mounted on the starter motor. The starter motor does not turn until the pinion is engaged with the flywheel ring gear. To provide for the possibility of over-run the pinion is driven through a one way roller clutch.

24. Starter Motors—M35J, M35K/PE—Testing in the Car

1. If the starter fails to turn (assuming the battery is in good condition) first listen for a loud click when the starter key is operated. A click indicates that the solenoid is operating. If no click is audible connect a voltmeter to the disconnected red/white wire and earth as shown in Fig.10.19. Operate the key-start switch and

a 12 volt reading should be obtained. If not the switch or wire is faulty.
2. Next connect the voltmeter across the main solenoid terminals as shown in Fig.10.20. A 12 volt reading should be obtained. (If not there is something wrong with the battery or main feeder cables and connections). When the key-start switch is now turned, the voltage reading should drop to zero. If it does not the solenoid switch is faulty and needs renewal. If the voltage drops and still the starter fails to turn, the starter motor itself must be examined.
3. To check that the coil start feed is operating (see Chapter 4) connect the voltmeter as shown in Fig.10.21. With the starter motor turning normally an 8 volt reading (approximately) should be obtained.

25. Starter Motors — M35J, M35K/PE — Removal & Replacement

1. Disconnect the earth lead from the negative battery terminal.
2. Disconnect the positive battery lead from the solenoid terminal by undoing the nut and pull off the other wires from the Lucar connectors on the solenoid.
3. Undo the two mounting bolts securing the starter motor to the bellhousing and remove the unit from underneath the car. Unlike other starter motors the exhaust manifold does not need to be removed to lift it out from above.
4. Replacement is a straightforward reversal of the removal procedure. Make sure that the electrical connections are re-made correctly. Refer to the wiring diagram if necessary.

26. Starter Motors — M35J, M35K/PE — Dismantling & Reassembly

1. It will be necessary to dismantle the starter motor if checks indicate that failure to turn the engine is due to faults with it. After some time the brushes will also wear sufficiently to warrant renewal.
2. The solenoid may be removed after detaching the short connecting cable from the other main terminal and removing the two securing nuts. If this is all that needs replacing a new one can be fitted over the existing plunger now.
3. To dismantle the motor further remove the short bolts, or through bolts, which hold the commutator end bracket with the brush gear to the main yoke. Also remove the split pin, washers and shims from the end of the shaft. The end bracket may then be carefully removed. Do not lose the thrust washer which is located over the end of the shaft inside.
4. Next remove the bolts holding the drive end cover in position (if necessary) and the end cover complete with armature and shaft may be drawn out of the yoke.
5. To separate the end cover from the armature it will be necessary to drive out the pin on which the engagement lever pivots. (See Fig.10.22).
6. To take the drive pinion and clutch assembly off the armature shaft it will be necessary to drive the thrust collar down the shaft with a piece of suitable tube and then remove the circlip which is exposed. (Fig.10.23). If the driving gear assembly is worn the whole unit should be renewed. To check that the roller clutch is in good condition it should lock and take up the drive in one direction immediately it is turned. When turned in the opposite direction it should rotate smoothly and evenly.

Fig.10.26. M35J Starter—location of field coil brushes.

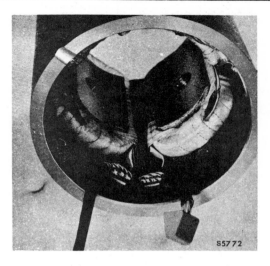

Fig.10.27. M35K starter—location of field coil brushes

Fig.10.28. Pre-engaged starters—Minimum thickness of commutator dimension 'A'

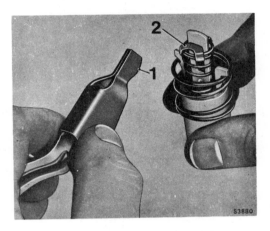

Fig.10.29. PRE-ENGAGED STARTERS—ASSEMBLY OF ENGAGEMENT LEVER TO SOLENOID PLUNGER

1. Chamfered corner   2. Retaining plate

Fig.10.30. Pre-engaged starters—Reassembling the commutator end cover assembly with the thrust washer (arrowed) in position.

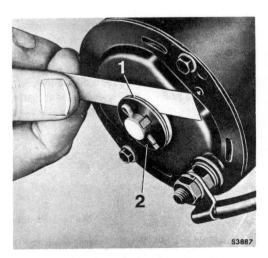

Fig.10.31. PRE-ENGAGED STARTERS — CHECKING END FLOAT OF THE ARMATURE SHAFT

1. Thrust washer   2. Shims

The whole clutch unit should also slide easily and without excessive play along the splines of the armature shaft.

7. Examine the brushes to ensure that they are not less than the permitted minimum length of .38 in. (9.5 mm). If they need renewal, obtain first the new ones. Two will be supplied complete with their terminal post and the other two separately for soldering to the field coil end tags. On the M35J starters which have an aluminium strip field winding, the old brushes should be cut off leaving a ¼ inch (7 mm) at least of the old copper wire to which the new brushes may be soldered. (You cannot solder aluminium!). Make sure the new brushes have sufficiently long leads and are in the proper position, (See Fig.10.26). On M35K starters, the field coils are made from copper strip and the new brushes may be soldered directly on to the tag ends (Fig.10.27).

8. Clean up the face of the commutator with a petrol moistened rag. Light scoring may be cleaned up with fine glass paper. If there is deep scoring the commutator face may be skimmed in a lathe, provided it does not diminish in thickness below .080 in. (2 mm). (See Fig.10.28). Do not undercut the segment insulation.

9. If it is suspected that the field coil insulation is gone it is recommended that they are removed, checked and repaired by specialists with the proper equipment.

10 Check that the shaft is a good fit into each of the end plate bushes and renew the brushes if necessary.

11 Assembly is a procedure that must be carried out in sequence with attention to several points to ensure that it is correct.

12 First assemble the engagement lever to the solenoid plunger so that the chamfered corner faces the solenoid. Then make sure that the retaining plate is correct, relative to the lever (Fig.10.29).

13 Next fit the drive pinion and clutch assembly on the armature shaft, fit the engagement lever fork to the clutch and assemble the whole lot together to the drive end cover. Then fit a new lever pivot pin and peen over the end to prevent it coming out.

14 Replace the yoke, and then lightly screw up the end cover bolts (if fitted).

15 Next place the thrust washer over the commutator end of the shaft, fit all the brushes into their appropriate holders in the end cover and replace the end cover on to the shaft (Fig.10.30). Both end covers have locating pips to ensure they are fitted correctly to the yoke.

16 Replace the through bolts or end cover bolts as appropriate and tighten them up at both ends.

17 Replace the thrust washer and shims to the end of the shaft, install a split pin, and then measure the end float gap between the thrust washer and the end cover with a feeler gauge. It should be no more than .010 in. (.25 mm) (Fig.10.31). Additional shims should be added to reduce the end float as required.

18 Next replace the rubber pad between the drive end bracket (under the solenoid plunger housing) and the yoke, and refit the solenoid. Reconnect the short cable to the solenoid terminal.

19 Before replacing the starter in the car after reassembly it is a good idea to check that it is functioning properly by connecting it temporarily to the battery.

27. Control Box (Dynamo) — General Description

The control box consists of three main parts, the cut-out relay, the current regulator and the voltage regulator. The whole unit controls the dynamo output so that it is correctly balanced between the requirements of the cars electrical equipment and the recharging requirement of the battery. The cut-out relay is basically an automatically operated switch which prevents current flowing the wrong way, from battery to dynamo, when the generator output is below 12 volts. The current regulator and voltage regulator work in conjunction to enable the generator to deliver its safe maximum output when necessary, and to reduce the current being delivered when the system or battery does not require it.

28. Control Box (Dynamo) — Checks & Adjustment

1. If the generator and battery are both known to be in good condition yet the battery gives indications of inadequate or excessive charge it may be assumed that the reasons are a fault or maladjustment in the control box. If an adjustment is necessary, (as revealed by the tests) the cover of the control box must first be removed by drilling out the rivets which hold it in position. All adjustments must be carried out in sequence given and quickly to prevent incorrect readings due to heating up of the appropriate coils.

29. Voltage Regulator (Dynamo)—Checks & Adjustment

1. To check the voltage regulator, first disconnect the brown wire from the 'B' terminal on the control box and make sure it is not allowed to touch anything.

2. Then connect a voltmeter to the 'WL' terminal and earth as shown in Fig.10.32.

3. Start the engine and slowly increase revolutions to 2,000 r.p.m. The voltage should reach between 14.3 to 15.5 volts according to air temperature as shown in the table in the specifications at the beginning of this chapter. Unsteady fluctuations (more than .3 volts) may be due to dirty contacts. A steady reading outside the range can be adjusted by turning the cam arrowed in Fig.10.32. Obtain the special toothed tool for this purpose. When the adjustment is completed, lower and raise the engine speed again to check the reading.

30. Cut-Out (Dynamo) — Checks & Adjustment

1. Connect the voltmeter as for the voltage regulator check but with all connections to the cut-out box left as they are (Fig.10.33).

2. Start the engine, and increase speed slowly. Check that the relay cuts in at between 12.6 and 13.4 volts. The cut-in is indicated by a flicker back of the voltmeter needle. If adjustment is required adjust the cam (arrowed) only when the engine is at idling speed. Then check by speeding the engine up.

3. Next disconnect the brown lead from terminal 'B' once more and connect an ammeter as shown in Fig.10.34. making sure that the loose tag does not touch anything.

4. Then switch on the headlamps, start the engine and increase the engine speed until a charge is indicated. Then gradually decrease engine speed and check that the discharge does not exceed 8 amps. If it does, bend the fixed contact (arrowed) back a little until it is correct.

31. Current Regulator (Dynamo) — Checks & Adjustment

1. Having completed the checks in Sections 20 and 21, leave the ammeter connected as in check 21, and hold the voltage regulator contacts together with a clip (Fig.10.35, Item 1).

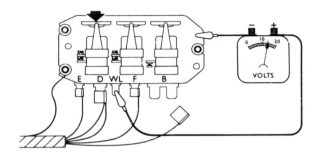

Fig.10.32. Connection of voltmeter to control box for voltage regulator check. Adjusting cam is arrowed.

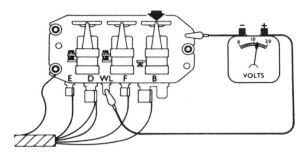

Fig.10.33. Connection of voltmeter to control box for cut-out check. Adjusting cam is arrowed.

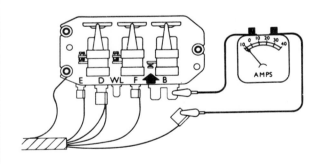

Fig.10.34. Connection of ammeter to control box for 2nd stage of cut-out check. Fixed contact is arrowed.

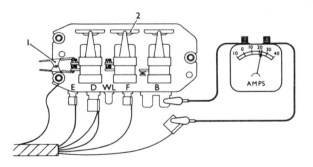

Fig.10.35. CONNECTION OF AMMETER TO CONTROL BOX FOR CURRENT REGULATOR CHECK

1. Regulator contacts held closed with clip

2. Adjusting cam

2. Start the engine and increase speed to 2750 r.p.m., when the ammeter should give a steady reading of 22 amps. Adjust by turning the cam (Item 2) if necessary.

32. Control Box Contacts (Dynamo) — Cleaning

1. The cut-out contacts (Fig.10.36, Item 3) may be cleaned in position by drawing very fine glass paper (not emery) between them.

2. The voltage and current regulator contacts (Items 1 and 2) must be removed and faced up on fine carborundum (stone or paper) and then cleaned off with methylated spirits. Whenever contacts are cleaned in this way the setting checks must afterwards be made as described in the previous sections and the mechanical settings as described in the next section.

33. Armature/Core Gaps & Cut-Out Contact Gap Setting — (Dynamo)

1. First check the gaps on the current and voltage regulators according to specifications. If adjustment is necessary, first turn the adjuster cams clockwise (Fig. 10.37, 1 and 2) so that the locknut on the adjustable contact can be reached with a tubular spanner in order to slacken it. Then place the feeler blade under the armature as far as the rivet heads allow, press the armature down and adjust the contact until they just touch. Re-check the armature core gap on release, and then tighten the locknut. The voltage and current regulator will need re-setting afterwards as described in Sections 20 and 22.

2. The cut-out relay contacts should just touch with a .015 inch feeler blade between the armature and core and the armature pressed down (Fig.10.38). The contacts are adjusted by bending the fixed contact. The armature to core gap should be between .035 inch and .045 inch and this is adjusted by bending the armature back stop. After adjustments are completed the settings should be re-checked as described in Section 21.

3. If the control box has been removed from the car it should be replaced before securing the cover with new rivets or nuts and bolts as convenient. Make sure that the wire connections are all re-made correctly as in Fig.10.39.

34. Fuses

1. Four fuses are fitted in a separate fuse holder positioned on the engine side of the dash panel. The area adjacent to each fuse is marked from 1 to 4 for easy identification.

2. 35 amp fuses are used. They protect the circuits as listed in the specifications at the beginning of the chapter.

3. If any of the fuses blow, check the circuits on that fuse to trace the fault, before renewing the fuse.

4. Headlamp and sidelamp circuits are protected by a thermal circuit breaker. This opens if the load exceeds 33 amps for ½ to 3 minutes. It can be tested by putting an ammeter and variable resistance in the circuit in series.

5. The fuse block is mounted on the right-hand side of the front wheel arch. The connectors to the fuse terminals, however, are inside underneath. The thermal circuit breaker is alongside the terminals.

35. Flasher Circuit — Fault Tracing & Rectification

1. The flasher unit is located in a clip behind the instrument panel which needs to be removed before it can be reached. See Section 45 for details of how to remove the instrument panel.

On later models a different type of flasher unit was used, and this is mounted on top of the heater control unit in some cars. Access to it is by lifting out the ash tray. This model lets you know if a bulb is defective by not flashing, although the indicator lamp will light.

Some models also have a hazard warning system fitted which will flash all four indicators, front and rear simultaneously. A separate unit (wired into the normal circuit) is clipped to the steering column support brackets behind the instruments. A switch, with a red indicator bulb in it is mounted in the lower steering column canopy. To remove the switch, the steering wheel and upper column canopy must be taken off.

2. If the flasher unit fails to operate, or works very slowly or very rapidly, check out the flasher indicator circuit as detailed below, before assuming there is a fault in the unit itself.

3. Examine the direction indicator bulbs front and rear for broken filaments.

4. If the external flashers are working but the internal flasher warning light has ceased to function, check the filament of the warning bulb and replace as necessary.

5. With the aid of the wiring diagram check all the flasher circuit connections if a flasher bulb is sound but does not work.

6. In the event of total direction indicator failure, check the No.2 fuse.

7. If all other items check out then the flasher unit itself is faulty and must be replaced.

36. Horn — Fault Tracing & Rectification

1. If the horn works badly or fails completely, check the wiring leading to it for short circuits and loose connections. Check that the horn is firmly secured and that there is nothing lying on the horn body.

2. If the horn still does not work or operates incorrectly it will be necessary to make adjustments.

3. Whether there are one or two horns, each is adjustable by means of a screw in the back.

4. Turn the screw anti-clockwise until no sound is heard. Turn it clockwise until the note is acceptable and then turn an additional quarter turn.

37. Headlamps & Sidelamps — Bulb & Lens Removal & Replacement

1. The pre-focus headlamp units are fitted with detachable bulbs and both side and headlamp bulbs are incorporated in the same housing.

2. To remove the bulb holder, raise the bonnet and pull the rubber cover off the back of the light unit (Fig.10.40). The lamp holder unit can then be detached and the bulb removed. The sidelamp bulb is a simple push fit into the unit below the headlamp bulb.

3. To remove the glass lens unit, it is first of all necessary to remove the radiator grille (See Chapter 12.20).

4. After the grille is removed a spring clip at the lower edge of the glass is accessible. Remove this and the glass may be lifted out.

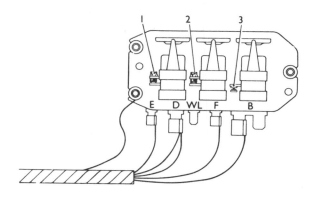

Fig.10.36. CONTROL BOX—CONTACT POINTS & CLEANING

1. Voltage regulator contacts)
2. Current regulator contacts)
   Remove & clean with fine
   carborundum & meths.
3. Cut-out relay contacts
   Clean in position with glass
   paper.

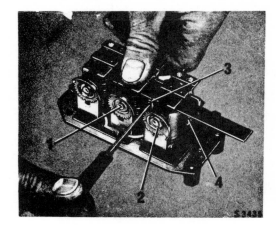

Fig.10.37. CONTROL BOX — CONTACT SETTINGS

1. Current regulator cam
2. Voltage regulator cam
3. Current regulator contact
4. Voltage regulator contact

Fig.10.38. CONTROL BOX — SETTING THE CUT-OUT CON-
TACTS

1. Cut-out relay contacts
2. Armature back stop

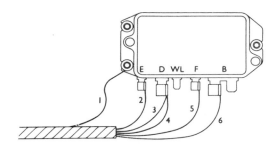

Fig.10.39. CONTROL BOX — WIRING CONNECTIONS
COLOUR CODE

1. Black
2. Black
3. Brown/yellow
4. Brown/Yellow
5. Brown/Green
6. Brown

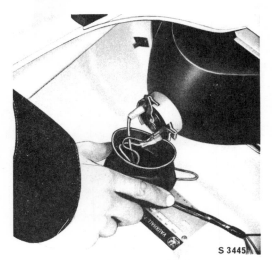

Fig.10.40. Removal of headlamp bulb-holder cover.

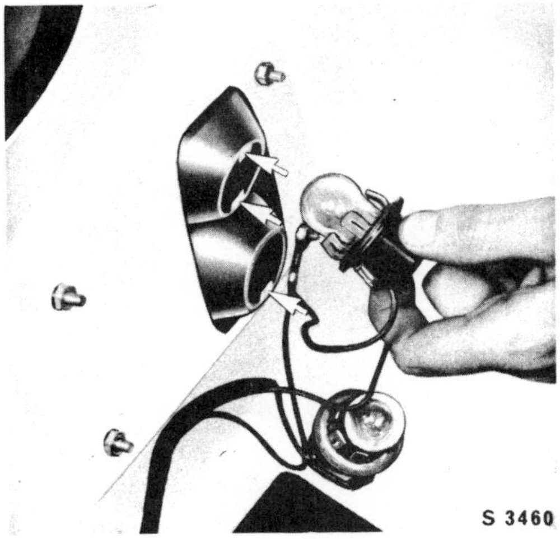

Fig.10.41. Fitting of rear lamp bulb holders. Locating tongues
are arrowed.

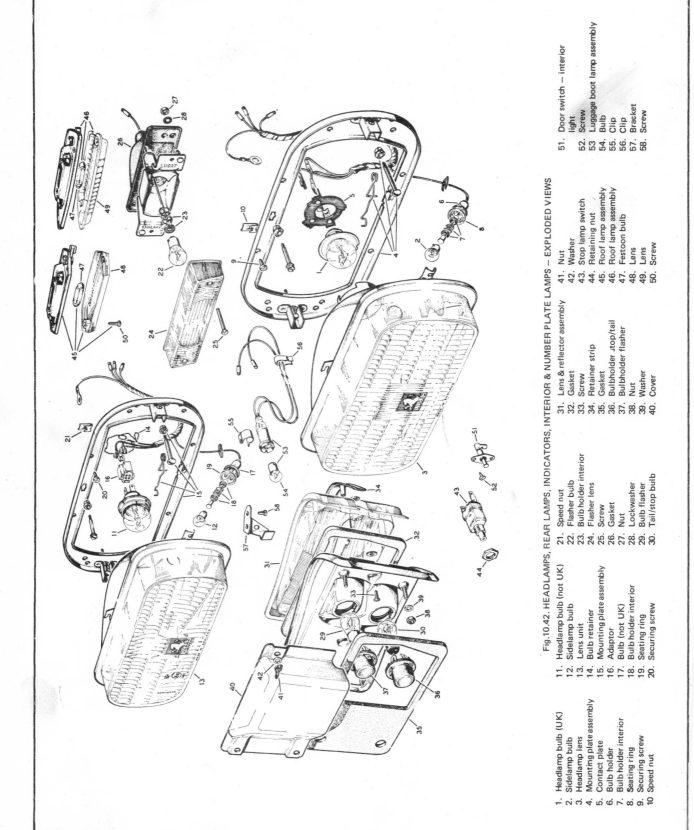

Fig.10.42. HEADLAMPS, REAR LAMPS, INDICATORS, INTERIOR & NUMBER PLATE LAMPS – EXPLODED VIEWS

1. Headlamp bulb (UK)
2. Sidelamp bulb
3. Headlamp lens
4. Mounting plate assembly
5. Contact plate
6. Bulb holder
7. Bulbholder interior
8. Seating ring
9. Securing screw
10. Speed nut

11. Headlamp bulb (not UK)
12. Sidelamp bulb
13. Lens unit
14. Bulb retainer
15. Mounting plate assembly
16. Adaptor
17. Bulb (not UK)
18. Bulb holder interior
19. Seating ring
20. Securing screw

21. Speed nut
22. Flasher bulb
23. Bulb holder interior
24. Flasher lens
25. Screw
26. Gasket
27. Nut
28. Lockwasher
29. Bulb flasher
30. Tail/stop bulb

31. Lens & reflector assembly
32. Gasket
33. Screw
34. Retainer strip
35. Gasket
36. Bulbholder stop/tail
37. Bulbholder flasher
38. Nut
39. Washer
40. Cover

41. Nut
42. Washer
43. Stop lamp switch
44. Retaining nut
45. Roof lamp assembly
46. Roof lamp assembly
47. Festoon bulb
48. Lens
49. Lens
50. Screw

51. Door switch – interior light
52. Screw
53. Luggage boot lamp assembly
54. Bulb
55. Clip
56. Clip
57. Bracket
58. Screw

176

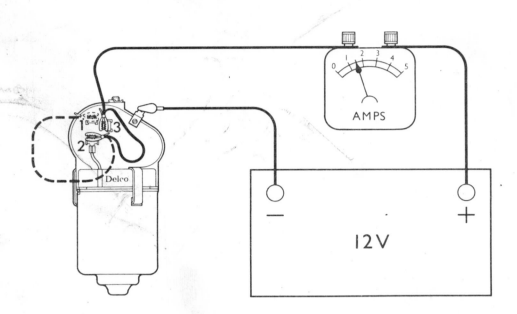

Fig.10.43. TEMPORARY HOOK UP OF LATER MODEL WIPER MOTORS TO CHECK END FLOAT & CURRENT
LOADING
A. Single speed. Dark line shows connection for continuous running. Dotted line shows additional connection for checking self-parking
B. Two speed. Dark line shows connection for continuous running at low speed. (large terminal 2 connection to terminal 4 for high
speed. To check self-parking move supply lead to terminal 3 and add lead (dotted line) between terminals 1 and 2

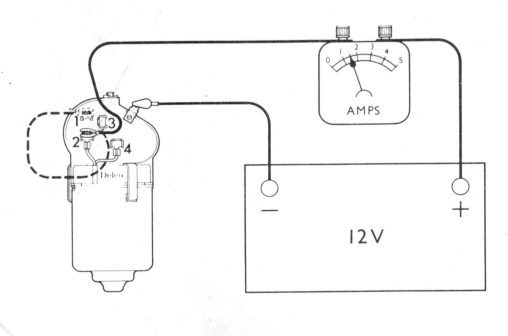

5. Replacements are a reversal of the removal procedures.

6. Headlamp beam adjustment is best done with proper equipment, but as a rough setting guide the centre bright spots should be 2½ inches below the height of the headlamp centre line when the lights are shining on to a vertical surface 25 feet in front of the car. The adjuster screw is located on the inside edge of the headlamp surround panel under the bonnet. It has a small rectangular headed shank and care should be taken not to damage it when adjustments are made.

38. Rear Lights & Flasher Bulbs — Removal & Replacement

1. Access to the rear lamp bulbs is from inside the luggage boot.

2. Remove the four nuts holding the cover in position and then pull out the appropriate bulb holder held in by spring clips round the edge of the holder.

3. Replace the bulb in the holder and then refit the holder so that the tongues locate in the spaces in the holder (See Fig.10.41).

39. Windscreen Wipers — Fault Finding

1. If the wipers do not work when they are switched on first check the No.2 fuse. If this is sound then there is either an open circuit in the wiring or switch, the wiper motor is faulty, or the pivot spindles or linkages may be binding.

2. If the wipers work intermittently then suspect a short circuit in the motor. Alternatively the armature shaft end float adjustment may be too tight or the wiper linkage may be binding.

3. Should the wipers not stop when they are turned off there must be a short circuit in the switch or wiring.

40. Windscreen Washer — Fault Finding

1. If the windscreen washers do not work when pumped, first check that there is water in the washer reservoir and that the jets in the discharge nozzles are clear (poke them with a pin).

2. Examine the water pipe connections at all junctions to ensure they are firmly fitted.

3. If there is still no jet from the screen nozzles detach the pipes from the pump unit and remove the unit from the dashboard.

4. In a bowl of water, submerge the inlet of the pump, operate it, and water should come from the outlet under reasonable pressure. Then operate the pump with the outlet only under water, when bubbles will come out. After a few strokes in this manner release the plunger and lift the outlet out of the water. If, on operating the pump again, some water comes from the unit then it means that the non-return valves inside are not functioning properly and the unit should be replaced. If the pump is satisfactory then the only possible faults can be in the suction and delivery pipes, unions or nozzles all of which must be carefully examined for splits, kinks, blockages or leaking connections.

5. On later models the pump is mounted on the escutcheon surrounding the heater/ventilator controls. On models fitted with two speed wipers the washer pump is electrically driven and is mounted on the ventilator panel under the bonnet. Fig.10.45 gives an exploded picture of the pump assembly. It is possible to renew a worn impeller by removing the end cover, seal, distance piece and washer.

41. Windscreen Wiper Motor — Self Parking Adjustment

1. If the windscreen wipers fail to park or park badly then alter the position of the switch contact on the wheelbox attached to the end of the wiper motor. To obtain access to the wiper motor, first disconnect the control cable from the heater water valve (if fitted) and also remove the air cleaner on HB22 engines. Then disconnect the heater wiring connections at the snap connectors (the green and black wires). If the screws holding the duct unit and panel are now removed, the whole unit may then be drawn back (fig.10.46).

2. The switch contact is moved by means of a hexagon headed pin held by a spring fixing plate.

3. Turn the wipers on and then off, noting where they come to rest. With a small 5/16 in. A.F. spanner turn the pin clockwise to make the blades park higher on the screen, and anti-clockwise to make the blades park lower. (Fig.10.47).

42. Windscreen Wiper Motor -- Removal & Replacement

1. The windscreen wiper motor has to be removed complete with the wiper operating links and arms, which are held in a rigid frame and comprise the complete windscreen wiper assembly, from under the bonnet on the drivers side by the scuttle.

2. Disconnect the battery and take off the windscreen wiper arms.

3. The frame is held at three points. At the top two points it is held by slotted rings (which in effect are nuts) positioned on the outside of the car just in front of the windscreen on the base of the splined pivots to which the wiper arms are attached.

4. Undo these nuts if possible using the special spanner to prevent damage to the rings. Alternatively use a screwdriver. Take off the outer sealing rings. (Fig.10.48).

5. Remove the heater and ventilator panel and duct as described in Section 30:1.

6. The wiper motor and crank assembly frame is secured with a slotted rubber stud to the dash panel. Disconnect this, and the whole assembly may now be withdrawn from the car after the wiper motor leads and earthing strap are disconnected. Undo the bolts holding the motor to the wiper mechanism frame.

7. Replacement is a reversal of the removal procedure. Make sure that when fitting the wiper pivot outer washers (Fig.10.48) that the curve of the washer follows the contour of the body panel. Do not tighten up the locking nuts until the frame has been refixed to the dash panel with the rubber stud.

43. Windscreen Wiper Motor — Dismantling, Inspection & Reassembly

Other than for normal wear, the bearings and gears in the motor should not deteriorate and if for any reason the motor should cease to function altogether, it is probably due to the wiper mechanism jamming or seizing which has over loaded the motor and burnt it out. In such instances the purchasing of either armature or field coils, and probably brushes as well, is hardly comparable to buying an exchange unit. If the motor

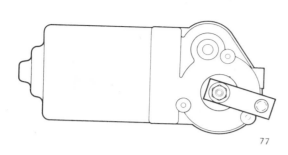

Fig.10.44. Later model wiper motor showing correct position crank when coming to rest on self-parking

Fig.10.45. ELECTRICALLY DRIVEN WASHER PUMP FITTED TO LATER MODELS

1. End cover and housing to body bolts
2. End cover
3. Seal
4. Distance piece
5. Nylon washer
6. Impeller
7. Housing
8. Motor body

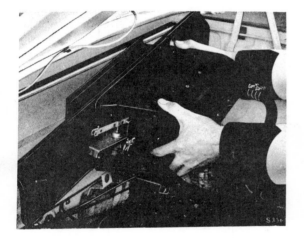

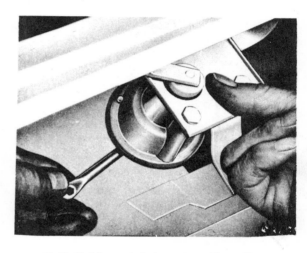

Fig.10.47. Adjustment of wiper motor parking position.

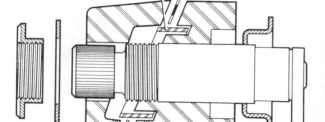

Fig.10.48. CROSS SECTION OF WIPER ARM PIVOT MOUNTING

1. Collar
2. Sealing rings

Fig.10.49. Later model wiper motors—Removal of armature shaft. Nylon thrust bearing is arrowed

179

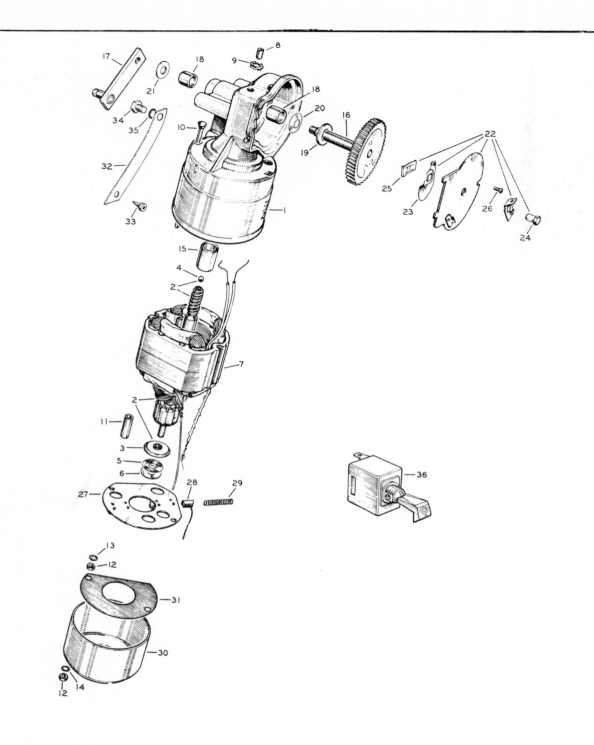

Fig.10.50. WINDSCREEN WIPER MOTOR — EXPLODED VIEW

1. Motor housing
2. Armature assembly
3. Oil slinger
4. Thrust ball
5. Fabric washer
6. Metal washer
7. Field coil assembly
8. Thrust screw
9. Locknut
10 Through bolt

11. Spacer
12. Nut
13. Washer
14. Lock washer
15. Armature bush
16. Cross shaft & gear
17. Crank and pin
18. Cross shaft bush
19. Thrust washer
20. Spring washer

21. Washer
22. Switch plate assembly
23. Parking contact spring
24. Parking contact adjust-
    ment pin
25. Retaining clip
26. Fixing screw
27. Brush plate
28. Brush
29. Spring

30. Commutator end frame
    and bearing
31. End frame insulator
32. Earth lead
33. Screw
34. Bolt
35. Star washer
36. Switch

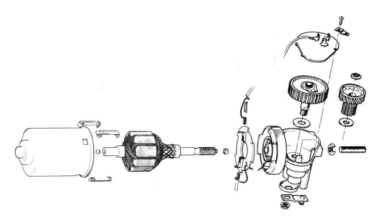

Fig.10.51. Wiper motor fitted to later models — Exploded view. Single speed version illustrated. (2 speed version has three brushes).

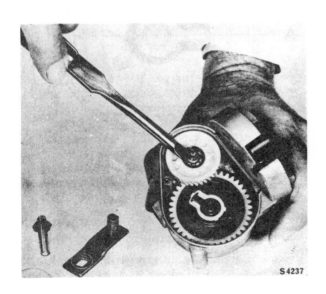

Fig.10.52. Later model wiper motors — Removal of worn wheel retainer.

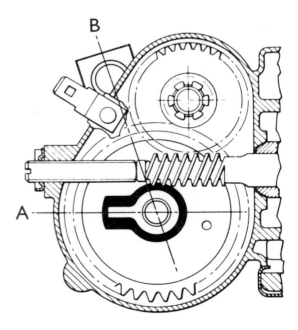

Fig.10.53. Later model wiper motors — Relative positions of self-parking contact (A) and crank (B) on reassembly

ceases to function for no immediately obvious reason proceed as follows:

1. Remove the motor from the mechanism as previously described and reconnect it to a 12-volt source to make sure that it is the motor at fault and not a jammed mechanism. NOTE: All bracketed numbers in this section refer to Fig.10.50.

2. Thoroughly clean the motor exterior, (use fluids very sparingly to prevent contamination of the interior).

3. Remove the switch plate screw (26) and lift off the switch plate and assembly. Examine the parking contact for condition. Replace if badly burnt or pitted.

4. Remove the nuts and washers (12 & 14) from the through bolts (10) and take off the end frame which also contains the spherical bearing for the commutator end of the armature.

5. Remove the end frame insulator (31) and examine the brushes (28) for condition and the commutator segments for burning or pitting. Clean the commutator with glass paper only. If the brushes need replacing remove the through bolt inner nuts and washers, (12 & 13) and withdraw the brush plate (27) to reveal the soldered brush connections. Unsolder these and resolder new ones with new springs.

6. If the commutator should be very badly burnt or pitted on any of the segments, it will almost certainly have broken down insulation on the windings and the best remedy is a new one.

7. To check the field coil (7) disconnect the leads from the switch plate and check for continuity and then ensure there is no short to earth. Field coils should not be loose around the pole pieces and the insulation should be visually examined for displacement or scorching.

8. Reassemble in the reverse order (if using the same armature) making sure that the end frame insulator (31) is replaced with the cut-away as shown.

9. Ensure that the spherical bearing re-seats properly in the end of the armature shaft.

10 To replace the armature, dismantle the motor as described in paragraphs 1—7, draw out the armature by revolving it anti-clockwise to clear the cross-shaft gear. Do not lose the ball (4) at the drive end. Slacken off the locknut and thrust screw (8 & 9) two or three turns and insert a new armature. Reassemble the brush gear and end cover as in paragraphs 8 and 9.

11 With a feeler gauge between the ball (4) and the screw (8) set the armature end float clearance to .002 inches and tighten the locknut (9).

12 Reassemble the switch plate having packed the gear housing 1/3rd full with recommended grease (see page 8). Re-test as before.

13 During examination of the bushes certain play may be apparent between the shafts and bushes (17 and 23). Theoretically the tolerances between them are 002 in.— 003 in. However, provided the play is not so great as to cause a possibility of jamming, or such as causes too great a variation in the wiper sweep and park position a certain discretion can be exercised regarding the necessity to replace them. If the cross shaft bush (18) is very badly worn the shaft can be withdrawn after removing the contact plate assembly (22) and the crank lever (17). The crank lever is secured to the shaft on a left-hand thread.

14 As mentioned earlier the motor will have been dismantled for some specific reason and if this was something other than the bushes — and the bushes are then found to be in need of renewal - it will probably be sensible economics to obtain a complete exchange motor.

15 Bushes can be replaced by drifting out and pressing in new ones.

16 When all repairs have been carried out and the unit reassembled, it is advisable to carry out some trial tests. Check the current consumption as an indication that there is no inherent overloading due to misalignment or tightness in bushes and thrust clearances. With an ammeter in circuit connect the BAT terminal to positive, the earth strip to negative, and the SW connection to the motor body. On free running the current should be 2.2 amps. If more, check for free rotation of shafts in the bushes. If less, then the motor cannot be running at full speed and the brushes will not be making proper contact, (or your battery has run down!).

17 On later models a new type of motor was fitted in both single and two speed versions (Fig.10.51). The self parking switch is not adjustable on these models.

18 It may be necessary to change brushes and adjust armature shaft end float. With the motor removed from the car, the end frame can be removed by prising off the spring clips. Then remove the screw holding the terminal plate to the gear wheel housing.

19 The end frame and armature shaft may be taken out next. Do not lose either the nylon bearing at the worm end of the shaft (Fig.10.49) or the ball at the other end.

20 Brushes may be renewed by soldering new ones on to the cut off tags of the old. If the shaft bearing bushes are badly worn the complete end cover will need replacing as bushes are not supplied separately. The worm wheel and cross shaft can be taken out after removing the motor crank arm and then prising off the retaining ring, (Fig.10.52).

21 When reassembling the motor make sure that all the thrust washers are correctly located. To ensure that the parking switch contact is in the right place make sure that the crank arm and self parking segment are aligned in relation to each other as shown in Fig.10.53.

22 The brushes will need to be held back when the armature is replaced in the end frame, and this can be done by hooking their leads over the tags on the brush holders. Then when the end frame cover is replaced they can be unhooked by using a piece of stiff wire through the holes for the securing clips.

23 When fully reassembled the end float needs checking and adjusting and this is best done when the motor is running. If it is connected up as shown in Fig.10.43 with an ammeter in circuit the end float thrust screw may be adjusted until current consumption increases by no more than 0.1 amps from the specified normal load after 5—10 minutes running. At the same time the self-parking position of the crank may be checked which should be as shown in Fig.10.43.

24 When reconnecting the wires to the motor on installation make sure that the correct leads are attached to the correct terminals.

Single speed motor	Two speed motor
1. Yellow	1. Yellow
2. Red	2. Red
3. Green	3. Green
Earth tag - Black	4. Blue
	Earth tag - Black

44. Wiper Mechanism — Inspection & Repair

1. Having removed the motor and mechanism assembly as described in Section 31, examine the wiper arm spindles for any signs of wear and looseness. If the whole unit is badly worn it is better to renew the

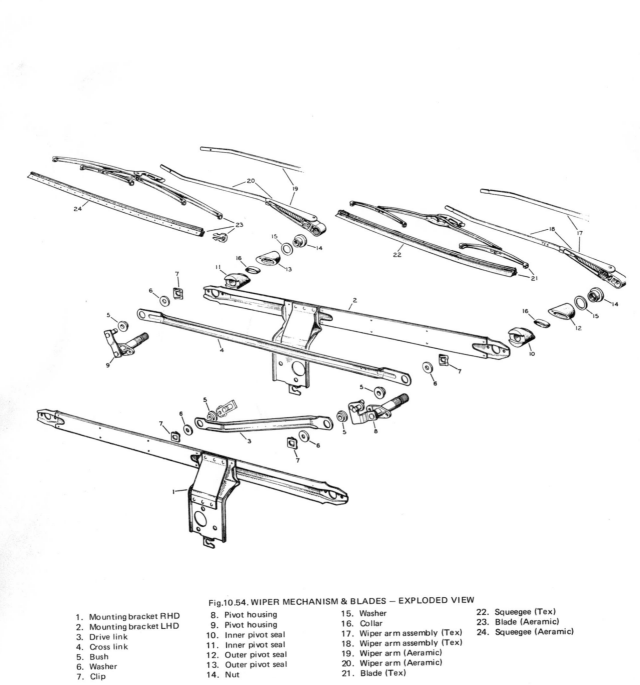

Fig.10.54. WIPER MECHANISM & BLADES — EXPLODED VIEW

1. Mounting bracket RHD	8. Pivot housing	15. Washer	22. Squeegee (Tex)
2. Mounting bracket LHD	9. Pivot housing	16. Collar	23. Blade (Aeramic)
3. Drive link	10. Inner pivot seal	17. Wiper arm assembly (Tex)	24. Squeegee (Aeramic)
4. Cross link	11. Inner pivot seal	18. Wiper arm assembly (Tex)	
5. Bush	12. Outer pivot seal	19. Wiper arm (Aeramic)	
6. Washer	13. Outer pivot seal	20. Wiper arm (Aeramic)	
7. Clip	14. Nut	21. Blade (Tex)	

complete assembly. Otherwise individual bushes may be renewed. If either of the wiper arm spindle units is worn, the rivets securing it should be drilled out and new units fitted. Grease all spindle bushes with Castrolease MS3, or equivalent.

45. Instrument Panel — Removal & Replacement

1. Disconnect the battery cables at the battery terminals. Also unscrew the speedometer cable union from the gearbox and unclip it from the engine. This is to enable it to be drawn through the scuttle a little way with the instrument panel so that no damage will occur before it is also unscrewed at the panel end.
2. Remove the centre and two end screws of the five screws along the top edge of the panel above the speedometer scale.
3. Pull the unit forward sufficiently far to enable the speedometer cable to be disconnected.
4. Lift the unit so that the lower edge becomes disengaged from the panel, pull off the multi-plug socket from the printed circuit and the unit is clear. Replacement is a reversal of the removal procedure.

46. Speedometer, Fuel Gauge, Temperature Gauge & Ignition & Oil Warning Lamps

1. Remove the instrument panel assembly as described in Section 35.
2. Referring to Fig.10.55, remove the screws (1) and clips (3). The printed circuit and instrument mounting plate can then be separated from the panel cover. The water temperature gauge or fuel gauge are held in place by nuts (2) and the speedometer head by two screws (4).
3. Before assuming that either the fuel gauge or temperature gauge is faulty make sure that the checks as described in Chapters 3/16 and 2/12 respectively are carried out.
4. When handling the individual instrument gauges be very careful and avoid bending or straining the pointers which might upset their delicate balance.
5. When refitting the instruments make sure that the earth tag on the printed circuit is located on the

appropriate terminal of the gauge so that it is correctly connected to the case of the instrument.
6. Later models had a single piece instrument panel assembly which incorporated the ignition, lighting and wiper switches. (Fig.10.56). Once the five screws are removed the panel is removed as was the earlier type. However to take it away completely the wires will have to be detached from the switches and a note should be taken of the correct connections. These are:—

Lighting Switch
Terminal 4 — Brown	Terminal 8 — Blue
Terminal 7 — Red/Brown	Others — Vacant

Wiper Switch (single speed)
Terminal 2 — Yellow
Terminal 4 — Green
Terminal 7 — Red

Wiper Switch (2 speed)
Terminal 2 — Yellow
Terminal 4 — Green
Terminal 6 — Red
Terminal 8 — Blue
Terminal 7 — Vacant

With the introduction of the new panel other controls were mounted below the heater and ventilation control unit.

47. Stop Lamp Switch

1. The stop lamp switch is mounted on the brake pedal support bracket adjacent to the brake pedal. It is operated mechanically on depression of the brake pedal.
2. The switch should operate when the brake pedal is depressed ½ inch (12 mm). It can be adjusted by slackening the retaining nut, and moving it in relation to the brake pedal.
3. If the switch is suspected of not working, first check that the circuit is working, by bridging the two terminals of the switch and noting whether the stop lights come on (with the ignition switched on). If they do, the switch is at fault. If not, check the stop lamp circuit wiring.

Fig.10.56. Instrument panel (later models). Arrows indicate securing screw.

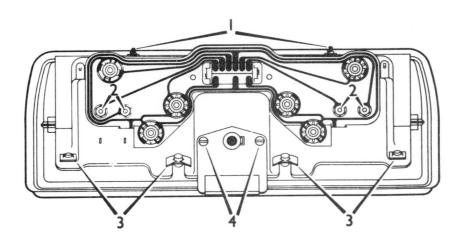

Fig.10.55. REAR VIEW OF INSTRUMENT PANEL

1. Securing screws - instrument panel
2. Mounting nuts-gauges
3. Clips - instrument panel to casing
4. Mounting screw - speed-ometer head

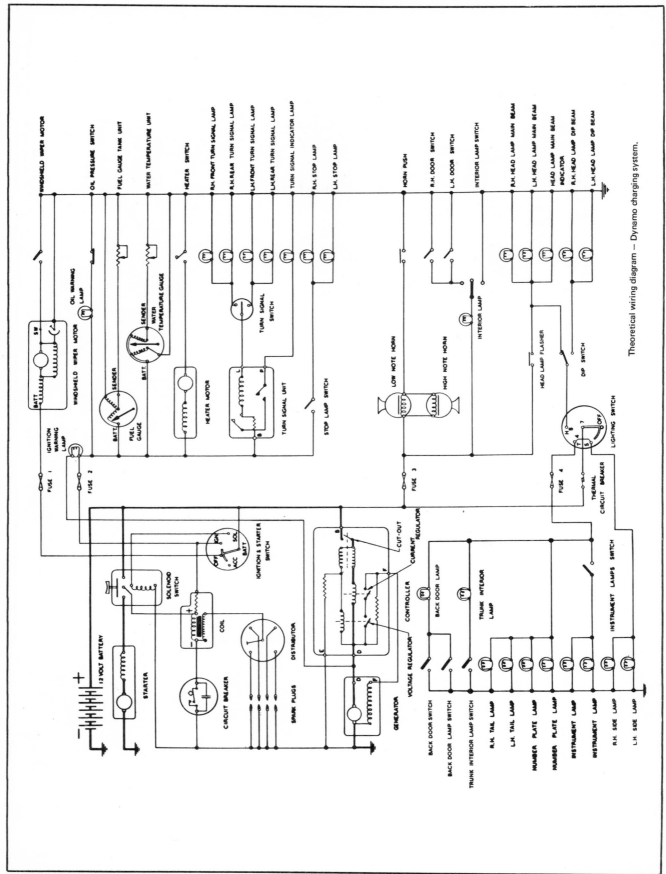

Theoretical wiring diagram – Dynamo charging system.

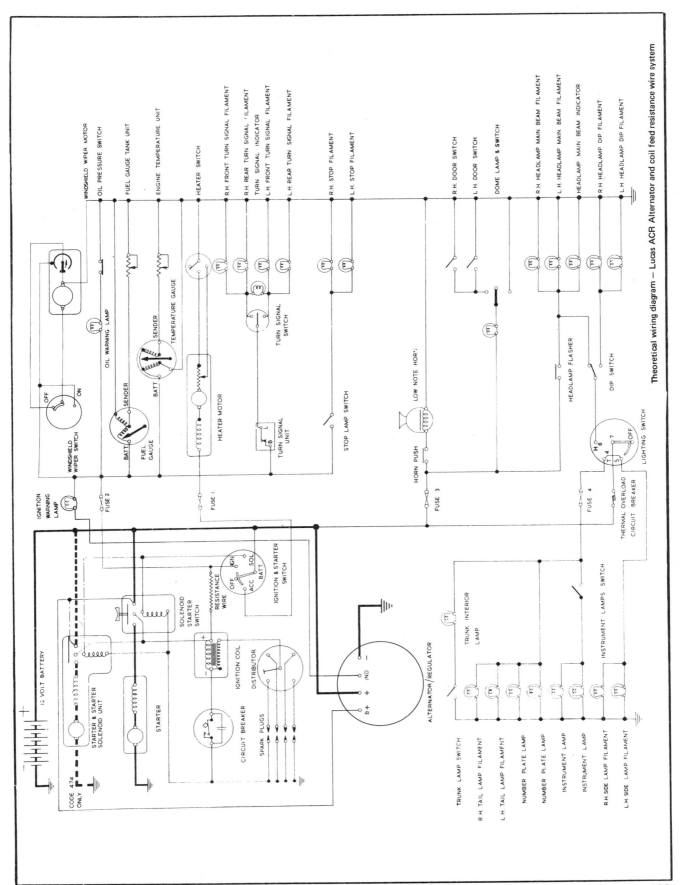

Theoretical wiring diagram – Lucas ACR Alternator and coil feed resistance wire system

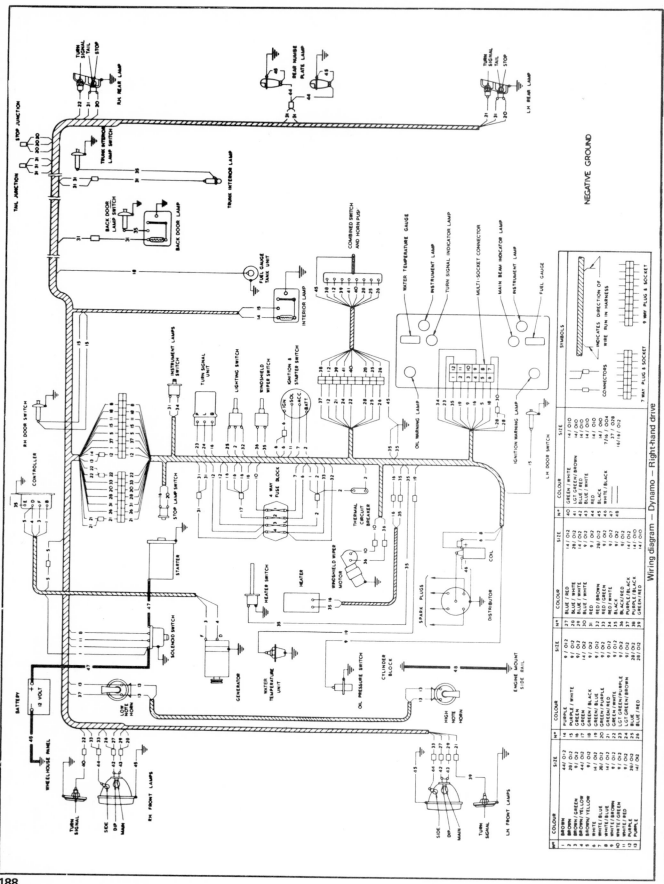

Wiring diagram — Dynamo — Right-hand drive

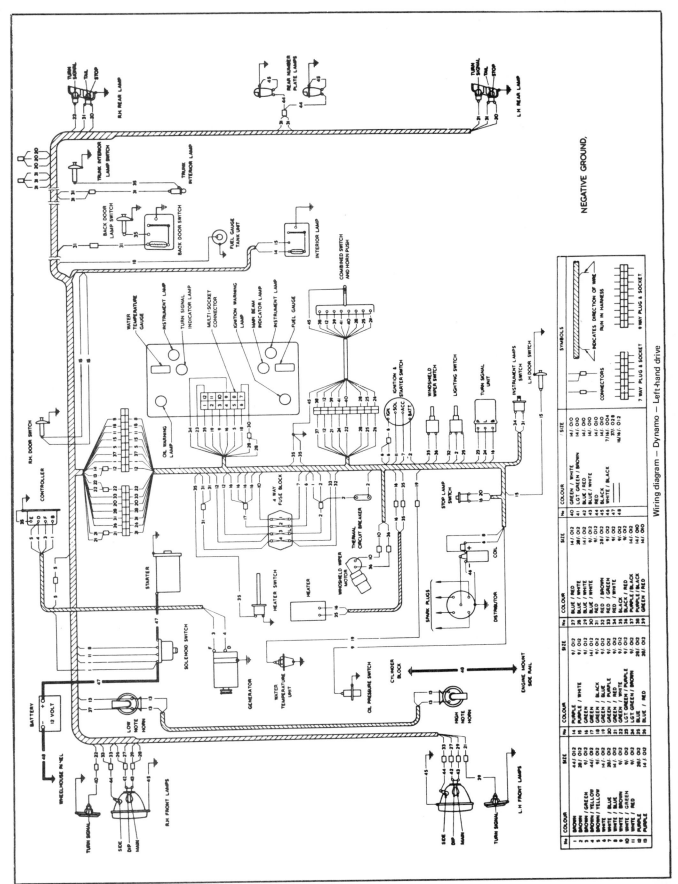

Wiring diagram — Dynamo — Left-hand drive

189

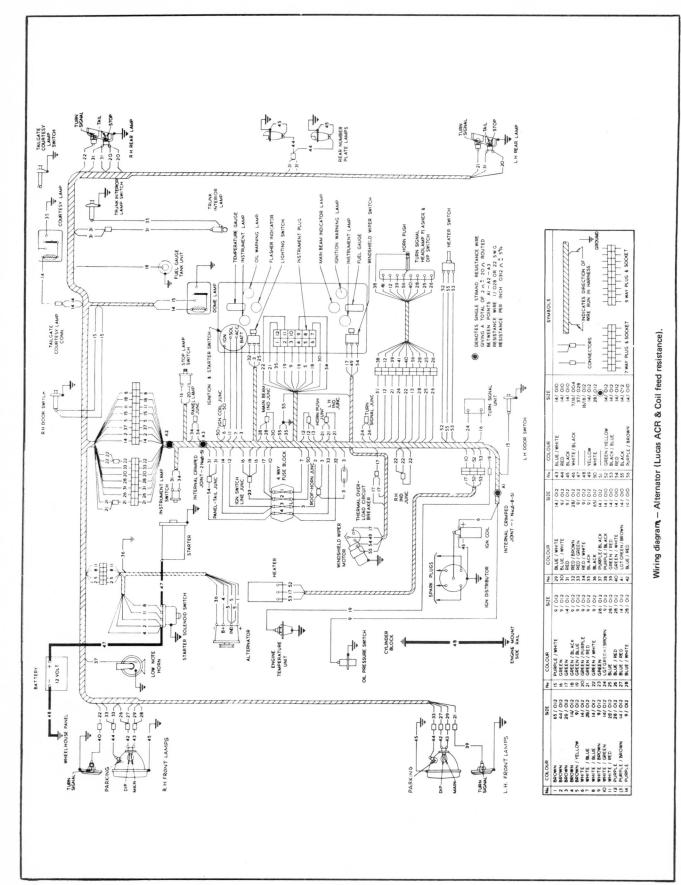

Wiring diagram — Alternator (Lucas ACR & Coil feed resistance).

190

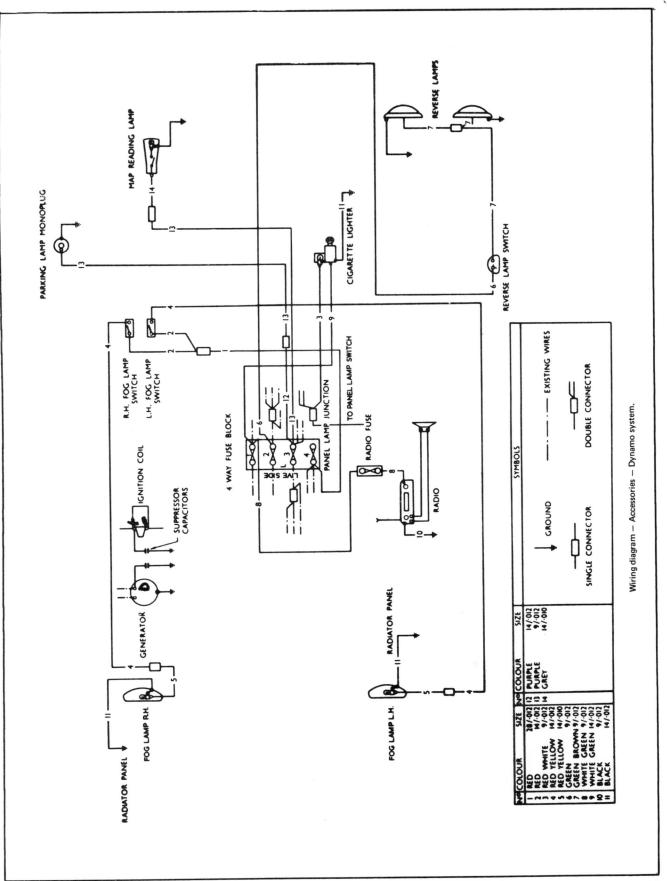

Wiring diagram — Accessories — Dynamo system.

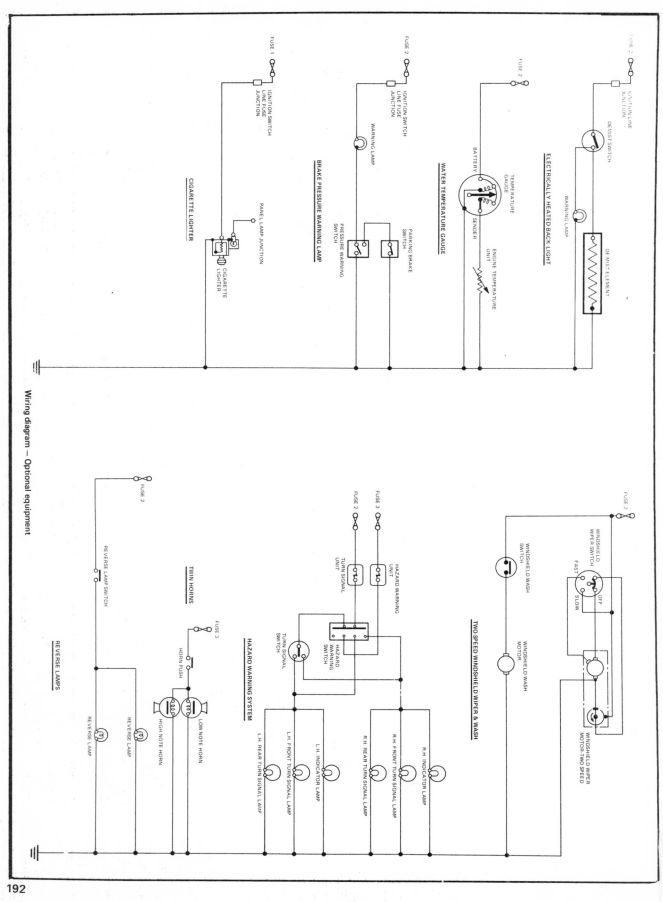

Wiring diagram – Optional equipment

CIGARETTE LIGHTER

BRAKE PRESSURE WARNING LAMP

WATER TEMPERATURE GAUGE

ELECTRICALLY HEATED BACK LIGHT

REVERSE LAMPS

TWIN HORNS

HAZARD WARNING SYSTEM

TWO SPEED WINDSHIELD WIPER & WASH

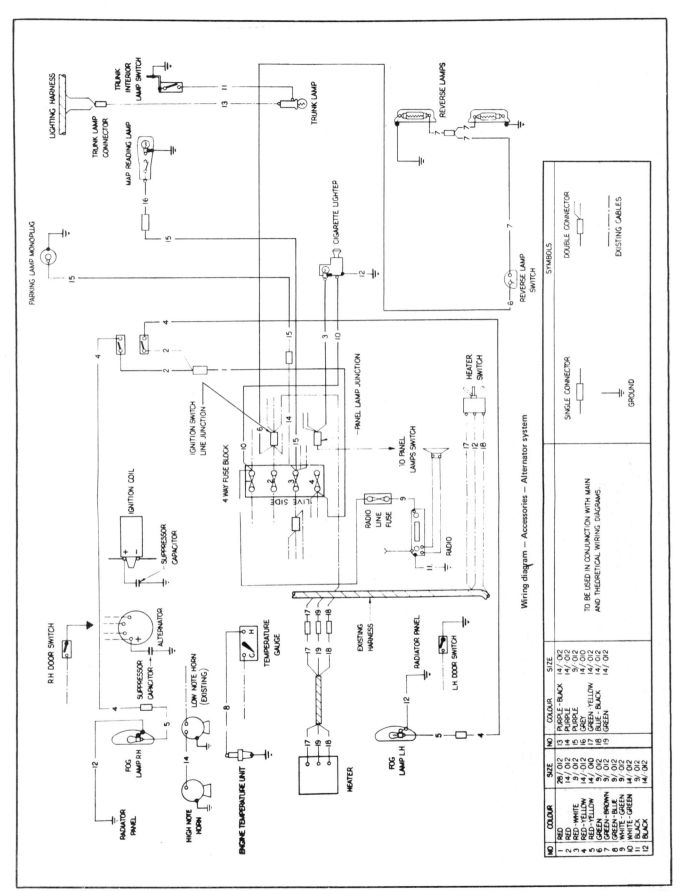

Wiring diagram – Accessories – Alternator system

TO BE USED IN CONJUNCTION WITH MAIN
AND THEORETICAL WIRING DIAGRAMS.

NO	COLOUR	SIZE
1	RED	28/.012
2	RED	14/.012
3	RED-WHITE	9/.012
4	RED-YELLOW	14/.012
5	RED-YELLOW	14/.010
6	GREEN	9/.012
7	GREEN-BROWN	9/.012
8	GREEN-BLUE	9/.012
9	WHITE-GREEN	14/.012
10	WHITE-GREEN	14/.012
11	BLACK	9/.012
12	BLACK	14/.012

NO	COLOUR	SIZE
13	PURPLE-BLACK	14/.012
14	PURPLE	14/.012
15	PURPLE	9/.012
16	GREY	14/.010
17	GREEN-YELLOW	14/.012
18	BLUE-BLACK	14/.012
19	GREEN	14/.012

SYMBOLS

DOUBLE CONNECTOR

EXISTING CABLES

SINGLE CONNECTOR

GROUND

Chapter 11/Suspension - Dampers - Steering

Contents

Specifications

Front Suspension

Type	Independent, coil springs with single lower arms and wishbone upper arms.
Front end standing height - Standard...	9.45 in. to 10.20 in.
- Heavy duty	9.95 in. to 10.70 in.

NOTE: Measured vertically from a level floor to the centre of the lower arm fulcrum bolt, unladen with fuel tank full. Each side should be within specification and the difference between them not exceed .24 inches.

Rear Suspension

Type	Coil spring, four arm location
Rear end standing height - Standard	7.96 in. to 8.76 in.
- Heavy duty	8.46 in. to 9.26 in.

NOTE: Measured vertically from a level floor to the centre of the lower arm front mounting bolt, unladen with a fuel tank full. Each side should be within specifications and the difference between them not exceed .24 inches.

Steering

Type	Rack and pinion
Make	Burman or Cam Gears
Oil capacity	¼ pint (Imperial)

Steering Geometry
(Up to Chassis Nos. OE339002 and OV252006)
(Maximum limits given)

Toe-in measured on rims at height of wheel centres	0 — 1/10 inch
Camber angle	0 — 2° 30' positive
Steering pivot (king pin) inclination	5° 38' to 8° 38'
Castor angle	2° to 2° 30'
Toe-out on turns	Outer wheel 18° 45' from straight with inner wheel at 20°

(Chassis Nos. OE339003 and OV252007 on)
(Maximum limits given)

Toe-in measured on rims at height of wheel centre	1/25 in. toe-in — 1/25 in. toe-out
Camber angle	1° 45' negative — 0° 45' positive
Steering pivot (king pin) inclination	7° 10' — 10° 10'
Castor angle	2° 30' — 4°

Toe-out on turns ... ...   Outer wheel 18° 45' from straight with inner wheel at 20°

Dampers

Type... ... ...   Telescopic double acting front and rear

Wheels & Tyres

Type... ... ...   Steel disc stud fixing
Tyres ... ...   5.50 x 12
Tyre pressures:—
    Standard suspension normal conditions ... ...   22 lbs/in.^{2} front and rear
    Standard suspension - prolonged speedometer full
    load conditions .. ..   24 lb/in.^{2} front   26 lb/in.^{2} rear
    Heavy duty suspension - all conditions.. ... ...   24 lb/in.^{2} front   28 lb/in.^{2} rear

Torque Wrench Settings

Front crossmember upper mounting to body nuts...	19 lb/ft.
Front crossmember rear mounting to body bolts	32 lb/ft.
Spring upper mounting to crossmember bolts	32 lb/ft.
Upper wishbone pivot bolt	37 lb/ft.
Lower arm pivot bolt	32 lb/ft.
Upper ball joint securing bolts (replacement)	22 lb/ft.
Steering knuckle to ball joint nuts	33 lb/ft. (tighten further for split pin)
Steering arm to steering knuckle	25 lb/ft.
Track rod end to steering arm nut	24 lb/ft.
Damper top mounting bolt...	32 lb/ft.
Damper lower mounting bolt	57 lb/ft.
Control rod to lower arm bolts	32 lb/ft.
Control rod rear end nut	32 lb/ft.
Rear suspension arms to hangars and axle mounting bolts..	38 lb/ft.
Rear spring to suspension arm mounting nut	19 lb/ft.
Steering wheel nut (Early Models)...	57 lb/ft.
Steering wheel nut with serrated flange (Later Models) ...	45 lb/ft.
Steering coupling to flanges	12 lb/ft.
Steering coupling cotter nut..	7 lb/ft.
Steering gear to crossmember bolts	19 lb/ft.

1. General Description

The HB series Viva was fitted with a completely re-designed suspension system which, together with the body styling change was the major difference from the previous HA model. Coil springs, wishbones and control rods replaced the transverse leaf at the front and at the rear, the conventional semi-elliptic leaf springs of the HA model were superseded by coil springs and radius arms. The improvement is very significant both in road holding and comfort and as far as the do-it-yourself owner is concerned the repairs, when necessary, are if anything easier than before. Double acting telescopic hydraulic dampers are used at both front and rear.

The steering is rack and pinion of conventional design and the products of either of two manufactures is fitted, namely Burman or Cam Gears. These can be identified by the manufacturers name cast on to the bottom of the gear housing. The assembly, comprising a housing, rack and pinion, is supported in rubber mountings on the front of the axle crossmember. The rack is mounted in one end of the housing by a bush, and at the other by a spring loaded adjustable yoke which also maintains engagement with the pinion. The pinion is mounted between ball thrust bearings, the pre-loading of which is also adjustable. The inner ends of the steering tie rods are attached to the rack by adjustable ball joints. The outer ends are fixed to the steering knuckle by sealed ball joints.

The steering column shaft is divided at its lower end by a flexible rubber coupling, the lower section of shaft being offset. This is a safety feature permitting the shaft to crumple on impact, rather than penetrate into the driving compartment. The column itself is clamped by a rubber insulated plate to the toe panel at the lower end and at the upper end to the dash panel. The shaft runs in spring loaded cup bearings at top and bottom.

2. Routine Maintenance

(a) Suspension & Dampers.

All wishbone fulcrum bushes at the front and radius arm bushes at the rear are rubber mounted and not subject to lubrication. Consequently maintenance consists simply of regular examination for any signs of deterioration or free play in the bushes. If any exists then the bushes must be renewed as described in the text.

(b) Steering.

The steering gear assembly is oil filled and needs no attention under normal circumstances. Periodical examination of the rubber boots at each end of the rack assembly is essential as if these deteriorate oil will leak out. If this should happen the assembly must be refilled with oil and new boots fitted without delay.

The upper and lower steering knuckles are provided with grease nipples. Apply grease every 12 months or 12,000 miles. Do not overgrease beyond the capacity of the retaining boots. These joints must be examined also for signs of excessive play and wear.

It must be emphasised that although at some points no maintenance is possible other than the replacement of the defective bush or knuckle, a car due for a roadworthiness test can be rejected if any of the items on the front suspension and steering are worn beyond a certain point. It is therefore, particularly important that owners do not fall into the trap of thinking that because their cars no longer need greasing they are no longer subject to wear in those places where grease was once applied routinely. The front wheel bearings relate to the condition of the steering and must be checked for wear regularly.

It is also recommended that the front wheel hub bearings are dismantled, flushed out and repacked with grease every 12 months or 12,000 miles although the manufacturers interval recommended is less frequent.

Defective steering is the most dangerous of any fault that may occur on a car, so regular attention is vital.

3. Springs & Dampers — Inspection

1. With the tyre pressures correct, fuel tank full and the car standing on level smooth ground, bounce it up and down a few times and let it settle. Then measure the distance from the lower arm fulcrum bolt centre to the ground (Fig.11.2), and from the rear longitudinal arm front bolt centre to the ground (Fig.11.3).

Make sure that any measurement outside specification is not affected by another before deciding how many springs may need renewal. This can be done by raising the car to the correct height on blocks at the faulty location and rechecking the remainder.

2. Dampers may be checked by bouncing the car at each corner. Generally speaking the body will return to its normal position and stop after being depressed. If it rises and returns on a rebound the damper should be suspect. Examine also the damper mounting bushes for any sign of looseness and the cylinders themselves for traces of hydraulic fluid leaks. If there is any sign of the latter, the unit must be renewed. Static tests of dampers are not entirely conclusive and further indications of damper failure are noticeable pitching; (bonnet going up and down when the car is braked and stopped sharply) excessive rolling on fast bends; and a definite feeling of insecurity on corners, particularly if the road surface is uneven. If you are in doubt it is a good idea to drive over a roughish road and have someone follow you to watch how the wheels behave. Excessive up and down 'patter' of any wheel is usually quite obvious, and denotes a defective damper.

4. Front Dampers — Removal & Replacement

All figures in text refer to Fig.11.1.
1. Removal of the dampers is made easier with the special Vauxhall tool VR2001 to compress the spring. but is not essential.
2. Jack up the car so that the front wheel is clear of the ground by a few inches.
3. Undo the three nuts (39,57) which hold the lower damper mounting plates to the lower suspension arm and also the nut (54) on the lower damper mounting bolt (51).
4. Place a block under the front wheel and then lower the car so that the brackets and lower damper mounting come clear of the arm. Remove the lower mounting pin and detach the brackets.
5. Remove the upper mounting bolt and nut (49,50) and the damper may be withdrawn from below.
6. The lower damper mounting bushes may be renewed separately if required but the top bush is part of the damper and is not supplied separately.
7. Reassembly is a reversal of the removal procedure but for convenience refit the lower mounting bushes and brackets loosely before reconnecting the top. Tighten all nuts to the specified torques.

5. Front Springs — Removal & Replacement

All figures in text refer to Fig.11.1.
1. Proceed as for front damper removal as described in Section 4, as far as paragraph 4 inclusive. Slacken also the nut (36) on the lower arm fulcrum pin (35). The coil spring is now held in compression by the lower suspension arm which is secured only by the lower steering joint (24) to the steering arm. Obviously the joint cannot be separated from the arm without taking measures to control the expansion of the spring when the lower arm is released. With a spring compressor this is no problem. A spring compressor can be made using short lengths of iron rod with the ends bent over to form hooks. Three of these will hold the coils of the spring sufficiently to enable the lower arm to be disengaged.
2. Alternatively one may proceed as follows. Jack the wheel up under the lower suspension arm and then support the car under the front crossmember.
3. Place a block of wood between the spring upper mounting and the upper wishbone to hold the wishbone up in position.
4. Disconnect the lower suspension arm ball joint as described in Section 6.
5. Lower the jack under the lower suspension arm until the spring is completely relaxed. The spring may then be detached.
6. Replacement is a reversal of this procedure. Make sure that the spring locates correctly in the lower arm seat and that the tapers of the ball joint pin and steering knuckle are perfectly clean and dry before reconnection.
7. When the weight of the car is finally resting on the suspension, retighten the lower arm fulcrum bolt to the recommended torque of 32 lb/ft.

6. Front Suspension Arm Ball Joints — Removal & Replacement

1. The front suspension ball joints will need renewal if they are worn beyond the acceptable limits. This wear is one of the items checked on the annual M.O.T. tests. The lower joint can be checked by jacking the car up so that the wheel hangs free and then placing another jack under the lower suspension arm and raising the arm so that the movement in the joint can be detected. It should not exceed .085 inch (2 mm). If there is any lateral movement the joint must be renewed anyway. On some later models a different type of ball joint was fitted and this can be identified by the fact that it has a self locking nut instead of a nut and split pin securing it. Fig.11.11 shows the difference between the two. The later type has no inbuilt vertical clearance whatsoever and if there are signs of vertical movement when it is checked then the joint must be renewed.
2. To remove the joint, first take off the split pin and nut (32) from the pin located in the steering knuckle.
3. Separate the joint from the knuckle. This can only be done with surety by using a claw clamp. However it is possible to drive through but only if the knuckle is firmly supported. It will almost certainly be damaged in the process so unless it is being renewed a claw clamp is essential. The lower suspension arm will only

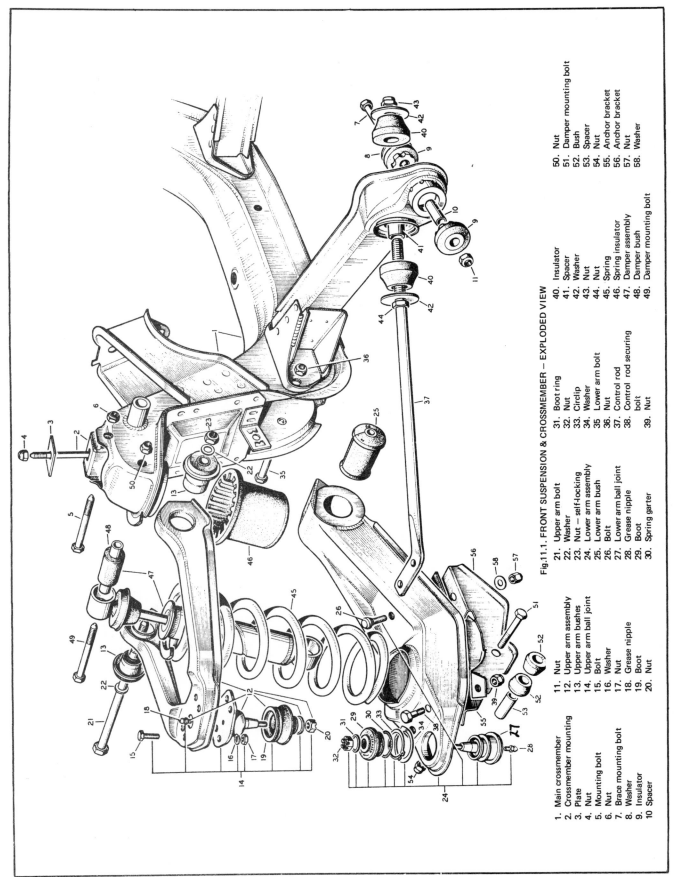

Fig.11.1.1. FRONT SUSPENSION & CROSSMEMBER – EXPLODED VIEW

1. Main crossmember	21. Upper arm bolt	40. Insulator
2. Crossmember mounting	22. Upper arm assembly	41. Spacer
3. Plate	23. Upper arm bushes	42. Washer
4. Nut	24. Upper arm ball joint	43. Nut
5. Mounting bolt	25. Lower arm assembly	44. Nut
6. Nut	26. Lower arm bush	45. Spring
7. Brace mounting bolt	27. Lower arm ball joint	46. Spring insulator
8. Washer	28. Grease nipple	47. Damper assembly
9. Insulator	29. Boot	48. Damper bush
10 Spacer	30. Nut	49. Damper mounting bolt
11. Nut	31. Boot ring	50. Nut
12. Upper arm assembly	32. Nut	51. Damper mounting bolt
13. Plate	33. Circlip	52. Bush
14. Bolt	34. Washer	53. Spacer
15. Bolt	35. Lower arm bolt	54. Nut
16. Washer	36. Nut	55. Anchor bracket
17. Nut	37. Control rod	56. Anchor bracket
18. Grease nipple	38. Control rod securing bolt	57. Nut
19. Boot	39. Nut	58. Washer
20. Nut	30. Spring garter	

197

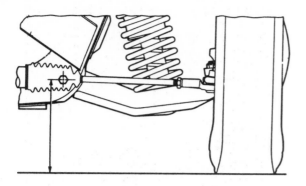

Fig.11.2. Diagram showing measurement point for front standing height check

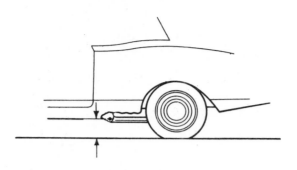

Fig.11.3. Diagram showing measurement point for rear standing height check

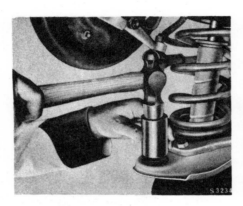

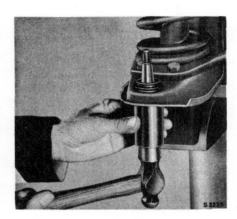

Fig.11.4. Driving out a lower arm ball joint with a suitable piece of tube and refitting a new one.

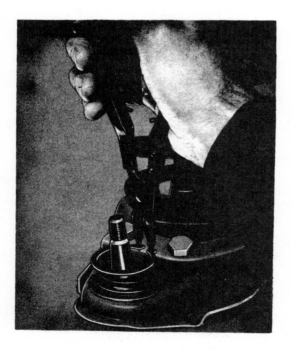

Fig.11.5. Front suspension lower arm ball joint removal of retaining circlip

Fig.11.6. Showing how the special washer is lined up when fitting a new lower arm ball joint

Fig.11.7. Detecting signs of play in an upper suspension arm ball joint

Fig.11.8. Front suspension bump stop as fitted to later model front crossmembers.

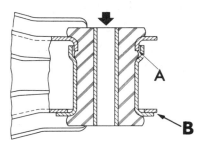

Fig.11.9. Cross section of suspension arm bush to show direction of removal

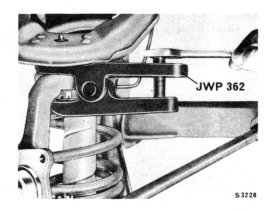

Fig.11.10. Disconnecting the upper ball joint from the steering knuckle using a special clamp

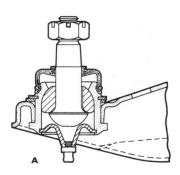

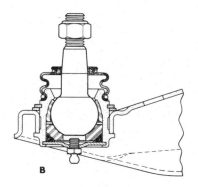

Fig.11.11. CROSS SECTION OF TWO TYPES OF LOWER SUSPENSION ARM BALL JOINTS USED
'A' has inbuilt vertical play. 'B' has none.

move a limited way as it is held by the front damper.

4. The car should then be jacked up under the front crossmember, a block placed under the wheel, and the car lowered again until the lower ball joint is clear of the knuckle and can be got at for removal from the arm.

5. To remove the joint from the arm, first remove the circlip (Fig.11.5) and washer.

6. Using a piece of tube, drive the joint out of the arm (Fig.11.4). It may be necessary to put a block of wood under the arm to provide a firm support for this.

7. Drive in a new joint so that the splines engage in the arm. Then fit the special washer with the flat lined up (Fig.11.6) and the concave side upwards and replace the circlip.

8. Reconnect the pin to the steering knuckle ensuring that the mating surfaces of the taper are clean. Replace the nut and split pin.

9. The upper arm ball joint (12) can be checked by jacking the car up and rocking the wheel whilst holding the joint to detect any play (Fig.11.7). If there is any play the joint must be renewed. This necessitates removal of the upper wishbone (See Section 7).

10 With the upper wishbone removed, the four rivets holding the joint must be drilled out without damaging the holes in the arm.

11 The holes in the arm must then be drilled out to 5/16th inch. The new joint will be supplied with the necessary mounting bolts. Install these with the heads uppermost and tighten the nuts to the specified torque of 22 lb/ft.

12 Replace the arm as described in Section 7.

7. Front Suspension Arms — Removal & Replacement

Figures in the text refer to Fig.11.1.

1. The suspension arms will need to be removed if the bushes are worn. Also the upper suspension arm needs to be removed in order to renew the ball joint.

2. To remove the upper arm, jack up the suspension under the lower arm and then remove the upper ball joint from the steering knuckle. This entails removal of the split pin and loosening the castellated nut followed by clamping the unit as shown. (Fig.11.10). There is virtually no other way of doing this without cutting the pin off, which of course can be done if the joint is being renewed.

3. Next, remove the long fulcrum bolt (21), and nut (23), which hold the upper arm to the crossmember. If necessary it is permissible to bend back the lashing eye (used for securing the car when carried on a transporter) which may get in the way when withdrawing the bolt. The arm can then be taken off.

4. To renew the bushes (13) calls for care as the arms of the wishbone must not be distorted during the course of removing and replacing the bushes. It is best to get the old ones out by cutting through them.

5. New bushes should be lubricated with soapy water and drawn in using a long nut and bolt together with a tubular spacer (on the inside of the arm) and large washers to ensure the bushes are drawn in square.

6. Replace the arm in the reverse order of removal but do not tighten the nut on the fulcrum bolt to the full torque until the weight of the car is resting on the suspension.

7. To remove the lower suspension arm proceed as for removal of the front spring as described in Section 5. Then remove the fulcrum bolt and the arm can be drawn away from the mounting brackets.

8. The single large bush needs careful treatment in removal if the arm is not to be distorted.

9. First cut off the flange of the old bush with a knife on the side of the arm as indicated in Fig.11.9. This side of the arm can be identified, being the one with a single plate thickness only round the bush, as opposed to double thickness (arrow B). Then, using a piece of tube and a suitable drive rod, press it out from the side where the flange has been cut off. Unless this is done the bush will bind on the flange inside the bush (arrowed A in the figure) and excessive force will distort the arm.

10 The new bush, well lubricated with soapy water must be pressed in, in the same direction as the old one was removed. On later models, the bush for the lower suspension arm is encased in a steel sleeve. This sleeve should be smeared with oil to aid fitment. When the bush being renewed is one of those with a steel jacket it is easier to draw in the new one and force out the old one in a single operation, using a long bolt and spacer tube. Otherwise difficulty may be encountered in getting the old steel sleeve out.

11 Replacement of the arm is in the reverse order of removal. Do not tighten the fulcrum bolt nut until the weight of the car is resting on the suspension.

8. Front Suspension Control Rods — Removal & Replacement

All numbers refer to Fig.11 1.

1. The front suspension lower arms are stabilised fore and aft by a rod (37) which is bolted to their outer ends and located in rubber bushes (40) at the other end into the front crossmember support stays. The length of the rod is adjustable to achieve the correct degree of castor angle on the front wheels.

2. If the control rod bushes need renewal it will be necessary to remove the rod first.

3. Jack up the suspension under the lower arm and remove the two nuts and bolts (38 and 39) securing the forward end to the suspension arm.

3. Slacken the two nuts (43 and 44) noting the position of the inner one first in relation to the thread. Then remove the end one (43) followed by the washer (42) and half bush. The rod may then be drawn out.

4. Return the inner nut to its original position before fitting new bushes and then replace the arm in the reverse order of removal.

5. Tighten the rear nut to 32 lb/ft.

6. It is advisable to have the steering geometry checked at a garage with suitable testing equipment after removal and replacement of these control rods.

9. Front Crossmember — Dimensions & Differences

Fig.11.12 shows the checking dimensions of the front crossmember on earlier models. When the steering geometry changes were made on later models the front crossmember was re-designed to provide for them and the dimensions were changed as shown in Fig.11.13. At the same time, the front suspension bump stops, previously incorporated in the dampers, were mounted on extension brackets of the crossmember as shown in Fig.11.8.

10. Rear Dampers — Removal & Replacement

1. The rear dampers will need removal if their mounting bushes are worn or if indications are that the unit is no longer performing properly.

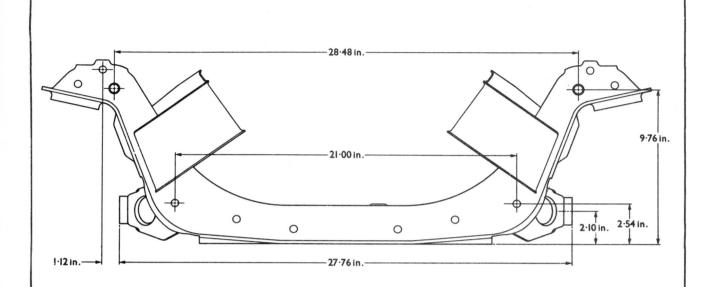

Fig.11.12. Front crossmember — early models

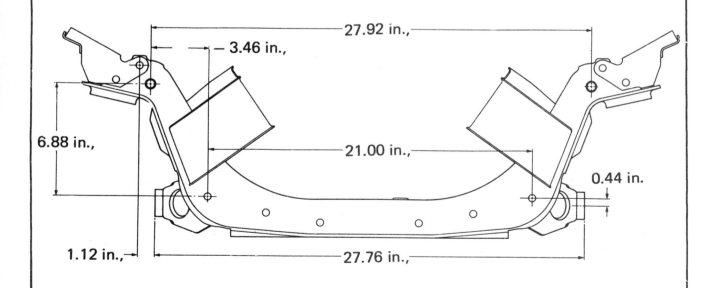

Fig.11.13. Front crossmember — later models

2. It is not necessary to raise the car to remove the dampers but if it is raised the axle should be supported as well.

3. To detach the top mounting, remove the rubber plug from the wheel arch inside the boot when the two upper nuts will be accessible. The slotted spindle will need holding firmly whilst the nuts are removed.

4. The lower mounting eye may be disconnected by removing the nut on the mounting pin and pulling it off.

5. Replacement is a reversal of the removal procedure. All bushes are renewable and care should be taken to arrange the bushes and washers correctly as shown in Fig.11.14.

6. Tighten the top securing nuts down to the bottom of the stud threads.

11. Rear Springs — Removal & Replacement

1. Jack up the car and support the body under the rear frame members on stands. Then support the axle on a jack.

2. Undo the lower spring mounting stud nut which is underneath the longitudinal suspension arm (See Fig. 11.14).

3. Lower the jack under the axle until the suspension arm is clear of the spring.

4. Using a socket wrench remove the upper bolt which is in the centre of the upper spring seat and fits into a captive nut in the side member.

5. Lift out the spring complete with the upper mounting seat.

6. New springs, spring seats, rubber insulators and retainers are supplied individually. They are all assembled and held together by the centre bush which is peened over on to the upper seat. Fig.11.15 shows a cross-section of the assembly with a special Vauxhall tool used to draw the new bush into position and peen over the top. If other improvised tools are used to carry out this job the main thing to remember is that the upper seat spring retainer must be held tightly together when the bush is being peened over.

7. Note that the upper seat has a dowel peg which locates in a corresponding hole in the side member. This must be correctly positioned when refitting the spring assembly which is otherwise a straightforward reversal of the removal procedure.

12. Rear Suspension Arms — Removal & Replacement

1. If the rubber mounting bushes at each end of any of the arms are worn it will be necessary to remove the arms to replace them.

2. The upper (radius) arms are bushed at the front end and bolted between brackets on the rear body frame member. The rear end locates over a lug on the rear axle, which is rubber bushed and is secured by a bolt and nut.

3. Simply by removing the nuts and bolts at each end the arm can be removed.

4. The front bush should be removed and replaced in exactly the same manner as described for the front suspension lower arm as described in Section 7.

5. The rear bush will need drawing out of the lug on the axle using a long nut and bolt with a tubular spacer and large flat washers. The new bush should be drawn in on the same manner after it has been well lubricated with soapy water.

6. Replace the arm and bolts but before tightening the nuts to the correct torque (38 lb/ft) let the weight of the car settle on the springs.

7. The lower (longitudinal) arms can be removed after first raising and supporting the car on stands under the body side frame members and placing a jack under the axle.

8. Remove the nut securing the lower spring mounting plate to the arm and then lower the jack until the arm is clear of the spring.

9. Remove the mounting bolts and nuts at each end and the arm can then be detached.

10 The same precautions for removal and replacement of the bushes apply as they do for the upper arms. In addition the front bush has two locating ridges which must be set correctly into the arm as shown in Fig. 11.16.

11 When refitting the arm, replace the mounting bolts but do not tighten the nuts to their correct torque (38 lb/ft) until the weight of the car is resting on the springs.

13. Front Wheel Hub Bearings — Inspection & Adjustment

1. The steering qualities of the car will deteriorate if the front wheel bearings are maladjusted or worn and can be a cause of rejection under the M.O.T. roadworthiness test.

2. To check the bearings, first jack up the car so that the wheel is clear of the ground. Check that the wheel spins freely with the brakes off.

3. Then grip the edge of the tyre at top and bottom and try and rock it in a vertical plane. If movement can be felt it is normally due to looseness in the bearing but at the same time it should be noted whether there is any sign of lateral movement in either the upper or lower suspension arm ball joints. (If there is they must be renewed as described in Section 6.).

4. There should be no detectable movement in the wheel bearings and if there is they should be adjusted. Fig.11.17 gives an exploded view of a front hub with either disc or drum brakes. Figures in the text refer to this drawing.

5. Remove the hub cap from the wheel and then tap the dust cover (18) out of the centre of the hub.

6. Remove the split pin from the nut (17) and, using a tubular spanner, tighten the nut whilst continuing to revolve the wheel. Then slacken the nut off and re-tighten it using only the tubular spanner without a tommy bar. This will provide the maximum permissible loading on the bearing.

7. The wheel should now spin freely with no indications of movement when rocked vertically. If any roughness is felt on spinning the wheel, the bearings should be removed for further examination.

8. Provided the adjustment is satisfactory fit a new split pin, backing off the nut to line up the hole if necessary. On later models the bearing nut is not slotted but is enclosed in a pressed steel retainer which has eight tags in it to provide more alternative positions for the split pin. This provides for finer adjustment of the wheel bearings. Replace the dust cap and hub cap and lower the wheel to the ground.

14. Front Wheel Hubs & Bearings — Removal, Inspection & Replacement

1. Jack up the car and remove the road wheel.

2. On drum brake models slacken off the brake adjusters as described in Chapter 9/3, on disc brake models

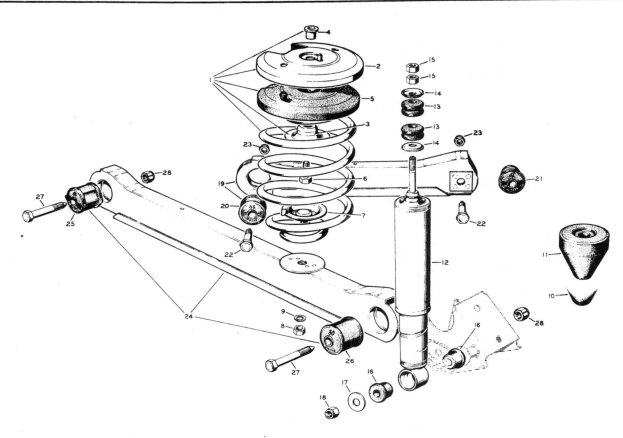

Fig.11.14. REAR SUSPENSION & RADIUS ARMS — EXPLODED VIEW

1. Spring and upper seat assembly	8. Nut	16. Bush - lower
2. Upper seat assembly	9. Spring washer	17. Washer
3. Upper retainer	10. Bump stop - normal	18. Nut
4. Upper bush	11. Bump stop - heavy duty	19. Upper arm and bush assembly
5. Rubber insulator	12. Damper	20. Bush-front upper arm
6. Mounting bolt-upper	13. Bush - upper	21. Bush - rear upper arm
7. Lower spring retainer	14. Retaining washers	22. Bolt
	15. Lock nuts	

23. Nut
24. Lower arm and bush assembly
25. Bush—front lower arm
26. Bush—rear lower arm
27. Bolt
28. Nut

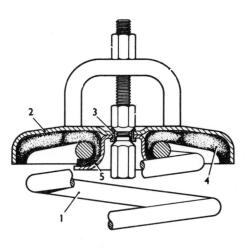

Fig.11.15. CROSS SECTION OF REAR SPRING UPPER MOUNTING

1. Spring   4. Rubber insulator
2. Upper seat   5. Spring retainer
3. Bush

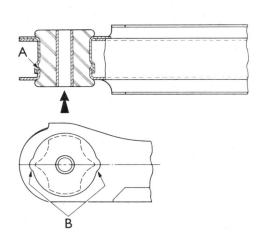

Fig.11.16. REAR SUSPENSION LOWER (LONGITUDINAL) ARM FRONT BUSH

A Lip requiring removal in direction of arrow

B Positioning lugs of bush when fitting new one

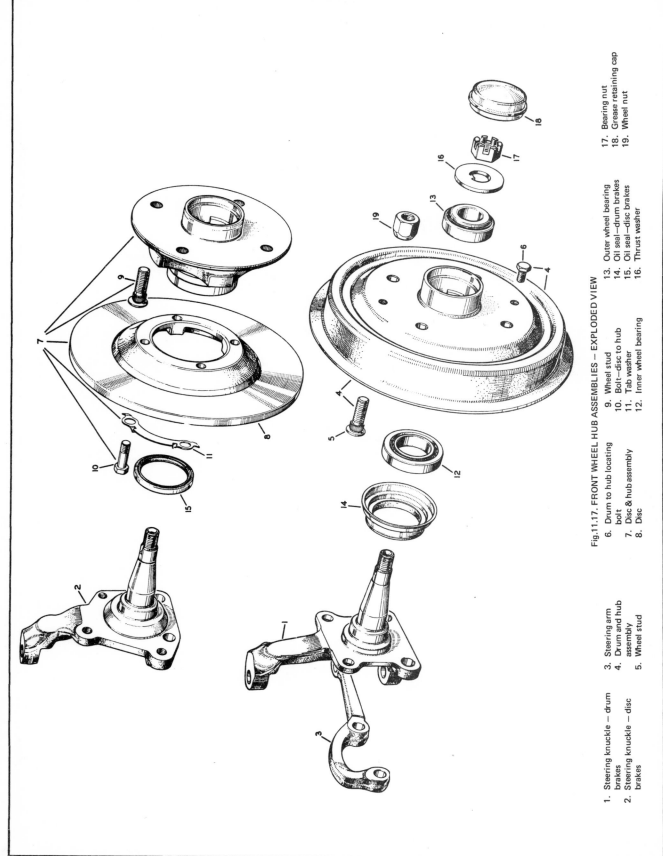

Fig.11.17. FRONT WHEEL HUB ASSEMBLIES – EXPLODED VIEW

1. Steering knuckle – drum brakes
2. Steering knuckle – disc brakes
3. Steering arm
4. Drum and hub assembly
5. Wheel stud
6. Drum to hub locating bolt
7. Disc & hub assembly
8. Disc
9. Wheel stud
10. Bolt–disc to hub
11. Tab washer
12. Inner wheel bearing
13. Outer wheel bearing
14. Oil seal–drum brakes
15. Oil seal–disc brakes
16. Thrust washer
17. Bearing nut
18. Grease retaining cap
19. Wheel nut

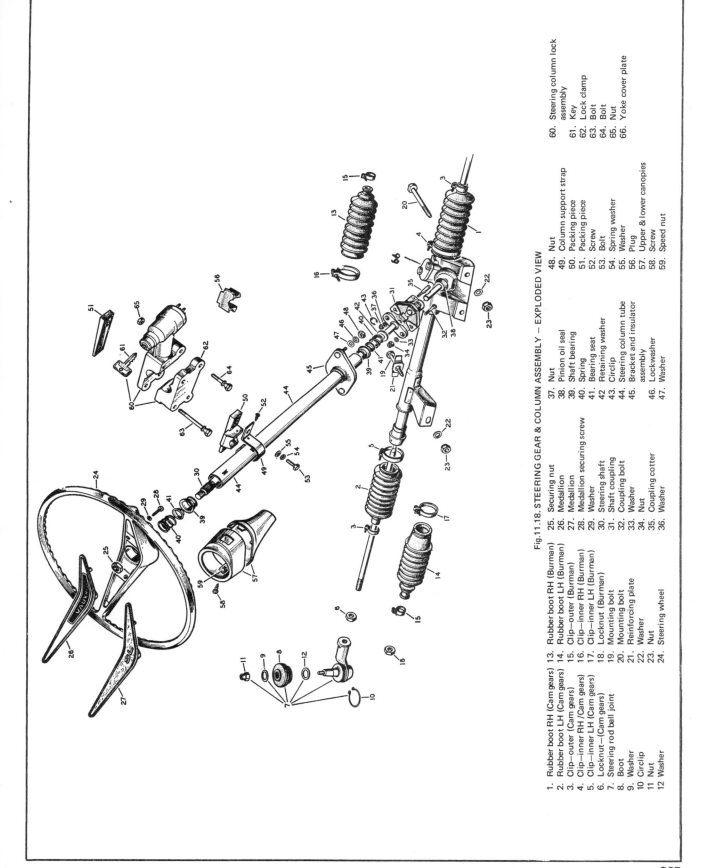

Fig.11.18. STEERING GEAR & COLUMN ASSEMBLY — EXPLODED VIEW

1. Rubber boot RH (Cam gears)
2. Rubber boot LH (Cam gears)
3. Clip—outer (Cam gears)
4. Clip—inner RH /Cam gears)
5. Clip—inner LH (Cam gears)
6. Locknut—(Cam gears)
7. Steering rod ball joint
8. Boot
9. Washer
10. Circlip
11. Nut
12. Washer

13. Rubber boot RH (Burman)
14. Rubber boot LH (Burman)
15. Clip—outer (Burman)
16. Clip—inner RH (Burman)
17. Clip—inner LH (Burman)
18. Locknut (Burman)
19. Mounting bolt
20. Mounting bolt
21. Reinforcing plate
22. Washer
23. Nut
24. Steering wheel

25. Securing nut
26. Medallion
27. Medallion
28. Medallion securing screw
29. Washer
30. Steering shaft
31. Shaft coupling
32. Coupling bolt
33. Washer
34. Nut
35. Coupling cotter
36. Washer

37. Nut
38. Pinion oil seal
39. Shaft bearing
40. Spring
41. Bearing seat
42. Retaining washer
43. Circlip
44. Steering column tube
45. Bracket and insulator assembly
46. Lockwasher
47. Washer

48. Nut
49. Column support strap
50. Packing piece
51. Packing piece
52. Screw
53. Bolt
54. Spring washer
55. Washer
56. Plug
57. Upper & lower canopies
58. Screw
59. Speed nut

60. Steering column lock assembly
61. Key
62. Lock clamp
63. Bolt
64. Bolt
65. Nut
66. Yoke cover plate

205

remove the brake calliper as described in Chapter 9/10.

3. Remove the grease cap and the split pin locking the castellated hub nut.

4. Remove the castellated hub nut and the washer behind it which is keyed to the shaft.

5. Withdraw the hub together with the brake drum, or disc, as appropriate.

6. Remove the bolts holding the disc or drum to the hub and separate the two.

7. The ball races will have come off with the hub, and the inner race of the outer bearing will be loose so that it can be taken out.

8. The inner bearing will need to be driven out with a drift from the inside of the hub. Locate the drift against the outside race. The oil seal will come out with the bearing. The outside race of the outer bearing should come out easily but may need tapping from the inside with a drift also.

9. Thoroughly clean the bearings and examine the rollers and races for signs of wear. If in doubt, renew them. Wear can be detected by running perfectly clean, lightly oiled bearings in their races and feeling for traces of roughness. Blue discolouration indicates overheating, but brown discolouration will only be lubricant stain and is not to be taken as an adverse indication.

10. Reassembly of the outer bearing races into the hub is a reversal of the removal procedure. Make sure that the open ends of the tapers of the outer races face outwards from the centre of the hub. Pack the inner bearing inner race and rollers with grease, and place it in position in the hub.

11 With the inner bearing fit a new seal, which on drum brake models fits over the hub boss and on disc brake types recesses into the hub behind the bearing. The lip of the seal should face to the centre of the hub on the latter.

12 Refit the brake drum or disc to the hub, and on disc brakes the bolts should be renewed on later models (they incorporate nylon thread inserts for self-locking purposes).

13 Pack the outer bearing inner race and rollers with the recommended grease, place it in position and refit the complete hub assembly to the spindle. Replace the washer and castellated nut and then adjust the bearings as described in Section 13.

14 Half fill the bearing cover cap with grease before replacement. Do not pack the hub itself in the space between the bearings.

15 Replace the disc calliper if appropriate as described in Chapter 9/10.

16 Adjust drum brakes as described in Chapter 9/3, having first replaced the road wheel.

15. Steering Mechanism — Inspection

All figures in text refer to Fig.11.18.
1. The steering mechanism on the Viva is uncomplicated and easy to check. As the statutory test for vehicles more than 3 years old pays particular attention to it, the owner can save himself a lot of trouble by regular examination, apart from, of course, keeping a check on his own safety.

2. Assuming that the suspension joints and bushes and front wheel bearings have been checked and found in order the steering check involves tracing the amount of lost motion between the rim of steering wheel and the road wheels. If the rim of the steering wheel can be moved more than 1 to 2 inches at its periphery with no sign of movement at either or both of the front wheels it may be assumed that there is excessive wear at some point. If there are signs of lost motion jack up the car at the front and support it under the front crossmember so that both wheels hang free.

3. Grip each wheel in turn and rock it in the direction it would move when steering. It will be possible to feel any play. Check first for any sign of lateral play in the ball joints (7) which connect the tie rods from the steering gear to the steering arms on the wheel knuckles. This is the more common area for wear to occur and if any is apparent the ball joint/s must be renewed.

4. Having checked the ball joints, next grip the tie rod and get someone to move the steering wheel. Do this with the bonnet open and if there is any play still apparent look first to see whether the flexible coupling (31) in the steering column shaft is causing the trouble. If it is it should be renewed.

5. Finally, if play still exists it must be in the steering gear itself. This is more serious (and expensive!). If either of the rubber boots (1 and 2) at each end of the gear housing is damaged, resulting in loss of oil from the unit then various bearings and teeth on the rack and pinion may have been severely worn. In such cases renewal of the complete steering gear assembly may be necessary. Certainly adjustments will be required.

16. Steering Gear — Examination, Adjustment & Replacement

1. Assuming that all ball joints and front wheel bearings are in order, it may be necessary to remove and replace, or renovate, the steering gear if there is excessive play between the steering shaft and the steering tie rods. This can be checked by gripping the inner end of both the rods in turn near the rubber boot, and getting someone to rock the steering wheel. If the wheel moves more than 1/16th of a revolution (11¼° in either direction) without moving the steering tie rod, then the wear is sufficient to justify overhaul. If the rubber boots have leaked oil they will also need renewal and, in order to do this and effectively refill the unit with the proper oil, it is easiest in the long run to remove the assembly from the car.

2. To remove the steering gear from the car first disconnect the lower half of the flexible coupling flange (Fig.11.18 item 31) from the pinion shaft by extracting the cotter pin (Fig.11.18 item 35) from the flange. Then disconnect both tie rod outer ball joints from the steering arms as described in Section 6.. The three mounting bolts (Fig 11.18, 19 and 20) holding the assembly to the front crossmember may then be removed and the unit taken off.

3. If it is necessary to replace only the rubber boots and refill the assembly with lubricant. Remove both outer ball joints from the tie rods together with the lock nuts, having noted their original position carefully. Slacken off the boot retaining clips noting their position in relation to the assembly housing. If the steering arms are dirty, clean them thoroughly and slide off the old boots.

4. Refit the clips to new boots and slide them onto the rods. Tighten the clips in position on one boot only. Stand the unit on end, refill the housing with ¼ pint of Castrol 'Hipress' (or equivalent EP SAE 140 oil), no more, and then refit the other boot and tighten the clips.

5. Service parts for the steering gear are not available for a complete overhaul. If the unit is very seriously worn or damaged therefore, it is recommended that a complete new unit is obtained.

Fig.11.19. Prising the direction indicator cancelling sleeve from the steering wheel

Fig.11.20. Showing a hose clip fitted round the steering shaft coupling to aid installation.

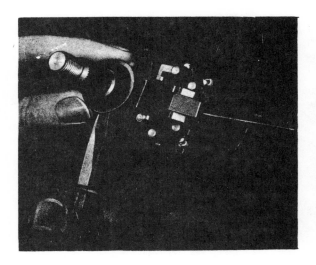

Fig.11.21. Prising the steering shaft top bearing out of the column

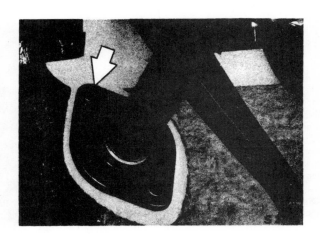

Fig.11.22. Showing how the stud nearest the edge of column locating plate (arrowed) fits uppermost on replacing the steering column assembly

6. It is possible to alleviate some of the play in the gear (between rack and pinion) by checking that the yoke pre-load is correct.

7. Remove the yoke cover plate (Fig.11.18, Item 66) and remove the shims and spring followed by the yoke.

8. Replace the yoke and cover without the spring or any shims and lightly tighten the bolts.

9. Measure the gap between the cover and the housing with a feeler gauge. The thickness of the shims should be the gap measurement PLUS .0005—.003 inch on Burman units or plus .0005—.006 inch on Cam Gear units. Make up the shim packs accordingly and re-assemble. Adjust the shims required to give a turning torque on the pinion of 12 lb/in.

10 Similarly, any sign of end float and slackness in the pinion shaft may be taken up by removing the cover opposite the pinion extension and reducing the thickness of the shims behind the cover accordingly. In this case the shims should be .001—.003 inch LESS than the measured clearance between the cover and housing.

11 It must be emphasised that the adjustments mentioned in this paragraph are not sufficient to compensate for extreme wear. Before making them, therefore, it must be decided whether the wear apparent is beyond adjustment, or sufficient to warrant adjustment anyway.

12 Any play in the tie rod INNER ball joints may be adjusted but involves drilling and re-pinning the joint and this calls for precision work.

13 Replacement of the assembly is a reversal of the procedure as described in paragraph 2. Make sure the assembly is centralised on the steering lock before attaching the pinion shaft to the steering column. Before tightening the cotter pin nut securing the coupling flange to the pinion shaft make sure that the hub of the steering wheel is not rubbing on the column shroud below it. This may be caused by the steering column dropping down a little when the steering gear unit was disconnected. Lift the steering wheel before tightening the cotter clamp nut. Tighten all nuts and bolts to the correct torques as specified.

14 The front wheel toe-in should then be checked at a garage with the proper equipment.

17. Steering Tie Rods Outer Ball Joints — Removal & Replacement

Figures in text refer to Fig.11.18.

1. The removal of the ball joints (7) is necessary if they are to be renewed, or if the rubber boots (2) on the steering gear are being renewed.

2. It is not necessary to jack the car up but the increase in height above ground level may make it more convenient to do so.

3. Slacken the self-locking nut (11) and completely remove it to clear the threads, and replace it after oiling them until the head of the nut is level with the end of the stud. This will protect the threads in subsequent operations if the same joint is being replaced.

4. If a claw clamp is being used to 'break' the taper of the joint pin from the steering arm the joint may be disconnected without further ado.

5. If no claw clamp is available and it is necessary to strike the pin out it is essential to provide a really firm support under the steering arm first. In the photo it can be seen how a socket on the top of a jack was used to achieve this. A firm tap with a normal weight hammer is all that is then necessary to move the pin out of the steering arm (photo).

6. If the nut now turns the pin when trying to remove

it, (despite the precaution taken in paragraph 3) jam the pin back into the arm with the jack to hold it whilst the nut is removed. If difficulty is experienced with a joint being renewed then cut it off.

7. Once the ball joint is clear of the arm, slacken the locknut (6) but leave it at its original position. The joint may then be removed and a new one fitted by screwing it up as far as the locknut. The pin should point upwards and then be fitted into the steering arm.

8. As the nut is self locking it will be necessary to prevent the pin turning whilst tightening it. This can be done by putting a jack under the joint so that the weight of the wheel rests on the taper.

9. Tighten the locknut on the tie rod.

10 It is advisable to have the front wheel alignment checked as soon as possible.

18. Steering Knuckle & Steering Arm

1. Neither the steering knuckle (or stub axle as it is sometimes called, from the name of a similar part on a beam front axle) nor steering arm, normally need any attention. It is possible, however, in the case of severe shock or damage to the front suspension and steering, that either or both of them could be bent or distorted. If it is necessary to remove them for checking or renewal proceed as follows:

2. Remove the front hub as described in Section 13.

3. Detach the upper and lower wishbone ball joints as described in Section 6.

4. Detach the steering arm outer ball joint as described in Section 16.

5. Disconnect the hydraulic brake pipe from the wheel cylinder mounted on the brake backplate (details in Chapter 9).

6. Remove the brake backplate and separate the steering arm from the knuckle by undoing the bolts and nuts joining them together.

7. Reassembly and replacement is a reversal of the procedure. Bleed the brake system when reassembly is complete (See Chapter 9).

19. Steering Geometry — Checking & Adjustment

1. Unless the front axle and suspension has been damaged the castor angle, camber angle and steering pivot angles will not alter, provided of course that the suspension ball joints and wishbone fulcrum pin bushes are not worn in any way.

2. The toe-in of the front wheels is a measurement which may vary more frequently and could pass unnoticed if, for example, a steering tie rod was bent. When fitting new tie rod ball joints, for example, it will always be necessary to reset the toe-in.

3. Indications of incorrect wheel alignment (toe-in) are uneven tyre wear on the front tyres and erratic steering particularly when turning. To check toe-in accurately needs optical aligning equipment, so get a garage to do it. Ensure that they examine the tie-rods for straightness and all ball joints and wheel bearings at the same time, if you have not done so yourself.

20. Steering Wheel — Removal & Replacement

Fig.11.18 refers.

1. The steering wheel is located on splines to the column shaft and secured by a nut.

2. First remove the centre medallion by undoing the

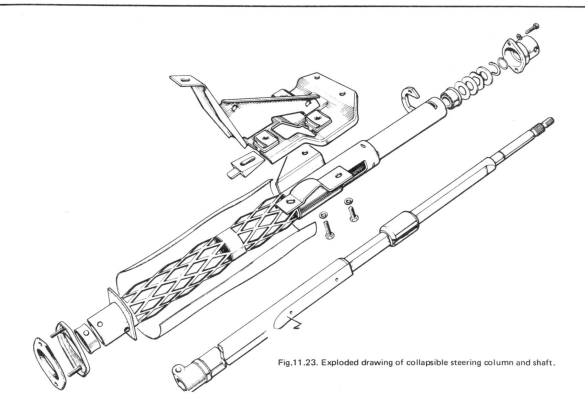

Fig.11.23. Exploded drawing of collapsible steering column and shaft.

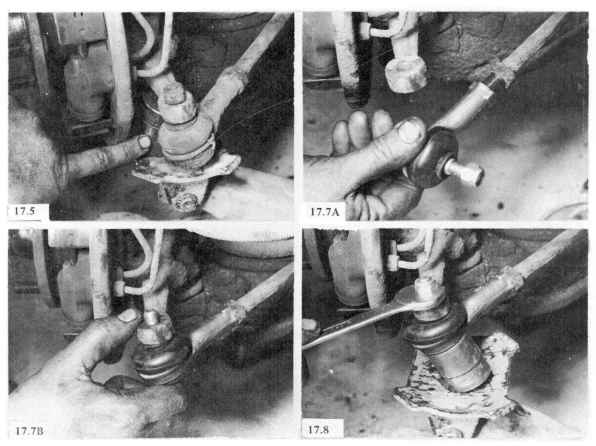

17.5

17.7A

17.7B

17.8

two screws (28) on the underside of the spoke.

3. Undo the nut (25) with a tubular spanner and then mark the relative position of the wheel to the shaft by making two marks with a centre punch. Then pull the wheel off.

4. The hub incorporates the trafficator cancelling sleeve which must be prised out (Fig.11.19) if it is being transferred to a new wheel.

5. Replacement is a straightforward reversal of the removal procedure.

21. Steering Shaft Flexible Coupling — Removal & Replacement

Fig.11.18 refers.

1. The flexible coupling is supplied complete and a new one should be fitted if any signs of wear are apparent.

2. First remove the cotter pin (35) which secures the lower coupling flange to the steering gear pinion.

3. Remove the nuts and bolts (32,34) which hold the steering shaft flange to the coupling.

4. Remove the circlip (43) from the shaft near the bottom bearing. This will enable the steering shaft to be lifted enough for the coupling to be drawn off the pinion shaft.

5. Replacement of the coupling is a reversal of the removal procedure. Before tightening the lower flange cotter nut, make sure that the steering wheel hub does not rub on the canopy (which means that the shaft is set too low). Also, if a new coupling has been fitted, remove the retention band from the coupling which is fitted to assist installation. If the existing coupling is being replaced it will aid installation if a hose clip is tightened round the flexible centre section to stress the rubber. Fig.11.20 shows how this may be done.

22. Steering Shaft Upper & Lower Bearings — Removal & Replacement (Early Models)

Fig.11.18 refers.

1. The upper shaft bearing (39) is a push fit into the top of the steering column. After the steering wheel has been removed (Section 20) the top canopy can be removed from the column and the bearing prised out (Fig.11.21).

2. Install the new bearing after greasing it and oiling the felt, replace the spring (40) and refit the steering wheel.

3. To replace the lower bearing it will first of all be necessary to remove the steering column and shaft from the car as described in Section 23.

4. When the column and shaft have been removed (and the steering wheel taken off) remove the circlip (43) and draw the shaft out from the bottom of the column.

5. Draw the old bearing and seal (39,40,41,42) from the shaft and fit new ones in their correct order after greasing the bearing and oiling the felt.

6. Replace the shaft in the column and refit the circlip.

7. Replace the column in the car (Section 23).

23. Steering Column — Removal & Replacement

Fig.11.18 refers.

1. The principal reason for removing the steering column other than for damage renewal, is to enable the bottom shaft bearing to be renewed.

2. Detach the shaft flange from the coupling (31) by

removing the two nuts and bolts (32,34).

3. Remove the instrument panel (See Chapter 12).

4. Disconnect the leads from the steering column indicator switch. If access is difficult it may be necessary to remove the lower panel as well.

5. Undo the nuts (48) holding the column lower mounting plate (45) to the toe panel and then remove the bolts (53) fixing the U strap at the upper end of the column to the dash.

6. The whole column may then be lifted out.

7. Replacement is a straightforward reversal of the foregoing procedure, bearing the following points in mind: Assemble all the nuts and bolts to their respective brackets before tightening up. Note also that the lower mounting bracket should be fitted so that the stud which is nearest the edge of the flange goes uppermost. (Fig.11.22).

24. Steering Column & Shaft Collapsible Type

See Fig.11.23.

1. On later models the steering column and shaft were re-designed so that they would collapse on heavy impact at the front of the car or on the steering wheel. The shaft is telescopic in design and D section in shape. To hold it rigid for normal use plastic is injected between the two sections and this shears under excessive end load on either the top or bottom of the shaft. The column has an open lattice work section which will collapse under impact. The column is attached to the dash panel on a bracket in which the bosses will shear under excessive load. In addition the steering shaft is shorter and there is an intermediate section between it and the coupling flange (Fig.11.24).

2. It should not be necessary to dismantle the column or shaft except for renewal of the lower shaft bearing or of course to replace a damaged column. In fact dismantling is to be discouraged as the components are relatively fragile and any careless handling or shock on the ends of the components could damage them to an extent where they need renewal.

3. To remove the column and upper shaft assembly, first disengage the intermediate shaft by removing the cotters at the end of the steering shaft and at the lower flange of the coupling. The shaft and coupling may then be slid down the pinion. If tight do NOT strike the coupling to force it down or the plastic in the upper shaft may be sheared. Hold the steering gear firm and move the steering wheel to ease the two shafts apart. The column and shaft assembly should then be removed as described in Section 23. The lower bearing is a nylon bush which can be prised out and renewed after removing the upper bearing as described in the next paragraph and drawing the shaft out.

4. The upper shaft bearing may be adjusted or renewed after removing the steering wheel, steering wheel circlip (or collars — See Fig.11.27), upper canopy and the switch sleeve. The switch sleeve is held by two screws to a horseshoe shaped collar around the shaft (See Fig.11.26) The bearing is located by a circlip. A wave washer and shims contact the pre-loading. The shim thicknesses may be varied to take up any noticeable slackness in the bearing. When the circlip is removed the shims may be detached and the bearing simply lifted out of the top of the column as it is a light push fit.

5. When reassembling the column assembly to the car the procedures given below must be followed carefully, to ensure correct alignment and even stresses. Fig.11.28 shows the upper mounting bracket. Screw the bolts (1) finger tight and then engage the steering shaft with the

Fig.11.24. Intermediate shaft fitted with collapsible steering shaft

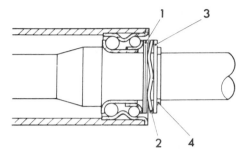

Fig.11.25. CROSS SECTION DRAWING OF UPPER BEARING FITTED WITH COLLAPSIBLE STEERING SHAFT

1. Shims   3. Plain washer
2. Wave washer   4. Circlip

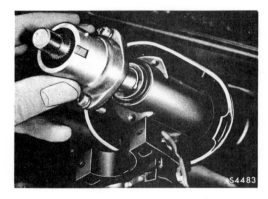

Fig.11.26. Showing removal of switch sleeve from upper end of steering column (collapsible type)

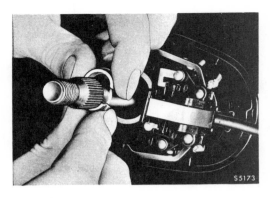

Fig.11.27. Showing the split collars on which the steering wheel seats on collapsible columns. Earlier versions had a circlip in place of the collars

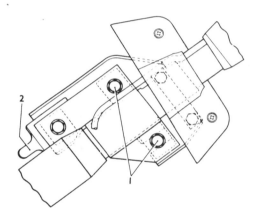

Fig.11.28. Drawing of upper mounting bracket for collapsible column showing bolts to be tightened first (1) and wedge (2).

intermediate shaft. Then tighten the upper cotter and tighten the bolts (1) to 17 lb/ft. Then install the coupling flange lower cotter, making sure it runs the same way as the upper one and tighten it. Then tighten up the nuts holding the flange at the bottom of the column to the toe panel. Next push the wedge (2) into position as far as it will go by hand, and refit and tighten the 3rd bolt in the upper mounting bracket to 17 lb/ft.

25. Wheels & Tyres

1. To provide equal, and obtain maximum wear from all the tyres, they should be rotated on the car at intervals of 6,000 miles to the following pattern:-

Spare to offside rear,
Offside rear to nearside front;
Nearside front to nearside rear;
Nearside rear to offside front;
Offside front to spare.

Wheels should be re-balanced when this is done. However, some owners baulk at the prospect of having to buy five new tyres all at once and tend to let two run on and replace a pair only. The new pair should always be fitted to the front wheels, as these are the most important from the safety aspect of steering and braking.

2. Never mix tyres of a radial and crossply construction on the same car, as the basic design differences can cause unusual and, in certain conditions, very dangerous handling and braking characteristics. If an emergency should force the use of two different types, make sure the radials are on the rear wheels and drive particularly carefully. If three of the five wheels are fitted with radial tyres then make sure that no more than two radials are in use on the car (and those at the rear). Rationalise the tyres at the earliest possible opportunity.

3. Wheels are normally not subject to servicing problems, but when tyres are renewed or changed the wheels should be balanced to reduce vibration and wear. If a wheel is suspected of damage - caused by hitting a kerb or pot hole which could distort it out of true, change it and have it checked for balance and true running at the earliest opportunity.

4. When fitting wheels do not overtighten the nuts. The maximum possible manual torque applied by the manufacturers wheel brace is adequate. It also prevents excessive struggle when the same wheel brace has to be used in emergency to remove the wheels. Overtightening may also distort the stud holes in the wheel causing it to run off centre and off balance.

211

Fault Finding Chart - Suspension - Dampers - Steering

Before diagnosing faults from the following chart, check that any irregularities are not caused by :-

1. Binding brakes.
2. Incorrect 'mix' of radial and cross-ply tyres.
3. Incorrect tyre pressures.
4. Misalignment of the body frame.

Symptom	Reason/s	Remedy
Steering wheel can be moved considerably before any sign of movement of the wheels is apparent.	Wear in the steering linkage, gear and column coupling	Check movement in all joints and steering gear and overhaul and renew as required.
Vehicle difficult to steer in a consistent straight line - wandering.	As above. Wheel alignment incorrect (indicated by excessive or uneven tyre wear).	As above. Check wheel alignment.
	Front wheel hub bearings loose or worn.	Adjust or renew as necessary.
	Worn ball joints or suspension arms.	Renew as necessary.
Steering stiff and heavy.	Incorrect wheel alignment (indicated by excessive or uneven tyre wear).	Check wheel alignment.
	Excessive wear or seizure in one or more of the joints in the steering linkage or suspension arm ball joints.	Renew as necessary or grease the suspension unit ball joints.
	Excessive wear in the steering gear unit.	Adjust if possible or renew.
Wheel wobble and vibration.	Road wheels out of balance.	Balance wheels.
	Road wheels buckled.	Check for damage.
	Wheel alignment incorrect.	Check wheel alignment.
	Wear in the steering linkage, suspension arm ball joints or suspension arm pivot bushes.	Check and renew as necessary.
	Broken front spring.	Check and renew as necessary.
Excessive pitching and rolling on corners and during braking.	Defective dampers and/or broken spring	Check and renew as necessary.

Chapter 12/Bodywork and Underframe

Contents

1. General Description

The combined body shell and underframe is an all welded unitary structure of sheet steel. Openings in it provide for the engine compartment, luggage compartment, doors and front and rear windows. The rear axle is attached to the body by arms bolted directly to it on rubber bushes and a detachable crossmember across the bottom of the engine compartment provides support for the engine and front suspension. A second detachable item is a central crossmember bridging the transmission tunnel which is the rear support of the engine/gearbox unit.

Early models had only two doors, but later on a four door version was produced.

Deluxe models have the heater and windscreen washer fitted as standard and on the S.L. versions more luxurious seats, twin horns and a water temperature gauge are also included.

2. Maintenance - Body Exterior

1. The general condition of a car's bodywork is the one thing that significantly affects its value. Maintenance is easy but needs to be regular and particular. Neglect, particularly after minor damage, can lead quickly to a further deterioration and costly repair bills. It is important also to keep watch on those parts of the car not immediately visible, for instance the underside, inside all the wheel arches and the lower part of the engine compartment. There is a feature of the HB series Viva which might be overlooked and that is the two fibre panels which are fitted behind the front wheels, one each side. These cover the large gap between the inner and outer body panels, and if they are broken or punctured, dirt will accumulate between the panels. The author retrieved one half bucket full of wet soil from one side alone, on the car used for this book. The panels are simply held by three self tapping screws and speed nuts and should be renewed if damaged. Take care not to damage the panels when struggling to extract the old and rusted screws. In addition, if your car is not fitted with mud flaps at the front, it is strongly recommended that they are installed. Vauxhall agents will supply them made to measure for the car at a very fair price. These protect the door undersills which are otherwise soon stripped to the bare metal by the water/grit slurry thrown up by the front wheels in wet weather.

2. The basic maintenance routine for the bodywork is washing - preferably with a lot of water, from a hose. This will remove all the loose solids which may have stuck to the car. It is important to flush these off in such a way as to prevent grit from scratching the finish. The wheel arches and underbody need washing in the same way to remove any accumulated mud which will retain moisture and tend to encourage rust. Paradoxically enough, the best time to clean the underbody and wheel arches is in wet weather when the mud is thoroughly wet and soft. In very wet weather the underbody is usually cleaned of large accumulations automatically and this is a good time for inspection.

3. Periodically it is a good idea to have the whole of the underside of the car steam cleaned, engine compartment included, so that a thorough inspection can be carried out to see what minor repairs and renovations are necessary. Steam cleaning is available at many garages and is necessary for removal of accumulations of oily grime which sometimes cakes thick in certain areas near the engine, gearbox and back axle. If steam facilities are not available, there are one or two excellent grease solvents available which can br beush applied. grease solvents available which can be brush applied. The dirt can then be simply hosed off.

4. After washing paintwork, wipe it off with a chamois leather to give an unspotted clear finish. A coat of clear protective wax polish will give added protection against chemical pollutants in the air. If the paintwork sheen

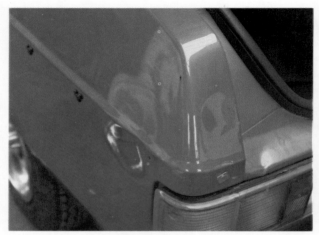

This sequence of photographs deals with the repair of the dent and scratch (above rear lamp) shown in this photo. The procedure will be similar for the repair of a hole. It should be noted that the procedures given here are simplified - more explicit instructions will be found in the text

In the case of a dent the first job - after removing surrounding trim - is to hammer out the dent where access is possible. This will minimise filling. Here, the large dent having been hammered out, the damaged area is being made slightly concave

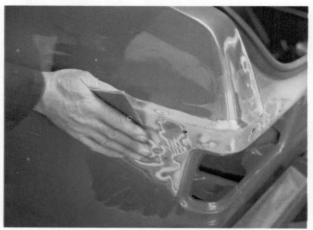

Now all paint must be removed from the damaged area, by rubbing with coarse abrasive paper. Alternatively, a wire brush or abrasive pad can be used in a power drill. Where the repair area meets good paintwork, the edge pf the paintwork should be 'feathered', using a finer grade of abrasive paper

In the case of a hole caused by rusting, all damaged sheet-metal should be cut away before proceeding to this stage. Here, the damaged area is being treated with rust remover and inhibitor before being filled

Mix the body filler according to its manufacturer's instructions. In the case of corrosion damage, it will be necessary to block off any large holes before filling - this can be done with zinc gauze or aluminium tape. Make sure the area is absolutely clean before ...

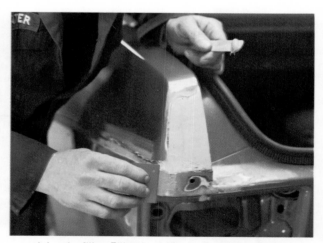

... applying the filler. Filler should be applied with a flexible applicator, as shown, for best results: the wooden spatula being used for confined areas. Apply thin layers of filler at 20-minute intervals, until the surface of the filler is slightly proud of the surrounding bodywork

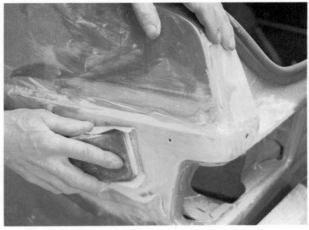

Initial shaping can be done with a Surform plane or Dreadnought file. Then, using progressively finer grades of wet-and-dry paper, wrapped around a sanding block, and copious amounts of clean water, rub-down the filler until really smooth and flat. Again, feather the edges of adjoining paintwork

The whole repair area can now be sprayed or brush-painted with primer. If spraying, ensure adjoining areas are protected from over-spray. Note that at least one-inch of the surrounding sound paintwork should be coated with primer. Primer has a 'thick' consistency, so will fill small imperfections

Again, using plenty of water, rub down the primer with a fine grade of wet-and-dry paper (400 grade is probably best) until it is really smooth and well blended into the surrounding paint-work. Any remaining imperfections can now be filled by carefully applied knifing stopper paste

When the stopper has hardened, rub-down the repair area again before applying the final coat of primer. Before rubbing-down this last coat of primer, ensure the repair area is blemish-free - use more stopper if necessary. To ensure that the surface of the primer is really smooth use some finishing compound

The top coat can now be applied. When working out of doors, pick a dry, warm and wind-free day. Ensure surrounding areas are protected from over-spray. Agitate the aerosol thoroughly, then spray the centre of the repair area, working outwards with a circular motion. Apply the paint as several thin coats.

After a period of about two-weeks, which the paint needs to harden fully, the surface of the repaired area can be 'cut' with a mild cutting compound prior to wax polishing. When carrying out bodywork repairs, remember that the quality of the finished job is proportional to the time and effort expended has dulled or oxidised, use a cleaner/polisher combination to restore the brilliance of the shine. This requires a little more effort, but is usually caused because regular washing has been neglected. Always check that door and ventilator opening drain holes and pipes are completely clear so that water can drain out. Bright work should be treated the same way as paintwork. Windscreens and windows can be kept clear of the smeary film which often appears if a little ammonia is added to the water. If they are scratched, a good rub with a proprietary metal polish will often clear them. Never use any form of wax or chromium polish on glass.

3. Maintenance - Interior

1. Mats and carpets should be brushed or vacuum cleaned regularly to keep them free of grit. If they are badly stained remove them from the car for scrubbing or sponging and make quite sure they are dry before replacement. Seats and interior trim panels can be kept clean by a wipe over with a damp cloth. If they do become stained (which can be more apparent on light coloured upholstery) use a little liquid detergent and a soft nail brush to scour the grime out of the grain of the material. Do not forget to keep the head lining clean in the same way as the upholstery. When using liquid cleaners inside the car do not over wet the surfaces being cleaned. Excessive damp could get into the seams and padded interior causing stains, offensive odours or even rot. If the inside of the car gets wet accidentally it is worthwhile taking some trouble to dry it out properly, particularly where carpets are involved. Do NOT leave oil or electric heaters inside the car for this purpose.

4. Minor Repairs to Bodywork

1. A car which does not suffer some minor damage to the bodywork from time to time is the exception rather than the rule. Even presuming the gatepost is never scraped or the door opened against a wall or high kerb, there is always the likelihood of gravel and grit being thrown up and chipping the surface, particularly at the lower edges of the doors and sills.
2. If the damage is merely a paint scrape which has not reached the metal base, delay is not critical, but where bare metal is exposed action must be taken immediately before rust sets in.
3. The average owner will normally keep the following 'first aid' materials available which can give a professional finish for minor jobs:

a) A resin based filler paste.
b) Matched paint either for spraying in a gun or in an aerosol can.
c) Fine cutting paste.
d) Medium and fine grade wet and dry abrasive paper.

4. Where the damage is superficial (i.e. not down to the bare metal and not dented), fill the scratch or chip with sufficient filler to smooth the area, rub down with paper and apply the matching paint.
5. Where the bodywork is scratched down to the metal, but not dented, clean the metal surface thoroughly and apply a suitable metal primer first, such as red lead or zinc chromate. Fill up the scratch as necessary with filler and rub down with wet and dry paper. Apply the matching colour paint.
6. If more than one coat of colour is required rub down each coat with cutting paste before applying the next.
7. If the bodywork is dented, first beat out the dent as near as possible to conform with the original contour.

Avoid using steel hammers - use hardwood mallets or similar and always support the back of the panel being beaten with a hardwood or metal 'dolly'. In areas where severe creasing and buckling has occurred it will be virtually impossible to reform the metal to the original shape. In such instances a decision should be made whether or not to cut out the damaged piece or attempt to re-contour over it with filler paste. In large areas where the metal panel is seriously damaged or rusted, the repair is to be considered major and it is often better to replace a panel or sill section with the appropriate part supplied as a spare. When using filler paste in largish quantities, make sure the directions are carefully followed. It is false economy to try and rush the job, as the correct hardening time must be allowed between stages or before finishing. With thick application the filler usually has to be applied in layers - allowing time for each layer to harden. Sometimes the original paint colour will have faded and it will be difficult to obtain an exact colour match. In such instances it is a good scheme to select a complete panel - such as a door, or boot lid, and spray the whole panel. Differences will be less apparent where there are obvious divisions between the original and re-sprayed areas.

5. Major repairs to Bodywork

1. Where serious damage has occurred or large areas need renewal due to neglect, it means certainly that completely new sections or panels will need welding in and this is best left to professionals. If the damage is due to impact it will also be necessary to completely check the alignment of the body shell structure. Due to the principle of construction, the strength and shape of the whole can be affected by damage to a part. In such instances the services of a Vauxhall agent with specialist checking jigs are essential. If a body is left mis-aligned, it is first of all dangerous as the car will not handle properly - and secondly, uneven stresses will be imposed on the steering, engine and transmission, causing abnormal wear or complete failure. Tyre wear will also be excessive.

6. Maintenance - Hinges, Door Catches & Locks ocks

1. Oil the hinges of the bonnet, boot and doors with a drop or two of light oil periodically. A good time is after the car has been washed.
2. Oil the bonnet release catch pivot pin and the safety catch pivot pin periodically.
3. Do not over-lubricate door latches and strikers. Normally a little oil on the end of the rotary pinion spindle and a thin smear of high melting point grease

on the striker pinion teeth and shoe spring plunger are adequate. Make sure that before lubrication they are wiped thoroughly clean and correctly adjusted. The excessive use of ordinary grease will result, most likely, in badly stained clothing.

7. Doors - Tracing of Rattles & Rectification

1. Check first that the door is not loose at the hinges and that the latch is holding it firmly in position, Check also that the door lines up with the aperture in the body.
6. If the hinges are loose or the door is out of alignment it will be necessary to detach it from the hinges as

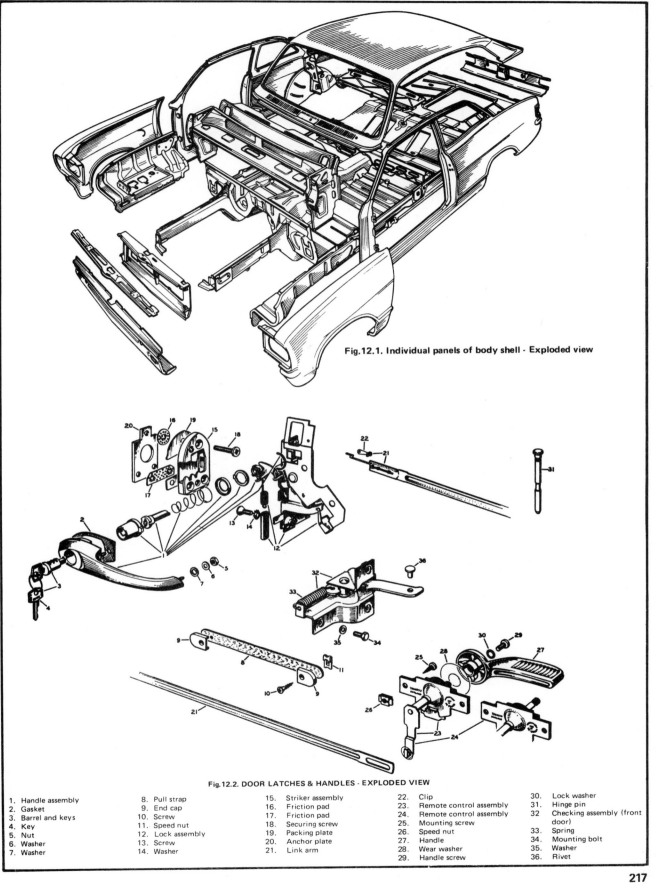

Fig.12.1. Individual panels of body shell - Exploded view

Fig.12.2. DOOR LATCHES & HANDLES - EXPLODED VIEW

1. Handle assembly	8. Pull strap	15. Striker assembly	22. Clip	30. Lock washer
2. Gasket	9. End cap	16. Friction pad	23. Remote control assembly	31. Hinge pin
3. Barrel and keys	10. Screw	17. Friction pad	24. Remote control assembly	32. Checking assembly (front
4. Key	11. Speed nut	18. Securing screw	25. Mounting screw	door)
5. Nut	12. Lock assembly	19. Packing plate	26. Speed nut	33. Spring
6. Washer	13. Screw	20. Anchor plate	27. Handle	34. Mounting bolt
7. Washer	14. Washer	21. Link arm	28. Wear washer	35. Washer
			29. Handle screw	36. Rivet

described in Section 8.

3. If the latch is holding the door correctly it should be possible to press the door inwards fractionally against the rubber weatherstrip. If not, adjust the striker plate as described in Section 9.

4. Other rattles from the door would be caused by wear or looseness in the window winder, the glass channels and sill strips, or the door handles and remote control arm; all of which are described in following sections.

8. Door Hinges – Pin Removal & Setting

1. The two halves of the door hinges are welded to the door and frame respectively.

2. To detach the doors, first drill out the pivot rivet from the door check link.

3. Support the bottom of the door on a suitable block and drive out the hinge pins. Once they have been moved sufficiently for the heads to get clear of the hinge butts a bar with a slot in the end can be fitted over the head and tapped with a mallet to draw the pin out. Get someone to hold the door while doing this or you could severely strain the second hinge or drop the door and damage it.

4. With the door off, the hinge butts on the body frame (NOT on the door) may be bent with a suitable lever in either direction to adjust the position of the door relative to the opening. Make sure that the two hinges stay in line with each other. It may be necessary to refit the door and hinge pins temporarily while adjusting the door position. Remove the latch striker from the door post while doing this. When replacing the door fit new hinge pins and install them with their heads facing each other, i.e. with the top pin head down and the bottom pin head up. Install a new rivet and reconnect the check link.

9. Door Latch Striker – Adjustment, Removal & Replacement

1. When the door is shut the panel should be flush with the bodywork and firm pressure on the door should move it inwards a fractional amount. If the door is difficult to latch or is loose when latched, slightly loosen the three striker plate fixing screws so that the striker plate will just move.

2. Shut the door carefully and, without touching the release button, move the door so that it is flush with the bodywork. Depress the button, open the door and tighten the fixing screws, making sure that the whole striker plate is square.

3. If there should be further indication of the door latch either hitting the inner recess of the striker or not latching firmly, check that the gap between the latch and the inner recess of the striker is correct at 1/5th in. (4 mm). This can be done by sticking a piece of plasticene in the striker recess and closing the door sufficiently to make a mark in it with the latch. If more or less than 1/5th inch then the packing behind the striker should be reduced or increased. If it cannot be reduced, then the door hinges must be reset. A large gap at the front edge of the door would indicate this latter situation.

4. To remove a striker which may be worn badly, first mark its outline in pencil (assuming it is correctly adjusted) and remove the three locating screws. Fit the new striker with the same shims and non-slip packing and if necessary adjust as described earlier in this section.

10. Door Trim Panel – Removal & Replacement

1. Remove the window regulator (winder) handle and remote control door latch handle by undoing the screw in each and pulling them off. Do not lose the wearing washers fitted behind them.

2. Remove the arm rest, where fitted, by undoing the mounting screws.

3. Slide a thin stiff blade (such as a putty knife) behind the edge of the trim and run it round next to each fixing clip in turn and prise the clip out of the hole in the door. Do not prise anywhere except next to a clip or the clip will probably tear out of the trim panel. Replace it by pushing the clips back in position and replacing the handles. When the window is closed, the winder handle, and latch handle normally lie horizontal facing forward.

11. Door Water Deflector – Removal & Replacement

1. To keep water from soaking the door trim panel a polythene sheet is stuck to the door behind it.

2. As it is difficult to remove the polythene material without ripping it, it is best to think always in terms of renewing it. It is cut to shape - the necessary holes for handles cut in it and then stuck on with a suitable adhesive such as Bostik No.3.

12. Door Window Regulator – Removal & Replacement

1. Remove the trim pad and water deflector as described in Sections 10 and 11.

2. Remove the window buffer bracket (Fig.12.3, Item 13) by removing the two mounting screws.

3. Lower the window (by temporarily replacing the handle) and with one hand supporting the glass, continue until the regulator arm comes out of the channel on the bottom of the glass.

4. Raise the glass by hand once more and prop it in position with a piece of wood or by jamming a wedge between it and the sill.

5. Remove the bolts holding the regulator and take it out through the lower opening in the inner door panel.

6. Replacement is a reversal of the removal procedure. Grease the window channel with high melting point grease.

13. Door Window Ventilator (Quarter Light) – Removal & Replacement

Fig.12.3 refers.

1. Remove the trim panel, deflector sheet, and window buffer bracket (13).

2. Lower the main window right to the bottom of the door and remove the sill sealing strips. The inner strip can be removed by driving it down into the door using a flat blade over the top of the securing clips. The outer rubber strip may be prised upwards out of the clips. Fig.12.4 gives a cross section of both strips as fixed and detail of a hook device for refitting the outer strip clips securely.

3. Undo the screw (7) in the inner door panel which secures the lower end of the window dividing channel (35).

4. Remove the two screws (49) which hold the ventilator frame to the door frame. These may be hidden under the

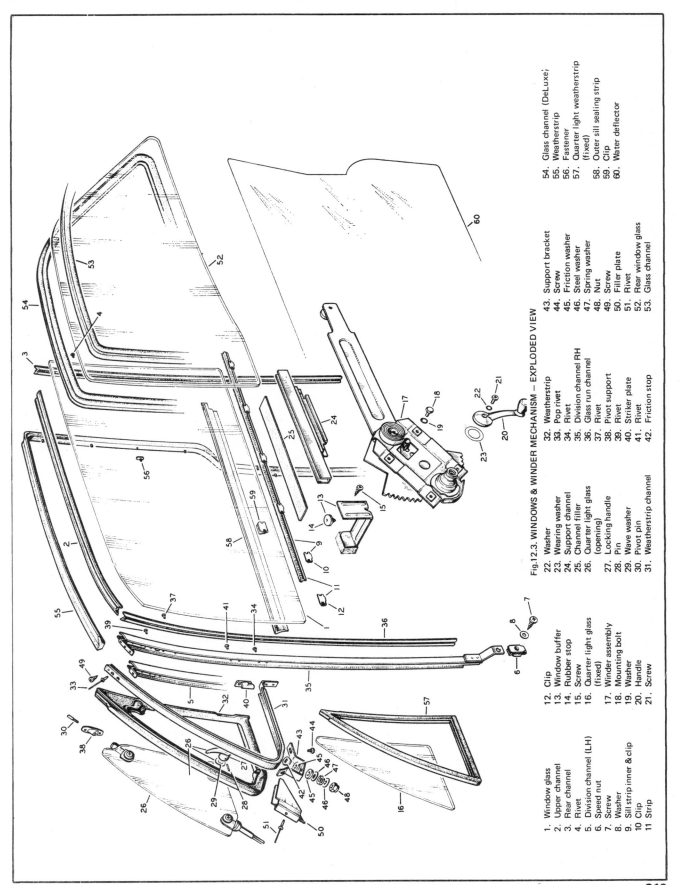

Fig.12.3. WINDOWS & WINDER MECHANISM – EXPLODED VIEW

1. Window glass	22. Washer	43. Support bracket	54. Glass channel (DeLuxe;
2. Upper channel	23. Wearing washer	44. Screw	55. Weatherstrip
3. Rear channel	24. Support channel	45. Friction washer	56. Fastener
4. Rivet	25. Channel filler	46. Steel washer	57. Quarter light weatherstrip
5. Division channel (LH)	26. Quarter light glass	47. Spring washer	(fixed)
6. Speed nut	(opening)	48. Nut	58. Outer sill sealing strip
7. Screw	27. Locking handle	49. Screw	59. Clip
8. Washer	28. Pin	50. Filler plate	60. Water deflector
9. Sill strip inner & clip	29. Wave washer	51. Rivet	
10. Clip	30. Pivot pin	52. Rear window glass	
11. Strip	31. Weatherstrip channel	53. Glass channel	
12. Clip	32. Weatherstrip		
13. Window buffer	33. Pop rivet		
14. Rubber stop	34. Rivet		
15. Screw	35. Division channel RH		
16. Quarter light glass	36. Glass run channel		
(fixed)	37. Pivot support		
17. Winder assembly	38. Rivet		
18. Mounting bolt	39. Rivet		
19. Washer	40. Striker plate		
20. Handle	41. Rivet		
21. Screw	42. Friction stop		

door sealing strip which will need lifting up to expose them (Fig.12.5).

5. If the whole unit is now tilted rearwards the glass and its frame may be lifted out of the door.

6. The glass may be removed from the frame by first dismantling the lower pivot bracket and friction assembly (Fig.12.6). Then undo the upper pivot pin (Fig.12.7) (which will need renewing) and lift out the glass. A new glass is supplied complete with pivot fittings and locking handle spindle. The handle itself can be removed by driving out the very small pin (Fig.12.8).

7. When reassembling the lower pivot bracket, make sure that the stop is correctly positioned against the bracket when the window is fully open and that the self locking nut is tightened sufficiently to prevent the window closing against air pressure.

8. Reassembly to the door frame is a reversal of removal. Before tightening the screw holding the lower end of the division channel run the main window up and down to ensure it runs freely.

14. Door Window Glass - Removal & Replacement

1. On the front doors it is first of all necessary to remove the quarter light assembly as described in Section 13.

2. Having detached the window lifting arm from the runner at the bottom of the glass lift the window up and out of the door, tilting it forward to enable it to clear the door frame. (This is the reason for removing the quarter light first).

3. If a new window is being fitted make sure that the lower support channel is fitted so that the open side of the runner faces inwards and that the rear end of the glass channel is 6¼ inches from the rear edge of the glass.

4. Replacement of the glass is the reverse of the removal procedure. Before tightening the dividing channel lower screw make sure the glass runs up and down smoothly.

15. Windscreen Glass & Rear Window Glass – Removal & Replacement

1. Unless the glass has been broken it is assumed that it is being removed because the sealing strip is leaking. If you are buying a secondhand screen from a breakers yard, ask them to remove it for you before paying for it. If the screen is already removed check the edges very carefully for signs of chipping. The screen should be smoothly ground all round the edge and any chip is a potential starter for a future crack.

2. Check whether the screen is made of toughened or laminated glass. Toughened glass has the mark shown in Fig.12.9. The toughened zone — approx. 45 x 6 inches extends across the wide screen.

3. Remove the windscreen wiper arms by slackening the wedge screw, tapping it to loosen the wedge and lifting the wiper off. Disconnect the battery and remove the interior mirror.

4. Toughened glass screens can be removed by bumping the glass from inside with the flat of the hand. Wear stout gloves as a precaution. If moderate bumping fails, use foot pressure with pads under the feet to distribute pressure.

5. With laminated glass remove the glazing channel insert strip, where fitted, and cut away the lip of the glazing channel on the outside of the glass. Apply firm steady pressure from inside. Do not bump the glass or it may crack.

6. If a broken screen is being removed, cover up the scuttle ventilation grille to prevent pieces falling into the heater or ventilator.

7. To replace the glass, first clean all old sealing compound off the frame and sealing strip, if the sealing strip can be re-used If the screen is being replaced because of vehicle damage, make sure the frame is not distorted in any way. This can be checked by carefully holding the new screen in position to see that its contour and shape is reasonably well matched. Take care not to chip the glass edges.

8. Fit the glazing channel to the screen with the securing lip towards the inner (concave) side. Fig.12.10 gives a cross-section showing chrome inserts where fitted.

9. Fit a piece of thin, strong cord into the inner groove so that a loop is left in the top centre and the ends come out at the bottom centre. Make sure that the cord crosses over in the channel at the loop and ends (otherwise the centre pieces of the glazing channel cannot be pulled over the flange with the cord). Identify each end and the halves of the loop so that the running direction of each piece of cord is known.

10 Using a suitable container fitted with a fine nozzle, apply sealer (Bostik No.6) to the bottom of the corner of the body frame flange and also round the front edge of the glass between the glass and the glazing strip.

11 Place the screen in position, pressing lightly from the outside, and pull the strings from the bottom edge so that the glazing channel comes over the edge of the bottom flange up to within six inches of each bottom corner. Make sure the glass is kept central and repeat the procedure along the top edge followed last of all by the sides. Check that the screen is properly seated both inside and out and clean away any sealing compound.

16. Rear Side Windows - Two Door Models - Removal & Replacement

1. Removal and replacement procedures follow exactly the same methods as for the windscreen described in Section 15. Where opening rear side windows are fitted (on S.L. models) the removal of the catch and hinge mounting screws enables the glass to be lifted out.

17. Weatherstrips – General

1. The weatherstrips round the doors and boot lid should be examined regularly for correct positioning and damage, and replaced if necessary.

2. The trunk lid strip is a press fit onto the flange and is quite simple to fit. Use adhesive (Bostik No.3) to retain the weatherstrips in position in addition to the fasteners.

3. The door weatherstrips are held in position by fasteners which are a pop fit into holes in the frame. The fastener is fitted into a slot in the weatherstrip. To remove them a metal blade with a slot in the end should be fitted round each fastener in turn to lift it out. Replacement is simply a matter of pressing them into the door, using suitable adhesive as additional security.

18. Bonnet Assembly Catch, Adjustment, Removal & Replacement

1. The bonnet is held to the hinges by two bolts on each side.

2. To remove the bonnet first mark the position of the hinges with a pencil. Remove one bolt from each side

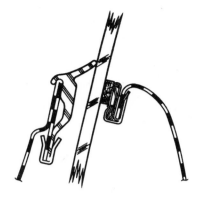

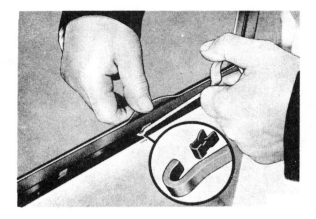

Fig.12.4. Door sill window sealing strips showing a cross section and also the use of a hook to fit the securing clips.

Fig.12.5. Removing the two screws (arrowed) holding the quarter light frame to the door frame

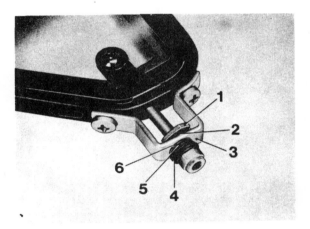

Fig.12.6. QUARTER LIGHT LOWER PIVOT FRICTION ASSEMBLY

1. Limit stop
2. Nylon washer
3. Support bracket
4. Spring
5. Washer
6. Nylon washer

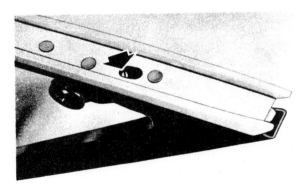

Fig.12.7. Quarter light upper pivot pin (arrowed)

Fig.12.9. Sign in centre lower edge of windscreen indicating it
is made of toughened glass

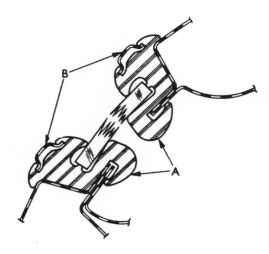

Fig.12.10. Cross section of windscreen glazing channel (A) and
moulding inserts on DeLuxe models (B)

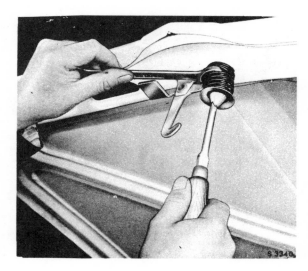

Fig.12.11. Adjustment of bonnet locking catch by altering length
of dovetail bolt

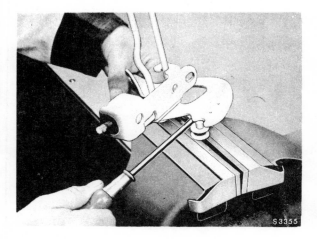

Fig.12.12. Fitting a new boot lid torsion bar to the right-hand
hinge

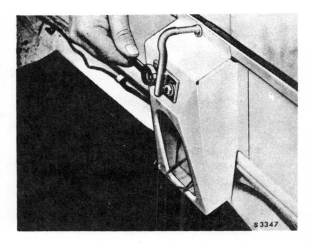

Fig.12.13. Adjusting the height of the boot lid striker loop.

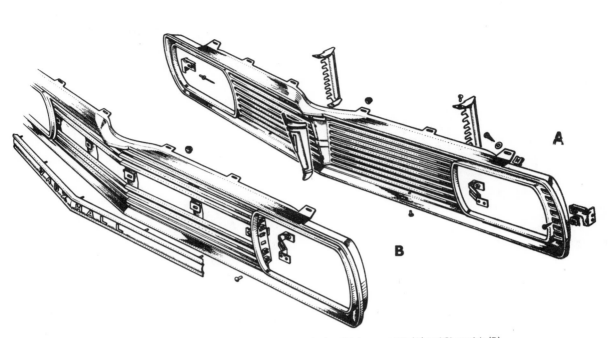

Fig.12.14. Radiator grille components as fitted to Standard and DeLuxe models (A) and SL models (B).

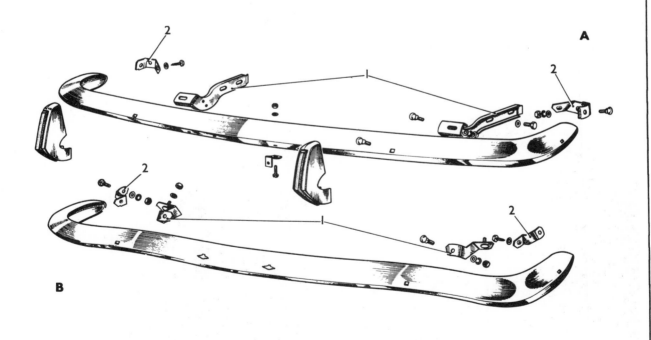

Fig.12.15. Front (A) and rear (B) bumper assemblies — Exploded view.

and then, with the help of someone, remove the other two, and lift the bonnet clear. Be careful when resting the bonnet against a wall, that the paint is not chipped, particularly at the back corners. Pad the edges resting against rough surfaces with some paper or old cloths.

3. Replacement is a straightforward reversal of the removal procedure, once again requiring assistance. Line up the hinges to the marks, nip the bolts up just enough to hold and close the bonnet. Check that it is central in the body opening and then tighten the bolts.

4. Should the bonnet require excessive pressure in order to engage the catch, or alternatively too light a force, meaning the catch spring is not compressed enough to prevent rattles, it may be adjusted.

5. Slacken the locknut on the dovetail bolt and with a screwdriver in the end slot, raise or lower the bolt as necessary. Retighten the locknut.

19. Boot Lid — Adjustments, Removal & Replacement

1. The weight of the boot lid is counter balanced by a torsion bar which is attached to the right-hand hinge and runs across the back of the luggage compartment.

2. To remove the boot lid, mark the position of the hinge arm with a pencil, pad the paintwork of the body near the hinges, remove the bolts with the help of someone and lift the lid away. Protect the paint from being scratched wherever the boot lid may be placed.

3. If the counterweight torsion bar should break, it can be renewed by removing the right-hand hinge from the car. First detach the right-hand hinge arm from the boot lid by unscrewing the two bolts, and support the lid in the open position.

4. Lift out the rear seat and then remove the squab by unclipping the two loops at the bottom and lifting it out.

5. Unfasten the rear parcel shelf trim.

6. The hinge bolts are then accessible from inside the car and can be removed, and the hinge/torsion bar assembly lifted out.

7. Remove the pieces of torsion bar from the hinge and fit the shorter arm of the new torsion bar into the eye on the hinge plate. Fit the rubber ring over the rod.

8. Clamp the longer end of the torsion rod in a vice so that the roller protrudes above the vice jaws. Turn the hinge arm, and lever the end over the torsion bar roller with a screwdriver (See Fig.12.12).

9. Replace the hinge.

10 Tighten the front attaching bolt only, until the boot lid is replaced and correctly positioned.

11 Replace the rear shelf trim and back seat.

12 The boot lid striker loop may need adjustment to keep the lid firmly closed. This can be done easily by slackening the two clamping bolts and raising or lowering the loop as necessary. (Fig.12.13).

20. Radiator Grille — Removal & Replacement

1. The radiator grille is held by 10 screws, 6 along the top edge, one at each end outside the headlamp and two inside the bonnet near the lower inside edge of the headlamp aperture. Removal of all the screws enables the grille to be lifted off.

21. Front & Rear Bumpers — Removal & Replacement

Fig.12.15. refers.
1. The front bumper is held by two brackets (A1) bolted

to each engine mounting side rail and at the ends by two more brackets (A2) to the wing panel. The rear bumper is similarly mounted by four brackets (B1,2).

2. When removing the bumpers it is best to detach the bumper and brackets together from the car. It is very difficult to separate the bumpers from the brackets whilst the brackets are attached to the car.

3. When refitting the rear bumper, make sure that the holes in the rear panel, to which the main support brackets (B1) are bolted, are sealed to prevent water entering the boot.

22. Heater & Ventilator Circuits — General Description & Operation

1. The heater is installed on all DeLuxe models or as an optional extra in standard models where it occupies the space above the scuttle ventilator. It comprises a radiator unit fed by hot water from the cooling system and an electrically driven fan of the squirrel cage type. With a ventilator only fitted there is a single knob on the dash which opens the duct flap and directs air to the screen or car interior. In addition, air entering through the scuttle grille can enter the car through ducts at each end of the dash panel. These ducts can be opened or closed as required by turning the hinged flaps.

Models fitted with a heater have a second control lever above the ventilator lever which operates the hot water control valve to the heater radiator. Also the ventilator lever can be pulled out to switch on the fan to boost air circulation in the main system.

2. Faults in the system are generally due to incorrect adjustment of the cables operating the ventilator flap and the heater control valve, or dislodged sealing pads in the ducting. Inadequate heating can also be due to a faulty thermostat or an air lock in the water circuit.

23. Heater Unit & Controls — Adjustment, Removal & Replacement

Fig.12.16 and 12.19. refers.
1. To check that the adjustment of the controls is correct, first set the ventilation lever to 'off' and the heater control knob to 'COLD'.

2. In these positions the ventilator flap should be shut (horizontal) and the water valve closed, i.e. the lever fully down. If otherwise the cable end stops should be adjusted. That for the ventilator flap can be reached by removing the parcel shelf and air distribution box from inside the car.

3. If either of the cables should break or become detached at the control lever end it will be necessary to withdraw the control lever assembly. To do this disconnect both ends of the cables at the ventilator flap and water valve. Remove the two knobs from the levers and take out the two screws holding the escutcheon to the dash. After disconnecting the fan heater wire the control unit can be withdrawn.

4. To remove the heater and fan assembly from the car, drain off sufficient water to clear the heater tank. Then disconnect the hoses, electrical wires and the cable to the water valve. By removing the seven securing screws the whole assembly may be lifted out.

5. The radiator tank can be separated after removing the water valve and clip and likewise the fan unit and motor can be removed by undoing the six screws which secure the mountings and bypass flap. With the motor removed it is possible to fit new carbon brushes, if

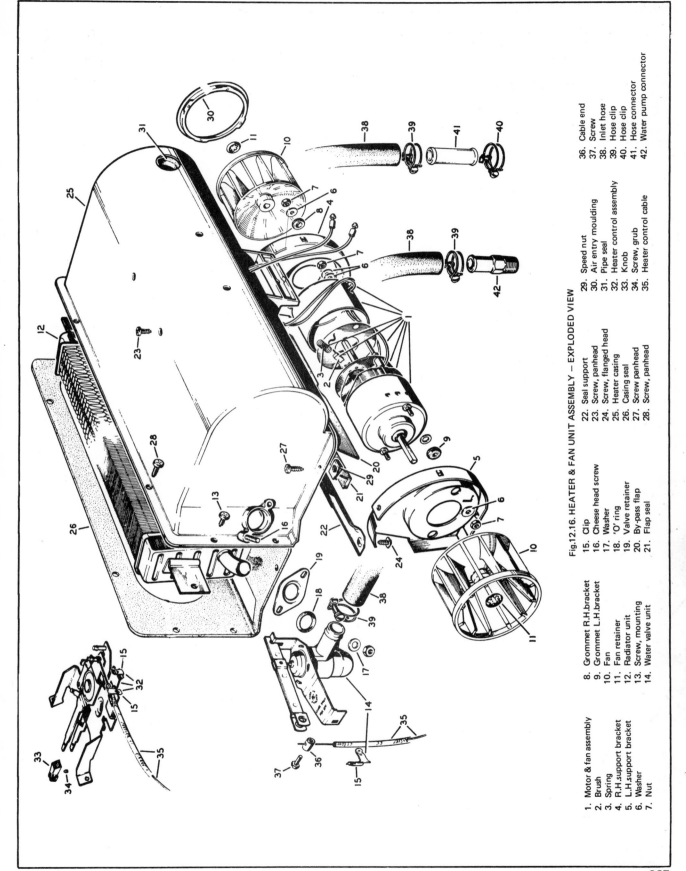

Fig.12.16. HEATER & FAN UNIT ASSEMBLY – EXPLODED VIEW

1. Motor & fan assembly
2. Brush
3. Spring
4. R.H.support bracket
5. L.H.support bracket
6. Washer
7. Nut

8. Grommet R.H.bracket
9. Grommet L.H.bracket
10. Fan
11. Fan retainer
12. Radiator unit
13. Screw, mounting
14. Water valve unit

15. Clip
16. Cheese head screw
17. Washer
18. 'O' ring
19. Valve retainer
20. By-pass flap
21. Flap seal

22. Seal support
23. Screw, panhead
24. Screw, flanged head
25. Heater casing
26. Casing seal
27. Screw panhead
28. Screw, panhead

29. Speed nut
30. Air entry moulding
31. Pipe seal
32. Heater control assembly
33. Knob
34. Screw, grub
35. Heater control cable

36. Cable end
37. Screw
38. Inlet hose
39. Hose clip
40. Hose clip
41. Hose connector
42. Water pump connector

required by removing the end cover.

6. When reassembling the fan motor to the housing the brackets must be positioned so that the 'L' stamped on one bracket is next to the ventilator holes in the motor casing and that the wires outlet also lines up in the correct position.

7. Do not refit the radiator into the housing but place it in position in the dash panel, complete with outlet hose and seal (Fig.12.18). Then offer the fan assembly up to it.

8. Before refitting the valve to the inlet pipe make sure the 'O' ring in the mounting flange is intact.

9. If the heater unit needs removal only to gain access to the ventilator securing screws it is not necessary to separate it from the panel or disconnect the water hoses. Simply disconnect the water valve cable and fan motor wires and remove the screws holding the whole panel to the dash. The unit can then be moved forward, (Fig.10.46). It is helpful to remove the carburetter air cleaner also.

10 When the radiator has been disconnected from the cooling system - or the system drained, any air locks can be cleared by disconnecting the heater outlet hose at the connector and pouring water via a funnel into the front section of hose until water comes out of the other section. This should be done with the radiator cap fitted and the water valve in the 'hot' position.

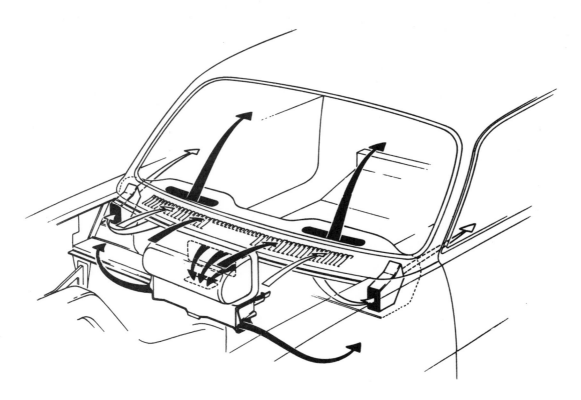

Fig.12.17. Diagram of air flow system; through the centre heater/distribution box (black arrows); and fresh air inlet only (white arrows).

Fig.12.18. Showing replacement of heater radiator prior to installation of fan unit

Fig.12.19. Withdrawal of heater and ventilator control assembly

Index

Printed by
Haynes Publishing Group
Sparkford Yeovil Somerset
England